# Visualizing Information with Microsoft® Office Visio® 2007: Smart Diagrams for Business Users

David J. Parker

McGraw Hill

New York   Chicago   San Francisco
Lisbon   London   Madrid   Mexico City   Milan
New Delhi   San Juan   Seoul   Singapore   Sydney   Toronto

*The McGraw·Hill Companies*

**Cataloging-in-Publication Data is on file with the Library of Congress**

McGraw-Hill books are available at special quantity discounts to use as premiums and sales promotions, or for use in corporate training programs. For more information, please write to the Director of Special Sales, Professional Publishing, McGraw-Hill, Two Penn Plaza, New York, NY 10121-2298. Or contact your local bookstore.

## Visualizing Information with Microsoft® Office Visio® 2007: Smart Diagrams for Business Users

1234567890 DOC DOC 01987

ISBN-13: 978-0-07-148261-5
ISBN-10: 0-07-148261-X

| | | |
|---|---|---|
| **Sponsoring Editor**<br>Wendy Rinaldi | **Technical Editor**<br>Bill Morein | **Composition**<br>International Typesetting and Composition |
| **Editorial Supervisor**<br>Patty Mon | **Copy Editor**<br>Marcia Baker | **Illustration**<br>International Typesetting and Composition |
| **Project Manager**<br>Vasundhara Sawhney<br>(International Typesetting and Composition) | **Proofreader**<br>Bev Weiler<br><br>**Indexer**<br>John Marshall | **Art Director, Cover**<br>Jeff Weeks |
| **Acquisitions Coordinator**<br>Mandy Canales | **Production Supervisor**<br>Jim Kussow | **Cover Designer**<br>Pattie Lee |

To my wife Beena and my children, Kryshnan and Alyesha.
"Look inside and see what I spend my time doing!"

# About the Author

**David J. Parker** was almost born four years before his actual birth, when his mother mistook his eldest sister for a boy and, temporarily, called her David. When David eventually was born in 1960, it was in the north Midlands of England (where you supported Nottingham Forest). David remembers The World Cup victory '66 in black-and-white, but he never thought it would not be repeated in color. When David's family moved further north, his red and white shirt was mistaken for a Manchester United strip, so he became a supporter, just in time for the first English team to win the European Cup. His footballing ambitions took a setback when he went to a grammar school where soccer was forbidden, so David became a field hockey player.

With a desire to combine art and mathematics, David studied architecture at Bath University, where he had to decide to stop playing hockey if he was to leave with a degree. Some computers were still being fed instructions punched into cards, David was introduced into programming for the first time.

David then worked as an architectural assistant and tested some early computer aided design (CAD) systems where the directions for drawing a circle were on the wall in a flowchart. David's second degree was at the Polytechnic of North London, where he lost the lottery for the 1 student out of 34 who would be allowed to use the brand new CAD system. He consoled himself with writing his thesis on a Spectrum 64 and making sprites race across the screen. The only printer was a smelly, sparkling thermal affair, so cassettes were dispatched to David's mother, who retyped everything on to proper paper.

Soon, David qualified as an architect and found himself in charge of a 3-D CAD system for an architectural practice, which mainly designed hospital extensions, trying to churn out drawings and reconcile lists of equipment in a spreadsheet. Frustration set in because of the inability of the two systems to communicate with each other in any way.

A short period as a partner in a start-up architectural practice left David convinced that he wanted to find out more about linking CAD to data. He offered his services to a company that had a UNIX-based system that could do just that, and David started to implement facilities and cable-management systems at merchant banks in the City of London. He left with the technical director to set up a consultancy company, and soon discovered that he was constantly writing code to clean up and import information into a database, to extract the data into reports, or to provide the glue between data and graphics.

When one particular client asked if he could come up with a way to create city trader desk layouts automatically from survey information, David found Visio was the only tool around that could provide the necessary accuracy and rapid development required.

Thus began David's love affair with a software application, and Visio was the first word his daughter learned to read from his shirt logo. He was an invited speaker at the first two Visio Solution Conferences in 1997 and 1998, where he met like-minded Visio-philes. This inspired David to set up his own company in 1998—bVisual ltd—to concentrate almost exclusively on Visio solutions.

David's eagerness to demonstrate the usefulness of Visio in business and his answering of public newsgroup questions led him to being made the first UK Most Valued Professional for Visio by Microsoft in 2005. David has taught Visio solution development in Europe and the Middle East, usually on behalf of Microsoft, and he has created Visio solutions that are in use all around the world.

David looks forward to a new era in Visio solutions, as Data Visualization becomes a recognized Microsoft competency, and Visio developers will soon be able to take a Microsoft Certification exam in the subject.

David has been married for over 20 years to Beena. He even found time to have two children—Kryshnan and Alyesha—neither of whom have any desire to emulate their father's meddling in IT. They all live near Reading in the UK . . . not far from Microsoft UK.

## About the Technical Editor

**Bill Morein** is a Program Manager Lead on the Visio team at Microsoft in the Office division, focusing on data visualization and extensibility features. Bill holds a master's degree in Computer Science from Columbia University.

# Contents

# Acknowledgments

This is my first book, so I apologize to all those people who expected me to write quicker than I did, especially Mandy Canales and Wendy Rinaldi.

Sorry to my family: namely, my wife Beena and my kids, Kryshnan and Alyesha, who eventually got used to seeing my laptop appearing at the slightest excuse.

Many thanks to my fellow Visio MVPs—Aviv Liberman and John Marshall—for reading through some chapters and their comments.

More thanks to Bill Morein for his patience and his insightful reviewing, and the rest of the Visio product team at Microsoft for producing a great visual information application.

Also, thank you to Vasundhara Sawhney, the project manager for this book, and to Marcia Baker, the copy editor.

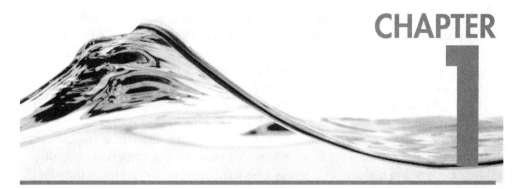

CHAPTER

1

# Review of Basics

The Visio Installation
Different Editions of Microsoft Visio
The User Interface
Types of Visio Documents
Types of Visio Pages
Mastering Visio Shapes
To Scale or Not to Scale
Layering Information
Outputs from Visio

1

Microsoft Visio is a data diagramming application that can be used for schematic or measured drawings. Visio is a general purpose tool that can be customised for particular tasks to focus the user's attention. It can also be programmed to create diagrams automatically from data supplied to it. The user can create many different categories of drawings with Microsoft Visio, but the ones I am interested in are those that contain data. Visio can provide a graphical representation of data, and it can be used to create it. This book is neither a beginner's guide to Visio—plenty of them should be around—nor is it a tutorial for graphic artists. Instead, it is intended for those who want to represent or model data visually, and for the myriad of budding developers who want to set up categories of drawings for others to use.

Before we get into the nitty-gritty of this, we should take a moment to check that you have a basic understanding of the anatomy of Visio. Without this, you may go off on a road to nowhere.

## The Visio Installation

Microsoft Visio is installed by default in C:\Program Files\Microsoft Office\OFFICE12\, and you should find a subfolder Samples\<LCID>\, which contains a few relevant files I refer to throughout this book. In my case, the Locale ID (LCID) is 1033, which is American English, although I am 2057, UK English (see http://www.microsoft.com/ globaldev/reference/lcid-all.mspx for a full listing). Friends have told me my accent changes depending on the person I am speaking to. Well, maybe this is the software equivalent. These LCID codes will be relevant in later sections of this book, especially if you have to create drawing templates for other languages than your own.

Each user needs the Visio application installed to manipulate the contents of a Visio document. This may sound obvious, but I have known developers who have tried to create installations for the Visio drawing control in a web page without Visio. They were gradually adding in dynamic link libraries (dlls) from their own Visio installation until they could get it working remotely. I quickly pointed out that not only is this illegal, but it will also result in an unsupportable mess. Microsoft kindly provides an ActiveX Microsoft Visio Drawing Control (VISOCX.DLL) with each copy of Visio, and it also provides an ActiveX Microsoft Office Visio Viewer (VVIEWER.DLL) with each copy of Microsoft Outlook 2007.

You can develop Windows Forms applications with the Microsoft Visio Drawing Control or with Visio Viewer, but the user needs a Microsoft Visio licence for the

Drawing Control. The Visio Viewer does, however, provide you with the capability to view certain pages, layers, shapes, properties, and hyperlinks, and I discuss this later in the book. This Drawing Control enables you to completely remove the standard user interface and to deliver an application based on Visio that does not necessarily look or feel like Visio. There are times when this is important, however, that is not the prime concern of this book. We shall examine the standard interface in Microsoft Visio because I am encouraging you to consider ways in which different types of diagrams can be linked together within business, in much the same way we can look at something from different angles until we can understand it better.

Therefore, you should understand some principles and patterns, so you can have consistency in your approach to data diagramming.

# Different Editions of Microsoft Visio

Microsoft Visio 2003 and 2007 are available as Standard or Professional editions, or you get Microsoft Visio 2003 Enterprise Architect with Visual Studio 2005 Team System (see http://www.microsoft.com/office/visio/prodinfo/editions.mspx). It is unlikely that you will deploy the latter within an organization, so we'll consider the former two editions. The drawing engine is the same among all editions, but the templates, stencils, and add-ons are different. The Professional edition contains all of the Standard edition, but then has some extra features such as network diagrams, floor plans, and database reverse engineering. I point out when a feature is only available in the Professional edition.

Unfortunately, Microsoft Visio 2002 Enterprise Edition was deployed with Visual Studio 2003, and Microsoft Visio 2003 Enterprise Edition is deployed with Visual Studio 2005. This has been the cause of much confusion within the Visio community. It is unlikely to change in the near future as the products are on different release cycles, so beware: your company may deploy Microsoft Office Visio 2007 to end users, but the development team may have Visual Studio 2005 Team Suite. They may think they are up-to-date with their edition of Visio, but they are, in fact, a product release behind. The good news is, however, that it should be possible for them to coexist on the same PC.

For completeness, know that Visio 2002 is Visio10 internally, Visio 2003 is Visio11, and Visio 2007 is Visio12. (Microsoft hiked the internal version number from 6 to 10 when it acquired the company to bring it into line with Office, so versions 7 to 9 never existed.)

# The User Interface

Some users find the user interface a bit daunting because only so much can be on display (see Figure 1-1). This is a result of so much capability within Visio. Microsoft Visio 2007 has not undergone the radical user interface changes *The Big Three* have . . . that may come one day! Until then, you need to understand the relevant areas of the standard interface.

## Selecting a Drawing Category

When you start Visio, you are normally presented with a list of drawing categories to choose from, down the left side of the screen (see Figure 1-2). When you select a Drawing Category, you are presented with a picture and title for each template within the category. You can then decide to create a drawing based on that category by choosing your measurement units, if you have both Metric and US units installed.

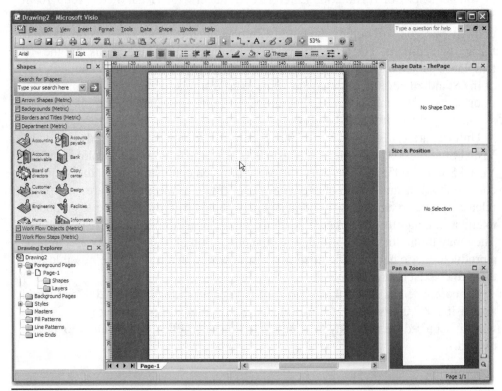

**Figure 1-1**    *The Microsoft Visio 2007 user interface*

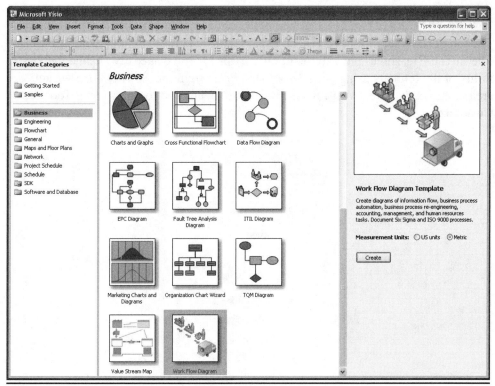

**Figure 1-2**    *Selecting a drawing template*

I will show you how you can create new categories and templates in Chapter 11 and this includes tips on getting an image as the preview picture for your template.

When a template opens, it normally displays a group of docked stencils down the left side and a single page. What you may not see is this: the template may also start a particular add-on, which listens for certain actions you perform. The add-on could cause a change in the user interface, and it may add or modify menus and toolbars. Many examples of this are in Microsoft Visio, for example, the Brainstorming Diagram, Organization Chart, and Space Plan each have their own add-ins that cause those types of diagrams to behave in particular, and distinct, ways. We investigate how this is done in Chapter 14. As a developer, you can create add-ons or COM add-ins for Visio, and either can change the user-interface or react to your actions.

## Menus and Toolbars

The top of the Visio interface has the usual menus and toolbars, like you used to find in The Big Three (pre-Microsoft Office 2007). You can easily change the visibility of the toolbars using View | Toolbars, or by right mouse clicking a vacant area in the toolbar area. You can customize the menus and toolbars using Tools | Customize.

We have a new main menu section and shape right-mouse menu item in Microsoft Visio 2007, called Data. This is fortunate, because most of this book is about the items on this menu.

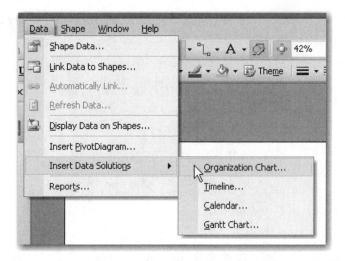

## Anchor Windows

You may, or may not, see some of the built-in anchor windows. Some of the add-ins also have their own anchor windows, but you need to know about six built-in ones. These anchor windows can be displayed or hidden by using the View menu.

### Shapes Window

The *Shapes window* is a docking area for stencils, but individual stencils can be dragged out from this window and floated around or docked. You can also add more stencils to this collection by using File | Shapes.

The shapes on the stencils are known as Masters, and they are usually dragged-and-dropped on to the drawing page.

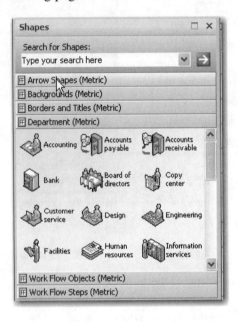

## Pan & Zoom Window

The *Pan & Zoom window* always shows the full drawing page and a red rectangle, which you can move or resize to change the area on view in the drawing page window.

## Shape Data Window

The *Shape Data window* displays the data for shape or shapes on the selected page. This is important for data diagramming, so you will see much more of this window later. It used to be called the Custom Properties window before Microsoft Visio 2007.

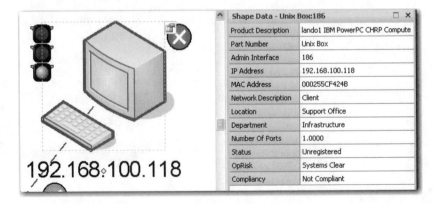

## Size & Position Window

The *Size & Position window* is quite cool because you can use it to add, subtract, multiply, or divide . . . and you can mix units, too! For example, if the width is "30 mm," you can simply type **+ 2 in** if you need to. This may not mean much on the west side of the Atlantic, but, in the U.K., lots of us speak in both languages!

In fact, Visio uses inches internally, so you do not have to add the units for inches, but you do need to explicitly type the units for anything else.

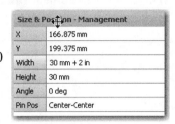

## Drawing Explorer Window

In my experience, this is an underused tool, but it is extremely useful. The *Drawing Explorer window* is a quick way of navigating elements within the Visio document, as you will see in Chapter 6.

## External Data Window

The External Data window is brand new in Microsoft Visio 2007, so we examine it in detail later in Chapter 3. The *External Data window* displays the contents of linked data lists, which may be connected to shapes within the document.

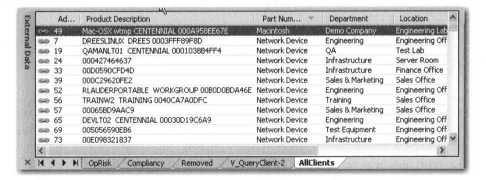

# Task Pane

The right-hand side of the screen is often occupied by one of the various task panes that can assist at various times. Microsoft Visio 2007 sees the introduction of the Themes task pane to enable you to apply color themes consistently, and many new shapes in the product (and old ones that have been reworked) work effectively with these themes. The *Data Graphics task pane* enables you to apply the wonderful new visualisations of information to your shapes. You also see the Reviewing, Document

Management, Document Updates, and Refresh Conflicts task panes in the relevant chapters.

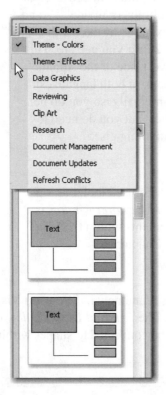

# The ShapeSheet Window

The ShapeSheet window is not normally displayed by users, unless they opened it by mistake using Window | Show ShapeSheet. In fact, I have seen users freeze when this window opens because they think something has gone wrong. The *ShapeSheet window* exposes why Visio is unique. It demonstrates that every line, text, or image within Visio has the potential to be smarter. It is the reason I use Visio.

To enable quick access to the ShapeSheet from the right-mouse menu of any page or shape selected, it is worthwhile switching on Run In Developer Mode on the Advanced tab of the Tools | Options dialog. *Run In Developer Mode* also enables other options, most noticeably on the Define Shape Data dialog.

While you have the Options dialog open, you may want to uncheck the Open in each ShapeSheet in the same window setting, but remember to close the ShapeSheet windows before saving the drawing. Otherwise, they will still be open (and probably hidden behind the drawing window) when the drawing is reopened.

The ShapeSheet is broken down into sections, rows, and cells (see Figure 1-3). Some of these sections are fixed in size, such as Shape Transform, and some sections are optional, such as Shape Data and Hyperlinks. Each of the cells can contain formulae, which can contain references to other cells, even in other shapes and pages.

Note to programmers who have never used the ShapeSheet: embrace it! Consider the ShapeSheet an extension to your object model. Encapsulate private methods and properties within the ShapeSheet, and send minimal messages to it through public properties. Understand the power of ShapeSheet formulae, and use it like your own favourite programming language.

I have been programming with various languages for over 20 years, but have never considered myself a hardcore programmer. People of my age never started in computing. Because the discipline never existed, we all came to it from something else. In my case, it was from a desire to extract data from drawings, so I am not puritanical about having to do something completely in C++, c#, or vb.net. I always look to exhaust the power of the ShapeSheet before resorting to other mainstream languages. Sometimes, this has the advantage that some of the required functionality of a diagramming solution is available without any external code.

As a simple example of this, use the Rectangle tool (on the Drawing toolbar) to draw a rectangle, just less than 1in or 25 mm in width. You can use the Size & Position window to check the width or even to type in the desired width. Then, open

**Figure 1-3**    *The smartness is in the ShapeSheet*

the ShapeSheet window and scroll down to the Fill Format section, and then type in **=Width** in the FillForegnd cell.

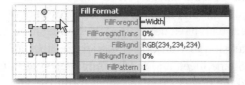

The fill will probably turn to black, but it will change when you stretch the width of the rectangle (or duplicate it and change the width of each rectangle). You will see the color changes from black to white, to red, to green, and so on as the shape gets wider. This may be a trivial example, but it demonstrates the innate power available to you.

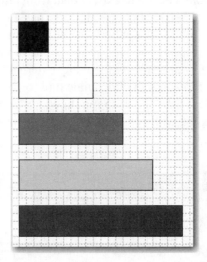

If you are curious, what is happening is the width of the shape is evaluating to a number in inches, and the FillForegnd cell accepts values in RGB(x,y,z), HSL(x,y,z), or, as in this case, Color Map index format. So, the inches are being interpreted as an index into the Color Map, which is between 0 and 23, In all versions of Visio before 2007, this index number was visible on the Format I Fill dialog, however, the number is no longer visible, and you are encouraged to the RGB() or HSL() formats from now on.

# Types of Visio Documents

There is only one type of Visio document!

Well, that is almost true. Six different file extensions are registered as Visio document types, so why did I say there is only one type?

## File Types

The drawing file, stencil, and templates just appear to be different because of the file extension used. So, the *vsd* and *vdx* file extensions are drawings, *vss* and *vsx* are stencils, and *vst* and *vtx* are templates. The Visio application decides how it is going to display the Visio document, largely based on the file extension, but also by content.

A stencil contains a number of shapes, called *Masters,* and either come with Microsoft Visio or are provided by a third-party, which could be you. You learn how to create these in Chapter 11. You will also see that even a stencil contains drawing pages, even though you cannot usually see them.

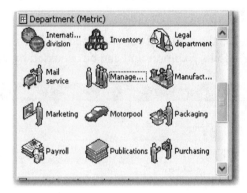

A drawing contains one or more pages, which are sized and scaled, and always contains its own stencil, called the Document Stencil, which you do not normally see. The *Document Stencil* is important in understanding the anatomy of a Visio document because it contains a local copy of every single Master used in the document. A drawing can also contain a group of stencils in its workspace.

A *template* is just a drawing with a different extension, so Visio knows to create a new drawing based on it by default. You learn how to categorize templates so your users can use them to create a new type of Visio drawing.

## File Formats

Visio files can exist in two formats, namely binary or XML. Before you get excited about the XML format, please remember that these files are seven to ten times larger than the same file in binary format, but they can sometimes compress to even smaller than the binary alternative. What is useful is that the .Net Framework includes the capability to compress and uncompress files (see http://msdn2.microsoft.com/en-us/ywf6dxhx.aspx).

Also, the XML format in the Visio 2003 and 2007 is not the new XML format used by the big three Microsoft Office 2007 applications (Word, Excel, and PowerPoint). The XML format currently in Visio is necessarily verbose to describe all the graphical information, along with all the other data that can be stored inside a Visio document. It can be a challenge to extract any information from the main body of the XML, but Microsoft has allowed programmers to use special sections, tagged as SolutionXML, that can be operated on much more easily. If you still want to store the Visio documents in binary format, it can be a useful technique to save this SolutionXML section as an external file whenever the drawing file is saved, thus enabling others access to salient data from standard XML tools.

## Document Properties

Every Visio document has the standard set of properties. They are useful, because they are exposed to Windows Explorer and can be accessed by other programs.

In addition, their values can be automatically linked to text in Visio shapes, which means you can use them to consistently label pages for viewing and printing. We show you how to do this in Chapter 10.

# Types of Visio Pages

A Visio document can have multiple pages, and each page can have a different size, orientation, and scale. This fact can make it a challenge to get a printout of the whole document on the same printer.

There are also three different types of Visio pages, which we describe now.

## Foreground Pages

Most users only work with Foreground pages, often because they do not realize about the other types. The Drawing Explorer can be used to navigate all the pages in a document, and it can even be used to reorder the pages. Each of the pages is shown as a page tab along the bottom of the drawing area.

Pages are named Page-1, Page-2, etc. by default, but you can rename them easily (see Figure 1-4). The page name used to be limited to 31 characters, but Visio 2007 allows much more than you should ever need.

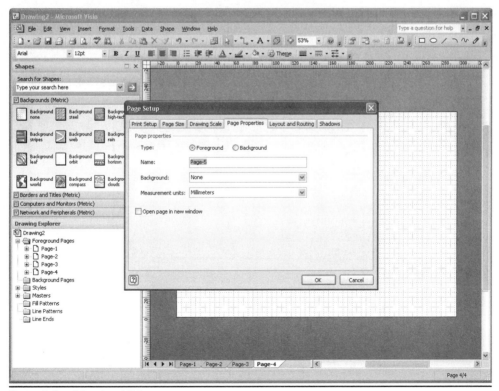

**Figure 1-4**   *Naming Visio pages*

When you insert a new page into the document, then the new page will have all the properties of the active page at the time of the insert action.

A Foreground page can have none or one associated Background page, and you can assign measurement units to be used. We look at the size and scale in the section titled To Scale or Not To Scale.

## Background Pages

A *Background page* does not print unless it is viewed through a Foreground page, and is usually used to hold background, borders, and title blocks, but it could be a floor layout. For example, a Background page can have a Background page, and so on.

If you drag a Master shape from the Backgrounds stencil on to a page, then it automatically creates a Background page, deletes the dropped shape from the page you dropped it on, and adds it to the Background page just created. These Background pages are named VBackground-1, VBackground-2, etc. and they appear as a page tab (see Figure 1-5) and as the Background page on the Page Properties dialog.

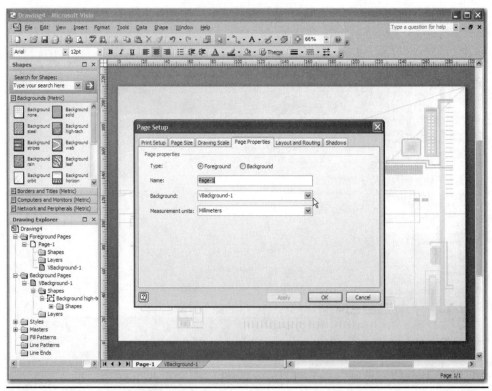

**Figure 1-5**    *Automatic backgrounds*

Or, you can create your own Background pages just by changing the type in the Page Properties dialog.

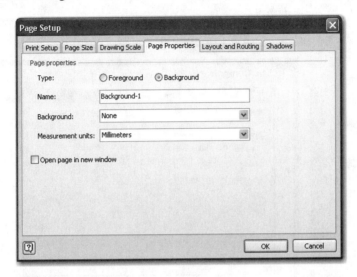

These pages are named Background-1, Background-2, etc. by default, but you can rename them (see Figure 1-6). You can then assign them as the background of any number of other pages, as required. This is an extremely useful way of having a consistent border and title block for a company documents. Indeed, if you choose to insert a new page from a page that has a Background page, then the new page also has the same background.

You can automatically link the Foreground page name and number to text in Visio shapes in the Background page, thus providing consistency for viewing and printing.

## Markup Pages

These pages are created when you decide to track markup (see Figure 1-7). Only one is created for each user on each page this is done for. They are named after the page they belong to, but with the user's initials, as entered on the Tools I Options I General tab.

Each user's markup page is shown as a tab at the top right-hand side of the drawing area, with the original page tab at the bottom right.

The reviewer's notes do not print when the page is printed, and no built-in report is in Microsoft Visio to do this. However, the information is quite easily read with some code, which we will examine in detail in Chapter 12.

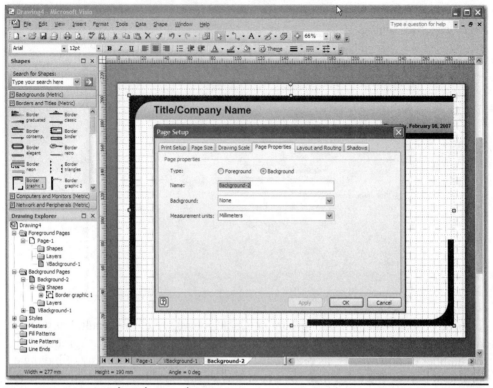

**Figure 1-6**   *A normal Background page*

# Mastering Visio Shapes

Here is a surprising fact: Visio documents and pages are just particular types of shapes—strange, but true. This is evident when you see you can open the ShapeSheet window for the document, page, or shape.

You need to understand a bit more about the shapes in a page before you can get the best from Visio.

## Using Master Shapes

Probably the first thing you do is to drag a Master shape from a global stencil and drop it on to a drawing page. What happens is the Master shape is copied onto the document stencil, and then an instance of the shape on the document stencil is created

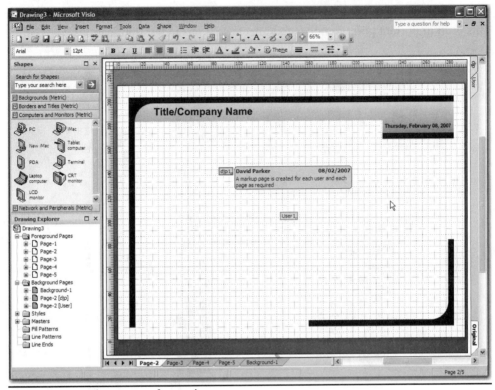

**Figure 1-7**   *Markup pages for each reviewer*

in the page. A good way to see this in action is to open the Drawing Explorer window before any shapes exist on the page . . .

. . . and then view it as a Master shape is dropped on to the page for the first time. This is an important point to understand because it has many implications.

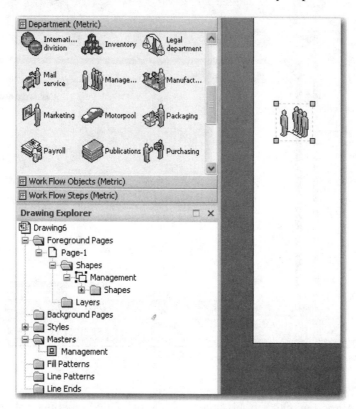

Rule 1: Editing a Master shape in a global stencil does not change any document in which the master shape has already been used. No method is supplied with Microsoft Visio for propagating any changes made to the Master shape in a global stencil to an instance in an existing document.

Rule 2: Editing the Master shape in a drawing document will (probably) propagate the changes to all instances in the drawing. Complex changes will not be propagated and neither will any cells that have been edited locally, such as the fill color.

Rule 3: Dragging-and-dropping a Master shape with the same name as one that has already been used in a document may create an extra, and unexpected, Master in the document.

If you have Microsoft Visio Professional, start a new Floor Plan diagram in the Maps and Floor Plans category. Drag-and-drop a Space shape from the Walls, Shell, and Structure stencil. Note, a Space Master is created in the Drawing Explorer window.

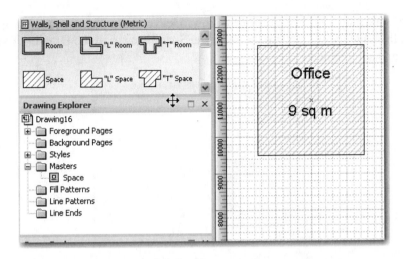

Open the Resources stencil. From the File | Shapes | Maps and Floor Plans | Building Plan category, drag a Space shape. Notice a second Master is created in the Drawing Explorer window.

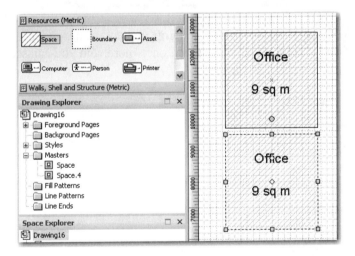

The second Master will have an extra number appended to differentiate it from the first one. This is usually not desirable, because Visio has to store an extra Master shape in the document, resulting in an increased file size, and possible confusion for any document-wide edits you may want to do.

There is a better way: undo the last action to leave you with only the first Space shape in the page. Now right-mouse click the Space Master in the Drawing Explorer window and select Master Properties.

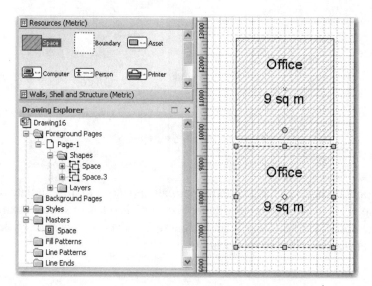

Now check Match Master by Name on Drop, and accept the change. Finally, drag the Space Master from the Resources stencil once more, and you can see an extra Space Master is not created this time.

Rule 4: Keep the number and depth of groups to a minimum, and use Combine rather than Group if you do not need to have different lines, colors, or text.

In the example with the Management shape, you can open its shape node in the Drawing Explorer to reveal this particular shape has other shapes within it, because it is a *Group* shape. Note, although the shape developer has created many subshapes, they have not been grouped further because this would cause Visio to have to perform more calculations.

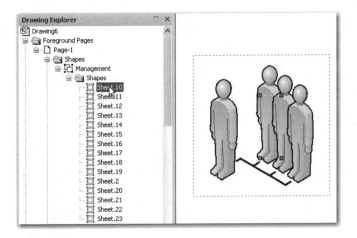

## Connecting Shapes

The next thing you might want to do is connect two shapes together (see Figure 1-8) using the Connector tool.

Notice this action automatically created the Dynamic connector Master in the Drawing Explorer.

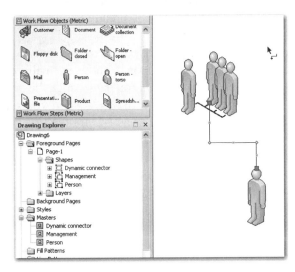

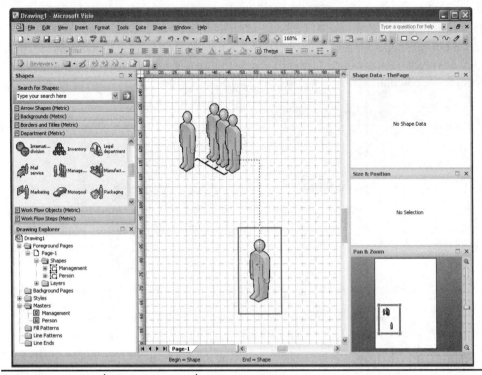

**Figure 1-8**   *Using the Connector tool*

Here is another important fact. The *Dynamic connector* is a special Master because it is automatically created, if it does not already exist, by several menu items and toolbar buttons in Visio.

When considering basic shape behavior types, here are just two: 1-D (Line) and 2-D (Box). The former shape is one-dimensional, and is normally used to connect between two 2-D() two-dimensional shapes. You can change the behavior of a shape between the two using the Format | Behavior dialog. Also, if you use the Line, Arc, or Freeform tools, then the drawn shape starts as 1-D for the first two vertices. But, if you add another vertex by continuing to draw, then the shape changes into 2-D automatically. This could be confusing for you if you are trying to use Visio because you expect to set the distance and angle to the next vertex. This could frustrate you and mistakenly make you believe Visio cannot draw accurately. Whereas, if you are shown the ShapeSheet, you could see the same thing can be achieved in Visio . . . and more!

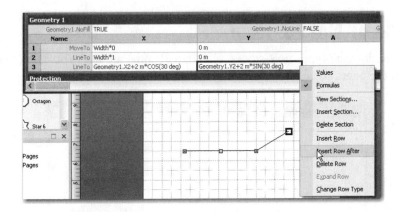

## Shapes Without a Master

Then, you may decide to write some text on the page as annotation. An examination of the Drawing Explorer reveals another truth: not all shapes are instances of a Master. If you use the buttons on the Drawing toolbar, just type in text or insert an object, such as an image or a Windows control, and then they all end up as shapes.

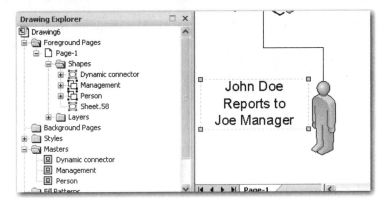

A block of text could easily have associated lines, arcs, etc. and a line, rectangle, arc, etc. can have a block of text. A normal mistake you might make is to write text adjacent to the shape you want to annotate, just as you would do in a CAD program or in PowerPoint. If you are an experienced Visio user, though, you would know to insert text into the shape, and then position it where required. This has the advantage of reducing the number of shapes in a document and permanently linking the text to the shape, so they either move together or are deleted together.

# To Scale or Not to Scale

Some of the drawing types in Visio are scaled, and some are not! You cannot tell by looking at the page, so you need to check the Page Properties dialog.

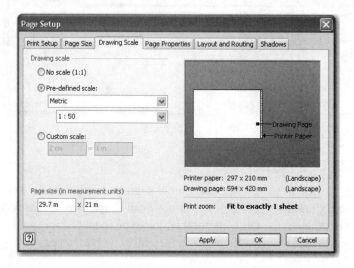

Or, you could drag-and-drop the Drawing scale Master shape from the Annotations stencil on to the page. The ShapeSheet for this shape reveals how it calculates the numbers to be displaced: it uses formulae in the User-defined Cells to calculate the ratio of the drawing scale and the page scale. This ShapeSheet uses a formula labelled as AntiScale, which is often used in Microsoft-supplied scaled Masters.

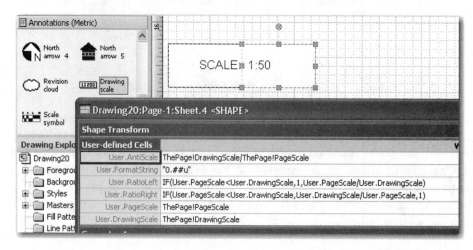

The reason for this is shapes need to be designed with scale in mind. Otherwise, you may get undesired results. The old rule-of-thumb is called the *Range of Eight*, which is that the scale of the Master must be no more than eight times larger or smaller than the page in which it is to be used. Consequently, all the network equipment shapes are created at 1:20, thus, they can be used safely up to 1:160, and down to 1:2.5. Since this rule was invented, Microsoft has introduced a new ShapeSheet function, *DropOnPageScale*, which helps adjust the properties of a shape to suit the scale of the page in which it is placed.

# Layering Information

All CAD programs I have used contain the capability to assign items to one layer or another, and then you can switch layer visibility on or off. Consequently, the items on those layers appear or disappear. Visio can also do that, but Visio has the extra complication that shapes, or shapes within those shapes, can be assigned to none, one, or multiple layers simultaneously.

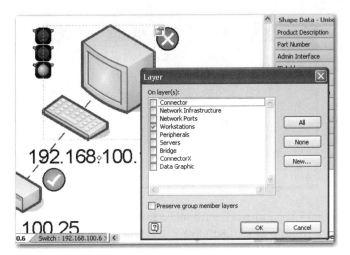

This can take some management, but it can be worth it because the usefulness of a document can be increased as items can be revealed or hidden as required using the Layer Properties dialog.

### NOTE

*The # column on this dialog shows the number of shapes on each layer, but do not rely on this for a count of shapes on the page because this includes subshapes of shapes and, as a shape can be on multiple layers, the same shape can be counted more than once.*

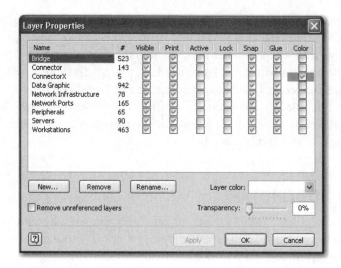

Moreover, layers can be used by Edit | Select by type to enable you to quickly select shapes on a particular layer.

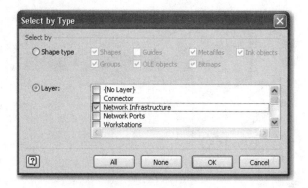

One CAD system I used to work with had a maximum of 255 layers. One of my colleagues set up a column of numbers from 1 to 255 down the edge of the page border, with each number on a particular layer, so you could tell which layers were on or off at the moment of printing. I think this was extremely smart, but a similar trick in Visio is problematical. First, layers are named in Visio, but these are converted to an index number in each page. Second, this index number could be different for the same layer name on each page because the index number is assigned sequentially. Users often ask how to transfer the layer setup from one page to another. One easy way to copy the layers from one page to another is to draw a rectangle, or a similar shape, on the first page, assign it to all layers on that page, move it to the second page, and then delete it (if required). Visio automatically creates all the layers on the second page in the same order as the first page.

You can then use a shape to display the name, visible, and printable status for each layer.

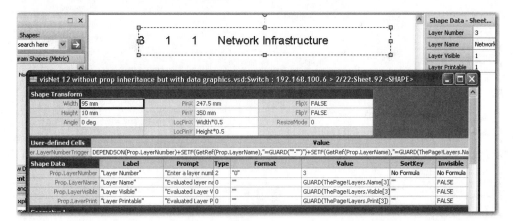

In this shape, I set up a shape data row to enter a layer number, and then a trigger responds to this number change to update the values of the remaining three shape data rows with the corresponding layer name, visibility, and printable status (and preventing them from being updated accidentally). The following shows the ShapeSheet formula for the User.LayerNumberTrigger to demonstrate a little of the power of Visio:

```
=DEPENDSON(Prop.LayerNumber)+SETF(GetRef(Prop.LayerName),"=GUARD(""-
"")")+SETF(GetRef(Prop.LayerName),"=GUARD(ThePage!Layers.Name["&Prop.LayerNumber
&"])")+SETF(GetRef(Prop.LayerVisible),"=GUARD(ThePage!Layers.Visible["&Prop.Laye
rNumber&"])")+SETF(GetRef(Prop.LaverPrint),"=GUARD(ThePage!Layers.Print["&Prop.
LayerNumber&"])")
```

Formulae can get quite long but, unfortunately, Visio only provides a single line to edit in. Sometimes, it is useful to use Notepad with text wrap on, and then cut-and-paste back into the ShapeSheet cell.

# Outputs from Visio

The best way to display a Visio document to someone is to use Visio! Unfortunately, not everybody has a copy of Visio to use, so the second best way should be the Microsoft Visio Viewer. Providing access to the original file is not always desirable, however, so there are many alternatives. You can save the pages of the document into a variety of formats or save the whole document to a web page (see Figure 1-9).

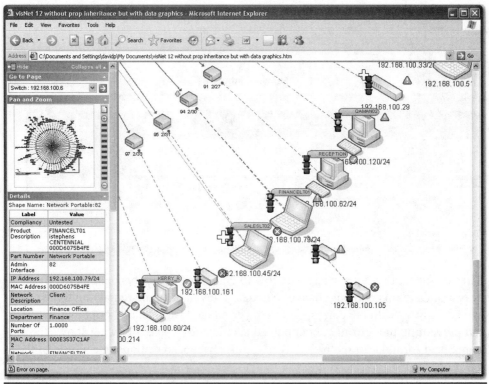

**Figure 1-9** *The Visio SaveAs Web feature*

And, new for Microsoft Visio 2007, as PDF or XPS, via a free download from the Microsoft web site. Adobe Acrobat, for example, does a better export into PDF because it preserves shape data and layers.

This latter option provides you with a document that can be printed with good fidelity, so it can be a better option than sending the original file for security and printability.

The *Visio Save As Web feature* creates a miniweb site, complete with an XML file that holds all the shape data. This file, data.xml, is stored in the subfolder created by the save routine, and is used by the details and search functions available in the web page.

We examine how to prepare Visio documents for the intended audience in Chapter 10, but, for now, you need to understand more about Shape Data.

# Shape Data and User-Defined Cells

S*hape data*, or custom properties, as it used to be called, is the key to visualising information with Microsoft Visio. If you want to see the information stored in a shape, or to use the built-in reporting, then you need to become familiar with shape data. If you want to have hidden information or to build in formulae that change shape data or parts of the graphics, then use *User-defined cells*. You can even use the right mouse menu to change shape data values by using the Action cells.

At times, you need to be able to edit shape data but, at other times, you need only to view it, or you may even want to make selected shape data invisible. You may want to have drop-down lists to select from, with the content of the list changed, depending on the value selected in another list. You can change the color of all or parts of a shape, or even change the appearance of a shape, in response to the value in a shape data row.

Customizing Visio shapes to suit your requirements reduces the time needed to create data diagrams, provides you with your corporate look and feel, and increases the insight of your audience.

Some tools within Microsoft Visio can create shape data automatically, so you need to understand what they are doing, so you can use them to your best advantage.

Some sections in the ShapeSheet are always there because they are required for every shape but, others, such as Shape Data, User-defined cells, or Actions are only created when they are required. Every cell can be identified by name or its Section Row Column (SRC) value.

# Creating Shape Data

You can create shape data rows on a shape in several ways, and many master shapes in stencils that come with Microsoft Office Visio already have some shape data in them. For example, if you drag a Process master from Basic Flowchart stencil on to a page, then you can see Shape Data rows are defined already (Cost, Duration, and Resources).

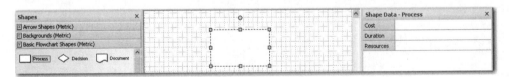

You can view (and edit) these rows in the Shape Data window or with the Shape Data dialog, which can be opened from the Data | Shape Data menu item.

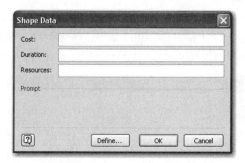

By default, you can open the Define Shape Data dialog from the Shape Data dialog or window.

However, the appearance of the Define Shape Data dialog is different if you are running in Developer mode. You can turn Developer mode on/off in the Tools | Options | Advanced tab.

If you are not running in Developer mode, then you do not see the Name, Sort Key, Ask On Drop, or Hidden controls. And you do not get the useful Show ShapeSheet menu item on the right mouse menu of a page or shape.

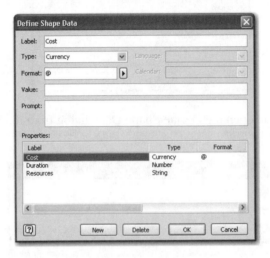

In fact, by setting the LockCustProp ShapeSheet cell to 1, you can make the Define Shape Data button on the Shape Data dialog invisible and disabled on the Shape Data window right-mouse menu. This cell is located in the Protection section of the ShapeSheet window.

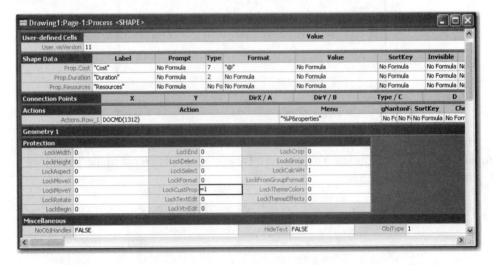

The ShapeSheet is often a better way to develop shape data rows because you can enter formulae into the cells directly. This is impossible with the Define Shape Data dialog because it assumes everything you type is just text.

# Shape Data Cells

Each section in the ShapeSheet has named cells. Table 2-1 shows lists of the cells that make up the Shape Data rows. Each cell can also be referenced by its Section/Row/Column numbers in code, but you must use the Prop.XXX.CellName in the ShapeSheet.

| Cell Name | Cell Index | Cell Description |
| --- | --- | --- |
| Name | | Default is Row_*n*, where *n* is the row number. Leaving this default row name unchanged can cause problems with automation, so the recommendation is to name the rows accordingly. You need to be in Developer mode to do this. |
| Label | visCustPropsLabel (2) | This appears as the visible name of a data row in the Shape Data window and dialog. It is also used for matching against column names when you use data linking. |
| Prompt | visCustPropsPrompt (1) | This is the longer description that appears at the bottom of the Shape Data dialog. Strangely, a lot of the supplied shapes do not have anything entered here, but it can help your users to understand the purpose of the data. |
| Type | visCustPropsType (5) | Table 2-2 lists the various types. The default is String (text). |
| Format | visCustPropsFormat (3) | Various formats can be applied to values, so that, for example, a date appears as 23 June 2006, or a number displays one decimal place. See the developer help for a full list. |
| | | Additionally, the format cell is used to store lists, normally separated by semicolons, for Fixed or Variable lists data types. |
| Value | visCustPropsValue (0) | The value of the data row: if you want your text data to appear to have no value when first opened, then it is best to enter "" (double-quote double-quote) as the value. The data row will default to 0.000 if you do not have anything entered (no formula). |
| | | For fixed list, you could enter the formula =""" & INDEX(0,Prop.XXX.Format) & """" if you want to default to the first value in the list, where XXX is the name of the row. |
| SortKey (Sort key) | visCustPropsSortKey (4) | This enables you to order the appearance of your data rows. An earlier tool in Visio (Network Properties) used this cell to group data rows together but, consequently, lost the capability to order them. |
| | | Note, the ordering is done on the text, not on the numbers, so use 01,02,03, etc. — not 1,2,3. Otherwise, 11 will appear before 2. |
| Invisible (Hidden) | visCustPropsInvis (6) | This enables you to toggle the visibility of selected data rows. This can be useful, as you can decide when to have certain rows on view for clarity or security. |
| Ask (Ask on drop) | visCustPropsAsk (7) | This determines whether the user should be prompted for input when a copy of the shape is added to a page. |
| | | Creating many copies in one action, however, will not cause the dialog to open for each shape. |
| LangID | visCustPropsLangID (14) | The language code identifier (LCID) used, for example, 1033 for U.S. English, 1036 for French, and 3082 for Spanish. |
| Calendar | visCustPropsCalendar (15) | This is the type of calendar, Western or other, to use for dates. The default is 0 (Western). |

**Table 2-1**   *Shape Data Cells*

The cell indices can be used in code as the last part of CellsSRC property. The section index (visSectionProp) is 243, but the row index can be more difficult to discover as you may need to use the row name.

## Shape Data Types

Specifying the correct type of data is important if you want Data Graphics to interpret the values properly. Table 2-2 shows a list of all the shape data types available to you.

## Templates and Add-Ons That Create Shape Data Rows Automatically

Scattered throughout Microsoft Visio are some drawing templates and add-ons that enable you to create shape data rows automatically. Unfortunately, they do not always create them in the same way, so if you intend to use them with other data, be aware of the differences.

Table 2-3 shows a list of the templates (drawing types) I could find that create shape data rows automatically.

In addition to the templates, Table 2-4 contains several add-ons that create shape data rows automatically, which can be called from any drawing type.

| Value | Type | Description |
| --- | --- | --- |
| 0 | String | Normal text (default). |
| 1 | Fixed List | The value must be from a list entered in the format cell, with values separated by semicolons. |
| 2 | Number | Any number. Use the format cell to specify the appearance, such as decimal places. |
| 3 | Boolean | TRUE or FALSE. |
| 4 | Variable List | The value must be from a list entered in the format cell, with values separated by semicolons. If it is not in the list, then the value is added to the list. |
| 5 | Date | Date or time. Use the Format cell to specify the appearance, such as the long or short date. |
| | | The earliest date that can be entered is 30/12/1899 00:00:00, so Visio time starts then. Thus, if you want to store earlier dates than that, use a string type or convert to a number. In fact, the datetime cell stores datetimes as a double number, that is, the days since 30/12/1899 before the decimal point, and the seconds in the day, after the decimal point. If you enter a number between 0 and 1, it is interpreted as time only. |
| | | You only get a date picker in the user interface, however, not a clock face. |
| 6 | Duration | Elapsed time. Use the format cell to specify the appearance. |
| 7 | Currency | Uses the current Regional settings. Use the Format cell to specify the appearance, while the Value cell can specify the currency, for example, =CY(200,"USD"). |

**Table 2-2**   *Shape Data Types*

| Template | Menu Item | Comments |
|---|---|---|
| Business/Brainstorming Diagram | Brainstorming/Import Data | Imports from an XML file in a particular format. Creates unnamed shape data rows. |
| Business/Organization Chart | Organization Chart/Import Organization Data | Imports from Microsoft Exchange Server directory, text, Excel, or ODBC-compliant data source. Enables you to choose which columns to import as shape data rows.<br><br>Creates named shape data rows. |
| Business/Organization Chart Wizard | As above | As above. |
| Business/PivotDiagram | Data/Insert PivotDiagram | New in Microsoft Visio 2007. Creates special summary data shapes from Excel, Access, SharePoint Service list, SQL Server, and other OLEDB or ODBC data source. A fuller description of this capability is in a later chapter, but it creates named shape data rows. However, it does not have a programmable interface. |
| Maps and Floor Plans/Space Plan | Plan/Import Data | Imports from Excel, Active Directory, Exchange Server, or ODBC. Enables you to choose columns and to filter the records to import.<br><br>You can also select the Master shape; the default label; and the Color By Value to use within the wizard.<br><br>Matches shape data rows with the same label where possible. Otherwise, it creates unnamed data rows. |
| Schedule/Calendar | Calendar/Import Outlook Data Wizard | Specialist import from Microsoft Outlook calendar. |
| Schedule/Gantt Chart | Gantt Chart/Import | Specialist import from Microsoft Project. |
| Schedule/Timeline | Timeline/Import Timeline Data | Specialist import from Microsoft Project. |
| Software and Database/Web Site Map | Generate Site Map | Specialist import from any web site. |

**Table 2-3**  *Templates That Automatically Create Shape Data*

In addition to the add-ons that create linked shape data, another one creates unlinked shape data—the *Number Shapes tool*—but it takes total control of the shape's text, so it is difficult to recommend its use with data-linked shapes.

| Menu Item | Comments |
|---|---|
| Data/Link Data to Shapes | New in Microsoft Visio 2007. Allows for multiple read-only links. A more in-depth description of this capability is in Chapter 3, but it links to the existing shape data rows using the label, or it creates named shape data rows and has a programmable interface. |
| Tools/Add-ons/Maps and Floor Plans/Import Data | This is a useful add-on even in nonfloor plan drawings, but duplicates some of the functionality in the previous add-on. |
| Tools/Add-ons/Visio Extras/Database Wizard | This long-standing add-on has many uses, which will be discussed in Chapter 6. It differs in some ways from the newer Link Data to Shapes because it uses the name of the shape data row to link to rather than the label.<br><br>This add-on can also be used to update an ODBC data source and to delete records (use with extreme caution).<br><br>It only allows for linking to a single ODBC data source. |
| Tools/Add-ons/Visio Extras/Link to ODBC Database... | See Database Wizard for comments, as they do the same, but with a different user interface. |

**Table 2-4**   *Add-ons That Create Shape Data*

## Reviewing Existing Shape Data

Before you embark on creating new shape data, you may want to review any existing Shape Data first. This could be because you want to adapt a Master provided by Microsoft or other third parties, or even previous developers within your company. Also, some organizations like to keep documentation of any custom development.

Fortunately, a basic, and verbose, tool is available in the Microsoft Visio SDK, called Print ShapeSheet that appears under Tools | Add-ons | SDK when installed.

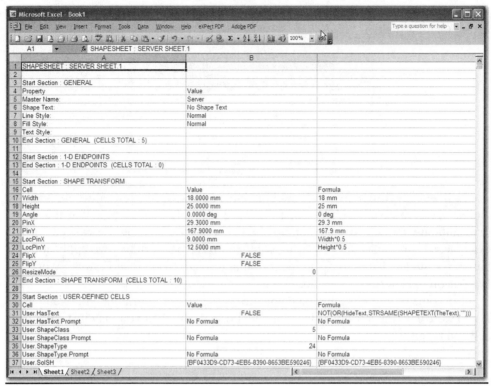

**Figure 2-1**    *Output from Print ShapeSheet*

*Print ShapeSheet* exports the selected ShapeSheet sections into the Clipboard, File, or Printer. Probably the most useful is the clipboard, because you can then paste the information into, say, Microsoft Excel, where you can analyze it more easily, as in Figure 2-1.

## Creating Shape Data Rows Manually

Unfortunately, you cannot copy a whole row from one ShapeSheet to another, so this must be done slowly and carefully. It is important that you name and label shape data rows consistently if you intend to use them with some of the other add-ons provided.

If you are copying shape data rows manually, then you need to be able to open at least two ShapeSheets simultaneously. The default setting is to open all ShapeSheets in the same window, so you need to uncheck the setting on the Advanced tab of the Tools | Options dialog.

The ShapeSheet supports inline editing, but you also have a line editor in the toolbar area. However, neither of these lets you see more than a single line at a time, although the cells can contain up to 64k characters. You can use Notepad, for example, as a formula editor by using copy-and-paste between the two applications, but do not put any hard returns in the formula. Instead, ensure that Format | Word Wrap is on in Notepad.

Also, some of the cells anticipate you are typing text or a formula. For example, if you were entering a list of values into the Format cell, then you may just enter the cell and type:

```
a;b;c
```

the interface assumes you are entering text and changes the entry to:

```
="a;b;c"
```

You may then tab into the next cell—Value—and want to enter the default value, so you type:

```
a
```

However, you then get an error because the interface is expecting a formula.

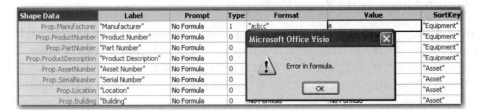

Instead, you must enter:

```
"a"
```

or

```
="a"
```

The ShapeSheet then knows you are entering text. This may seem strange, but it is logical. This is because the Value cell holds all different data types, so it doesn't know if you are entering text, a number, a date, or even a formula.

# Creating Shape Data Rows Automatically

If you are a SmartShape designer, you will often have to repeat the same shape data rows on similar shapes. Automating some of the actions is useful, but not that simple because references often occur from cell-to-cell, so the order in which formulae are added becomes important. A tool—Shape Data Sets—in Microsoft Visio can help with this, but it is limited in its usefulness to serious developers.

## Shape Data Sets

*Shape Data Sets* provides you with the capability to copy sets of shape data rows from one shape to another. It is only accessible from the right-mouse menu on the Shape Data Window title bar.

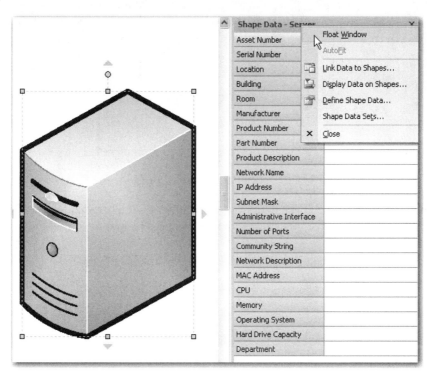

This tool copies data rows, but it orders them alphabetically on the target shape. This means you must use the Sort key consistently if you want the data rows to appear in the same order on similar shapes. To try this yourself:

1. Create a new Basic Network Diagram and drag a Server on to the page.
2. Open the Shape Data window, if you do not have it open already.
3. Select Shape Data Sets… from the right-mouse menu of the Shape Data Window title bar.
4. Select Add.. in the Shape Data Sets window.
5. Name the new set Network Properties, or something similar.
6. Draw a new shape (for example, a rectangle or an ellipse from the Drawing toolbar).
7. Check the Network Properties in the Shape Data Sets window, leave the default settings, and then select Apply.

Notice the order of the shape data rows is different on the original Server shape and on your new shape because this can be confusing to users.

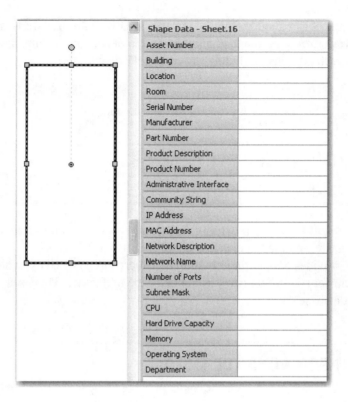

You need to edit the SortKey cells if you want them to be in the same order.

## Using Code to Copy Shape Data Rows

The Microsoft Visio SDK contains a Code Library with examples of how to create shape data (Custom Properties). This could be used in, say, a Microsoft Excel macro to reproduce shape data rows on any shape. In practice, though, you may want to be able to reproduce more than just the shape data, because quite often they are combined with User-defined cells, Action rows, and Smart Tags. Therefore, you need a tool to be able to transfer any or all of these at the same time.

Microsoft Excel is a good method of storing, reviewing, or transferring ShapeSheet rows from one shape to another, and, indeed, some companies on the Web provide such add-ons, including my own, *celMaker.*

| | A | B | C | D | E | F | G | H | I | J | K |
|---|---|---|---|---|---|---|---|---|---|---|---|
| 1 | *Mast* | Mast | Secti | CellName | Value | S | Pro | Label | T | f | SortKey |
| 2 | Server | Drag ont | Prop | Manufacturer | | | | "Manufacturer" | 0 | | "Equipment" |
| 3 | Server | Drag ont | Prop | ProductNumber | | | | "Product Number" | 0 | | "Equipment" |
| 4 | Server | Drag ont | Prop | PartNumber | | | | "Part Number" | 0 | | "Equipment" |
| 5 | Server | Drag ont | Prop | ProductDescription | | | | "Product Description" | 0 | | "Equipment" |
| 6 | Server | Drag ont | Prop | AssetNumber | | | | "Asset Number" | 0 | | "Asset" |
| 7 | Server | Drag ont | Prop | SerialNumber | | | | "Serial Number" | 0 | | "Asset" |
| 8 | Server | Drag ont | Prop | Location | | | | "Location" | 0 | | "Asset" |
| 9 | Server | Drag ont | Prop | Building | | | | "Building" | 0 | | "Asset" |
| 10 | Server | Drag ont | Prop | Room | | | | "Room" | 0 | | "Asset" |

Using Microsoft Excel for recording shape data rows, and others, can make the design and transfer to other shapes less painful.

Microsoft provides *ShapeStudio,* within the Microsoft Visio SDK, which can also be used to transfer shape data rows from one shape to another. This uses a Microsoft SQL Server database.

# User-Defined Cells for Data

*User-defined cells* are general purpose cells that can be used to store hidden data or to contain *triggers,* formulae that evaluate when values in other cells change.

If you use them to store data, then you cannot specify the data type, but you can label it in the Prompt cell. Many examples in the Master shapes are provided by Microsoft. For example, if you examine the User-defined section of any of the Organization Chart Masters, you will see the User-defined section has many rows. Some of them are storing data values, such as User.Solsh, while others are dynamically calculating values, such as User.Margin, in the following example.

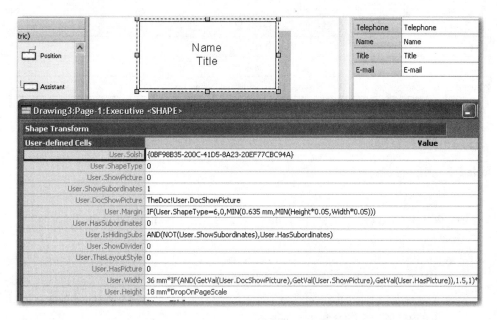

User-defined cells can be used in Reports, but it can be difficult to clearly see which cells are being used for data values, and which are being used for calculations of one sort or another. I recommend you name the rows accordingly and, if it is not clear, use the Prompt cell to describe the purpose of any formula in the Value cell.

You will find that some Microsoft Visio-provided shapes also use the Scratch section to store values or to make calculations. Sometimes, this is because Scratch cells predate User-defined cells; at other times, it is because the Scratch section contains special cells that can store geometric points.

# Using ShapeSheet Formulae

Some ShapeSheet functions get used more than others. For example, the LOOKUP function returns the 0-based index number of a value within a list. You can then use that number with the INDEX function to return a value from another list. In this way, you can change the color of a fill, line, or text, depending on the selected value.

So, if you have a shape data row that is a fixed-list type, let's call it *Priority,* with values Low, Medium, High, you could cause the lines to change between Green, Yellow, Red.

| Cell | Formula |
| --- | --- |
| Name | Priority |
| Label | Priority |
| Prompt | Select the priority from the list |
| Type | 1 |
| Format | ";Low;Medium;High" |
| Value | "" |

**Table 2-5**    *Priority Shape Data*

First, you need to create a shape data row, as Table 2-5 shows, for the Priority selection.

**NOTE**

*A semicolon is before the word "Low." This is because the default value is unset and, because this is a fixed-list, any value must be in the list.*

Then you need to create some User-defined cells, as Table 2-6 shows. The first one of these simply gets the index position of the selected Priority.

This index is used to get a color definition from a list of colors, as you can see in Table 2-7. In fact, I specified that the new THEME function should be applied if the Priority is not set (the first item in the list is a zero-length string).

| Cell | Formula |
| --- | --- |
| Name | PriorityIdx |
| Value | LOOKUP(Prop.Priority,Prop.Priority.Format) |
| Prompt | "The index of the Priority property" |

**Table 2-6**    *Get the Index of the Selected Priority*

| Cell | Formula |
| --- | --- |
| Name | PriorityColor |
| Value | INDEX(User.PriorityIdx,"THEME(""LineColor"")";RGB(0,255,0);RGB(255,255,0);RGB(255,0,0)") |
| Prompt | "Priority" |

**Table 2-7**    *Get a Color for the Selected Priority*

| Cell | Formula |
|------|---------|
| Name | PriorityTrigger |
| Value | DEPENDSON(User.PriorityIdx)+SETF(GetRef(LineColor),User. PriorityColor) |
| Prompt | Set Priority |

**Table 2-8**  *Set the Line Color Value According to the Priority*

The color formula could be put into any one of several cells, but because the foreground and background fill colors can be used by the Data Graphics later, I will set the line color to give visual indication of the Priority. See Table 2-8.

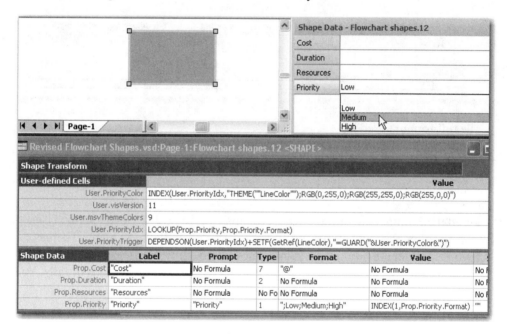

In the previous example, I chose to set the formula for the line color by pushing in the value. I could have chosen to pull the value in by having a formula in the LineColor cell directly, but then the value would need to be guarded against changes from the UI, otherwise the Priority color could not be reapplied.

# Respecting Themes

The new Themes in Microsoft Visio 2007 changes the formula of a few color cells and inserts a new User row, msvThemeColors. Now, if you want to have a formula that does one thing if a theme is used, and another if it is not, then you need to be able to detect the presence of the User. msvThemeColors cell. Most functions refer directly to a cell, but the SETF function (which is used for setting formulae in other cells) expects the name string, therefore, you can write a formula that uses the SETF function, regardless of whether or not the cell exists. So, if the SETF succeeds, it will not cause an error, but if it fails, then it will report an error. Fortunately, you can detect this with the ISERRVALUE function. However, it will not reevaluate automatically, so I set the formula to reevaluate whenever there is a change in the value of the FillForegnd cell. It is safe to refer to this cell directly because it is a built-in cell, unlike the rows of shape data or User-defined cells.

Thus, you can amend the formula in the User.PriorityTrigger to respect the possible use of themes.

| | |
|---|---|
| ✗ ✓ | =DEPENDSON(User.PriorityIdx)+IF(AND(User.PriorityIdx=0,User.HasTheme=0),SETF(GetRef(LineColor),"=THEME(""LineColor""))"),SETF(GetRef(LineColor),"="&User.PriorityColor&"")) |

| Shape Transform | |
|---|---|
| **User-defined Cells** | **Value** |
| User.PriorityColor | INDEX(User.PriorityIdx,";GUARD(RGB(0,255,0));GUARD(RGB(255,255,0));GUARD(RGB(255,0,0))") |
| User.visVersion | 11 |
| User.msvThemeColors | 9 |
| User.PriorityIdx | LOOKUP(Prop.Priority,Prop.Priority.Format) |
| User.PriorityTrigger | DEPENDSON(User.PriorityIdx)+IF(AND(User.PriorityIdx=0,User.HasTheme=0),SETF(GetRef(LineColor),"=THEME(""LineColor""))"),SETF(GetRef(LineColor),"="&User.PriorityColor |
| User.HasTheme | DEPENDSON(FillForegnd)+ISERRVALUE(SETF("User.msvThemeColors.Prompt","1")) |

The full formula used is:

```
=DEPENDSON(User.PriorityIdx)+IF(AND(User.PriorityIdx=0,User.HasTheme=0)
,SETF(GetRef(LineColor),"=THEME(""LineColor"")"),SETF(GetRef(LineColor)
,"="&User.PriorityColor&""))
```

I used the Prompt cell, of the User.visVersion row, to push a value into the User. visThemeColors.Prompt cell because it is unimportant and unused by the Themes.

If you enter the previous formula into a new User-defined cell, say, HasTheme, then the resultant value will be 0 or 1, depending on whether it succeeds or fails. You can use this elsewhere in your ShapeSheet.

### NOTE

*I increased the line weight in the previous example, so the color is more visible.*

## Making Read-Only Shape Data Rows

Microsoft Visio contains a useful Reports tool, but this requires the shapes to contain the data you want to report on. This sounds straightforward, but there are some values you may want to have in Reports, but you cannot normally find them in the shape data.

For example, the page name and number do not appear in the list of properties of a shape. However, you can modify your shapes to include these values. All you need to do is to add rows to your Master shape, and then they will be available to you in reports that contain the instances of these Master shapes.

The only problem is you want these rows to be noneditable because they will contain formulae, so you should either guard the formula or create a fixed list with just one entry. The former has the disadvantage that you can overtype the entry, but it will revert to the original value when you exit the cell in the Shape Data window or dialog. The latter has this disadvantage: you need to have identical formulae in the Format and Value cell, and there is a pull-down arrow in the left edge of the cell. Another drawback of this is you cannot apply a data type to the value—they are all strings (text).

## Creating Calculated Values

At other times, you need to display the result of a calculation based on the values in other cells. For example, you may have a shape data row for Duration and one for DailyRate, and you want to display the Cost, as the product of Duration * DailyRate.

To do this, drag a Process shape from the Basic Flowchart stencil. It already has the Cost, Resources, and Duration shape data, but you need to modify it to add another shape data row: DailyRate. Then you have a choice: you can either *pull* the result into the DailyRate cell or you can *push* it in.

To pull the data in, you can enter the formula Prop.DailyRate * Prop.Duration into the Prop.Cost.Value cell. If you enclose the formula with the GUARD function, then you make it noneditable.

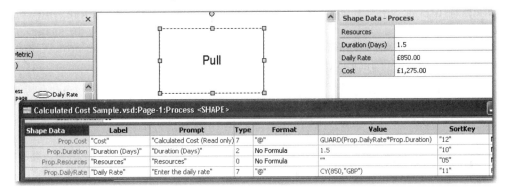

| Shape Data | Label | Prompt | Type | Format | Value | SortKey | |
|---|---|---|---|---|---|---|---|
| Prop.Cost | "Cost" | "Calculated Cost (Read only)" | 7 | "@" | GUARD(Prop.DailyRate*Prop.Duration) | "12" | |
| Prop.Duration | "Duration (Days)" | "Duration (Days)" | 2 | No Formula | 1.5 | "10" | |
| Prop.Resources | "Resources" | "Resources" | 0 | No Formula | "" | "05" | |
| Prop.DailyRate | "Daily Rate" | "Enter the daily rate" | 7 | "@" | CY(850,"GBP") | "11" | |

To push the data in, you can create a new User-defined cell, called, say, CostTrigger, and then enter the formula

```
=DEPENDSON(Prop.Duration,Prop.DailyRate)+SETF(GETREF(Prop.Cost),Prop.
DailyRate*Prop.Duration)
```

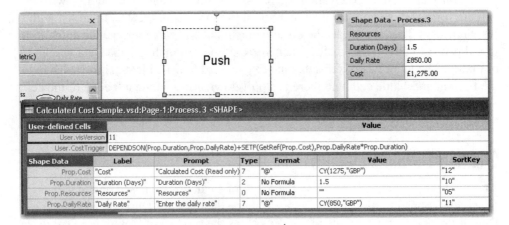

This has the effect of pushing the result of the calculation into the Prop.Cost.Value cell whenever the Cost or DailyRate is changed. This makes the Cost editable, but it will be updated if the Duration or DailyRate is changed.

# Creating Intershape References

In the previous Cost example, referring to a centralized value for the DailyRate would be useful, rather than having to maintain it in many places. Therefore, you could create a shape data row in the page, and then the DailyRate cell in the shape can refer to it with the formula ThePage!Prop.DailyRate. Again, you can protect this from being edited by enclosing the formula with the GUARD function.

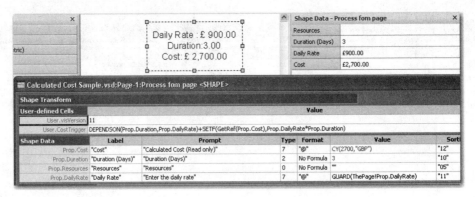

If you anticipate you might have more than one page in your document, then you could create a new shape data row or User-defined cell in the document ShapeSheet. To do this, you need to open the ShapeSheet from the document node on the Drawing Explorer window.

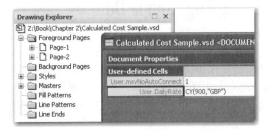

Once you create the cell, you need to refer to it from the DailyRate cell in the shape, with the formula TheDoc!User.DailyRate.

# Shapes to Edit Document Level Variables

I have always thought it strange that you can only create shape data rows for the document with the ShapeSheet: there is no Shape Data window or dialog. Therefore, little advantage usually exists in creating shape data rows rather than User-defined cells. Because you do not have a built-in method of inputing a document level value, other than using the ShapeSheet, you may need to create one. Of course, you could write a Windows application or add-in that provides a totally new window or dialog, but you can achieve the same end with another custom shape.

If you create a shape with a Daily Rate shape data row, then you can add a User-defined cell that has a trigger to update the document's User-defined cell. Then, all cells that refer to the document level DailyRate cell are automatically updated.

The only problem with this approach is you could have many copies of the trigger shape, which will update the document's DailyRate value. Therefore, it is useful to display the current value in the trigger shape, as well as the new rate you want to apply. You can then easily see if a difference exists between the two.

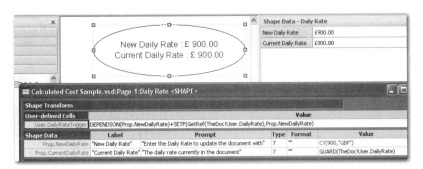

Remember, we set this up to change the document level value whenever the new daily rate is changed, so you need to change the new daily rate value to cause the document level value to be updated.

## Automatically Creating Page Shape Data

If you have a shape that contains cell formulae with references to shape data rows or User-defined cells in the page, then those referred to page rows are automatically created whenever the shape is dropped onto a page that does not contain them.

In one of the previous calculated cost examples, the DailyRate refers to the page's DailyRate so, consequently, that Shape Data row is added to any new page when the shape is added to it.

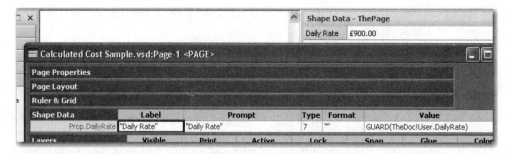

One drawback to adding shape data rows to pages in this manner is you can have many shapes, all trying to add page-level shape data rows, and they can be added in any order. Therefore, if you want to have some consistency in appearance of the shape data rows from one page to another, use the SortKey cell to ensure the rows are in the same order.

## Rolling Up Values

Sometimes, it is useful to be able to have the value of shape data on one shape to sum the shape data rows from several other shapes. You can do this manually, but it is usually much easier to have a little automation. In the calculated cost example, summing the duration from other shapes would be sufficient to provide the rollup cost in the selected shape (the rollup shape).

The end result is this: you can change the value of the Duration shape data in any of the child shapes, and the Duration value in the rollup shape is automatically updated.

## Manual Rollup

As previously mentioned, the Shape Data window and dialog cannot be used to enter formulae, so you have to use the ShapeSheet to enter the rollup formula. Also, you need to know the unique shape IDs (known as the *sheet IDs*) or the NameU of the shapes with the data you want to roll up.

The simplest way to find the ID is to select Special from the Format menu (which you will not see unless you are in Developer mode).

You can also see the name of the shape on the Special dialog, and you can rename a shape manually with it. Please note, the first time you rename a shape with this dialog, the underlying universal name is also changed (the *NameU*). However, the NameU will not be changed if you subsequently rename the shape with this dialog again. The Name of the shape will be different from the NameU of the shape, unless you use code to change it. This is to allow different languages to be used.

Consequently, it is preferable to use the NameU of a shape in code, because the Name could have been changed. Similarly, a Shape Data row has a NameU and Name property.

## Automated Rollup

There are many scenarios where you would like a rollup shape to display the sum of shape data in other shapes. In a complete solution, you may want to update the rollup shape formula whenever it is connected or disconnected to other shapes, but we will take the simple case where you create a multiple shape selection and the first shape selected is the rollup shape.

The example is shown in Visual Basic for Applications (VBA) because it is a good way of testing code but, of course, you must have VBA enabled to try this.

```
Public Sub RollupDuration()
    'Pass the shape data name to the helper function
    RollupData "Prop.Duration"
End Sub


Private Sub RollupData(ByVal cellName As String)
Dim rollupShape As Visio.Shape
Dim childShape As Visio.Shape
Dim rollupList As String

If Visio.ActiveWindow.Selection.Count < 2 Then
    'Not enough selected shapes to continue
    Exit Sub
End If
```

```
If Visio.ActiveWindow.Selection.PrimaryItem.CellExists( _
        cellName, Visio.visExistsAnywhere) Then
    Set rollupShape = Visio.ActiveWindow.Selection.PrimaryItem
Else
    'The first shape does not contain the correct shape data row
    Exit Sub
End If


'Loop through the selection
For Each childShape In Visio.ActiveWindow.Selection
    If Not childShape Is rollupShape _
        And childShape.CellExists( _
            cellName, Visio.visExistsAnywhere) Then

        If Len(rollupList) = 0 Then
            'This is the start of the list
            rollupList = childShape.NameU & "!" & cellName
        Else
            'Append to the list
            rollupList = rollupList & "," & _
                childShape.NameU & "!" & cellName
        End If

    End If
Next


'Finally, update the rollup shape formula
'GUARD the formula to protect from overtyping
'Use FormulaForce for subsequent reruns
rollupShape.Cells(cellName).FormulaForce = _
    "=GUARD(SUM(" & rollupList & "))"


End Sub
```

I have used FormulaForce, rather than just Formula, because it is necessary to force a formula into a cell when it contains the GUARD function.

This macro is available from the Tools | Macros menu, but you need to select the summary shape, followed by all the other shapes that contain a Duration property.

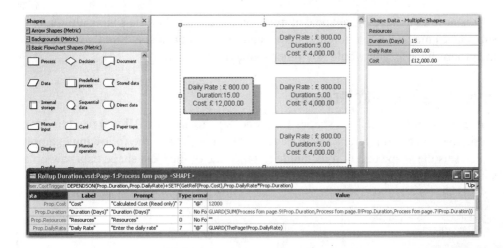

### NOTE

*The primary shape has a thicker magenta-colored rectangle, and the formula pushed into the primary shape's Duration cell sums the Duration cells of the other shapes. Because the intershape reference has been set, changing the duration in one of the subshapes will cause the summary shape's Duration to be updated automatically. There is no need to run the macro again.*

## Group Shape References

We have demonstrated the capability to reference cells in other shapes, the page, or documents, but sometimes users get confused about references within a shape, when that shape is a group.

First, grouping should be done with caution. Why? Because users often forget what is grouped, and then they group groups or they ungroup too far, thus destroying the behavior and data of the original shapes. Sometimes, it is necessary to create grouped shapes and to have cell references in the grouped shapes to cells in the group shapes. In general, if you need multiple text blocks, different line or fill patterns, within the same shape, then it is necessary to have a grouped shape, otherwise use the Shape / Operations to create more efficient shapes. In addition, you should keep the number of groups within groups to an absolute minimum because the Visio engine needs to recalculate values through each group.

It is normal to have the shape data rows on the top level of the shape, although sub-shapes may need to reference shape data in the group shape. Simply reference the group shape as you would any other shape on the page.

## Inter-Page Shape References

You can also refer to cells in shapes from one page to another. All you need to do is prefix the shape cell reference with Pages[page name]!, as in the following example, which sets the shape text of a rectangle to the value of the Cost shape data row on a shape in another page:

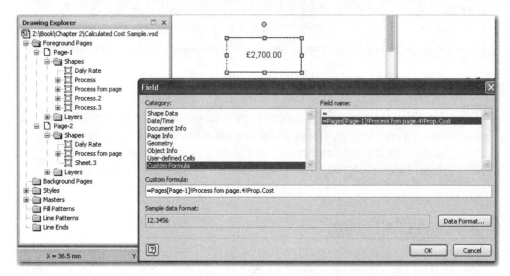

# Right-Mouse Menu Items from Shape Data Lists

An interesting Master, called *Flowchart Shapes*, is on the Basic Flowchart Shapes stencil. What makes this interesting is the way the shape changes appearance, depending on a selection of Process, Decision, Document, or Data. This is quite an old shape, and I think it is due for an upgrade.

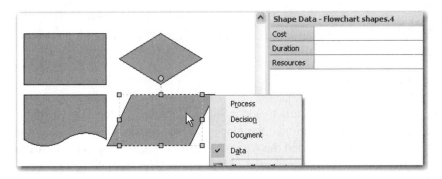

For example, the shape does not display which type it is, so it is difficult to create reports filtered by the type. If you look at the ShapeSheet of this shape, you can see four rows are in the Actions section, which sets the formula of a cell in the Scratch section to a value from 1 to 4.

| User-defined Cells | | | | | Value | | | | |
|---|---|---|---|---|---|---|---|---|---|
| User.msvThemeColors | 9 | | | | | | | | |
| User.visVersion | 11 | | | | | | | | |

| Shape Data | Label | Prompt | Type | Format | Value | | | | |
|---|---|---|---|---|---|---|---|---|---|
| Prop.Cost | "Cost" | No Formula | 7 | "@" | No Formula | | | | |
| Prop.Duration | "Duration" | No Formula | 2 | No Formula | No Formula | | | | |
| Prop.Resources | "Resources" | No Formula | No Formula | No Formula | No Formula | | | | |

| Connection Points | X | Y | DirX / A | DirY / B | Type / C | D | | |
|---|---|---|---|---|---|---|---|---|

| Actions | Action | Menu | gNantonF; SortKey | Checked | Disabled | ReadOnly |
|---|---|---|---|---|---|---|
| Actions.Row_1 | SETF("Scratch.A1",1) | "P&rocess" | No Fc No F; No Formula Scratch.A1=1 | No Formula | No Formula | |
| Actions.Row_2 | SETF("Scratch.A1",2) | "Decisio&n" | No Fc No F; No Formula Scratch.A1=2 | No Formula | No Formula | |
| Actions.Row_3 | SETF("Scratch.A1",3) | "Doc&ument" | No Fc No F; No Formula Scratch.A1=3 | No Formula | No Formula | |
| Actions.Row_4 | SETF("Scratch.A1",4) | "D&ata" | No Fc No F; No Formula Scratch.A1=4 | No Formula | No Formula | |
| Actions.Row_5 | DOCMD(1312) | "%P&roperties" | No Fc No F; No Formula No Formula | No Formula | No Formula | |

| Geometry 1 | | | | | | | | | |
|---|---|---|---|---|---|---|---|---|---|
| Geometry1.NoFill | FALSE | | | Geometry1.NoLine | FALSE | Geometry1.NoShow | NOT(Scratch.A1=4) | | Geometry1. |
| Name | X | | Y | | A | B | C | | D |
| 1 | MoveTo | Width*0-Scratch.B1 | Height*0 | | | | | | |
| 2 | LineTo | Width*1-Scratch.B1 | Height*0 | | | | | | |
| 3 | LineTo | Width*1+Scratch.B1 | Height*1 | | | | | | |
| 4 | LineTo | Width*0+Scratch.B1 | Height*1 | | | | | | |
| 5 | LineTo | Geometry1.X1 | Geometry1.Y1 | | | | | | |

| Geometry 2 | | | | | | | | | |
|---|---|---|---|---|---|---|---|---|---|

| Geometry 3 | | | | | | | | | |
|---|---|---|---|---|---|---|---|---|---|

| Geometry 4 | | | | | | | | | |
|---|---|---|---|---|---|---|---|---|---|

| Scratch | X | Y | A | B | C | D | |
|---|---|---|---|---|---|---|---|
| 1 | MIN(MIN(Width,Height)/8,Scratch.Y1) | Width/12 | 4 | MIN(Height/4,Width/4) | No Formula | No Formula | |

The Set Formula (SETF) sets the value of the quoted cell, for example:

```
=SETF("Scratch.A1",1)
```

The Menu cell displays the shape type, so you can select which shape type you want to use. The Checked cell displays which shape type is selected.

```
=Scratch.A1=1
```

Four geometry sections are in the ShapeSheet, but only one of them is displayed at any one time. This is because their NoShow cell is set according to the value in the Scratch.A1 cell.

```
=NOT(Scratch.A1=4)
```

My suggested improvement is to add a Shape Data row, called Type, with a fixed list. I suggest you should minimize the places where any language-dependent text is written. Therefore, I amended the Action cells to reference Format cell of Prop. Type, and the Menu to read the Prompt cell of a new User-defined cell called User. TypeIdx.

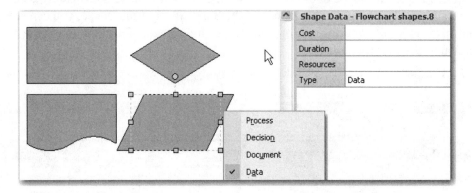

The formula in the Value cell of User.TypeIdx row looks up the zero-based index of the value of Prop.Type in the list defined in the Prop.Type.Format cell.

```
=LOOKUP(Prop.Type,Prop.Type.Format)
```

This index is used in the Action cells to set the formula of the shape data row, Prop.Type.

```
=SETF(GetRef(Prop.Type),"="""""&INDEX(0,Prop.Type.Format)&"""""")
```

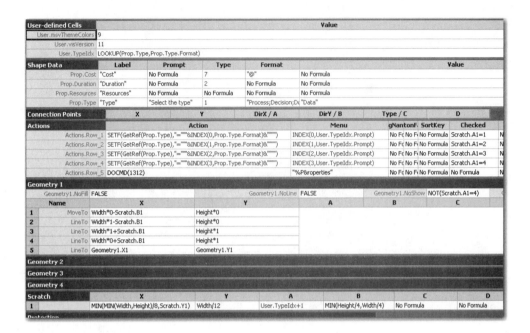

| User-defined Cells | | | | Value | | | | | |
|---|---|---|---|---|---|---|---|---|---|
| User.msvThemeColors | 9 | | | | | | | | |
| User.visVersion | 11 | | | | | | | | |
| User.TypeIdx | LOOKUP(Prop.Type,Prop.Type.Format) | | | | | | | | |

| Shape Data | Label | Prompt | Type | Format | | Value | | | |
|---|---|---|---|---|---|---|---|---|---|
| Prop.Cost | "Cost" | No Formula | 7 | "@" | No Formula | | | | |
| Prop.Duration | "Duration" | No Formula | 2 | No Formula | No Formula | | | | |
| Prop.Resources | "Resources" | No Formula | No Formula | No Formula | No Formula | | | | |
| Prop.Type | "Type" | "Select the type" | 1 | "Process;Decision;D{ | "Data" | | | | |

| Connection Points | X | | Y | | DirX / A | DirY / B | Type / C | D | |
|---|---|---|---|---|---|---|---|---|---|

| Actions | | Action | | | Menu | gNantonF | SortKey | Checked | |
|---|---|---|---|---|---|---|---|---|---|
| Actions.Row_1 | SETF(GetRef(Prop.Type),"="""&INDEX(0,Prop.Type.Format)&"""") | | | INDEX(0,User.TypeIdx.Prompt) | No Fc | No Fi | No Formula | Scratch.A1=1 | N |
| Actions.Row_2 | SETF(GetRef(Prop.Type),"="""&INDEX(1,Prop.Type.Format)&"""") | | | INDEX(1,User.TypeIdx.Prompt) | No Fc | No Fi | No Formula | Scratch.A1=2 | N |
| Actions.Row_3 | SETF(GetRef(Prop.Type),"="""&INDEX(2,Prop.Type.Format)&"""") | | | INDEX(2,User.TypeIdx.Prompt) | No Fc | No Fi | No Formula | Scratch.A1=3 | N |
| Actions.Row_4 | SETF(GetRef(Prop.Type),"="""&INDEX(3,Prop.Type.Format)&"""") | | | INDEX(3,User.TypeIdx.Prompt) | No Fc | No Fi | No Formula | Scratch.A1=4 | N |
| Actions.Row_5 | DOCMD(1312) | | | "%P&roperties" | No Fc | No Fi | No Formula | No Formula | N |

| Geometry 1 | | | | | | | | | |
|---|---|---|---|---|---|---|---|---|---|
| Geometry1.NoFill | FALSE | | | Geometry1.NoLine | FALSE | | Geometry1.NoShow | NOT(Scratch.A1=4) | |
| | Name | X | | Y | | A | B | C | |
| 1 | MoveTo | Width*0-Scratch.B1 | | Height*0 | | | | | |
| 2 | LineTo | Width*1-Scratch.B1 | | Height*0 | | | | | |
| 3 | LineTo | Width*1+Scratch.B1 | | Height*1 | | | | | |
| 4 | LineTo | Width*0+Scratch.B1 | | Height*1 | | | | | |
| 5 | LineTo | Geometry1.X1 | | Geometry1.Y1 | | | | | |

| Geometry 2 | | | | | | | | | |
|---|---|---|---|---|---|---|---|---|---|

| Geometry 3 | | | | | | | | | |
|---|---|---|---|---|---|---|---|---|---|

| Geometry 4 | | | | | | | | | |
|---|---|---|---|---|---|---|---|---|---|

| Scratch | X | | Y | | A | B | C | | D |
|---|---|---|---|---|---|---|---|---|---|
| 1 | MIN(MIN(Width,Height)/8,Scratch.Y1) | | Width/12 | | User.TypeIdx+1 | MIN(Height/4,Width/4) | No Formula | | No Formula |

**NOTE**

*I used the Get Reference (GETREF) function to obtain the name of the Prop.Type cell because the SETF function requires the name, and you could possibly change the name of the Prop.Type row. Using the GETREF function ensures the reference is not broken.*

Also, note the text being pushed into the Value cell must be enclosed in double-quotes, because the Value cell does not know what the data type is.

The overall effect is that you can select the type of an individual shape by using either the right mouse menu or by changing the shape data type. The extra benefits are the Prop.Type can be used in reports and you can change the type of multiple shapes simultaneously by using the Shape Data window.

In Chapter 8, you learn how you can combine smart tags and right-mouse menu items. But, in Chapter 3, we delve deeper into data linking.

# Linking Data to Shapes

**IN THIS CHAPTER**

Creating Linked Data

Labeling Shapes from Shape Data

Enhancing Shapes with Color, Icons, and Data Bars

The Link Data to Shapes tool is the backbone of the new features in Microsoft Visio 2007. It may not have the immediate impact of the flashy Data Graphics tool, but they are of no use without the data in the shapes in the first place. The data in Visio is what makes it so suitable for use as a corporate tool.

The *Link Data to Shapes tool* is only for viewing information from a data source—it does not let you edit the data, and then update the data source. The older tool, Database Wizard, has that capability, but Link Data also allows a shape to be linked to multiple data sources. This is a crucial difference because it means you can overlay, say, a list of designated fire marshals from a departmental spreadsheet on personnel shapes from the corporate HR database. Then, if your personnel are laid out on a floor plan, you could use the new Data Graphics tool to highlight the fire marshals, and you can visually check that their distribution is satisfactory. Similarly, you could identify PCs that are missing a required software patch.

The list of useful scenarios for simple visualization of data is endless, but their usefulness is constrained by the veracity of the supplied data.

A variety of types of data can be linked to Visio, including Microsoft Excel, Microsoft Access, Microsoft SQL Server and SharePoint Services Lists, or any suitable OLEDB or ODBC data source. Although you can easily link to Microsoft Excel, I prefer to use a data source that can identify the data type in each column explicitly. In particular, I have had trouble where a few numbers, as well as text, were in a single column.

Microsoft Visio 2007 installs a sample Access database (DBSample.mdb), usually found in C:\Program Files\Microsoft Office\Office 12\1033, and accessible via the ODBC User DSN called *Visio Database Samples*. This database has a few sample tables we can use to demonstrate linking data with, as you can see in Figure 3-1.

# Creating Linked Data

Linked data can be created manually, by picking existing shapes in a drawing or by associating data rows with a selected Master, or automatically when the unique identifier values exist already in shape data rows of existing shapes. In either case, the process will map fields to shape data rows or create any missing shape data rows, as required.

We are going to link some computer shapes to the Network—Computers table. If you examine the 15 fields in this table, you can see they are of a variety of data types.

| Field Name | Data Type |
|---|---|
| MachineSN | Text |
| Owner | Text |
| Manufacturer | Text |
| Machine Type | Text |
| Machine Type code | Number |
| Hard Disk Space | Number |
| Memory | Number |
| Processor | Text |
| Screen Size | Text |
| Network Card | Yes/No |
| Modem | Yes/No |
| Sound Card | Yes/No |
| Cost | Currency |
| XLocation | Text |
| YLocation | Text |

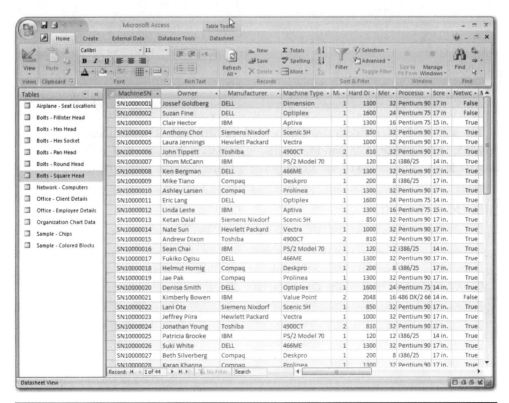

**Figure 3-1**    *The sample Access database in Microsoft Visio 2007*

Create a new Basic Network Diagram, drag a PC shape off the Computers and Monitors stencil, and then open the ShapeSheet to examine its shape data rows.

| Shape Data | Label | PromptType | Format | Value | SortKey | |
|---|---|---|---|---|---|---|
| Prop.Manufacturer | "Manufacturer" | No For 0 | No Formul. | No Fc | "Equipment" | F |
| Prop.ProductNumber | "Product Number" | No For 0 | No Formul. | No Fc | "Equipment" | F |
| Prop.PartNumber | "Part Number" | No For 0 | No Formul. | No Fc | "Equipment" | F |
| Prop.ProductDescription | "Product Description" | No For 0 | No Formul. | No Fc | "Equipment" | F |
| Prop.AssetNumber | "Asset Number" | No For 0 | No Formul. | No Fc | "Asset" | F |
| Prop.SerialNumber | "Serial Number" | No For 0 | No Formul. | No Fc | "Asset" | F |
| Prop.Location | "Location" | No For 0 | No Formul. | No Fc | "Asset" | F |
| Prop.Building | "Building" | No For 0 | No Formul. | No Fc | "Asset" | F |
| Prop.Room | "Room" | No For 0 | No Formul. | No Fc | "Asset" | F |
| Prop.Department | "Department" | No For 0 | No Formul. | No Fc | No Formula | F |
| Prop.NetworkName | "Network Name" | No For 0 | No Formul. | No Fc | "Network" | F |
| Prop.IPAddress | "IP Address" | No For 0 | No Formul. | No Fc | "Network" | F |
| Prop.SubnetMask | "Subnet Mask" | No For 0 | No Formul. | No Fc | "Network" | F |
| Prop.AdminInterface | "Administrative Interface" | No For 0 | No Formul. | No Fc | "Network" | F |
| Prop.NumberofPorts | "Number of Ports" | No For 0 | No Formul. | No Fc | "Network" | F |
| Prop.CommunityString | "Community String" | No For 0 | No Formul. | No Fc | "Network" | F |
| Prop.NetworkDescription | "Network Description" | No For 0 | No Formul. | No Fc | "Network" | F |
| Prop.CPU | "CPU" | No For 0 | No Formul. | No Fc | "Workstation" | F |
| Prop.Memory | "Memory" | No For 0 | No Formul. | No Fc | "Workstation" | F |
| Prop.OperatingSystem | "Operating System" | No For 0 | No Formul. | No Fc | "Workstation" | F |
| Prop.BelongsTo | "Belongs To" | No For 0 | No Formul. | No Fc | No Formula | 1 |
| Prop.ShapeClass | "ShapeClass" | No For 0 | No Formul. | "Equi | No Formula | 1 |
| Prop.ShapeType | "ShapeType" | No For 0 | No Formul. | "Com | No Formula | 1 |
| Prop.SubShapeType | "SubShapeType" | No For 0 | No Formul. | "Desk | No Formula | 1 |
| Prop.MACAddress | "MAC Address" | No For 0 | No Formul. | No Fc | "Network" | F |
| Prop.HardDriveSize | "Hard Drive Capacity" | No For 0 | No Formul. | No Fc | "Workstation" | F |

You will see 26 shape data rows, all with Type = 0 (text). Four of them are invisible in the Shape Data window or dialog, however, because they either store classification information or the BelongsTo data (used by the Space Plan add-in).

# Link Data Manually

Now, select Data | Link Data to Shapes… and in the Data Selector dialog, select the sample Access database, DBSample.mdb, and the Network—Computers table. For now, do not bother to change the columns or filter the data; you should see (All Columns) and (All Data) in the Data Selector dialog. Then, click the Finish button.

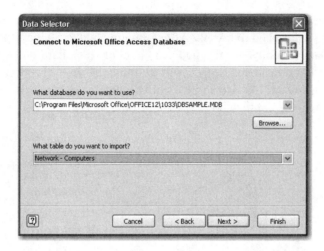

The External Data window automatically opens, and it displays the rows and columns of data from the database table. The data is copied locally into the Visio file as XML, which you can now link to shapes in the diagram.

| | MachineSN | Owner | Manufacturer | Machine Type | M... | Hard... | Memory | |
|---|---|---|---|---|---|---|---|---|
| | SN10000001 | Jossef Gold... | DELL | Dimension | 1 | 1300 | 32 | F |
| | SN10000002 | Suzan Fine | DELL | Optiplex | 1 | 1600 | 24 | F |
| | SN10000003 | Clair Hector | IBM | Aptiva | 1 | 1300 | 16 | F |
| | SN10000004 | Anthony Chor | Siemens Nixdorf | Scenic 5H | 1 | 850 | 32 | F |
| | SN10000005 | Laura Jenni... | Hewlett Packard | Vectra | 1 | 1000 | 32 | F |
| | SN10000006 | John Tippett | Toshiba | 4900CT | 2 | 810 | 32 | F |
| | SN10000007 | Thom McCann | IBM | PS/2 Model 70 | 1 | 120 | 12 | ï |
| | SN10000008 | Ken Bergman | DELL | 466ME | 1 | 1300 | 32 | F |
| | SN10000009 | Mike Tiano | Compaq | Deskpro | 1 | 200 | 8 | ï |
| | SN10000010 | Ashley Larsen | Compaq | Prolinea | 1 | 1300 | 32 | F |
| | SN10000011 | Eric Lang | DELL | Optiplex | 1 | 1600 | 24 | F |
| | SN10000012 | Linda Leste | IBM | Aptiva | 1 | 1300 | 16 | F |
| | SN10000013 | Ketan Dalal | Siemens Nixdorf | Scenic 5H | 1 | 850 | 32 | F |
| | SN10000014 | Nate Sun | Hewlett Packard | Vectra | 1 | 1000 | 32 | F |
| | SN10000015 | Andrew Dixon | Toshiba | 4900CT | 2 | 810 | 32 | F |

Network - Computers

Now, ensure that you have the PC Master selected, and then drag-and-drop the top row from the External Data window into the drawing page. The PC shape will now be populated with the data from the row you just dropped, and a chain-link symbol will appear in the first column of the External Data window. If, and probably when (unless you have unchecked the Apply After Linking Data to Shapes option at the bottom of the Data Graphics panel), the Data Graphics Task Pane automatically appears, just close it down because you will examine that in the section "Labeling Shapes from Shape Data." Notice 35 items of shape data are now visible, as some new data rows are added at the end of the shape data section.

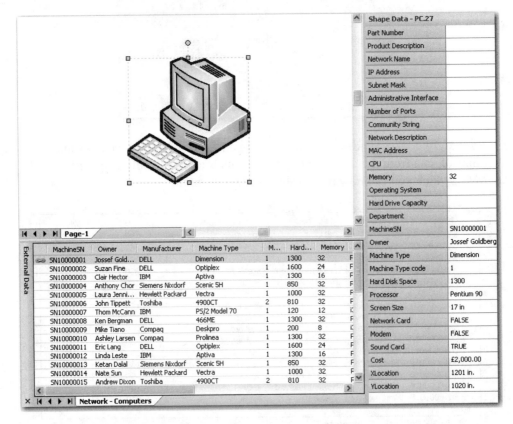

Open the ShapeSheet for this shape and you can see what happened. In my case, you can easily spot the affected shape data rows because the LangID column has the code 2057 (English UK) rather than 1033 (English US).

| Shape Data | Label | PromptType | Type | Format | Value | SortKey | Invisible | Ask | LangID |
|---|---|---|---|---|---|---|---|---|---|
| Prop.Manufacturer | "Manufacturer" | No For | 0 | No Formul | "DELL" | "Equipment" | FALSE | FALSE | 2057 |
| Prop.ProductNumber | "Product Number" | No For | 0 | No Formul | No Formula | "Equipment" | FALSE | FALSE | 1033 |
| Prop.PartNumber | "Part Number" | No For | 0 | No Formul | No Formula | "Equipment" | FALSE | FALSE | 1033 |
| Prop.ProductDescription | "Product Description" | No For | 0 | No Formul | No Formula | "Equipment" | FALSE | FALSE | 1033 |
| Prop.AssetNumber | "Asset Number" | No For | 0 | No Formul | No Formula | "Asset" | FALSE | FALSE | 1033 |
| Prop.SerialNumber | "Serial Number" | No For | 0 | No Formul | No Formula | "Asset" | FALSE | FALSE | 1033 |
| Prop.Location | "Location" | No For | 0 | No Formul | No Formula | "Asset" | FALSE | FALSE | 1033 |
| Prop.Building | "Building" | No For | 0 | No Formul | No Formula | "Asset" | FALSE | FALSE | 1033 |
| Prop.Room | "Room" | No For | 0 | No Formula | No Formula | "Asset" | FALSE | FALSE | 1033 |
| Prop.Department | "Department" | No For | 0 | No Formul | No Formula | No Formula | FALSE | FALSE | 1033 |
| Prop.NetworkName | "Network Name" | No For | 0 | No Formul | No Formula | "Network" | FALSE | FALSE | 1033 |
| Prop.IPAddress | "IP Address" | No For | 0 | No Formul | No Formula | "Network" | FALSE | FALSE | 1033 |
| Prop.SubnetMask | "Subnet Mask" | No For | 0 | No Formul | No Formula | "Network" | FALSE | FALSE | 1033 |
| Prop.AdminInterface | "Administrative Interface" | No For | 0 | No Formul | No Formula | "Network" | FALSE | FALSE | 1033 |
| Prop.NumberofPorts | "Number of Ports" | No For | 0 | No Formul | No Formula | "Network" | FALSE | FALSE | 1033 |
| Prop.CommunityString | "Community String" | No For | 0 | No Formul | No Formula | "Network" | FALSE | FALSE | 1033 |
| Prop.NetworkDescription | "Network Description" | No For | 0 | No Formul | No Formula | "Network" | FALSE | FALSE | 1033 |
| Prop.CPU | "CPU" | No For | 0 | No Formul | No Formula | "Workstation" | FALSE | FALSE | 1033 |
| Prop.Memory | "Memory" | No For | 0 | No Formul | "32" | "Workstation" | FALSE | FALSE | 2057 |
| Prop.OperatingSystem | "Operating System" | No For | 0 | No Formul | No Formula | "Workstation" | FALSE | FALSE | 1033 |
| Prop.BelongsTo | "Belongs To" | No For | 0 | No Formul | No Formula | No Formula | TRUE | FALSE | 1033 |
| Prop.ShapeClass | "ShapeClass" | No For | 0 | No Formul | "Equipment" | No Formula | TRUE | FALSE | 1033 |
| Prop.ShapeType | "ShapeType" | No For | 0 | No Formul | "Computer" | No Formula | TRUE | FALSE | 1033 |
| Prop.SubShapeType | "SubShapeType" | No For | 0 | No Formul | "Desktop" | No Formula | TRUE | FALSE | 1033 |
| Prop.MACAddress | "MAC Address" | No For | 0 | No Formul | No Formula | "Network" | FALSE | FALSE | 1033 |
| Prop.HardDriveSize | "Hard Drive Capacity" | No For | 0 | No Formul | No Formula | "Workstation" | FALSE | FALSE | 1033 |
| Prop._VisDM_MachineSN | "MachineSN" | No For | No Fc | No Formul | "SN10000001" | No Formula | No Formula | No Formula | 2057 |
| Prop._VisDM_Owner | "Owner" | No For | No Fc | No Formul | "Jossef Goldber | No Formula | No Formula | No Formula | 2057 |
| Prop._VisDM_Machine_Type | "Machine Type" | No For | No Fc | No Formul | "Dimension" | No Formula | No Formula | No Formula | 2057 |
| Prop._VisDM_Machine_Type_code | "Machine Type code" | No For | 2 | No Formul | 1 | No Formula | No Formula | No Formula | 2057 |
| Prop._VisDM_Hard_Disk_Space | "Hard Disk Space" | No For | 2 | No Formul | 1300 | No Formula | No Formula | No Formula | 2057 |
| Prop._VisDM_Processor | "Processor" | No For | No Fc | No Formul | "Pentium 90" | No Formula | No Formula | No Formula | 2057 |
| Prop._VisDM_Screen_Size | "Screen Size" | No For | No Fc | No Formul | "17 in" | No Formula | No Formula | No Formula | 2057 |
| Prop._VisDM_Network_Card | "Network Card" | No For | 3 | No Formul | FALSE | No Formula | No Formula | No Formula | 2057 |
| Prop._VisDM_Modem | "Modem" | No For | 3 | No Formul | FALSE | No Formula | No Formula | No Formula | 2057 |
| Prop._VisDM_Sound_Card | "Sound Card" | No For | 3 | No Formul | TRUE | No Formula | No Formula | No Formula | 2057 |
| Prop._VisDM_Cost | "Cost" | No For | 7 | No Formul | CY(2000,"GBP") | No Formula | No Formula | No Formula | 2057 |
| Prop._VisDM_XLocation | "XLocation" | No For | No Fc | No Formul | "1201 in." | No Formula | No Formula | No Formula | 2057 |
| Prop._VisDM_YLocation | "YLocation" | No For | No Fc | No Formul | "1020 in." | No Formula | No Formula | No Formula | 2057 |

The Manufacturer and Memory rows have values, but the data type for Memory is incorrect, as it has not been changed from 0 (text) to 2 (number).

There are 13 new rows, but some of them are not required (XLocation and YLocation), and some could have been mapped to existing Shape Data rows.

## Column Settings

You can change the mapping of columns using the Column Settings... dialog that can be opened from the right mouse menu of the External Data window.

The column mapping is based on the Label cell in the shape data rows, so all you need to do is rename some of the column names to match those already existing in the PC shape, as Table 3-1 shows.

In addition, you can uncheck the XLocation and YLocation columns, as they are not required in this example.

Now delete the PC shape you just dragged on to the page, and redrag the first data row back on to the page (first, ensure the PC Master is selected in the stencil). This time, you should get only 27 visible shape data rows, but you should also get a warning that data was linked to hidden shape data fields in some of your shapes. This refers to the Belongs To row because it is currently set to invisible.

| Old Label | New Label | Existing Data Row Name |
|---|---|---|
| MachineSN | Serial Number | SerialNumber |
| Machine Type | Product Number | ProductNumber |
| Machine Type code | Part Number | PartNumber |
| Processor | CPU | CPU |
| Hard Disk Space | Hard Drive Capacity | HardDriveSize |
| Owner | Belongs To | BelongsTo |

**Table 3-1**  *Suggested Column Name Changes*

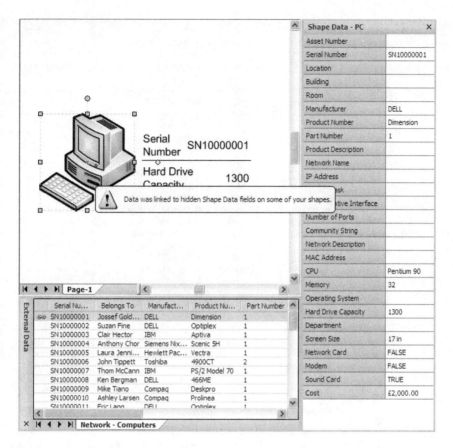

You can now see the data from the remapped columns are going into the pre-designated shape data rows. Again, if you look at the ShapeSheet of this shape, you can see six new rows, each of which has shape data row names, which begin with _visDM_. These rows have the correct Type code (although _visDM_Screen_Size does not show 0, it will be interpreted as 0).

| Shape Data | Label | PromptType | Format | Value | SortKey |
|---|---|---|---|---|---|
| Prop.Manufacturer | "Manufacturer" | No For 0 | No Formul "DELL" | | "Equipment" |
| Prop.ProductNumber | "Product Number" | No For 0 | No Formul "Dimension" | | "Equipment" |
| Prop.PartNumber | "Part Number" | No For 0 | No Formul "1" | | "Equipment" |
| Prop.ProductDescription | "Product Description" | No For 0 | No Formul No Formula | | "Equipment" |
| Prop.AssetNumber | "Asset Number" | No For 0 | No Formul No Formula | | "Asset" |
| Prop.SerialNumber | "Serial Number" | No For 0 | No Formul "SN10000001" | | "Asset" |
| Prop.Location | "Location" | No For 0 | No Formul No Formula | | "Asset" |
| Prop.Building | "Building" | No For 0 | No Formul No Formula | | "Asset" |
| Prop.Room | "Room" | No For 0 | No Formul No Formula | | "Asset" |
| Prop.Department | "Department" | No For 0 | No Formul No Formula | | No Formula |
| Prop.NetworkName | "Network Name" | No For 0 | No Formul No Formula | | "Network" |
| Prop.IPAddress | "IP Address" | No For 0 | No Formul No Formula | | "Network" |
| Prop.SubnetMask | "Subnet Mask" | No For 0 | No Formul No Formula | | "Network" |
| Prop.AdminInterface | "Administrative Interface" | No For 0 | No Formul No Formula | | "Network" |
| Prop.NumberofPorts | "Number of Ports" | No For 0 | No Formul No Formula | | "Network" |
| Prop.CommunityString | "Community String" | No For 0 | No Formul No Formula | | "Network" |
| Prop.NetworkDescription | "Network Description" | No For 0 | No Formul No Formula | | "Network" |
| Prop.CPU | "CPU" | No For 0 | No Formul "Pentium 90" | | "Workstation" |
| Prop.Memory | "Memory" | No For 0 | No Formul "32" | | "Workstation" |
| Prop.OperatingSystem | "Operating System" | No For 0 | No Formul No Formula | | "Workstation" |
| Prop.BelongsTo | "Belongs To" | No For 0 | No Formul "Jossef Goldberg" | | No Formula |
| Prop.ShapeClass | "ShapeClass" | No For 0 | No Formul "Equipment" | | No Formula |
| Prop.ShapeType | "ShapeType" | No For 0 | No Formul "Computer" | | No Formula |
| Prop.SubShapeType | "SubShapeType" | No For 0 | No Formul "Desktop" | | No Formula |
| Prop.MACAddress | "MAC Address" | No For 0 | No Formul No Formula | | "Network" |
| Prop.HardDriveSize | "Hard Drive Capacity" | No For 0 | No Formul "1300" | | "Workstation" |
| Prop._VisDM_Screen_Size | "Screen Size" | No For No Fc | No Formul "17 in" | | No Formula |
| Prop._VisDM_Network_Card | "Network Card" | No For 3 | No Formul FALSE | | No Formula |
| Prop._VisDM_Modem | "Modem" | No For 3 | No Formul FALSE | | No Formula |
| Prop._VisDM_Sound_Card | "Sound Card" | No For 3 | No Formul TRUE | | No Formula |
| Prop._VisDM_Cost | "Cost" | No For 7 | No Formul CY(2000,"GBP") | | No Formula |

You could edit the ShapeSheet here to make the changes you want, such as the visibility of Belongs To and the type of Memory, but this would mean you would need to make these changes for each PC you link. So, instead, you should edit the Master in the document stencil. In a complete solution, you would probably save these amended Masters to a stencil as part of a custom template.

Delete the PC shape you just dropped on to the page again, and then navigate to the PC Master in the Drawing Explorer window. First, ensure the Match Master by Name on Drop Setting is checked in the Master Properties dialog. This ensures that the local, amended version of the PC Master will be used, even when the PC Master on the global stencil Computers and Monitors is selected.

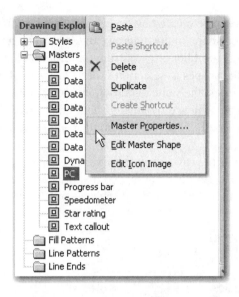

Expand the Masters branch in the Drawing Explorer window, and select the PC Master node. Now, select Edit the Master Shape from the right mouse menu of the PC Master, and a new window will open. Select the PC shape and open the ShapeSheet. Next, change the Type cell of the Memory and HardDriveSize Shape Data rows to 2 (numeric), and the Invisible cell of the BelongsTo row to FALSE.

This is also your opportunity to alter the display order of the shape data rows by changing the values in the SortKey cells. Remember, the sort keys are alphabetic order (thus, use 01, 02, etc. rather than 1,2).

This time, when you drag-and-drop a row from the External Data window, you will get the desired number of visible shape data rows, as you should see the Belongs To shape data row.

| CPU | Pentium 90 |
| Memory | 32 |
| Operating System | |
| Hard Drive Capacity | 1300 |
| Department | |
| Belongs To | Jossef Goldberg |
| Screen Size | 17 in |
| Network Card | FALSE |
| Modem | FALSE |
| Sound Card | TRUE |
| Cost | £2,000.00 |

Manual links to data can be created by dragging a data row from the External Data window on to an existing shape in the diagram. Indeed, if you have multiple shapes selected before you drag a number of rows from the External Data window, then the rows will be linked to the shapes in selection order. One note of caution: if you select fewer data rows than shapes, the same data row will be applied to multiple shapes.

The same action can be achieved by having shapes and rows selected, and then choosing the Link to Selected Shapes item from the right mouse menu of the External Data window.

You can also drag multiple rows from the External Data window with a Master selected in the stencil. You will get a cascaded display of linked data shapes, one for each row connected to an instance shape of the selected Master.

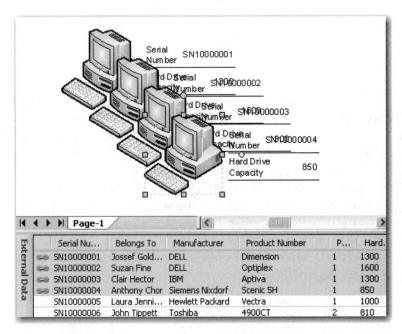

Another note of caution: do not select multiple Masters because you will get far too many shapes. In fact, you will get (number of selected rows) × (number of selected Masters). Apparently, it is supposed to work this way.

The layout of shapes created using this method will need some manual rearrangement because the cascaded layout invariably overlaps shapes.

# Filtering Rows

Your data source usually has more rows than you require, so you may want to filter the data source as you create the link using the Select Rows button on the Data Selector Wizard. If you need to change the settings after you create the link, then you open the Data Selector again from the Change Data Source button on the Configure Refresh dialog. This can be opened from the right mouse menu of the External Data window.

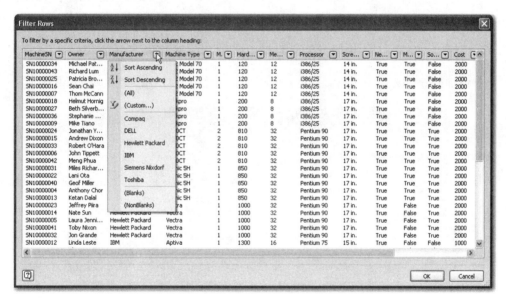

The Filter Rows dialog presents a preview of the data and enables you to filter and/or sort the data, as required.

If you select the arrow on a column heading and the select (Custom) from the pop-up menu, you will open the Filter and Sort dialog. You can add multiple filter criteria, which can be *And* or *Or* statements.

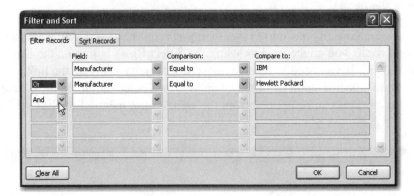

You can sort the rows in ascending or descending order by up to three columns.

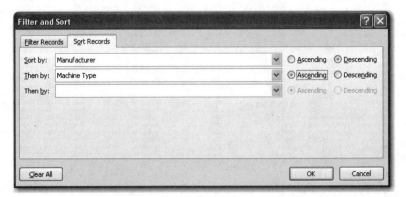

# Link Data Automatically

If you have shapes in a drawing that already have shape data rows, and one or more of them have values that uniquely describe the shape in an External Data window row, then you can automatically link the data row to the shape.

In the example table, Network—Computers, the MachineSN field is the primary key, but it is the SerialNumber shape data row in the PC shape. You can change the column, or columns, that define each row uniquely (usually the primary key) using the Configure Refresh dialog, which can be opened from the right mouse menu of the External Data window.

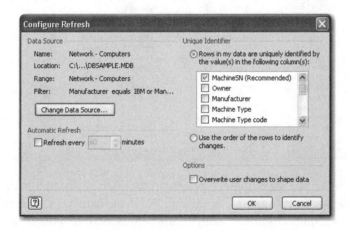

The unique identifier can consist of multiple columns, just as the primary key in the database table can be comprised of multiple fields.

So, in our example, you can have multiple PC shapes already placed within the drawing page and, if you enter valid Serial Numbers, such as SN10000006, SN10000007, etc., you can merely select Automatically Link... from the right mouse menu of the External Data window. Then, all the shapes with valid SerialNumber/MachineSN values will be automatically linked to the related data row.

## Merging Data from Other Sources

Not only can you use multiple Link Data sources per drawing, but you can also have multiple Link Data sources per shape.

Thus, in the network PC example we have been exploring, we can merge the personnel information from the Office—Employee Details table, so each PC displays the Department, Employee Title, and Extension, all useful information for your helpdesk. Select Data | Link Data to Shapes… again, and use the sample database as before but, this time, choose the Office—Employee Details table.

| Belongs To | Title | Department | Extension |
|---|---|---|---|
| Andrew Dixon | QA team lead | Product Development | 286 |
| Anthony Chor | IS | IS | 243 |
| Ashley Larsen | Operations | Operations | 240 |
| Beth Silverberg | Tech support engineer | Customer Services | 243 |
| Clair Hector | Documentation | Product Development | 224 |
| David Jaffe | Applications Engineer | Product Development | 200 |
| Denise Smith | Applications Engineer | Product Development | 213 |
| Eric Lang | Temporary QA Engineer | Product Development | 222 |
| Fukiko Ogisu | Receptionist | Operations | 202 |
| Helmut Hornig | QA student | Product Development | 212 |
| Jae Pak | Operations | Operations | 205 |
| Jeffrey Piira | Human Resources | Human Resources | 204 |
| John Tippett | Database Analyst | Customer Services | 301 |
| Jolie Lenehan | Finance | Finance | 222 |
| Jon Grande | QA student | Product Development | 241 |
| Jonathan Young | QA Engineer | Product Development | 222 |

Network - Computers    **Office - Employee Details**

This table contains each employee's name in the Name column, but this is equivalent to the Belongs To column in our existing PC shape data rows. Therefore, you must rename the Name column as Belongs To in the Column Settings dialog, before we link any data rows.

Also, you can uncheck the XLocation and YLocation columns, as they are not required in this example.

Ensure that you have a few PC shapes linked to rows in the Network—Computers table before selecting Automatically Link… from the right mouse menu of the Office—Employee Details tab in the External Data window. After ensuring that All Shapes on Page is selected, proceed to the link where the Belongs To Data Column equals the Belongs To Shape Field in the Automatic Link dialog.

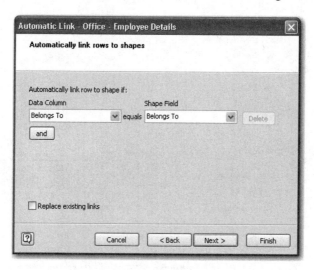

You should end up with two extra Shape Data rows—Title and Extension—added to each PC shape that was linked.

| Hard Drive Capacity | 850 |
| --- | --- |
| Department | IS |
| Belongs To | Anthony Chor |
| Screen Size | 17 in. |
| Network Card | TRUE |
| Modem | TRUE |
| Sound Card | TRUE |
| Cost | £2,000.00 |
| Title | IS |
| Extension | 243 |

Only two extra rows are there because both the Belongs To and Department Shape Data rows existed already, so it was unnecessary to create them.

## Navigating to/from Linked Data

When a shape in a drawing is linked to a row in an External Data window, it is often useful to be able to find the row or rows from the shape . . .

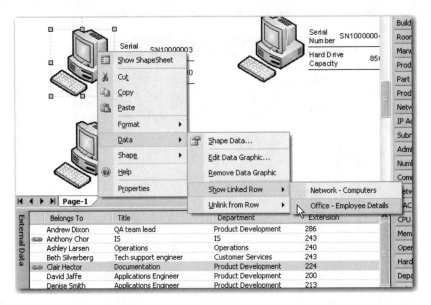

. . . or to find the shape or shapes from the row.

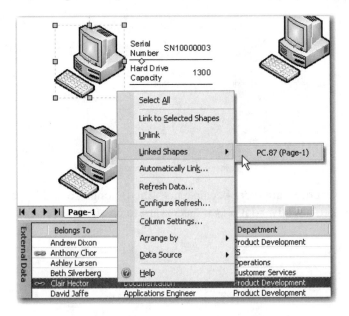

# Refreshing the Data

Because you can have multiple Link Data sources per drawing, you may not want to refresh your data from all sources at the same time. Therefore, you can select Refresh Data from the right mouse menu of each External Data Window tab.

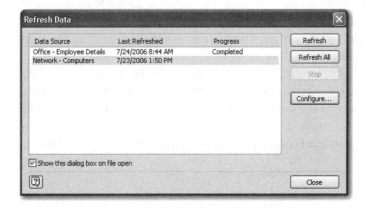

Or, you can configure the settings for the refresh with the Configure Refresh dialog that is available from the right mouse menu of the External Data window.

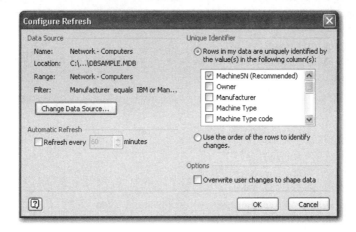

The Configure Refresh dialog enables you to change the data source, which can be useful if the file is moved, or to change the unique identifier. It also lets you set the refresh interval (which must be between 1 and 32,767 minutes) if you want the drawing to be refreshed automatically at all. Finally, you can decide whether any changes the user makes to data in the shape manually will be overwritten from the data source. Remember, this is a one-way link only—you cannot update the data source from the shapes.

# Creating Data Connections in Code

You can create DataRecordsets in code, which are presented as tabs in the External Data window in the Visio user interface. Each DataRecordset has DataColumns, each of which are mapped to corresponding fields in the data source.

A DataConnection object is created for each of these DataRecordsets (except for XML data). The DataRecordsets can only be updated from the data source by refreshing the DataRecordset. You cannot update the data from the shapes; it is a one-way connection.

The Data Selector Wizard provides the capability to create simple connections, but you may need to read data via a stored procedure, for example, in a SQL Server database. You can only do this with custom code. The following example has the normal SELECT method commented out, but the alternative Stored Procedure method demonstrates how easy it is to send parameters to the server.

```
Public Sub CreateRecordset()
Dim dds As Visio.DataRecordset   'The data recordset
Dim ary() As String 'An array to hold the unique identifier columns
Dim SQLConnStr As String    'The connection string for the SQL Server
Dim SQLCommStr As String    'The Command string
Dim datasetName As String   'The dataset name
    SQLConnStr = "Provider=SQLOLEDB.1;" & _
            "Integrated Security=SSPI;" & _
            "Persist Security Info=True;" & _
            "Data Source=localhost;" & _
            "Initial Catalog=Northwind"

    'A SELECT statement
    'SQLCommStr = "SELECT * FROM Customers"
    'ary() = Split("CustomerID", ";")
    'datasetName = "Customers"

    'Or a Stored Procedure
    SQLCommStr = "EXEC SalesByCategory 'Beverages',1996"
    ary() = Split("ProductName", ";")
    datasetName = "SalesByCategory"

    Set dds = Visio.ActiveDocument.DataRecordsets.Add(SQLConnStr, SQLCommStr, _
        Visio.VisDataRecordsetAddOptions.visDataRecordsetDelayQuery, datasetName)
    dds.SetPrimaryKey visKeySingle, ary()
    dds.Refresh
End Sub
```

The previous example requires the Northwind database to be installed, but it is simple to change it for your own database.

# Linking XML Data

The Data Selector dialog offers you five ways of creating data sources, and the capability to select a previously created connection. It does not offer you the chance to select an XML document, but you can link XML, as long as you do it in code.

The XML document must be in "classic" ADO RowsetSchema form. For example, if the following data was stored in a file called PATTested.xml . . .

```
<xml xmlns:s='uuid:BDC6E3F0-6DA3-11d1-A2A3-00AA00C14882'
        xmlns:dt='uuid:C2F41010-65B3-11d1-A29F-00AA00C14882'
        xmlns:rs='urn:schemas-microsoft-com:rowset'
        xmlns:z='#RowsetSchema'>
<s:Schema id='RowsetSchema'>
        <s:ElementType name='row' content='eltOnly' rs:updatable='true'>
                <s:AttributeType name='c0' rs:name='_Visio_RowID_' rs:number='1'
                        rs:nullable='true' rs:maydefer='true' rs:writeunknown='true'>
                        <s:datatype dt:type='int' dt:maxLength='4' rs:fixedlength='true'/>
                </s:AttributeType>
                <s:AttributeType name='SerialNumber' rs:number='2' rs:nullable='true'
                        rs:maydefer='true' rs:writeunknown='true'>
                        <s:datatype dt:type='string' dt:maxLength='16'/>
                </s:AttributeType>
                <s:AttributeType name='PATTested' rs:number='3' rs:nullable='true'
                        rs:maydefer='true' rs:writeunknown='true'>
                        <s:datatype dt:type='string' dt:maxLength='8'/>
                </s:AttributeType>
                <s:extends type='rs:rowbase'/>
        </s:ElementType>
</s:Schema>
<rs:data>
        <z:row c0='1'  SerialNumber='SN10000003' PATTested='Yes'/>
        <z:row c0='2'  SerialNumber='SN10000004' PATTested='No'/>
        <z:row c0='3'  SerialNumber='SN10000013' PATTested='Yes'/>
        <z:row c0='4'  SerialNumber='SN10000014' PATTested='Yes'/>
</rs:data>
</xml>
```

. . . then the following VBA code would load the file into the Visio document as a new Data Recordset. To run the following code, you need to have a reference to Microsoft Scripting Runtime and Microsoft XML. These can be added from Tools | References in the Visual Basic for Applications (VBA) Editor environment. The Scripting Runtime is required for the FileSystemObject.

### Code Listing for CreateXMLRecordset

```
Public Sub CreateXMLRecordset()
Dim doc As Visio.Document
Dim dst As Visio.DataRecordset
Dim xmlFile As String
Dim oFS As New FileSystemObject
Dim fil As File
Dim dom As New MSXML2.DOMDocument
Dim OK As Boolean
    Set doc = Visio.ActiveDocument
        xmlFile = "PATTested.xml"
    If Len(Dir(xmlFile)) = 0 Then
        Exit Sub
    Else
        Set fil = oFS.GetFile(xmlFile)
        OK = dom.Load(xmlFile)
        If OK = False Then
            Exit Sub
        End If
    End If
    Set dst = doc.DataRecordsets.AddFromXML(dom.XML, 0, "PAT Tests")
End Sub
```

# Refreshing XML Data

XML DataRecordsets are connectionless (they do not have a DataConnection object), but you can update the source XML file, and then use RefreshUsingXML. The following example code shows how an XML file can be used to update the DataRecordset. It works better if you first edit the PATTested.xml file by altering a PATTested='Yes' to PATTested='No'.

### Code Listing for RefreshXML

```
Public Sub RefreshXML()
Dim doc As Visio.Document
Dim dst As Visio.DataRecordset
Dim xmlFile As String
Dim oFS As New FileSystemObject
Dim fil As File
Dim dom As New MSXML2.DOMDocument
Dim OK As Boolean
```

```
Set doc = Visio.ActiveDocument
    xmlFile = "PATTested.xml"
If Len(Dir(xmlFile)) = 0 Then
    Exit Sub
Else
    Set fil = oFS.GetFile(xmlFile)
    OK = dom.Load(xmlFile)
    If OK = False Then
        Exit Sub
    End If
End If

For Each dst In Visio.ActiveDocument.DataRecordsets
    If dst.Name = "PAT Tests" Then
        dst.RefreshUsingXML dom.XML
        Exit For
    End If
Next

End Sub
```

## Link Data Legends

If you publish a data-linked diagram without a legend stating its source, date, and explanation, it is almost worthless. Legends are essential for any business diagram. Unfortunately, there is no legend for the Link Data records, so you may have to create one. The Data Source | Properties right mouse menu displays the name of the data source and how many records are linked in the document (but you cannot see how many are in the active page). You can also see when the Data Source was last refreshed (see the Refreshed value).

I believe you should have a legend for each page with linked data shapes. Therefore, the audience knows when the data was refreshed from the data source. The Visio user can see the External Data window and can find which shapes are linked to which data source. But, the viewer of a printed or Web-published diagram does not have the full Visio client and cannot see where the data came from. Of course, you may not want to display the actual database name or spreadsheet, but you should at least display when each data source was last refreshed.

Two data sets are in the example of the network PCs you have been using: one for the Computers and the other for Employee Details. So, the legend will consist of two rows below the header. I decided there should be a count of the number of shapes linked to each data set.

In this case, both data sets come from the same data source—the sample Access database—but that is not always true.

## Creating Link Data Legends

I decided to write a bit of VBA code to display the following details for each data set. You can use the programming language of your choice, so the code can reside in an add-on or COM add-in, but this VBA can just be stored in the Visio document. ALT+F11 gets you into the VBA Editor (or Tools | Macros | Visual Basic Editor), so you can enter the following subfunction into a module or the ThisDocument class.

The code collects a count of shapes linked to each data set in the active page, and then displays the count, the last refresh date, and the data set name and data source filename. It displays the results in a pop-up window and, if you have a shape selected already and choose to do so, refreshes the text with the details.

A suitable shape to add the text to would be a rectangle because you can change the tab stops to make it more legible.

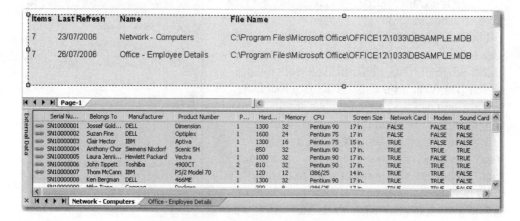

Of course, you can change the code to suit your requirements.

## Code Listing for ListActivePageDataLinks and ListPageDataLinks

```
Public Sub ListActivePageDataLinks()
'Purpose : To call ListPageDataLinks with a shape selected
'          to make it into a legend

    ListPageDataLinks Visio.ActivePage

End Sub

Public Sub ListPageDataLinks(ByVal pag As Visio.Page)
'Purpose : To refresh a list of data sets used in a page
Dim drs As Visio.DataRecordset
Dim aryIDs() As Long      'Collects the shape IDs used by a specific RecordDataSet
Dim retVal As Integer     'Return value from MessageBox
Dim txt As String    'List of used DataRecordsets
Dim title As String
Dim shpLegend As Visio.Shape

    'I hate doing On Error Resume Next,
    'but VBA does not have a simple way to test if the array is empty
    On Error Resume Next

    title = "Data Recordsets in Page"
    'Create the header text
    txt = "Items" & vbTab & _
          "Last Refresh" & vbTab & _
          "Name" & vbTab & _
          "File Name"

    For Each drs In Visio.ActiveDocument.DataRecordsets
        ReDim aryIDs(0)
        pag.GetShapesLinkedToData drs.ID, aryIDs()
        'If there is no error, then txt will be appended to
        If Len(drs.CommandString) > 0 Then
            txt = txt & vbCrLf & _
                UBound(aryIDs) + 1 & vbTab & _
                Format(drs.TimeRefreshed, "ddddd") & vbTab & _
                drs.Name & vbTab & _
                drs.DataConnection.FileName
        Else
            txt = txt & vbCrLf & _
                UBound(aryIDs) + 1 & vbTab & _
                "(unknown)" & vbTab & _
```

```
                drs.Name & vbTab & _
                "unknown XML file"
        End If
    Next drs


    'The next statement will fail if it does not find a shape named DataRecordsetsLegend
    Set shpLegend = pag.Shapes("DataRecordsetsLegend")
    If Not shpLegend Is Nothing Then
        shpLegend.text = txt
    Else
        'Optionally update the text of a selected (legend) shape
        If Visio.ActiveWindow.Page Is pag And Visio.ActiveWindow.Selection.Count > 0 Then
            retVal = MsgBox(txt & vbCrLf & "Update text of selected shape?", vbYesNo, title)
            If retVal = vbYes Then
                Visio.ActiveWindow.Selection.PrimaryItem.text = txt
                Visio.ActiveWindow.Selection.PrimaryItem.NameU = "DataRecordsetsLegend"
            End If
        Else
            MsgBox txt, vbOKOnly, title
        End If
    End If

End sub
```

## Automating Link Data Legends

I have shown you the main principles of creating a Link Data Legend, but you could
go further and have a Link Data Legend Master, which you drag-and-drop on to each
relevant page in your document. The Link Data Legend Master could be available
from a global stencil and this could contain the VBA code to refresh the text.

If you do not like VBA, then you could have a COM add-in that performs the
same task, and the COM add-in could be listening for the relevant events in the
document, such as DataRecordsetChanged and BeforeDataRecordsetDelete.

An automatic refresh is preferable to a manual one, because people always forget
to refresh data. Perhaps the simplest automation is to perform the refresh of legend
shapes on all pages whenever the document is saved. This can be done easily in the
ThisDocument class in VBA, because it already holds the Visio.Document object with
events. All you need to do is enter the following code in the Document_DocumentSaved
subfunction:

```
Private Sub Document_DocumentSaved(ByVal doc As IVDocument)
    Dim pag As Visio.Page
    For Each pag In ThisDocument.Pages
```

```
        If pag.Type = visTypeForeground Then
            ListPageDataLinks pag
        End If
    Next pag
End Sub
```

Consequently, all the shapes called DataRecordsetsLegend have their text updated whenever the document is saved.

# Labeling Shapes from Shape Data

You can label shapes that contain shape data using several methods. Some may be more suitable than others for your type of diagrams. The main principle is to have labels that are automatically updated whenever the data changes. This removes the possibility of error in data entry.

## Using Data Graphics to Update Labels

Microsoft Visio 2007 introduces a new, and superior, method for labeling shapes that have shape data. Among its capabilities, *Data Graphics* can be used to label shapes quite effectively. The labels can include both the shape data row names and values.

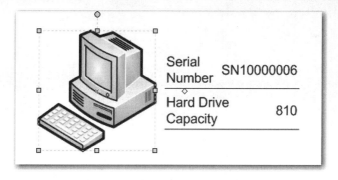

This is done by editing an existing Data Graphic or by creating a new Data Graphic from the Data Graphics panel, which is opened with the Data | Display Data on Shapes menu item.

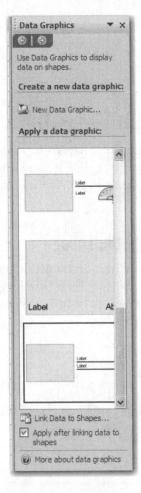

The Edit Data Graphics dialog enables you to create and edit four types of Data Graphics, with Text being the first. You learn about the others in the section "Enhancing Shapes with Color, Icons, and Data Bars". You can add as many Text items as you require, by simply creating a new Text item and selecting a shape data field, or by selecting any other cell from the Field dialog that is opened by More Fields… at the end of the pull-down list of fields.

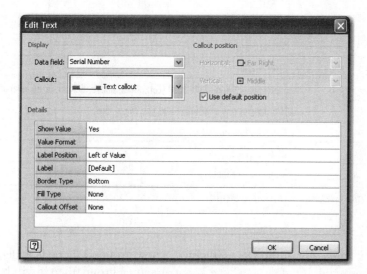

The Edit Text dialog provides you with the capability to select a type of Callout, specify its position relative to the shape, and to change the Details.

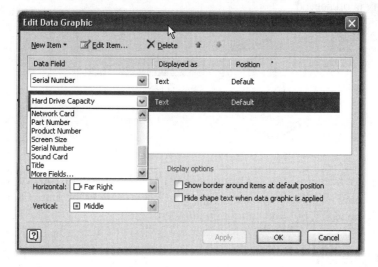

You have great flexibility in the definition of the detail of each label. See Table 3-2.

The resultant Data Graphics from these simple changes, such as selecting Heading 3 (a simple colored bar with white text), rather than Text Callout, can add much greater clarity.

| Detail | Comment |
|---|---|
| Show Value | True or False |
| Value Format | Enter a valid |
| Label Position | Select the position of the label (Left, Right, Above, Below), or no label at all |
| Label | [Default] or any alternative text you would like |
| Border Type | None, Bottom, or Top |
| Fill Type | None or Filled |
| Callout Offset | None, Left, or Right |

**Table 3-2** *Data Graphic Callouts Detail*

When you apply any of the Data Graphics, a new grouped shape is added to the target shape and, if the target shape is not already a group, then it will be automatically turned into one. The smart thing is that the new subshapes are linked to a Master in the document stencil and, if the target shape is an instance of a Master, then the link is preserved.

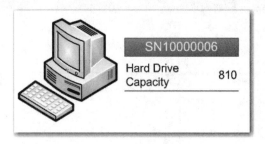

If you do not need any compatibility with versions earlier than 2007 of Microsoft Visio, then Data Graphics is the way to go. You can still view the Data Graphics in Microsoft Visio 2003, but you cannot create them.

## Label Shapes Add-In

Microsoft Visio Professional provides you with the Label Shapes Add-In available from Tools | Add-Ons | Maps and Floor Plans. This is not part of the new Data Graphics in Microsoft Visio 2007, but rather it exists in both Microsoft Visio 2003 and 2007.

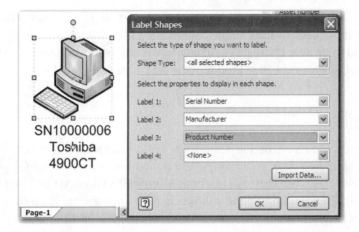

This is limited to a maximum of four shape data rows and you cannot include the name of the shape data row. However, it can be applied to any selected shape and can be reapplied multiple times.

This creates a new User-defined cell named visCustomLabel at the bottom of the User-defined Cells section in the ShapeSheet, and then references this in the Value cell of the first row in the Text Fields section.

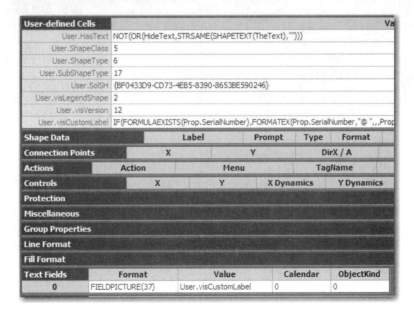

The formula in User.visCustomLabel includes multiple IF statements that test if there is an entry in each desired shape data row.

If you need to be able to create or update labels easily in Microsoft Visio 2003, then the Label Shapes Add-in is probably the way to go.

## Custom Callouts

Three Custom Callouts are on the Visio Extras | Callouts stencil that you can use to label shapes with their data. Again, these are not part of the new Data Graphics in Microsoft Visio 2007, but they exist in both Microsoft Visio 2003 and 2007.

The only difference among these callouts is their appearance. Each of them has the capability to automatically display selected shape data, with or without the name along with the value.

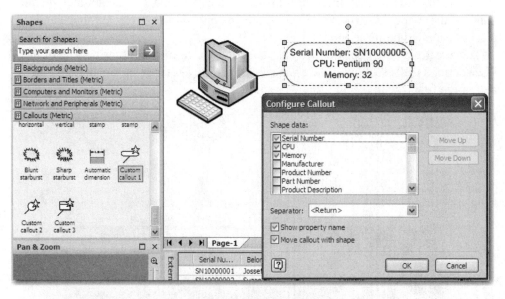

The callouts can be duplicated and linked to other shapes and, thus, they will display the selected shape data. The display changes whenever the shape data changes. These callouts could be used to highlight particular shapes in conjunction with the other methods of labeling.

## Manually Editing Associated Text Blocks

Every shape in Visio has the capability of displaying text and the text can be multiple lines, and can optionally include references to ShapeSheet cells. Paragraphs,
sentences, lines, words, or individual characters can be formatted to suit.

In the Network—Computers example we have been constructing, the PC shape
already has an associated text block, complete with a control handle (the yellow
diamond) to reposition it. Simply select a PC shape, select Insert | Field, then select
Shape Data, and then Serial Number.

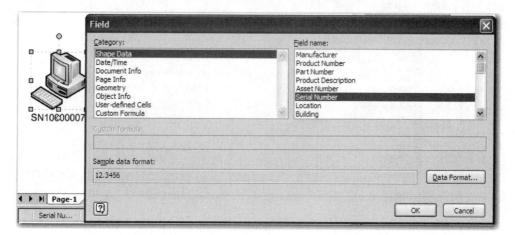

You can format the value, if required, according to the type of data.

The result is that the selected shape data cell reference is inserted into the Text
Fields section in the ShapeSheet, and these Text Fields are embedded within the
paragraph you write. So, this is the great flexibility of this method. You have the
freedom to embed shape data cell references, as well as any other cell reference while
you are at it.

The disadvantage of this method is that it is more suited to labeling individual
shapes or prelabeling Masters before they are used in a document. In the latter case, it
can be used effectively in grouped shapes where you need automatic labels in different
areas.

For example, drag the Title Block Corporate 2 Master from the Visio Extras |
Borders and Titles stencil on to a drawing page, and then delete it. This copies the
Master into the document, so open the Drawing Explorer window and expand the

Master's node. Edit the Master Properties and ensure that Match Master by Name on Drop is checked.

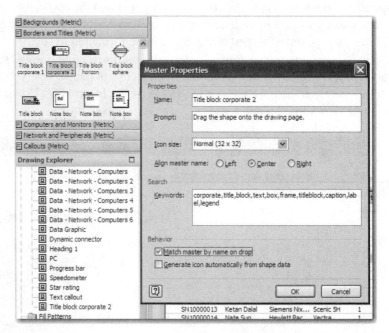

Now, select Edit Master Shape and select the Company Name shape within the main shape. Select Insert | Field to open the Field dialog, and then select the Category Document Info and the field name Company.

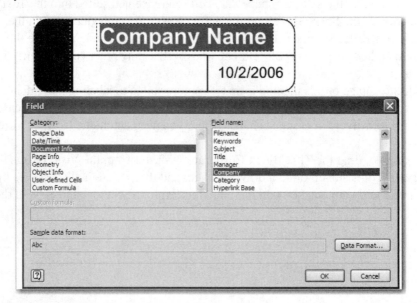

Close the Master Edit window. Now, you can drag the Master from the stencil on to multiple pages within the document. If you edit the File Properties | Company value, it will now automatically be displayed in all instances of the Master in all pages in the document.

# Enhancing Shapes with Color, Icons, and Data Bars

Coloring shapes according to data values can be an effective way to communicate information quickly, and now you can also add icons and data bars.

## Setting Color to Shape Data Values

You can set formulae to change the display color of different elements within a shape to reflect different data values. In the previous chapter, we changed the line color to reflect the different Priority Status for a Process shape. The same principle can be applied to the foreground fill, the background fill, or the shadow color. In fact, you can have subshapes within your shapes that reflect different shape data values.

In the following example of a risk model, the Capacity and Operational Risk rectangles on the right of each shape reflect their status.

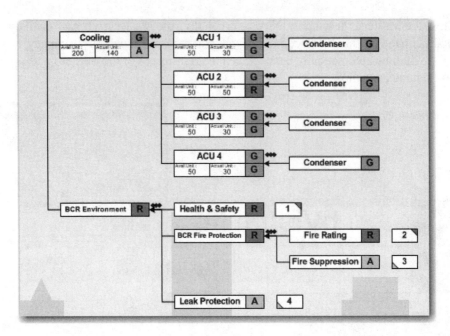

The next example is variance on risk, which displays the details of an application on a server, and the associated business continuity management level, the criticality, the status, and the IT ownership is the fill color of main body of the shape.

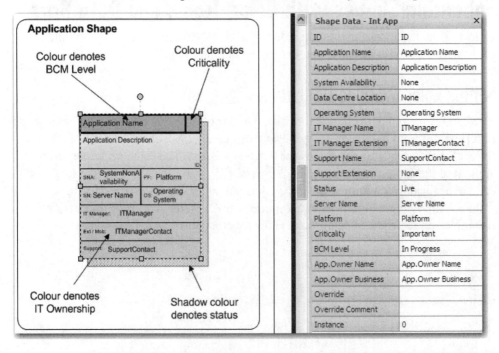

This shape was designed prior to Microsoft Visio 2007, thus, the color fill does not use Data Graphics. All the colors apart from the IT ownership are from a fixed list, similar to the Priority Status example, but the IT ownership fill color is read from a database.

## Predefining Fills in a Database

You can use Visio to update a database with the settings for color fills and patterns. This can make your diagrams consistently use the same graphics for the same entity, such as Department, in a variety of diagram types. We examine this in more detail when we use the Database Wizard in Chapter 6.

## Space Plan — Color By Value

The Space Plan Add-in—Color By Value—can be used in any type of diagram, if you have Microsoft Visio 2003 Professional, or later. *Color By Value* also creates a legend automatically that displays the color, count of shapes in the page, and the value. This is not part of the new Data Graphics, but it can be updated by Visio 2003 users.

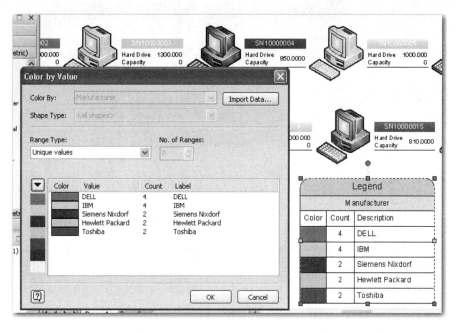

The right mouse menu for the legend shape provides the capability to Edit Legend or to Refresh Legend. You can also decide whether or not to display the count.

The colors will not automatically refresh as you add more relevant shapes to the drawing page. You need to do this manually, using the right mouse menu of the legend, unlike in the new Data Graphics, where colors can be automatically applied as the shapes are dropped.

# Data Graphics—Color By Value

The new Data Graphics also has the capability to color shapes by value, but it does not create a legend automatically. This is an omission that needs to be overcome for serious business use, so we will take some time to examine how this can be done.

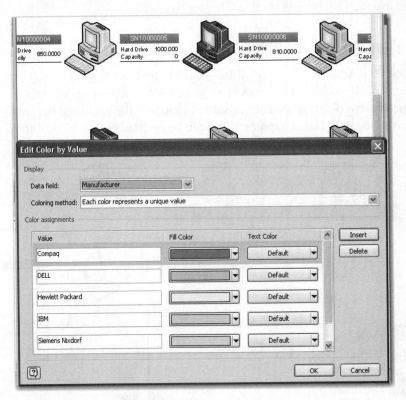

These Color ByValue Data Graphics allow the suggested colors for each data value to be overridden by custom colors.

### Creating Data Graphic Color By Value Legends

The color formulae are stored in a User-defined cell in the Data Graphic Master shape. Consequently, any code that needs to read or update the colors associated with any values must first determine which Data Graphic Masters are used for Color By Value, and then interpret the shape data row (or other formula) being used for coloring. Then, the shapes in the page must be examined to see how many there are for each color and value.

Finally, the results need to be displayed on the page, so any viewer can understand what the colors represent. The Space Plan Color By Value Add-in presents a reasonable legend, so this is used as a model.

The Color By Value part of Data Graphics can understand if the shape data type is text or numbers by checking the Prop.MyData.Type cell. Thus, it is able to provide the capability to display colors for discrete values . . .

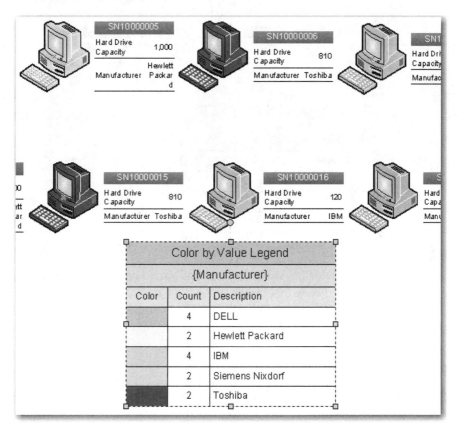

. . . or, for numbers, you can enter ranges of values.

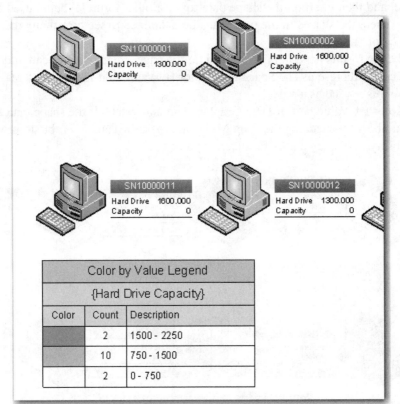

Using more than one Color By Value set in a page would be extremely confusing, so I have put a check in the code that aborts if you have multiple Color By Value sets.

The VBA code for this is too long to list here, but it is available from the companion website: www.visualizinginformation.com.

## Data Graphic Icons Sets

You can use multiple *Data Graphic Icon Sets* in the same page and, indeed, you can have multiple sets per shape. This is because you have a variety of icon sets to choose from, and you can create your own. Icon sets can be used in conjunction with Color By Value to enhance the display even further. However, there is no built-in capability to create legends for Icon Sets either, so I extended the sample VBA legend code to include Icon Sets.

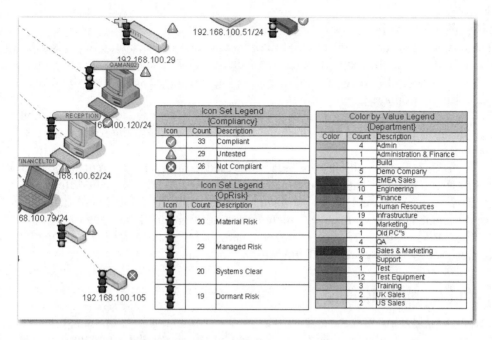

Icon Sets can have a maximum of five different icons, so you need to provide criteria for no more than this number, but you do not have to use them all.

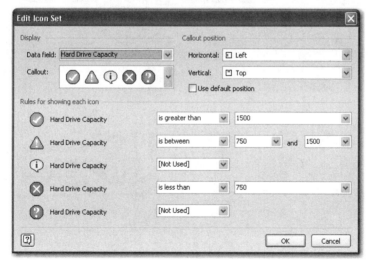

Later, in Chapter 7, you learn how to create your own Icon Sets.

### Creating Data Graphic Icon Set Legends

The essential concept here is to recognize that a Master for each Icon Set exists in the document, and the shapes that use the Icon Sets have a shape inserted into them. A User-defined cell, called msvCalloutIconNumber, is in the subshape, which stores the currently displayed icon number.

Thus, the code iterates through each of the shapes in the page to check if an Icon Set Master is incorporated as a subshape. If it exists, then the count for that icon is incremented.

The code handles multiple Icon Sets being used to represent different shape data values, but it does not handle the same Icon Set being used to represent different shape data, as that would be too confusing. Consequently, multiple Icon Set Legends can be created on the same page, which the user must manually arrange.

The VBA code for this is too long to list here, but it is also available from the companion website: www.visualizinginformation.com.

## Data Graphic Data Bars

*Data Graphic Data Bars* are another way to display numeric data in a shape They can also be used with the other types of Data Graphics, as in the following example:

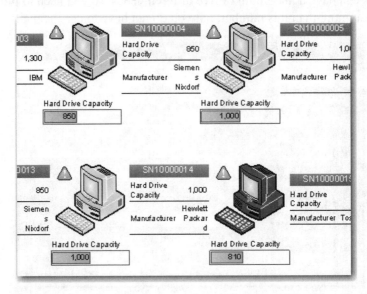

A variety of Data Bars are provided, including some that allow the data from multiple fields to be combined into, say, a bar chart.

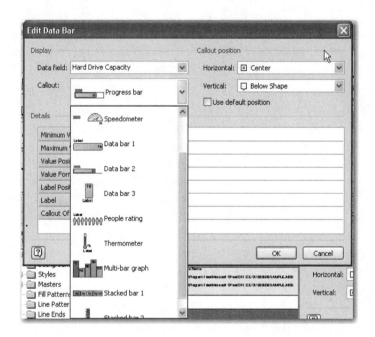

You have great flexibility in the definition of the detail of each Data Bar. See Table 3-3.

So, you now have a variety of methods to display information within your Microsoft Visio 2007 shapes, and I hope you will use them to clarify, rather than confuse.

| Detail | Comment |
| --- | --- |
| Minimum Value | Default 0, but you can edit to any number |
| Maximum Value | Default 100, but you can edit to any number |
| Value Position | Not Shown, Left, Right, Top, Bottom, or Interior |
| Value Format | Either enter valid format codes or open the Data Form dialog |
| Label Position | Not Shown, Left, Right, Top, Bottom, or Interior |
| Label | [Default] or any alternative text you would like |
| Callout Offset | None, Left, or Right |

**Table 3-3**  *Data Graphic Data Bars Details*

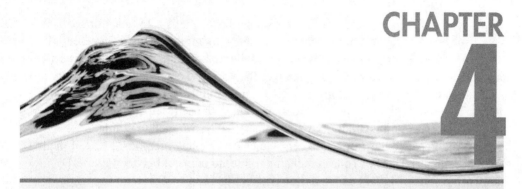

# Connecting Items to Each Other

One of the key factors in Visio's success over the last 15 years or so, has been its capability to connect one shape to another. This is an essential factor in creating useful business diagrams, such as organization charts, process flows, and network diagrams. Over the years, Visio added the capability to create database entity relationships, UML, and brainstorming diagrams, among others. Together with the capability to store data with each shape, Visio defined a new data-diagramming paradigm, which others have struggled to emulate.

You can create connections between shapes using many methods. Most of them involve using a 1-D shape (one-dimensional line) to connect between two 2-D shapes (two-dimensional boxes). These connections can be *Dynamic* (no need for a connection point in the 2-D shape) or *Static* (glued to a connection point in the 2-D shape or page).

Unfortunately, in the 2003 version, Microsoft decided to retire two of the most used wizards, which were able to create certain types of network diagrams or to read the connections from a diagram back into a database.

At some point, the Visio development team recognized the need to connect two 2-D shapes together in uses such as laying out office worktops or HVAC ductwork, so they also added this capability.

In all these cases, the visual connection of shapes can represent the logical or physical connection of the elements these shapes represent, such as the reporting hierarchy in an organization, the flow of a process, or the cable between an outlet and a PC. Some of these connections have a direction, often represented by arrows, and some may represent different types of connections, often indicated by changing the line type or color.

# Making Shapes Connectable

For a connection to be made between shapes, the shapes being connected and the shape being used to make the connection need to have certain properties.

If you were simply to draw two shapes, and then draw a line between them, they would not connect together because the line has not been configured as a dynamic connector.

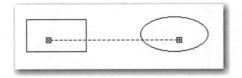

If you were to use the Connector tool to draw a line between them, or select the Connect Shapes button with both shapes selected, then they would be connected together.

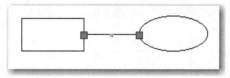

This demonstrates the difference between 1-D shapes that can be used with dynamic glue and those that cannot. This is because the lines drawn by the Connector tool and Connect Shapes are, by default, using the Dynamic Connector Master.

You could add a connection point to each of the two shapes, however, and then you would be able to draw a simple line between these points, but this would be using static glue instead of dynamic glue.

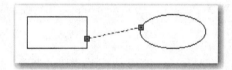

Now, you will discover what makes shapes connectors and connectable.

## 2-D Shape Options

When you draw a rectangle, ellipse, or any irregular-shaped polygon in Visio, then you automatically create a 2-D shape. You can see this by selecting the shape, and then selecting Format | Behavior and viewing the Interaction style.

You can modify this behavior for a shape, and change a rectangle into a 1-D shape, for example. This is generally how rack-equipment shapes that need to connect to bolt holes in a vertical elevation of a network-equipment rack are built. You cannot change a shape from 2-D to 1-D in the ShapeSheet, but you can 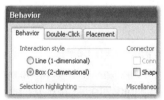 recognize the difference because a 1-D shape has an extra section at the start called *1-D Endpoints*. You can toggle the interaction style between 1-D and 2-D in code using Shape.OneD = True or False.

You can also define the Placement behavior of a shape with the Format | Behavior dialog. If you want a 2-D shape to accept dynamic glue, then it must not have the placement behavior of Do Not Lay Out and Route Around. The default is Let Visio

Decide, but select Layout and Route Around if you need the shapes always to be able to have dynamic glue capability.

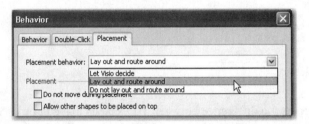

In fact, the normal user interface only shows three alternative placement behaviors for 2-D shapes, whereas in the ShapeSheet, the ObjType cell in the Miscellaneous section, reveals five options in all, because one is only for 1-D shapes, and one is only for group shapes.

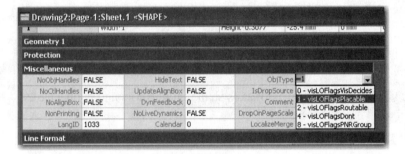

The Layout and Routing tab on the File | Page Setup dialog enables you to define the way that dynamic connectors interact with the shapes and with each other. These settings can make radical changes to the position and angle of dynamic connector ends on the outline of a shape.

## Connection Points

*Connection Points* can be added to any shape (1-D or 2-D) or to a page to provide the capability to connect the ends of a 1-D shape with static glue; to provide the preferred location of the ends of a dynamically glued routable 1-D shape; or to control the gluing angle of two 2-D shapes abutted together.

**Static Glue Points**   Connection Points can be added to any shape or page with the Connection Points tool, but if you want to position the points accurately within the shape, then you need to use the ShapeSheet to enter the X/Y coordinates. You can also name the connection points in the ShapeSheet, and change their Type from the default of 0—Inwards, which has a blue diagonal-cross appearance.

Unfortunately, you cannot change the visibility of a connection point, but you can change its position and type with a formula. The normal method of appearing to make connection points invisible is to make them be in the same position as another, if they are not required because of some other cell value within the shape. For example, the Rack and Cabinet Masters on the Rack-mounted Equipment stencil have a varying number of connection points dependant on the height of the rack.

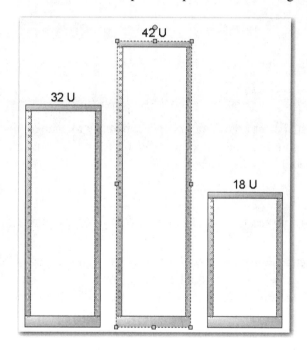

This height is governed by the Shape Data row Prop.UCount value, so the *Y* coordinate formula is as follows:

```
=User.BaseHeight+IF(Prop.UCount>n,1,Prop.UCount)*User.OneUHeight
```

Where *n* is the *U* Position or vertical row position, not forgetting there are two connection points per row as one is on each side of the rack. So, if the height of the rack is, say, 12 Us, then every connection point where *n* is greater than 5 is effectively invisible because it is at the bottom of the rack or, more precisely, at the value of the User.BaseHeight cell.

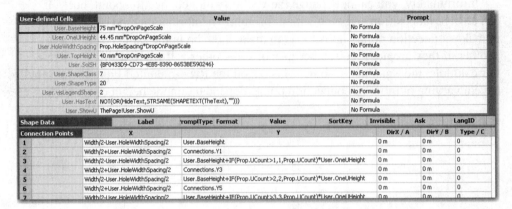

| User-defined Cells | Value | Prompt |
|---|---|---|
| User.BaseHeight | 75 mm*DropOnPageScale | No Formula |
| User.OneUHeight | 44.45 mm*DropOnPageScale | No Formula |
| User.HoleWidthSpacing | Prop.HoleSpacing*DropOnPageScale | No Formula |
| User.TopHeight | 40 mm*DropOnPageScale | No Formula |
| User.SolSH | {BF0433D9-CD73-4EB5-8390-8653BE590246} | No Formula |
| User.ShapeClass | 7 | No Formula |
| User.ShapeType | 20 | No Formula |
| User.visLegendShape | 2 | No Formula |
| User.HasText | NOT(OR(HideText,STRSAME(SHAPETEXT(TheText),""))) | No Formula |
| User.ShowU | ThePage!User.ShowU | No Formula |

| Shape Data | Label | PromptType | Format | Value | SortKey | Invisible | Ask | LangID |
|---|---|---|---|---|---|---|---|---|

| Connection Points | X | | | Y | | DirX / A | DirY / B | Type / C |
|---|---|---|---|---|---|---|---|---|
| 1 | Width/2-User.HoleWidthSpacing/2 | User.BaseHeight | | | | 0 m | 0 m | 0 |
| 2 | Width/2+User.HoleWidthSpacing/2 | Connections.Y1 | | | | 0 m | 0 m | 0 |
| 3 | Width/2-User.HoleWidthSpacing/2 | User.BaseHeight+IF(Prop.UCount>1,1,Prop.UCount)*User.OneUHeight | | | | 0 m | 0 m | 0 |
| 4 | Width/2+User.HoleWidthSpacing/2 | Connections.Y3 | | | | 0 m | 0 m | 0 |
| 5 | Width/2-User.HoleWidthSpacing/2 | User.BaseHeight+IF(Prop.UCount>2,2,Prop.UCount)*User.OneUHeight | | | | 0 m | 0 m | 0 |
| 6 | Width/2+User.HoleWidthSpacing/2 | Connections.Y5 | | | | 0 m | 0 m | 0 |
| 7 | Width/2-User.HoleWidthSpacing/2 | User.BaseHeight+IF(Prop.UCount>3,3,Prop.UCount)*User.OneUHeight | | | | 0 m | 0 m | 0 |

The previous shape could also include the capability to change the Type of the connection point, so it becomes unconnectable (Type = 1 – Outwards, which has a blue dot appearance).

### NOTE

*Some users may want to measure the U Position from the top rather from the bottom of the rack.*

**Dynamic Glue Preferred Position**   At times, you might want dynamically glued lines to appear to come from a particular position on a shapes edge. Most of the Master shapes on the Basic Flowchart stencil, for example, have connection points predefined at the center of each side of the shape. This has the effect of grouping any dynamically glued connection lines to these positions, rather than at some arbitrary position along each face, or on a vertex.

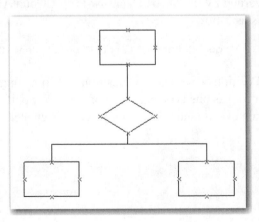

Therefore, it is seldom necessary to glue the dynamic connectors between process flowchart shapes to static connection points on the shapes. This is because dynamic glue makes the connectors appear to be from the nearest connection point anyway. Using dynamic glue means you can easily reposition these flowchart shapes relative to each other, and the connectors automatically decide which side of the shape to connect to.

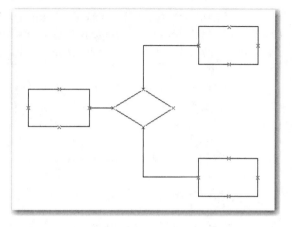

The Layout and Routing style of the page (File | Page Setup) affects the way the dynamic connectors arrange themselves.

**2-D Shape Abutment Angle**    As an example of gluing two 2-D shapes together, start a new diagram by selecting File | New | Maps and Floor Plans | Home Plan. Then, drag a Base corner Master from the Cabinets stencil. Next, drag-and-drop a Base 1 Master near to the top edge of the Base corner where the blue asterisk connection point is located. You should get a red square when you are in the correct position for gluing, so let go to leave it glued there. Then, drag another Base 1 to the right edge of the corner shape and move the Base 1 shape around until you get the red square again. This time, the Base 1 shape will be rotated 90 degrees. If the drawer line is showing on the bottom edge, rather than the top edge, you can flip the shape through 180 degrees by means of the right mouse action, Flip Depth.

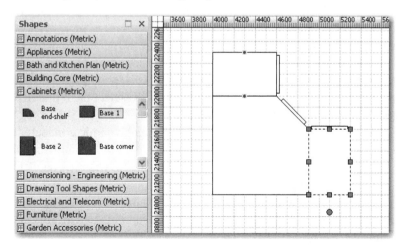

This behavior is possible because the Connection Points have Type = 2 (Inwards & Outwards) and the *angle of dangle* is defined by the DirX/A and DirY/B cells, where DirX and DirY define the coordinate of an arbitrary point on the line to describe the abutment angle.

In the previous example, the Base corner is the primary shape. If it is moved or rotated, then both of the Base 1 shapes will be moved and rotated in their relative position. Conversely, if you were to move either of the secondary shapes, then their connection to the primary shape is easily broken. The primary shape is the one at the start of the chain of glued 2-D shapes.

# 1-D Shape Options

When you draw a single line in Visio with the Line tool, then its default behavior is that it can be connected between two connection points. The single line is not routable (it will not automatically arrange itself around placeable 2-D shapes), and it is not capable of being glued dynamically to shapes.

However, if you were to open the ShapeSheet for the line, and then enter a **2** in the Miscellaneous/ObjType cell, then it would make the line "Routable." This has the immediate effect that the line will automatically be able to connect two simple shapes together, such as a rectangle or an ellipse, with dynamic glue. It will automatically try to avoid 2-D shapes that have the Layout and Route Around The Format behavior setting (it also adds three new right-mouse menu actions to let you choose the style of the connector— right-angled, straight, or curved).

## The Dynamic Connector

A special Master shape, called the *Dynamic connector,* is in Visio, which is automatically created in your Document Stencil by several actions (if you have not already selected a 1-D Master in a stencil).

For example, if you select the Connector tool to draw a connection between two shapes, then you automatically are using the Dynamic connector Master *unless* you have preselected a 1-D Master in the active stencil. This is, perhaps, the most frequent error I make when I use Visio manually and I forget to preselect the required Master before using the Connector tool.

However, knowing how Visio behaves regarding *the* Dynamic connector can be used to your advantage if you want to have your own default Dynamic connector. If your template document already contains a Master called Dynamic connector, then it will be used instead of the one created by Visio. You should ensure that your version of the Dynamic connector has its Match Master by Name on Drop property checked, and you can also make the Master invisible in the document stencil. This is done in code by setting the Master.Hidden = True.

# Layout and Routing Styles

The style of placement shapes and connectors can be selected from the dialog that can be opened from the Shape | Configure Layout ... menu item. These settings can be applied to the selected shapes or to the whole page.

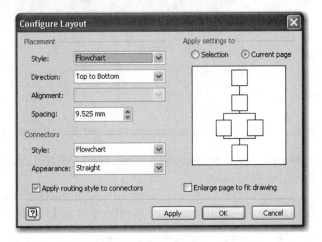

In fact, you can also alter the page settings from the Layout and Routing tab on the Page Setup dialog that can be opened from the File menu.

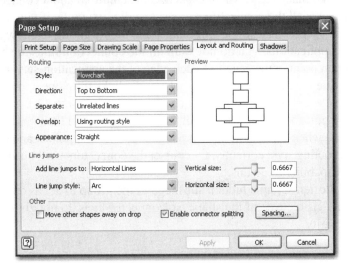

The routing style can have a drastic effect on the legibility of a diagram as it controls the way that dynamic connectors appear. Moreover, you can define the spacing between connectors and shapes, both horizontally and vertically.

Sometimes, it is necessary to set these settings in code, so you can set the values in the ShapeSheet of the page. All the relevant cells are in the Page Layout section and can be accessed in code using, for example:

```
Visio.ActivePage.PageSheet.Cells("PlaceStyle").Formula = "=2"
```

| Page Layout | | | | | | | |
|---|---|---|---|---|---|---|---|
| PlaceStyle | 1 | BlockSizeX | 6.35 mm | LineToNodeX | 3.175 mm |
| PlaceDepth | 1 | BlockSizeY | 6.35 mm | LineToNodeY | 3.175 mm |
| PlowCode | 0 | AvenueSizeX | 9.525 mm | LineToLineX | 3.175 mm |
| ResizePage | FALSE | AvenueSizeY | 9.525 mm | LineToLineY | 3.175 mm |
| DynamicsOff | FALSE | RouteStyle | 5 | LineJumpFactorX | 0.6667 |
| EnableGrid | FALSE | PageLineJumpDirX | 0 | LineJumpFactorY | 0.6667 |
| CtrlAsInput | FALSE | PageLineJumpDirY | 0 | LineJumpCode | 1 |
| LineAdjustFrom | 0 | LineAdjustTo | 0 | LineJumpStyle | 0 |
| PlaceFlip | 0 | LineRouteExt | 0 | PageShapeSplit | 1 |

In fact, the number 2 is the constant VisCellVals.visPLOPlaceLeftToRight, and many more start with visPLOPlace.

Similarly, the RouteStyle cell takes the values of one of the constants that begins VisCellVals.visLORoute...—in this case, the number 5 is visLORouteFlowchartNS.

## Spacing out Connections for Clarity

I have encountered many cases where users became confused about connecting shapes in a way that shows all the connections to a shape. For example, if you are modeling applications on a server as a single 2-D shape, and then wanting to show the links between these applications, you do not want all the connection lines to show as a single connection point in the center of each edge of the application-server shape. This would not provide the capability to visually trace the links from one application-server to another. Most users start adding many connection points to the 2-D shapes, and they often want guidance on how to equally space them around their shapes. They are always surprised when I recommend removing all connection points, and configuring the layout and routing style correctly. Of course, the connectors used need to have dynamic glue capability to do this.

In addition, I often set up a hidden subshape in the group to act as an exclusion zone around the visible part of the shape, so connector lines do not go too close to the edges for clarity.

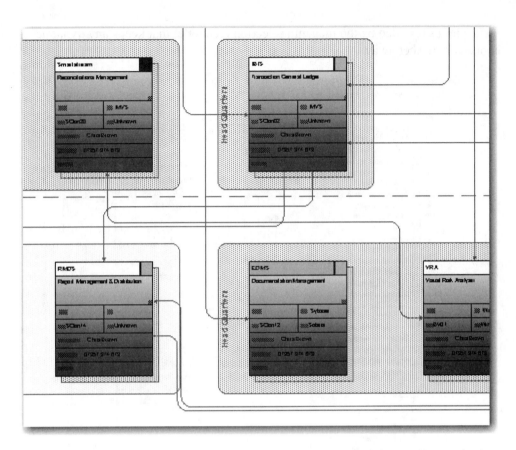

   This technique requires the main shape to be a group, which is usually required
because you need to have multiple text labels or multiple colors to represent different
data. Two squares are in the following example: No Exclusion Zone and With
Exclusion Zone. The *No Exclusion Zone* shape only keeps the dynamic connectors
away a short distance. The group shape, With *Exclusion Zone,* contains a hidden

rectangle (as revealed by the magenta selection rectangle) that keeps any dynamic connectors further away.

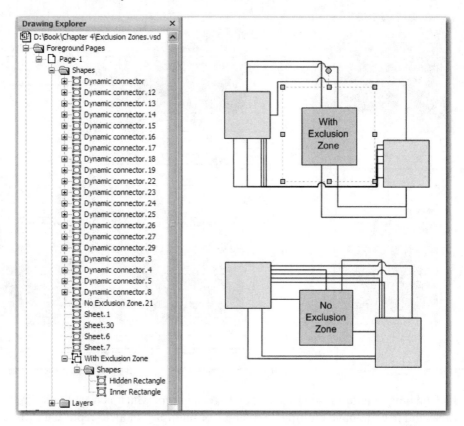

You can make the lines of any shape invisible by setting the value of the NoLine cell of its geometry section to TRUE and, you can also turn off any fill or both, using the NoFill and NoShow options. In addition you can also prevent any snapping to a geometry section by setting NoSnap to TRUE. *Snapping* is the capability of elements to be attracted by other elements, without gluing. For example, the end of a dynamic connector is attracted to the snappable elements within range as you move it with the cursor close to those elements. The dialog opened by Tools | Snap & Glue enables you to change the settings, and even switch off snap and/or glue.

# Manual Methods of Connecting Shapes

Microsoft Visio 2007 has introduced a new way of connecting shapes together called *AutoConnect* to add to the other methods.

## Drag-and-Drop

You can simply drag-and-drop a connector Master from a stencil, and then connect each end of the connector to a suitable shape or to connection points in shapes or pages.

If you were drawing an elevation of a network equipment rack or cabinet using File | New | Network | Rack Diagram, then you could simply drag a network equipment Master on to a rack. It should connect at either side to imitate connecting to a bolt hole at a given *U* height.

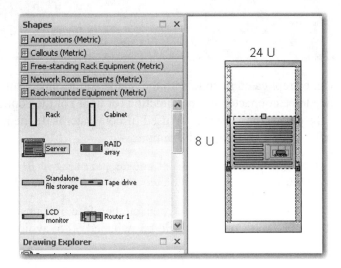

In this case, each end of the equipment shape is statically glued to different connection points on the same rack shape, but often connections are made between two different shapes.

## AutoConnect

The Visio application has to have AutoConnect enabled for it to work. This is normally done by depressing the AutoConnect button on the Standard toolbar or by checking Enable AutoConnect on the General tab on Tools | Options dialog. You can set ApplicationSettings.EnableAutoConnect in code to True or False, but you must also change the User.msvNoAutoConnect cell in the DocumentSheet to 0 or 1 to switch the AutoConnect on or off.

This method enables you to create connections by either dragging-and-dropping one 2-D shape on to the AutoConnect blue arrow of another 2-D shape, or by clicking the desired blue AutoConnect arrow of one 2-D shape pointing toward the 2-D shape to connect to.

If you have a dynamic connector (not necessarily *the* Dynamic connector Master) selected in the active stencil, then it is used as the connector shape.

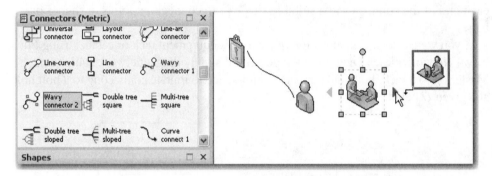

This action can be replicated in code with the Shape.AutoConnect function that requires the shape to be connected to, the direction (or none) of the connector, and, optionally, the connector Master to be used (if no Master is defined, then the Dynamic connector Master is used). For example:

```
'AutoConnect with a connector Master, and no particular direction
shpFrom.AutoConnect shpTo, visAutoConnectDirNone, mstConnector
```

You cannot create static glue with AutoConnect, therefore, it is unsuitable for some types of diagrams. AutoConnect should be switched off to avoid confusion and to speed processing.

If you want to prevent a document from ever having the capability to use AutoConnect, then enter the following formula in the User.msvNoAutoConnect. Prompt cell of the document DocumentSheet:

```
=DEPENDSON(User.msvNoAutoConnect)+SETF(GetRef(User.msvNoAutoConnect),1)
```

This formula sets the value of User. msvNoAutoConnect cell back to 1 if someone tries to use the user interface to switch on AutoConnect.

## Connector Tool

You can use the Connector tool, with or without a selected 1-D connector Master, to connect dynamically between shapes or statically between connection points.

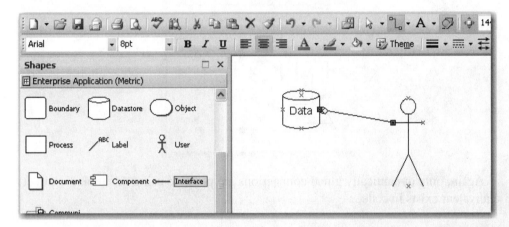

These types of connections can be made in code using the Cell.Glue method, which requires the target cell as an argument. In this case you are defining the connection from an existing 1-D shape (actually the BeginX or EndX cell normally) to a cell on a 2-D shape (usually a connection point for static glue, or PinX for dynamic glue). Thus, the code for making a connection with a 1-D shape between two 2-D shapes requires more than one line, for example:

```
'Drop a new connector shape
Set shpConnector = pag.Drop(mstConnector, 0, 0)
'Glue start to first shape cell
shpConnector.Cells("BeginX").GlueTo shpFrom.Cells("PinX")
'Glue end to second shape cell
shpConnector.Cells("EndX").GlueTo shpTo.Cells("PinX")
```

## Connect Shapes

The *Connect Shapes tool* is on the Action toolbar and can be applied to multiple selected shapes simultaneously. It goes through the selected shapes, in selection order, connecting them in series and using the selected 1-D connector Master, if possible. Otherwise, it uses the Dynamic connector.

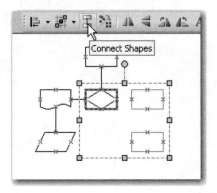

Again, only dynamically glued connections are possible using this tool. No direct equivalent exists in code.

## Using Controls to Connect

You can construct shapes with Controls (the small yellow diamonds) that can be used to connect to other shapes. For example, the Ring Network or Ethernet Masters on the Network and Peripherals stencil in the File | New | Basic Network Diagram has a number of Controls you can drag on to connection points on other shapes.

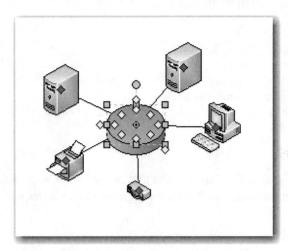

These connections are all done with static glue and, although it may seem the radial lines from the hub shape are connecting, the Control cells are connected to connection points on the equipment shapes.

# Automating Connections

Visio does not have a general automation tool for shape-to-shape connectivity. This section explores ways of automating connections, but the first requirement is to be able to find the shapes to be connected at either end of a connector.

## Finding Shapes by Shape Data

Visio offers many ways of selecting shapes, for example, you can use Edit | Select by Type ... to select by shape type or by layer and Edit | Find ... to find shapes. In code, you can also use the CreateSelection method to get a list of shapes by layer, data graphic, master, or type. No user interface exists for this method, unfortunately, and, moreover, none of the find shapes functions provide the capability to get a list of shapes that satisfy given shape data criteria. This is unfortunate because the *Save As Web* tool does at least provide the capability to search for shapes that have particular criteria for shape data (and it provides a useful flashing pointer in the VML version).

So, I feel compelled to introduce a coded method for selecting shapes, so they can be automatically connected together. The code is presented without error trapping, to save space, and is written within the limitations of VBA. The purpose of the code is to provide shape data criteria that can return a shape ID (or a list of shape IDs) on the active page (or in the whole document). Additionally, it allows for the first level of subshapes of a group to be included in the search, and you can specify whether you are providing the name or the label of the Shape Data row.

Table 4-1 shows the main function GetShapesByData with the following parameters:

| Parameter | Data Type | Usage |
|---|---|---|
| findFirstOnly | Boolean | True to return the first found shape ID |
| activePageOnly | Boolean | True to search only the active page |
| includeSubShapes | Boolean | True to include first level of subshapes in a group |
| aryCriteria | Variant | A two-dimensional string array of shape data criteria, where the first dimension is the criterion index and the second dimension has three criteria elements: 1 = True to use shape data row name, False to use the label 2 = The shape data row name or label 3 = The value to search for |
| returnArray() | Long | The returned long array of page IDs and shape IDs that match the criteria |

**Table 4-1**  *Parameters for GetShapesByData Function*

The function returns True if the search has been successful, so you can then explore the returned array of page IDs and shape IDs.

## Code Listing for GetShapesByData and Support Functions

```
Public Function GetShapesByData(ByVal findFirstOnly As Boolean, _
    ByVal searchScope As Byte, _
    ByVal includeSubShapes As Boolean, _
    ByVal aryCriteria As Variant, _
    ByRef returnArray() As Long) As Boolean

'To return the page and shape IDs found that meets the given criteria
Dim pag As Visio.Page
Dim shp As Visio.Shape
Dim foundShapes As Integer
Dim subShp As Visio.Shape
Dim retVal As Boolean
Dim endSearch As Boolean

Select Case searchScope
    Case 0  'Selection
        For Each shp In Visio.ActiveWindow.Selection
            If checkShapeForMatch(shp, findFirstOnly, _
                includeSubShapes, aryCriteria, _
                returnArray, foundShapes) = True Then
                Exit For
            End If
        Next shp

    Case 1  'Active Page
        For Each shp In Visio.ActivePage.Shapes
            If checkShapeForMatch(shp, findFirstOnly, _
                includeSubShapes, aryCriteria, _
                returnArray, foundShapes) = True Then
                Exit For
            End If
        Next shp

    Case 2  'All foreground pages
        For Each pag In Visio.ActiveDocument.Pages
            If pag.Type = visTypeForeground Then
                For Each shp In pag.Shapes
                    If checkShapeForMatch(shp, findFirstOnly, _
                        includeSubShapes, aryCriteria, _
                        returnArray, foundShapes) = True Then
                        endSearch = True
                        Exit For
                    End If
                Next shp
            End If
```

```
        If endSearch = True Then
            Exit For
        End If
    Next pag

End Select

    'Set the returned value
    If foundShapes > 0 Then
        GetShapesByData = True
    Else
        GetShapesByData = False
    End If

End Function

Private Function checkShapeForMatch(ByVal shp As Visio.Shape, _
    ByVal findFirstOnly As Boolean, _
    ByVal includeSubShapes As Boolean, _
    ByVal aryCriteria As Variant, _
    ByRef returnArray() As Long, _
    ByRef foundShapes As Integer) As Boolean
Dim endSearch As Boolean    'Return this value
Dim subShp As Visio.Shape

    If matchCriteria(shp, aryCriteria, foundShapes, returnArray) = True Then
        If foundShapes = 1 And findFirstOnly = True Then
            endSearch = True
        End If
    End If

    If includeSubShapes = True And endSearch = False Then
        For Each subShp In shp.Shapes
            If matchCriteria(subShp, aryCriteria, foundShapes, returnArray) = True Then
                If foundShapes = 1 And findFirstOnly = True Then
                    endSearch = True
                    Exit For
                End If
            End If
        Next subShp
    End If

    checkShapeForMatch = endSearch
End Function

Private Function matchCriteria(ByVal shp As Visio.Shape, _
    ByVal aryCriteria As Variant, _
    ByRef foundShapes As Integer, ByRef returnArray() As Long) As Boolean

Dim subShp As Visio.Shape
Dim criterion As Integer
Dim rowIndex As Integer
```

```
Dim celProp As Visio.Cell
Dim rowType As Integer
Dim isMatch As Boolean

    For criterion = 1 To UBound(aryCriteria)
        isMatch = False 'Reset for each criterion to test
        If aryCriteria(criterion, 1) = "True" Then
            If shp.CellExistsU("Prop." & aryCriteria(criterion, 2),
                            Visio.visExistsAnywhere) = True Then
                rowIndex = shp.Cells("Prop." & aryCriteria(criterion, 2)).Row
                isMatch = matchCell(shp, rowIndex, aryCriteria(criterion, 3))
            End If
        Else
            For rowIndex = 0 To shp.RowCount(Visio.visSectionProp) - 1
                If shp.CellsSRC(Visio.visSectionProp, rowIndex, Visio.visCustPropsLabel)
                    .ResultStr("") = aryCriteria(criterion, 2) Then
                    isMatch = matchCell(shp, rowIndex, aryCriteria(criterion, 3))
                    Exit For
                End If
            Next rowIndex
        End If

        'Abort if any criteria do not match or shape does not contain the property
        If isMatch = False Then
            Exit For
        End If
    Next criterion

    If isMatch = True Then
        foundShapes = foundShapes + 1
        ReDim Preserve returnArray(1 To 2, 1 To foundShapes)
        returnArray(1, foundShapes) = shp.ContainingPageID
        returnArray(2, foundShapes) = shp.ID
    End If

    matchCriteria = isMatch

End Function

Private Function matchCell(ByVal shp As Visio.Shape, _
    ByVal rowIndex As Integer, ByVal criteria As String) As Boolean

Dim celProp As Visio.Cell
Dim rowType As Integer
Dim retVal As Boolean

    Set celProp = shp.CellsSRC(Visio.visSectionProp, rowIndex, Visio.visCustPropsValue)

    'Check the Shape Data Type of the row
    rowType = shp.CellsSRC(Visio.visSectionProp, rowIndex, Visio.visCustPropsType)
                        .ResultIU
```

```
Select Case rowType
    Case 0, 1, 4  'String, Fixed List, Variable
        'Often developers forget to set the type correctly so double check
        If celProp.ResultStr("") = criteria Then
            retVal = True

        ElseIf IsNumeric(celProp.ResultStr("")) = True _
                And IsNumeric(criteria) = True Then
            If celProp.ResultIU = CDbl(criteria) Then
                retVal = True
            End If

        ElseIf IsDate(celProp.ResultStr("")) = True _
                And IsDate(criteria) = True Then
            If CDate(celProp.ResultStr("")) = CDate(criteria) Then
                retVal = True
            End If

        End If

    Case 2, 6, 7 'Numeric, Duration, Currency
        If celProp.ResultIU = CDbl(criteria) Then
            retVal = True
        End If

    Case 3    'Boolean
        If Abs(celProp.ResultIU) = Abs(CDbl(criteria)) Then
            retVal = True
        End If

    Case 5    'Date
        If CDate(celProp.ResultStr("")) = CDate(criteria) Then
            retVal = True
        End If

End Select

matchCell = retVal

End Function
```

# Connecting Between Found Shapes

The *GetShapeByData function* enables you to get a list of shapes that contain given shape data values, so now you need to be able to use these lists to create connections automatically.

## Creating Dynamic Glue

The example database contains a table called Organization Chart Data, which contains employee names and their manager's name, among other information.

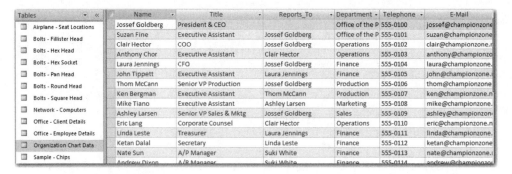

| Tables | Name | Title | Reports_To | Department | Telephone | E-Mail |
|---|---|---|---|---|---|---|
| Airplane - Seat Locations | Jossef Goldberg | President & CEO | | Office of the P | 555-0100 | jossef@championzone |
| Bolts - Fillister Head | Suzan Fine | Executive Assistant | Jossef Goldberg | Office of the P | 555-0101 | suzan@championzone |
| Bolts - Hex Head | Clair Hector | COO | Jossef Goldberg | Operations | 555-0102 | clair@championzone.r |
| Bolts - Hex Socket | Anthony Chor | Executive Assistant | Clair Hector | Operations | 555-0103 | anthony@championzo |
| Bolts - Pan Head | Laura Jennings | CFO | Jossef Goldberg | Finance | 555-0104 | laura@championzone. |
| Bolts - Round Head | John Tippett | Executive Assistant | Laura Jennings | Finance | 555-0105 | john@championzone.( |
| Bolts - Square Head | Thom McCann | Senior VP Production | Jossef Goldberg | Production | 555-0106 | thom@championzone |
| Network - Computers | Ken Bergman | Executive Assistant | Thom McCann | Production | 555-0107 | ken@championzone.n |
| Office - Client Details | Mike Tiano | Executive Assistant | Ashley Larsen | Marketing | 555-0108 | mike@championzone. |
| Office - Employee Details | Ashley Larsen | Senior VP Sales & Mktg | Jossef Goldberg | Sales | 555-0109 | ashley@championzon( |
| Organization Chart Data | Eric Lang | Corporate Counsel | Clair Hector | Operations | 555-0110 | eric@championzone.n |
| Sample - Chips | Linda Leste | Treasurer | Laura Jennings | Finance | 555-0111 | linda@championzone. |
| | Ketan Dalal | Secretary | Linda Leste | Finance | 555-0112 | ketan@championzone |
| | Nate Sun | A/P Manager | Suki White | Finance | 555-0113 | nate@championzone.( |
| | Andrew Dixon | A/R Manager | Suki White | Finance | 555-0114 | andrew@championzoi |

We shall use this table along with the Person Master on the Resources stencil to create a number of data-linked shapes to demonstrate the automated connections.

Start a File | New | Maps and Floor Plans | Space Plan diagram, but cancel the Space Plan Startup Wizard that pops up, as we are demonstrating the principal. Use Data | Link Data to Shapes to select the Access database C:\Program Files\Microsoft Office\OFFICE12\1033\DBSAMPLE.MDB and the table Organization Chart Data, and then continue to accept all defaults to the finish of the wizard.

The filed names do not quite match the labels of the shape data rows on the Person Master, so you need to edit the Column Settings from the right-mouse menu of the External Data Window.

Simply rename the Reports_To, Telephone, and E-Mail columns to Manager, Phone Number and, E-mail Alias, and you can uncheck the Master_Shape column.

If you now select the Person Master on the Resources stencil, then select all the rows in the External Data Window and drop them on to the top-left corner of the page. You get a cascaded display of data-linked Person shapes.

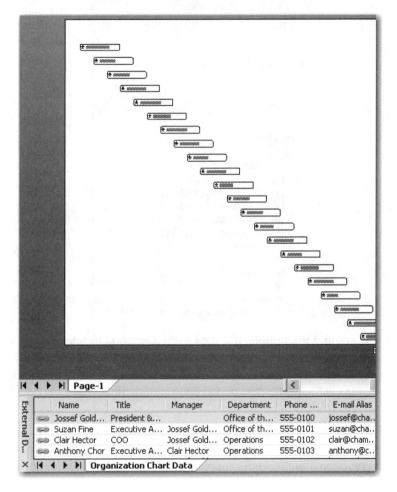

You do not need any Data Graphics at this point and, of course, in a real scenario, these Person shapes will be located at desks on a floor plan, but the cascaded arrangement is sufficient for this example.

Now, open the Organization Chart Shapes stencil from File | Shapes | Business | Organization Chart, drag the Dotted-line report Master on to the page, and then delete it (do not use UNDO or CTRL-Z). This copies the Master to the document, so you can use it more easily in code.

In code, you could, for example, use the OpenEx method to open a copy of a stencil docked.

Finally, open the VBA Editor (ALT + F11), and create a new module in this document, and then paste the GetShapesByData and supporting functions into its code window.

## Using GetShapesByData for Dynamic Glue

Create a new module in the VBA Editor, and then cut-and-paste the ConnectSub-Ordinates subfunction along with its support function FindMySubordinates into the new module's code window.

The ConnectSubOrdinates subfunction loops through all the shapes on the active page to check if the shape qualifies as a Person (it includes Name and Manager shape data). Then, for each qualifying shape, the FindMySubordinates, which calls the GetShapesByData function with particular parameters, returns a list of all shapes that have the current Person as a manager, and then connects the Dotted-line report Master between the manager and the subordinate.

Two alternative methods of creating dynamically glued connections with a designated Master are included in the code. The first uses AutoConnect, in which case you need to get hold of the last shape in the page, and the second uses GlueTo. Simply change the commenting out to try the alternatives.

Finally, the connector shape is modified by changing its line color, begin, and end arrows.

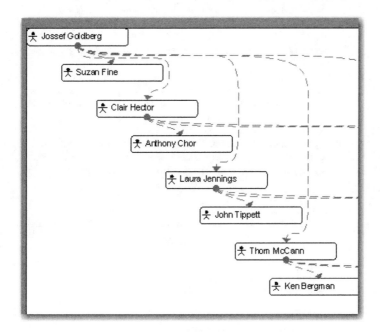

The Dotted-line report Master could be enhanced to include a layer and shape data rows, and the code could be enhanced to include shape data values, thus enabling the connectors themselves to be data linked.

## Code Listing for ConnectSubOrdinates and Support Function

```
Public Sub ConnectSubOrdinates()
Dim pag As Visio.Page
Dim shp As Visio.Shape
Dim subshp As Visio.Shape
Dim shpConnector As Visio.Shape
Dim shapeCounter As Integer
Dim manager As String
Dim mst As Visio.Master

    Set mst = ThisDocument.Masters("Dotted-line report")
    Visio.Application.EventsEnabled = False
```

```
For Each shp In Visio.ActivePage.Shapes
    'Check that the shape qualifies
    If shp.CellExists("Prop.Name", Visio.visExistsAnywhere) = True _
        And shp.CellExists("Prop.Manager", Visio.visExistsAnywhere) = True Then
        manager = shp.Cells("Prop.Name").ResultStr("")
        'Get a list of subordinate shapes
        Dim foundShapes()  As Long
        If FindMySubordinates(manager, foundShapes) = True Then
            For shapeCounter = 1 To UBound(foundShapes, 2)
                Set pag = Visio.ActiveDocument.Pages.ItemFromID(foundShapes(1,
                                                        shapeCounter))
                Set subshp = pag.Shapes.ItemFromID(foundShapes(2, shapeCounter))

                'EITHER use AutoConnect
                'AutoConnect will cause the page layout to be triggered
                'AutoConnect without a Master will use Dynamic connector
                'shp.AutoConnect subshp, visAutoConnectDirDown
                'AutoConnect with a connector Master
                shp.AutoConnect subshp, visAutoConnectDirNone, mst
                'Get a reference to the last shape (the connector)
                Set shpConnector = pag.Shapes(pag.Shapes.Count)

                'OR use GlueTo
'                'Drop a new connector shape
'                Set shpConnector = pag.Drop(mst, shp.Cells("PinX").ResultIU, shp.
                                        Cells("PinY").ResultIU)
'                'Glue start to manager
'                shpConnector.Cells("BeginX").GlueTo shp.Cells("PinX")
'                'Glue end to subordinate
'                shpConnector.Cells("EndX").GlueTo subshp.Cells("PinX")

                'Set any connector shape properties that you want
                'for example, the line color
                shpConnector.Cells("LineColor").Formula = "2" 'Red
                shpConnector.Cells("BeginArrow").Formula = "10" 'Small circle
                shpConnector.Cells("EndArrow").Formula = "2" 'Small triangle
                'Other properties to consider are layer, hyperlinks and shape data

            Next shapeCounter
        End If
    End If
Next shp
Visio.Application.EventsEnabled = True
End Sub

Private Function FindMySubordinates(ByVal manager As String, _
    ByRef foundShapes() As Long) As Boolean
Dim aryCriteria() As String
'Array dimensions:
' 1 = UseName = "True", UseLabel = "False"
' 2 = Data Name or Label
' 3 = Value (as string)
```

```
ReDim aryCriteria(1 To 1, 1 To 3)

aryCriteria(1, 1) = "False"
aryCriteria(1, 2) = "Manager"
aryCriteria(1, 3) = manager

FindMySubordinates = GetShapesByData(False, 1, False, _
    aryCriteria, foundShapes)

End Function
```

## Creating Static Glue

The scenario of a network equipment shape in a rack or cabinet is a good example of when you may need to automate the connection of items to particular connection points.

To try this example, you need to create a list of equipment in an Excel spreadsheet.

### NOTE

*You only need to type the first three rows in Excel, and then highlight the second and third rows of text cells and drag this selection box down as far as is required to create the right number of rows. The numbers are automatically incremented where necessary (see E04-Rack Equipment.xlsx).*

| | A | B | C | D | E |
|---|---|---|---|---|---|
| 1 | Asset Number | Equip Type | Height in U's | Rack | U Position |
| 2 | CT-01 | Cable Tray | 2 | RACK-01 | 0 |
| 3 | PP-01 | Patch Panel | 2 | RACK-01 | 2 |
| 4 | CT-02 | Cable Tray | 2 | RACK-01 | 4 |
| 5 | PP-02 | Patch Panel | 2 | RACK-01 | 6 |
| 6 | CT-03 | Cable Tray | 2 | RACK-01 | 8 |
| 7 | PP-03 | Patch Panel | 2 | RACK-01 | 10 |
| 8 | CT-04 | Cable Tray | 2 | RACK-01 | 12 |
| 9 | PP-04 | Patch Panel | 2 | RACK-01 | 14 |
| 10 | CT-05 | Cable Tray | 2 | RACK-01 | 16 |
| 11 | PP-05 | Patch Panel | 2 | RACK-01 | 18 |
| 12 | CT-06 | Cable Tray | 2 | RACK-01 | 20 |
| 13 | PP-06 | Patch Panel | 2 | RACK-01 | 22 |
| 14 | CT-07 | Cable Tray | 2 | RACK-01 | 24 |
| 15 | PP-07 | Patch Panel | 2 | RACK-01 | 26 |
| 16 | CT-08 | Cable Tray | 2 | RACK-01 | 28 |
| 17 | PP-08 | Patch Panel | 2 | RACK-01 | 30 |
| 18 | CT-09 | Cable Tray | 2 | RACK-01 | 32 |
| 19 | PP-09 | Patch Panel | 2 | RACK-01 | 34 |
| 20 | CT-10 | Cable Tray | 2 | RACK-01 | 36 |
| 21 | PP-10 | Patch Panel | 2 | RACK-01 | 38 |
| 22 | CT-11 | Cable Tray | 2 | RACK-01 | 40 |

Start a new File | Network | Rack Diagram, and then select Data | Link Data to Shapes to link the Excel spreadsheet. Drag a Rack Master shape from the Rack-mounted Equipment stencil on to the page, and type **RACK-01** into its Asset Number shape data.

Then click the Equip Type column header to order by it. Select the Cable Tray/Spacer Master on the stencil, and then select all the Cable Tray rows in the External Data Window and drag on to the left of the Rack shape. Repeat for the Patch Panel Master and rows.

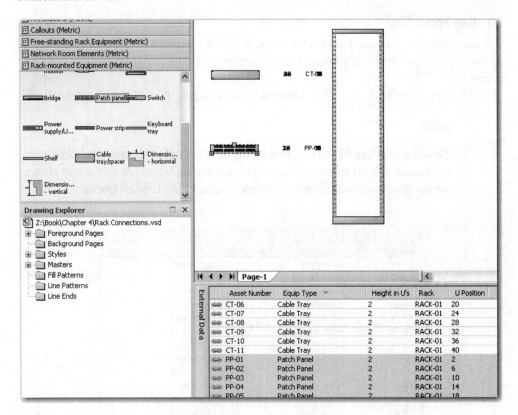

In fact, I edited the Data Graphic in the previous example to display the *U* Position and Asset Number shape data to the right of the shapes.

So, you now have all the equipment for this rack on the page, but not yet connected to the rack at the correct *U* Position.

## Using GetShapesByData for Static Glue

Create a new module in the VBA Editor, and then cut-and-paste the *ConnectRack-Equipment* subfunction along with its support function *FindMyRackEquipment* into the new module's code window.

The *ConnectRackEquipment* loops through all the shapes on the active page to check if the shape qualifies as a *Rack* (if it includes Prop.HoleSpacing shape data). Then, for each qualifying shape, the *FindMyRackEquipment*, which calls the GetShapesByData function with particular parameters, returns a list of all shapes that belong to the current Rack, and then reads the *U* Position and connects the equipment item to the rack's connection points.

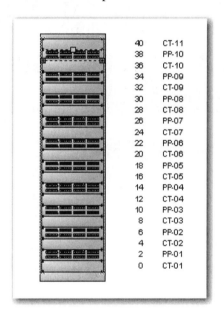

## Code Listing for ConnectRackEquipment

```
Public Sub ConnectRackEquipment()
Dim pag As Visio.Page
Dim shp As Visio.Shape
Dim subshp As Visio.Shape
Dim shapeCounter As Integer
Dim rack As String
Dim UPosition As Integer
Dim ptLeft As Integer

    Visio.Application.EventsEnabled = False
    For Each shp In Visio.ActivePage.Shapes
```

```
                'Check that the shape qualifies as a rack or cabinet
            If shp.CellExists("Prop.HoleSpacing", Visio.visExistsAnywhere) = True Then
                rack = shp.Cells("Prop.AssetNumber").ResultStr("")
                'Get a list of rack equipment shapes
                Dim foundShapes()  As Long
                If FindMyRackEquipment(rack, foundShapes) = True Then
                    For shapeCounter = 1 To UBound(foundShapes, 2)
                        Set pag = Visio.ActiveDocument.Pages.ItemFromID(foundShapes(1,
                                                                shapeCounter))
                        Set subshp = pag.Shapes.ItemFromID(foundShapes(2, shapeCounter))
                        'Get the U Position
                        If subshp.CellExists("Prop._VisDM_U_Position", Visio.
                                            visExistsAnywhere) = True Then
                            UPosition = subshp.Cells("Prop._VisDM_U_Position").ResultIU
                            'Convert the U Position to the Connection on the left
                            ptLeft = (2 * UPosition) + 1
                            'Use GlueTo
                            'Glue start to left Connection Point
                            subshp.Cells("BeginX").GlueTo shp.Cells("Connections.X"
                                                            & CStr(ptLeft))
                            'Glue end to right Connection Point
                            subshp.Cells("EndX").GlueTo shp.Cells("Connections.X"
                                                            & CStr(ptLeft + 1))
                        End If
                    Next shapeCounter
                End If
            End If
        Next shp
        Visio.Application.EventsEnabled = True
End Sub


Private Function FindMyRackEquipment(ByVal rack As String, _
    ByRef foundShapes() As Long) As Boolean
Dim aryCriteria() As String
'Array dimensions:
' 1 = UseName = "True", UseLabel = "False"
' 2 = Data Name or Label
' 3 = Value (as string)

    ReDim aryCriteria(1 To 1, 1 To 3)

    aryCriteria(1, 1) = "False"
    aryCriteria(1, 2) = "Rack"
    aryCriteria(1, 3) = rack

    FindMyRackEquipment = GetShapesByData(False, 1, False, _
        aryCriteria, foundShapes)


End Function
```

# Ideas for Enhancing Connectors

We have seen that 1-D connectors can be created between shapes and with a little automation, they can be modified as they are created, and the connector Master could be premodified to behave in particular ways.

## Adding Hyperlinks to Connectors

If I am creating a large diagram that has shapes connected via 1-D connectors, then I often add hyperlinks to the connectors automatically. Consequently, each connector has two hyperlinks—one for each shape at either end—so the user can navigate quickly from one end to the other, even when zoomed in close to one end, just by selecting the connector and selecting the hyperlink to the opposite end. In the example, Page-1/A:2 and Page-1/A:18 are hyperlinks to the shapes at either end of the selected connector.

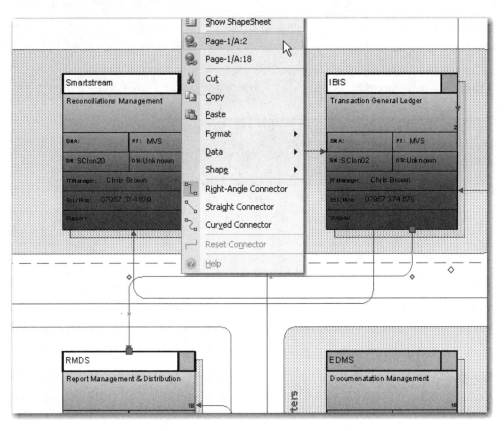

Of course, if the user decides to modify the diagram, you need to handle the removal or the update of hyperlinks.

## Updating Connection Point Labels

Sometimes, it is useful to update the labels associated with the connection point or shape, which is connected to with the Shape Data from the shape connected to the other end of the connector, as in this example of a desk wiring loom.

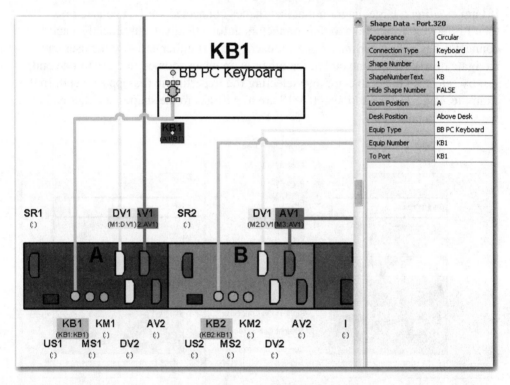

In this example, code is listening for the connections being made or deleted, and then the shape data of the shape at the opposite end is copied to each connected shape. This enables the shape data labels to be updated automatically. Additionally, the code checks that the correct type of ports are being connected and, if successful, the connector line color is updated to reflect the type of connection being made.

## Displaying Duplex Data

Sometimes, 1-D connectors represent flow in either direction, and the user would like to see, for example, the remaining capacity represented as differently colored arrows at each end of the connector. This can be seen in the following example of a network capacity-planning diagram.

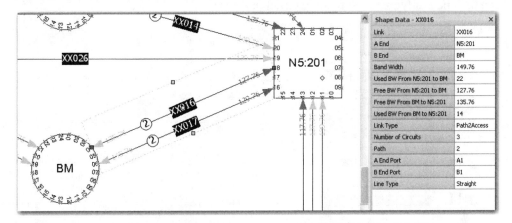

The important part of this technique is to ensure the 1-D connector shape is a group shape that contains at least three, almost identical, lines occupying the same space. There is a line for each direction, so they can respond to the shape data of the group independently, and so they show different color arrows at each end of the line.

# Reading Connections

Microsoft Visio has no automated export of connections within it, so you need to decide how you will do this. The method employed usually depends on the needs of the user.

If you need to use the Visio reports to display connectivity, for example, the equipment items in each rack—or the steps in a process diagram—then it is necessary to write code to create or update shape data and/or User-defined cells with the required information.

## Updating Network Rack Connections

Earlier, you saw how you can update a network equipment arrangement from a spreadsheet that has a list of equipment at *U* positions in a rack. However, the rack diagrams may be manually drawn in Visio, with equipment being dragged-and-dropped at *U* positions, and then you want to be able to read these positions into a spreadsheet or database.

In this case, you need to have code that will read what is connected to the racks, and then add or update the shape data in each item with the rack and *U* Position. This can then be easily exported to an external database.

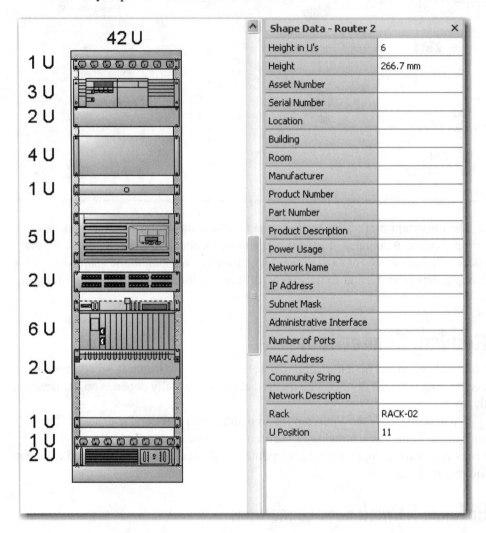

| Shape Data - Router 2 | ✕ |
|---|---|
| Height in U's | 6 |
| Height | 266.7 mm |
| Asset Number | |
| Serial Number | |
| Location | |
| Building | |
| Room | |
| Manufacturer | |
| Product Number | |
| Part Number | |
| Product Description | |
| Power Usage | |
| Network Name | |
| IP Address | |
| Subnet Mask | |
| Administrative Interface | |
| Number of Ports | |
| MAC Address | |
| Community String | |
| Network Description | |
| Rack | RACK-02 |
| U Position | 11 |

In addition to the following code listing, you need to copy-and-paste three functions from the Microsoft Visio SDK Code Library:

1. Custom Property Add (modAddingACustProp)
2. Cell Value as String (modSetCellValueToString)
3. String To Formula (modStringToFormulaForString)

## Code Listing for UpdateRackEquipment and Support Function

```
Public Sub UpdateRackEquipment()
Dim pag As Visio.Page
Dim shp As Visio.Shape
Dim cnx As Visio.Connect
Dim UPosition As Integer
Dim rack As String
Dim shpEquip As Visio.Shape

    Set pag = Visio.ActivePage

    For Each shp In pag.Shapes
        If shp.CellExists("Prop.HoleSpacing", Visio.visExistsAnywhere) = True Then
            rack = shp.Cells("Prop.AssetNumber").ResultStr("")
            Debug.Print rack
            'Check what is connected to it
            For Each cnx In shp.FromConnects
                'Only need to read connections on one side
                If cnx.ToCell.Row Mod 2 = 0 Then
                    'Get the U Position
                    UPosition = (cnx.ToCell.Row / 2)
                    Set shpEquip = cnx.FromSheet
                    updateData shpEquip, "Rack", rack
                    updateData shpEquip, "U Position", UPosition
                End If
            Next cnx
        End If
    Next shp
End Sub

Private Sub updateData(ByVal shp As Visio.Shape, _
    ByVal propLabel As String, ByVal value As String)

Dim propName As String
Dim celProp As Visio.Cell
Dim rowCounter As Integer

    'Remove special characters from label
    propName = Replace(Replace(propLabel, " ", "_"), "'", "_")

    If shp.CellExists("Prop." & propName, Visio.visExistsAnywhere) = True Then
        'Check for simply named
        Set celProp = shp.Cells("Prop." & propName)
    ElseIf shp.CellExists("Prop._visDM_" & propName, Visio.visExistsAnywhere) = True Then
        'Check for the default created by Link Data
        Set celProp = shp.Cells("Prop._visDM_" & propName)
    Else
        'Check through all Shape Data Rows in case it wasn't named
        For rowCounter = 0 To shp.RowCount(Visio.visSectionProp) - 1
```

```
            If shp.CellsSRC(Visio.visSectionProp, rowCounter, _
                    Visio.visCustPropsLabel).ResultStr("") = propLabel Then
                Set celProp = shp.CellsSRC(Visio.visSectionProp, rowCounter, _
                    Visio.visCustPropsLabel)
                Exit For
            End If
        Next rowCounter
    End If

    If celProp Is Nothing Then
        'Add the Shape Data row
        If AddCustomProperty(shp, propName, propName, propLabel) = True Then
            Set celProp = shp.Cells("Prop." & propName)
        End If
    End If

    If Not celProp Is Nothing Then
        'Update the value
        Select Case shp.CellsSRC(Visio.visSectionProp, celProp.Row, _
                Visio.visCustPropsType).ResultIU
        Case 0, 1, 4
            SetCellValueToString celProp, value
        Case Else
            celProp.Formula = "=" & value
        End Select
    End If

End Sub
```

# Updating Process Connectors

The *Microsoft Visio 2007 SDK Code Library* contains code to create a small process diagram.

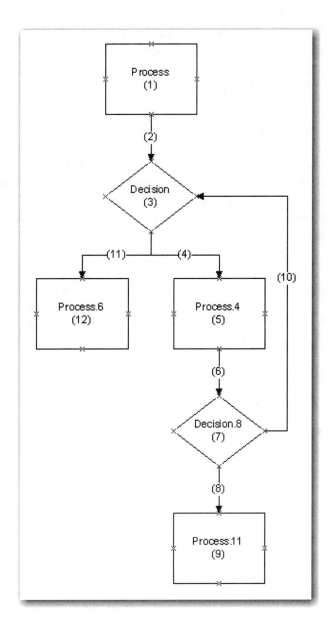

This code is:

1.  Drawing Navigator Using Connections (modDrawingNavigator)
2.  Dynamic Glue Connections (modDynamicConector)

If you remove the parameter from the subfunction DemoDrawingNavigator and add the following two lines at the top of the sub instead . . .

```
Dim vsoApplication as Visio.Application
Set vsoApplication = Visio.Application
```

. . . you can then run the DemoDrawingNavigator function to create the process flow diagram (see E04-CreateProcessDrawing.vsd) in a new drawing.

In the new drawing, you can add the *UpdateConnectorData* subfunction to update the connectors between the process flow shapes with the unique IDs and/or selected shape data (or the shape name) of the shapes at either end. You can then export these connections more easily, and you can interrogate a connector with the mouse to see what it is connected to. Of course, in a complete solution, you need to blank out the connection data for any connectors that are no longer connected properly.

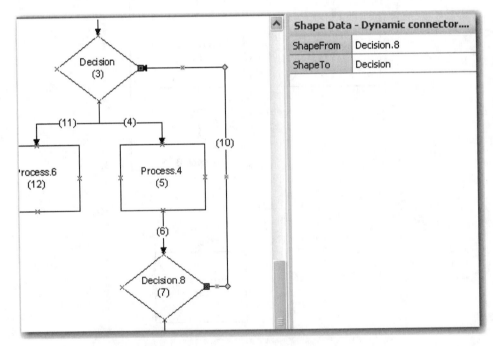

In addition to the following code listing, you need to copy-and-paste three functions from the Microsoft Visio SDK Code Library:

1. Custom Property Add (modAddingACustProp)
2. Cell Value as String (modSetCellValueToString)
3. String To Formula (modStringToFormulaForString)

## Code Listing for UpdateConnectorData and Support Functions

```
Public Sub UpdateConnectorData()
Dim shpConnector As Visio.Shape
Dim cnx As Visio.Connect
Dim shpFrom As Visio.Shape
Dim shpTo As Visio.Shape
Dim rowUserGUIDFrom As Integer
Dim rowUserGUIDTo As Integer
Dim rowUserFrom As Integer
Dim rowUserTo As Integer
Dim rowPropFrom As Integer
Dim rowPropTo As Integer

    For Each shpConnector In Visio.ActivePage.Shapes
        If shpConnector.OneD = True Then
            Set shpFrom = Nothing
            Set shpTo = Nothing
            For Each cnx In shpConnector.Connects
                If cnx.FromCell.Name = "BeginX" Then
                    Set shpFrom = cnx.ToSheet
                ElseIf cnx.FromCell.Name = "EndX" Then
                    Set shpTo = cnx.ToSheet
                End If
            Next cnx

            If Not shpFrom Is Nothing And Not shpTo Is Nothing Then
                'You could also check if the From and To shapes are the correct type
                'Update a User-defined cell with the GUID of the shape
                rowUserGUIDFrom = getUserRow(shpFrom, "ShapeID")
                shpFrom.CellsSRC(Visio.visSectionUser, rowUserGUIDFrom, _
                            Visio.visUserValue).Formula = _
                    "=" & StringToFormulaForString(shpFrom.UniqueID _
                                            (Visio.visGetOrMakeGUID))

                rowUserGUIDTo = getUserRow(shpTo, "ShapeID")
                shpTo.CellsSRC(Visio.visSectionUser, rowUserGUIDTo, _
                            Visio.visUserValue).Formula = _
                    "=" & _
                StringToFormulaForString(shpTo.UniqueID(Visio.visGetOrMakeGUID))

                'Update the connector User-defined cells with the From/To shape GUIDs
                rowUserFrom = getUserRow(shpConnector, "ShapeFrom")
                shpConnector.CellsSRC(Visio.visSectionUser, rowUserFrom, _
                                Visio.visUserValue).Formula = _
                    "=" & _
                StringToFormulaForString(shpFrom.UniqueID(Visio.visGetGUID))
                rowUserTo = getUserRow(shpConnector, "ShapeTo")
                shpConnector.CellsSRC(Visio.visSectionUser, rowUserTo, Visio. _
                                visUserValue).Formula = _
                    "=" & _
                StringToFormulaForString(shpTo.UniqueID(Visio.visGetGUID))
```

```
                       'Additionally you can update the connector Shape Data
                       rowPropFrom = getPropRow(shpConnector, "ShapeFrom")
                       shpConnector.CellsSRC(Visio.visSectionProp, rowPropFrom, Visio.
                                      visCustPropsValue).Formula = _
                          "=" & StringToFormulaForString(shpFrom.Name)

                       rowPropTo = getPropRow(shpConnector, "ShapeTo")
                       shpConnector.CellsSRC(Visio.visSectionProp, rowPropTo, Visio.
                                      visCustPropsValue).Formula = _
                          "=" & StringToFormulaForString(shpTo.Name)


                End If

            End If
        Next shpConnector

End Sub

Private Function getUserRow(ByVal shp As Visio.Shape, ByVal rowName As String) As Integer
Dim sectUser As Integer

    If shp.SectionExists(Visio.visSectionUser, Visio.visExistsAnywhere) = False Then
        sectUser = shp.AddSection(Visio.visSectionUser)
    Else
        sectUser = Visio.visSectionUser
    End If

    If shp.CellExists(«User.» & rowName, Visio.visExistsAnywhere) = False Then
        getUserRow = shp.AddNamedRow(sectUser, rowName, 0)
    Else
        getUserRow = shp.Cells(«User.» & rowName).Row
    End If
End Function

Private Function getPropRow(ByVal shp As Visio.Shape, ByVal rowName As String) As Integer
Dim sectProp As Integer

    If shp.SectionExists(Visio.visSectionProp, Visio.visExistsAnywhere) = False Then
        sectProp = shp.AddSection(Visio.visSectionProp)
    Else
        sectProp = Visio.visSectionProp
    End If

    If shp.CellExists(«Prop.» & rowName, Visio.visExistsAnywhere) = False Then
        AddCustomProperty shp, rowName, rowName, rowName
    End If

    getPropRow = shp.Cells(«Prop.» & rowName).Row


End Function
```

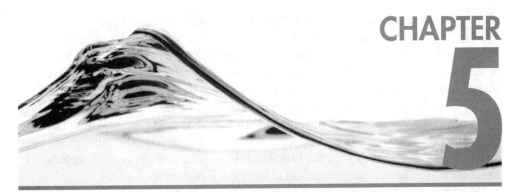

# Summarizing Information with PivotDiagrams

PivotDiagrams are a great new way to summarize data in Microsoft Visio. *PivotDiagrams* can be used for dynamic analysis; to visually present aggregate information, and even to navigate linked data shapes on the same, or different pages (with a little bit of code). You can combine PivotDiagrams with Linked Data and Data Graphics to provide integrated data dashboards.

The PivotDiagrams are created with data sources, just like Link Data to Shapes, but the Data Recordsets are not displayed within the External Data window. The PivotDiagram solution is an add-on to Visio, so you do not have the same programmatic control as you have with the Link Data. However, you can employ techniques to enhance your user's experience and to increase productivity.

PivotDiagrams let you select columns, usually non-numeric ones, as Categories into which you can breakdown the data. These Categories are presented as Breakdown Shapes, below which Nodes display the aggregate data. These nodes can be broken down into further categories, and so on until all rows from the Data Recordset are displayed as single nodes . . . if you want to go that far.

PivotDiagrams work particularly well with aggregations of numeric and currency data. In the sample database, *C:\Program Files\Microsoft Office\ OFFICE12\1033\DBSAMPLE.MDB,* the Network—Computers table has the Number data type fields, Machine Type code, Hard Disk Space and Memory, while, the Cost field is Currency data type.

| Field Name | Data Type |
|---|---|
| Owner | Text |
| Manufacturer | Text |
| Machine Type | Text |
| Machine Type code | Number |
| Hard Disk Space | Number |
| Memory | Number |
| Processor | Text |
| Screen Size | Text |
| Network Card | Yes/No |
| Modem | Yes/No |
| Sound Card | Yes/No |
| Cost | Currency |
| XLocation | Text |
| YLocation | Text |

A query called Network—Details, in the database, summarizes the numeric fields and provides a count of machines from the Network—Computers table.

Network - Computers

| MachineSN | Owner | Manufacturer | Machine Type | Mac | Hard Disk Spa | Memc | Processo | Scree |
|---|---|---|---|---|---|---|---|---|
| SN10000001 | Jossef Goldberg | DELL | Dimension | 1 | 1300 | 32 | Pentium 90 | 17 in |
| SN10000002 | Suzan Fine | DELL | Optiplex | 1 | 1600 | 24 | Pentium 75 | 17 in |
| SN10000003 | Clair Hector | IBM | Aptiva | 1 | 1300 | 16 | Pentium 75 | 15 in |
| SN10000004 | Anthony Chor | Siemens Nixdorf | Scenic 5H | 1 | 850 | 32 | Pentium 90 | 17 in |
| SN10000005 | Laura Jennings | Hewlett Packard | Vectra | 1 | 1000 | 32 | Pentium 90 | 17 in |
| SN10000006 | John Tippett | Toshiba | 4900CT | 2 | 810 | 32 | Pentium 90 | 17 in |
| SN10000007 | Thom McCann | IBM | PS/2 Model 70 | 1 | 120 | 12 | i386/25 | 14 in |
| SN10000008 | Ken Bergman | DELL | 466ME | 1 | 1300 | 32 | Pentium 90 | 17 in |

The query does not show the breakdown by the fields Manufacturer and Machine Type, for example, but this could easily be added to provide the following breakdown.

| Manufacturer | Machine Type | SumOfHard Disk Space | SumOfMemory | SumOfCost | CountOfMachineSN |
|---|---|---|---|---|---|
| Compaq | Deskpro | 800 | 32 | £8,000.00 | 4 |
| Compaq | Prolinea | 5200 | 128 | £8,000.00 | 4 |
| DELL | 466ME | 6500 | 160 | £10,000.00 | 5 |
| DELL | Dimension | 1300 | 32 | £2,000.00 | 1 |
| DELL | Optiplex | 8000 | 120 | £10,000.00 | 5 |
| Hewlett Packard | Vectra | 5000 | 160 | £10,000.00 | 5 |
| IBM | Aptiva | 5200 | 64 | £7,000.00 | 4 |
| IBM | PS/2 Model 70 | 600 | 60 | £10,000.00 | 5 |
| IBM | Value Point | 2048 | 16 | £1,500.00 | 1 |
| Siemens Nixdorf | Scenic 5H | 4250 | 160 | £10,000.00 | 5 |
| Toshiba | 4900CT | 4050 | 160 | £10,000.00 | 5 |

You could use a Pivot Table in Microsoft Excel to display similar information. This has the advantage of being able to be easily manipulated by users for analysis.

| Row Labels | Sum of Hard Disk Space | Sum of Memory | Sum of Cost | Count of MachineSN |
|---|---|---|---|---|
| Compaq | 6000 | 160 | 16000 | 8 |
| Deskpro | 800 | 32 | 8000 | 4 |
| Prolinea | 5200 | 128 | 8000 | 4 |
| DELL | 15800 | 312 | 22000 | 11 |
| 466ME | 6500 | 160 | 10000 | 5 |
| Dimension | 1300 | 32 | 2000 | 1 |
| Optiplex | 8000 | 120 | 10000 | 5 |
| Hewlett Packard | 5000 | 160 | 10000 | 5 |
| Vectra | 5000 | 160 | 10000 | 5 |
| IBM | 7848 | 140 | 18500 | 10 |
| Aptiva | 5200 | 64 | 7000 | 4 |
| PS/2 Model 70 | 600 | 60 | 10000 | 5 |
| Value Point | 2048 | 16 | 1500 | 1 |
| Siemens Nixdorf | 4250 | 160 | 10000 | 5 |
| Scenic 5H | 4250 | 160 | 10000 | 5 |
| Toshiba | 4050 | 160 | 10000 | 5 |
| 4900CT | 4050 | 160 | 10000 | 5 |
| Grand Total | 42948 | 1092 | 86500 | 44 |

The PivotDiagrams in Microsoft Visio 2007 are also able to be used dynamically, so you can easily use the diagrams to analyze data graphically.

# Creating a PivotDiagram

You can start a new PivotDiagram drawing from the New | Business category, or you can insert a PivotDiagram into any existing Visio document using Data | Insert Pivot-Diagram. You can also insert multiple PivotDiagrams into a single page.

When you start a new PivotDiagram, drag-and-drop the Pivot Node Master on to the page or select Insert PivotDiagram. You need to select the data to use from the Data Selector. For example, select the sample Access database *C:\Program Files\Microsoft Office\OFFICE12\1033\DBSAMPLE.MDB*, and the table Network—Computers. As with Link Data to Shapes, you can filter the records, if you want to.

Initially, a single Total Pivot Node is shown with the Pivot Title above it and the Pivot Info to the right. The PivotDiagram window is shown docked on the left in Figure 5-1, where you can see the Categories that can be added and the available Totals.

View the Shape Data window in the top right (if it is not there, use View | Shape Data Window to open it) and notice how the numeric and currency fields have been automatically aggregated as Shape Data rows on the root Pivot Node. The summation of the values is shown with the same default label as the Shape Data row name, but the Average is shown with (Avg) appended to the label. In this particular case, the

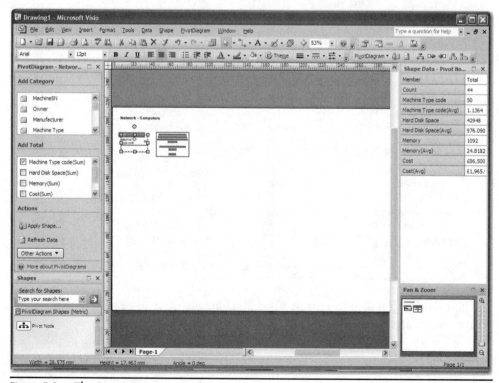

**Figure 5-1** *The PivotDiagram root*

PivotDiagram add-on has incorrectly chosen to display the sum of the Machine Type code Shape Data, so this should be changed to display the Count in the Add Total list in the PivotDiagram panel.

# Enhancing the Default Data Graphics

We could take the opportunity to amend the default Data Graphics for this PivotDiagram by adding three extra Data Graphic items at the same time as changing Machine Type code to Count. Simply select Pivot | Edit Data Graphic while one of the PivotDiagram shapes is selected (or select the desired Data Graphic from the Data Graphics panel).

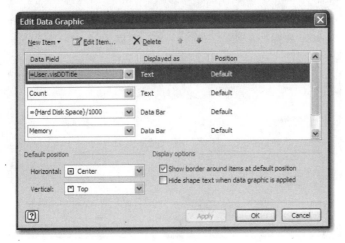

The Hard Disk Space Shape Data row contains values in large numbers of Gigabytes, so it could be better to divide the number by 1000 and to display only one decimal place. You can do this by selecting More fields from the bottom of the drop-down list on the Data field control in the Edit Data Graphic dialog.

**NOTE**

*The field name is enclosed in curly brackets, { }. The changing of a field name to a formula means the Label cannot be automatically assigned, so you need to enter your own, for example, Disk Space.*

The Speedometer Data Bar has been selected, and the Minimum and Maximum values have been left at their default, which means the arrow never quite reaches halfway because the highest value is 42.9, as seen on the Total Pivot Node. So, changing the Maximum to 50 would make the gauge swing more appropriately.

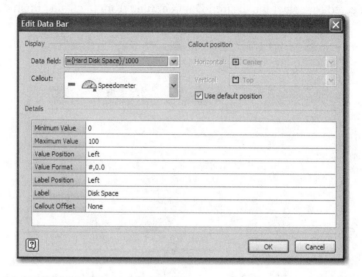

The Progress Bar has been used for the Memory Shape Data row, and the Label is positioned in the Interior.

The Maximum value for the Progress Bar could also be set to just above the underlying Shape Data row on the Total Pivot Node, to, say, 1100. This ensures the Total Pivot Node is nicely showing the maximum, while all breakdown Pivot Nodes always show part of the totals.

Finally, the Cost Shape Data has been added at the bottom as a Text item.

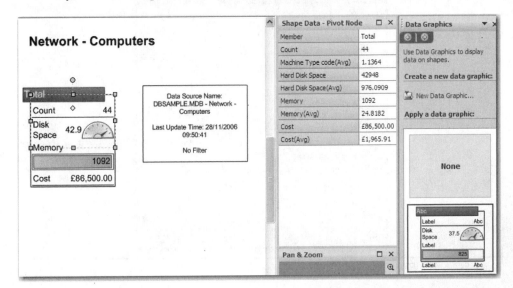

Note that the formula for the first Data Graphic row (not shown in the illustration) is:

```
=User.visDDTitle
```

A number of User-defined cells are in each type of PivotDiagram shape, which can be useful for Data Graphics or for use in code, so they are listed in the following PivotDiagram Masters.

## PivotDiagram Options

The PivotDiagram Options dialog can be opened from the PivotDiagram | Options menu, but you need to have at least one of the PivotDiagram shapes selected. This is because you could have more than one PivotDiagram per page (see Figure 5-2).

In this dialog, you can edit the title of the PivotDiagram, control the visibility of most of the components of a PivotDiagram, limit the number of items in each break-down, and set the underlying data to be refreshed periodically.

## Breaking Down the PivotDiagram

You can then drill down to the next level by adding a Category to breakdown from either the right mouse menu of the Pivot Node or from the Add Category panel of the

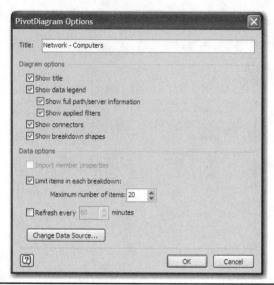

**Figure 5-2** *The PivotDiagram Options dialog*

PivotDiagram window. In this case, I selected Manufacturer, and then, with all the Manufacturer Pivot Nodes selected, another category, Machine Type, was selected.

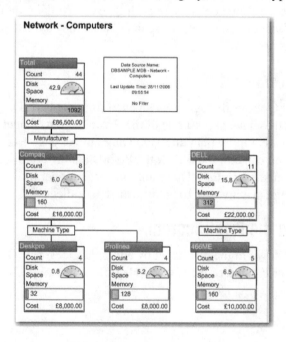

If you were to select the Breakdown Node, Manufacturer, for example, then you could decide to Sort (using the right mouse menu) the Manufacturers in Ascending or Descending order or even limit the number of items shown (the default is 20).

In addition, you could Filter the Manufacturers shown with the Configure Column dialog, which also lets you rename the Breakdown Node.

Further than that, you can break down to individual computers by selecting the Machine Type Pivot Nodes, and then selecting to add the category MachineSN.

When you have added all the MachineSN breakdowns, then the diagram looks too wide:

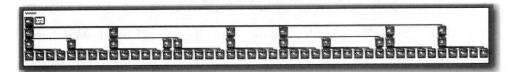

You can remedy this by selecting the menu item PivotDiagram | Layout Direction | Left-to-Right, or equivalent on the PivotDiagram toolbar. You need to have the MachineType nodes selected first (this is more easily done by first selecting any Manufacturer Pivot Node, and then running the SelectSameBreakdownName macro listed in the section "Making Selections").

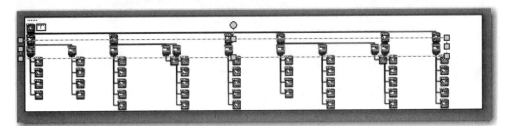

The PivotDiagram is now too widely spaced, but selecting PivotDiagram | Re-layout all can make them more compact. This still leaves the page too wide, as Visio automatically resized the page when you added the breakdown, but it did not bother to reduce it.

You can now either change the page size from the File | Page Setup | Page Size tab, or you can press CTRL while you select the right edge of the page and manually move it to the left.

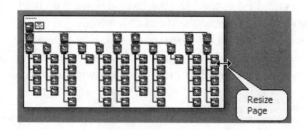

We have now been able to break down the data all the way to individual machines.

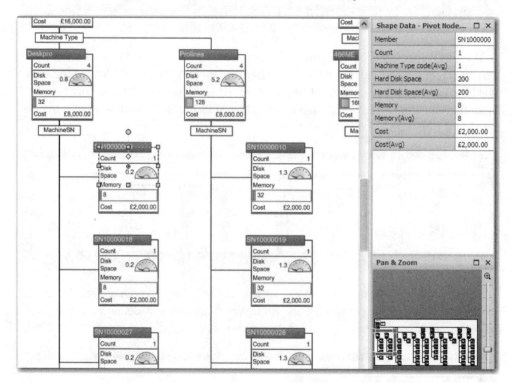

# Applying Shapes

You can enhance the appearance of Pivot Nodes by adding shapes from any stencil to them. For example, if you select all the Pivot Nodes that represent Manufacturers (this is more easily done by first selecting any Manufacturer Pivot Node, and then running the Select-SameBreakdownName macro listed later in this chapter), you can then select PivotDiagram | Apply Shape menu item to open the Apply Shape dialog.

The Departments and Workflow Objects stencils are automatically opened, if they are not already present, and you can select which of these stencils to browse with the pull-down list. In fact, the pull-down list shows any stencils you opened with the diagram, so you can include the graphics from any Master into your Pivot Nodes. In this case, we have selected the Manufacturing shape from the Departments stencil.

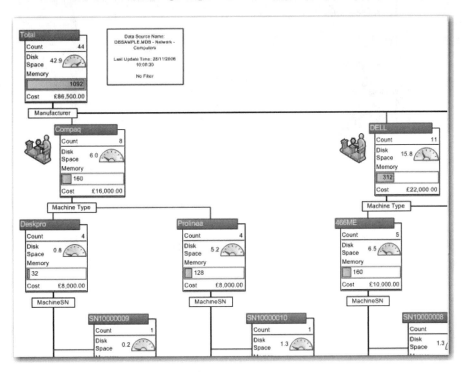

This can have the effect of changing the bounding box of the Pivot Node shape. You can use the Reset Shape button on the Apply Shapes dialog to remove the applied shape.

In fact, the Apply Shape action adds a subshape into the Pivot Node group, and this new subshape will be an instance of a Master in the document stencil, just as the Data Graphic items are. Thus, the required Master is added to the Document Stencil first, if it does not exist already.

Once you apply a shape to a Pivot Node in this way, any subsequent Add Categories you perform with the same Category will have the Apply Shape Master included already.

## Adding Link Data

Now that we have drilled right down to the individual machines, it is a simple matter to use the Data | Link Data to Shapes menu item to open the same source data recordset as an External Data window, and then to automatically link the Data Column MachineSN to the Shape Field Member.

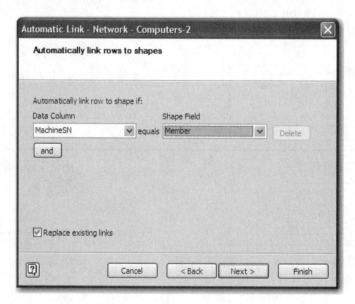

This adds all the Shape Data for the individual PCs.

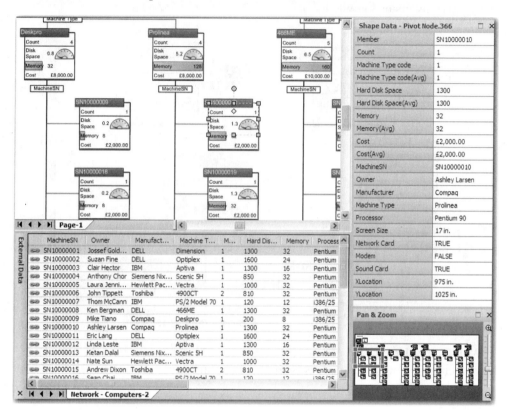

This provides you with all the Shape Data you need to apply any further Data Graphics.

# Merging Data

Sometimes, you could have breakdown members with too few Pivot Nodes on their own, so you can merge them together. In our example, you can select the last two

Manufacturer Pivot Nodes, Siemens Nixdorf and Toshiba (just as an example—I don't really have any inside knowledge!).

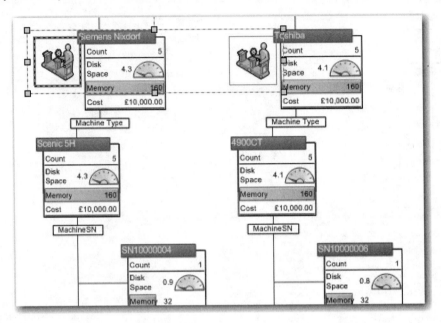

With them selected, you can use PivotDiagram | Merge to combine the two. The Manufacturer Pivot Node displays both of the manufacturers.

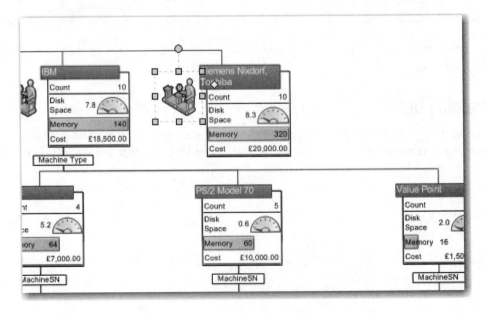

If you do not like the default appearance of node text, which is simply a comma-separated list of the values, then you can edit the Member Shape Data row item to be whatever you like. This does not affect the capability to Unmerge the node, as the FilterClause tag in the Solution XML contained within the User.visDDNormQueryStr cell holds the actual values used.

# Duplicating Data Graphics

You can use more than one Data Graphic set in the same PivotDiagram. If you duplicate the existing Data Graphic, you can apply the duplicate Data Graphic to the MachineSN Pivot Nodes. The SelectSameBreakdownName macro, as you can see in the section titled "Making Selections",  is useful to ensure that only the required shapes are selected. You can then edit the new Data Graphic to include, for example, a Data Icon to show what size screen is attached.

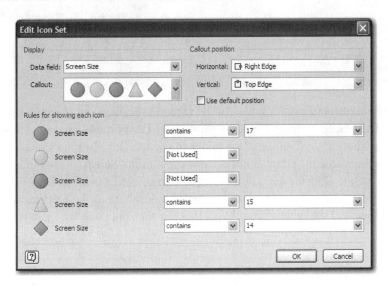

When this is applied to the Pivot Node shapes, you can then see a different Data Graphic is applied to the same PivotDiagram.

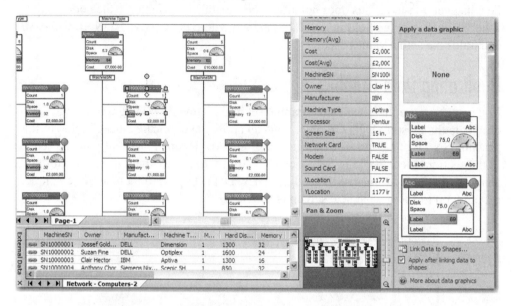

If you use multiple Data Graphics in the same PivotDiagram, then be careful not to edit the Data Graphic from PivotDiagram | Edit Data Graphic because this will apply to the whole PivotDiagram. It is better to use the Data Graphics panel to select the one you want to edit. You can always use the option "Select Shapes that use this Graphic" from the Data Graphic item. Or, you can select Data | Edit Data Graphic from the right mouse menu of one of the Pivot Nodes that has the Data Graphic you want to change. All the other Pivot Nodes that use the same one will also be changed.

# PivotDiagram Masters

The PivotDiagrams work with a number of different Masters, all of which can be made invisible, except for the Pivot Nodes (see Figure 5-2).

## Pivot Title

The Pivot Title for each PivotDiagram can be modified with the PivotDiagram Options dialog to show or hide the full path of the data file, the server information, or the applied filters. Table 5-1 contains the relevant User-defined cells in this shape.

| Cell | Example |
|------|---------|
| visDDIsTitleShape | 1 |
| visDDInstanceIndex | 2 |
| visDDShapeType | 4 |
| visDDSelfShapeID | -1 |

**Table 5-1**   *Pivot Title Master Shape User-Defined Cells*

# Pivot Info (Data Legend)

The Pivot Title for each PivotDiagram can be modified with the PivotDiagram Options dialog to show or hide the full path of the data file or the server information, or the applied filters. It always displays the name of the data source and when it was last updated.

The relevant User-defined cells in this shape are shown in Table 5-2.

# Pivot Node

The right-mouse menu of each Pivot Node is modified to add Categories for each column within the recordset to provide a drill down. This is done with the following formula, where $x$ is the column number:

```
RUNADDONWARGS("Drilldown","/cmd=33 /column=x")
```

The Member cell is updated with the column name.

The Shape Data section is updated with the numeric aggregate values for the requested columns in the source table(s), but there are always the _VisDM_Member and _VisDM_Count Shape Data rows. The member contains the value to pivot on.

The shape has right mouse menu actions to Collapse (if there are any child nodes that can be removed), to Apply Shapes, and a list of all the shape fields that can be pivoted on.

| Cell | Example |
|------|---------|
| visDDRootShape | 16 |
| visDDInstanceIndex | 2 |
| visDDIsTitleShape | 1 |
| visDDInstanceIndex | 2 |
| visDDBreakdownShape | 15 |
| visDDConnectionID | 3 |

**Table 5-2**   *Pivot Info Master Shape User-Defined Cells* (continued)

| Cell | Example |
|------|---------|
| visDDEncodedSchema | `"<SolutionXML><qm:VisioQueryManager xmlns:qm=""http://`<br>`schemas.microsoft.com/visio/2005/QueryManager""/><SchemaField`<br>`Name=""Name"" NameU=""Name"" Index=""0"" Ordinal=""-1""`<br>`Type=""0"" TypeChangeable=""0"" TimeDimension=""0""`<br>`Levels=""1"" Provider=""1"" DBType=""3""><SchemaLeve`<br>`l Name=""Name"" NameU=""Name"" DisplayName=""Name""`<br>`HierNameU=""Name"" ShortName="""" Index=""0"" Ordinal=""-1""`<br>`Type=""202"" AggType=""0""/></SchemaField><SchemaField`<br>`Name=""Title"" NameU=""Title"" Index=""1"" Ordinal=""-1""`<br>`Type=""0"" TypeChangeable=""0"" TimeDimension=""0""`<br>`Levels=""1"" Provider=""1"" DBType=""3""><SchemaLevel`<br>`Name=""Title"" NameU=""Title"" DisplayName=""Title""`<br>`HierNameU=""Title"" ShortName="""" Index=""0"" Ordinal=""-1""`<br>`Type=""202"" AggType=""0""/></SchemaField><SchemaField`<br>`Name=""Department"" NameU=""Department"" Index=""2""`<br>`Ordinal=""-1"" Type=""0"" TypeChangeable=""0""`<br>`TimeDimension=""0"" Levels=""1"" Provider=""1"" DBType=""3"">`<br>`<SchemaLevel Name=""Department"" NameU=""Department""`<br>`DisplayName=""Department"" HierNameU=""Department""`<br>`ShortName="""" Index=""0"" Ordinal=""-1"" Type=""202""`<br>`AggType=""0""/></SchemaField><SchemaField Name=""Extension""`<br>`NameU=""Extension"" Index=""3"" Ordinal=""-1"" Type=""0""`<br>`TypeChangeable=""0"" TimeDimension=""0"" Levels=""1""`<br>`Provider=""1"" DBType=""3""><SchemaLevel Name=""Extension""`<br>`NameU=""Extension"" DisplayName=""Extension""`<br>`HierNameU=""Extension"" ShortName="""" Index=""0"" Ordinal=""`<br>`-1"" Type=""202"" AggType=""0""/></SchemaField><SchemaField`<br>`Name=""XLocation"" NameU=""XLocation"" Index=""4"" Ordinal=""`<br>`-1"" Type=""0"" TypeChangeable=""0"" TimeDimension=""0""`<br>`Levels=""1"" Provider=""1"" DBType=""3"">`<br>`<SchemaLevel Name=""XLocation"" NameU=""XLocation""`<br>`DisplayName=""XLocation"" HierNameU=""XLocation""`<br>`ShortName="""" Index=""0"" Ordinal=""-1"" Type=""202""`<br>`AggType=""0""/></SchemaField><SchemaField Name=""YLocation""`<br>`NameU=""YLocation"" Index=""5"" Ordinal=""-1"" Type=""0""`<br>`TypeChangeable=""0"" TimeDimension=""0"" Levels=""1""`<br>`Provider=""1"" DBType=""3""><SchemaLevel Name=""YLocation""`<br>`NameU=""YLocation"" DisplayName=""YLocation""`<br>`HierNameU=""YLocation"" ShortName="""" Index=""0"" Ordinal=""`<br>`-1"" Type=""202"" AggType=""0""/></SchemaField><SourceInfo`<br>`FullPathName=""C:\Program Files\Microsoft Office\`<br>`OFFICE12\1033\DBSAMPLE.MDB"" ServerName="""" DatabaseName=""""`<br>`CountColumnName=""Count"" MemberColumnName=""Member"" LastMod`<br>`ified=""30/09/1996 14:01:00""/></SolutionXML>"` |

**Table 5-2** *Pivot Info Master Shape User-Defined Cells* (continued)

| Cell | Example |
|---|---|
| visConnectionString | `"Provider=Microsoft.ACE.OLEDB.12.0;User ID=Admin;Data Source=C:\Program Files\Microsoft Office\OFFICE12\1033\ DBSAMPLE.MDB;Mode=Read;Extended Properties="""";Jet OLEDB: System database="""";Jet OLEDB:Registry Path="""";Jet OLEDB:Engine Type=5;Jet OLEDB:Database Locking Mode=0;Jet OLEDB:Global Partial Bulk Ops=2;Jet OLEDB: Global Bulk Transactions=1;Jet OLEDB:New Database Password="""";Jet OLEDB:Create System Database=False;Jet OLEDB:Encrypt Database=False;Jet OLEDB:Don't Copy Locale on Compact=False;Jet OLEDB:Compact Without Replica Repair=False;Jet OLEDB:SFP=False;Jet OLEDB:Support Complex Data=False"` |
| visDDInitQueryString | `"select * from `Office - Employee Details`  WHERE `Department` LIKE '%a%'"` |
| visDDLastRefreshTime | `"02/09/2006 18:52:54"` |
| msvLayoutSortIndex | `2` |
| visDDShapeType | `3` |
| visDDBreakdownShapeRef | `Pivot Breakdown.15!PinX` |
| visDDDocGUID | `"{E4DC0F1D-BF89-44FC-B126-0FB115757348}"` |
| visDDSelfShapeID | `-1` |

**Table 5-2**    *Pivot Info Master Shape User-Defined Cells*

The relevant User-defined cells in this shape are in Table 5-3.

## Pivot Connector

The Pivot Connector links the Pivot Nodes together. You can change the layout style of each connector from its right mouse menu.

You can see the relevant User-defined cells in this shape in Table 5-4.

## Pivot Breakdown

The Pivot Breakdown shape is automatically positioned between the parent and child Pivot Nodes. It displays the field used for the breakdown. The Pivot Breakdown shape has right mouse actions to Collapse (remove the child nodes), Sort (the order of child nodes),

| Cell | Example |
| --- | --- |
| visDDInfoShape | 2 |
| visDDBreakdownShape | 139 |
| visDDIsRoot | 0 |
| visDDHasChildren | 1 |
| visDDIsMerged | 0 |
| visDDIsTopN | 0 |
| visDDSelfShapeID | 66 |
| visDDParentDDShape | 55 |
| visDDInstanceIndex | 0 |
| visDDParentDDShape | 13 |
| msvLayoutSortIndex | 2 |
| visDDShapeType | 1 |
| visDDImageName | Sheet.69!PinX |
| visDDRecordsetID | -1 |
| visDDQueryID | -1 |
| visDDNormQueryStr | -1 |
| visDDParentBDShapeRef | Pivot Breakdown.55!PinX |
| visDDBreakdownShapeRef | Pivot Breakdown.139!PinX |
| visHasText | NOT(OR(HideText,STRSAME(SHAPETEXT(TheText),""))) |
| visDGDefaultPos | PNT(3,4) |
| visDGDisplayFormat | USE({xxxxxxxxxxxxxxxxxxxxxxxxxxxxxxxx}) |
| msvLayoutIncludeSubshapes | IF(TRUE,1,SETATREFEXPR(0)) |
| visDDMergedTitle | -1 |
| visDDTitle | IF(STRSAME(Prop._VisDM_Member,""),"(empty)",Prop._VisDM_Member) |

**Table 5-3**  *Pivot Node Master Shape User-Defined Cells*

| Cell | Example |
|------|---------|
| visDDInstanceIndex | 2 |
| visDDShapeType | 5 |
| visDDConnHideAlways | 0 |
| visDDTrackX | `COS(User.visDDNormalAngle)*ThePage!AvenueSizeX/2+BeginX` |
| visDDTrackY | `SIN(User.visDDNormalAngle)*ThePage!AvenueSizeY/2+BeginY` |
| visDDNormalAngle | `ATAN2(Geometry1.Y2-Geometry1.Y1,Geometry1.X2-Geometry1.X1)` |
| visDDSelfShapeID | `-1` |

**Table 5-4**   *Pivot Connector Master Shape User-Defined Cells*

edit Data Graphics (for the child nodes), or to Configure Column (to relabel or to filter the child nodes):

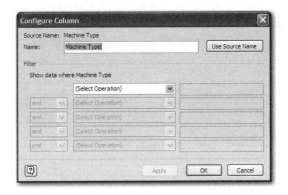

Table 5-5 shows the User-defined cells for the Master.

# Making Selections

Sometimes, you need to be able to select a Pivot Node, and then add all other Pivot Nodes in the same group, level, or with the same breakdown. Unfortunately, this capability is unavailable out of the box so, again, we can supplement Visio capability with a little custom code (see the file E05-PivotSelections.vsd).

| Cell | Example |
|---|---|
| **visDDParentShape** | 13 |
| **visDDInfoShape** | 2 |
| **visDDQueryID** | 4 |
| **visDDRecordsetID** | 4 |
| **visDDNormQueryStr** | `"<SolutionXML><qm:VisioQueryManager xmlns:qm="" http://schemas.microsoft.com/visio/2005/QueryManager ""/><Filters><Filter Field=""Manufacturer"" Level="" Manufacturer""><FilterClause Operator=""EQUAL_SEL"" Value=""Compaq"" Linkage=""AND"" ParenBefore=""0"" ParenAfter=""0""/></Filter></Filters><Axis Field="" Machine Type"" Level=""Machine Type""/></SolutionXML>` |
| **visDDInstanceIndex** | 0 |
| **visDDIsRootDB** | 0 |
| **visDDColumIndex** | 3 |
| **visDDShapeType** | 2 |
| **visDDGraphicMasterID** | -1 |
| **visDDShapeImageMasterID** | -1 |
| **visDDIsSortedBD** | 0 |
| **visDDSelfShapeID** | 55 |
| **visDDBDRefPntErr** | `ISERR(Pivot connector.63!PinX)` |
| **visDDDeltaX** | 0 mm |
| **visDDDeltaY** | 0 mm |
| **visDDTopNNormQueryStr** | `"<SolutionXML><qm:VisioQueryManager xmlns:qm =""http://schemas.microsoft.com/visio/2005/ QueryManager""/><Filters><Filter Field=" "Manufacturer"" Level=""Manufacturer""><Filter Clause Operator=""EQUAL_SEL"" Value=""Compaq"" Linkage=""AND"" ParenBefore=""0"" ParenAfter =""0""/></Filter></Filters><Axis Field=" "Machine Type"" Level=""Machine Type""/><Limit MaxReturn=""-1"" MaxReturnDir=""TOP"" OverLimit=""1""/></SolutionXML>` |
| **visDDSortIndexCounter** | 2 |

**Table 5-5**  *Pivot Breakdown Master Shape User-Defined Cells*

# Recognizing a Pivot Shape

When writing code with PivotDiagrams, it is useful to have some support functions that enable you to recognize if the shape is the right sort of PivotDiagram shape. Consequently, I have included some Public functions in the following that all call the isPivotShapeType function to test what type of shape is being examined. The function checks the value of the User.visDDShapeType, if it exists.

## Code Listing for isPivotShapeType Ad Calling Functions

```
Public Const UserDDShapeType As String = "User.visDDShapeType"

Public Enum ePivotShapeType
    Node = 1
    Breakdown = 2
    Info = 3
    Title = 4
    Connector = 5
End Enum

Public Function IsPivotTitle(ByVal shape As Visio.shape) As Boolean
    IsPivotTitle = isPivotShapeType(shape, ePivotShapeType.Title)
End Function

Public Function IsPivotInfo(ByVal shape As Visio.shape) As Boolean
    IsPivotInfo = isPivotShapeType(shape, ePivotShapeType.info)
End Function

Public Function IsPivotNode(ByVal shape As Visio.shape) As Boolean
    IsPivotNode = isPivotShapeType(shape, ePivotShapeType.Node)
End Function

Public Function IsPivotConnector(ByVal shape As Visio.shape) As Boolean
    IsPivotConnector = isPivotShapeType(shape, ePivotShapeType.Connector)
End Function

Public Function IsPivotBreakdown(ByVal shape As Visio.shape) As Boolean
    IsPivotBreakdown = isPivotShapeType(shape, ePivotShapeType.Breakdown)
End Function

Private Function isPivotShapeType(ByVal shape As Visio.shape, _
    ByVal pivotShapeType As ePivotShapeType) As Boolean

    If Not shape.CellExists(UserDDShapeType,
Visio.VisExistsFlags.visExistsAnywhere) = 0 Then
```

```
           If shape.Cells(UserDDShapeType).ResultIU = pivotShapeType Then
               isPivotShapeType = True
           Else
               isPivotShapeType = False
           End If
       Else
           isPivotShapeType = False
       End If
End Function
```

# Getting the Breakdown ID

To get the unique ID of the parent Breakdown or Drilldown shapes, you can simply read the values from the relevant User-defined cell.

## Code Listing for GetBreakdownID

```
Public Const UserParentBDShape As String = "User.visDDParentBDShape"
Public Const UserParentDDShape As String = "User.visDDParentDDShape"

Public Function GetBreakdownID(ByVal shape As Visio.shape) As Integer
    If shape.CellExists(UserParentBDShape, _
Visio.VisExistsFlags.visExistsAnywhere) = 0 Then
        GetBreakdownID = 0
    Else
        GetBreakdownID = CInt(shape.Cells(UserParentBDShape).ResultIU)
    End If
End Function
Public Function GetParentNodeID(ByVal shape As Visio.shape) As Integer

    If shape.CellExists(UserParentDDShape, _
Visio.VisExistsFlags.visExistsAnywhere) = 0 Then
        GetParentNodeID = 0
    Else
        GetParentNodeID = CInt(shape.Cells(UserParentDDShape).ResultIU)
    End If

End Function
```

# Selecting Shapes in the Same Group

If you select a Pivot Node shape, then you may need to extend your selection to include the other Pivot Nodes in the same group. The *SelectSameGroup* subfunction does this.

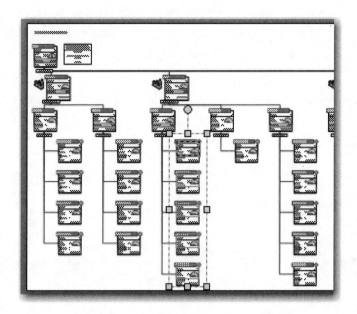

## Code Listing for SelectSameGroup and Support Functions

```
Public Sub SelectSameGroup()
'Select all shapes that belong to the same group as the primary selected shape
Dim shp As Visio.shape
Dim vsoWindow As Visio.Window
Dim parentNodeID As Integer

    Set vsoWindow = Visio.Application.ActiveWindow
    If vsoWindow.Selection.Count > 0 Then
        Set shp = vsoWindow.Selection.PrimaryItem
        If IsPivotNode(shp) = True Then
            parentNodeID = GetParentNodeID(shp)
        End If
        If parentNodeID > 0 Then
            For Each shp In Visio.ActivePage.Shapes
                If IsPivotNode(shp) = True Then
                    If parentNodeID = GetParentNodeID(shp) Then
                        Visio.ActiveWindow.Select shp, Visio.visSelect
                    End If
                End If
            Next shp
        End If
    End If

End Sub
```

```
Public Function GetBreakdownID(ByVal shape As Visio.shape) As Integer

    If shape.CellExists(UserParentBDShape, _
            Visio.VisExistsFlags.visExistsAnywhere) = 0 Then
        GetBreakdownID = 0
    Else
        GetBreakdownID = CInt(shape.Cells(UserParentBDShape).ResultIU)
    End If

End Function

Public Function GetParentNodeID(ByVal shape As Visio.shape) As Integer

    If shape.CellExists(UserParentDDShape, _
            Visio.VisExistsFlags.visExistsAnywhere) = 0 Then
        GetParentNodeID = 0
    Else
        GetParentNodeID = CInt(shape.Cells(UserParentDDShape).ResultIU)
    End If

End Function
```

## Selecting Shapes with the Same Breakdown

If you want to apply the same Data Graphic, Layout Direction, or format to the child
nodes of a particular breakdown, then it is convenient to be able to select a Pivot
Node, and then run the *SelectSameBreakdownName* subfunction to extend the selection to all the Pivot Nodes with the same breakdown parent.

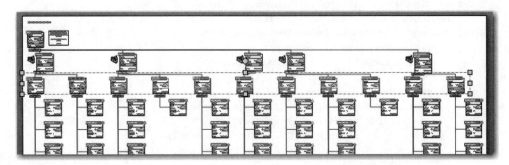

### Code Listing for SelectSameBreakdownName and Support Functions

```
Public Sub SelectSameBreakdownName()
Dim shp As Visio.shape
Dim vsoWindow As Visio.Window
Dim breakdownName As String
```

```
    Set vsoWindow = Visio.Application.ActiveWindow
    If vsoWindow.Selection.Count > 0 Then
        Set shp = vsoWindow.Selection.PrimaryItem
        If IsPivotNode(shp) = True Then
            breakdownName = GetGroupNameByID(GetBreakdownID(shp))
            SelectByBreakdownName breakdownName
        End If
    End If

End Sub

Public Sub SelectByBreakdownName(ByVal breakdownName As String)
Dim shp As Visio.shape
Dim vsoWindow As Visio.Window
Dim vsoPage As Visio.Page

    Set vsoWindow = Visio.Application.ActiveWindow
    Set vsoPage = Visio.ActivePage

    For Each shp In vsoPage.Shapes
        If IsPivotNode(shp) = True Then
            If GetGroupNameByID(GetBreakdownID(shp)) = breakdownName Then
                vsoWindow.Select shp, Visio.VisSelectArgs.visSelect
            End If
        End If
    Next shp

End Sub

Public Function GetGroupNameByID(ByVal parentBDShapeID As Integer) As String
Dim groupShape As Visio.shape
Dim parentText As String
Dim shp As Visio.shape
Dim vsoPage As Visio.Page

    Set vsoPage = Visio.Application.ActivePage
    For Each shp In vsoPage.Shapes
        If shp.ID = parentBDShapeID Then
            Set groupShape = shp
            parentText = groupShape.Characters.Text
            Exit For
        End If
    Next

    GetGroupNameByID = parentText

End Function
```

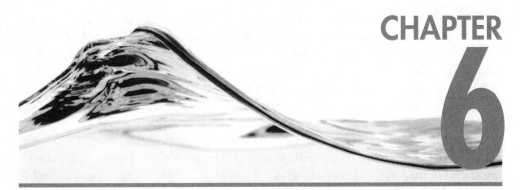

# Database Wizard

**IN THIS CHAPTER**

The Database Wizard has been around for a good few years. In fact, I was a beta tester of the add-on back in 1996 for Visio 4.5 (long before Microsoft bought the product/company). The *Database Wizard* was a key element that distinguished Visio from any other drawing package and, although it has not been brought right up-to-date, it remains the only out-of-the box tool that provides two-way communication with a database. Thus, it has its uses, even with the advent of the new Link Data technology.

The particular diagrams I was setting up in those days were floor plans for merchant banks, both in London and New York. The personnel changes on the desk layouts were frequent, and the help desk needed to know where everyone was, so I used the Database Wizard to link over 500 desks on each floor to a view in a Sybase database. Then, at a push of a button, the labels and colors of the desks changed to reflect the current location of the staff. Moreover, a legend for the cost-center colors was created.

There were some challenges to be overcome, for example, the Database Wizard has an option to include an action to refresh a page, but not a document. And, the Database Wizard can take a while to perform its actions on large documents, but it also has its merits.

I was able to set up an administrator's Visio document, which was used to define the color fills and patterns for each cost center. This was linked to a specific table in the database, so the user could use standard Visio-formatting options, and then update the database with these settings. The desk layout documents would be linked to a database view that included these colors for the cost center of each person, therefore, the desks were always colored and patterned according to a predefined and consistent appearance. The desk layouts were only able to read the database, not write, as the writing of desk to personnel associations was done through a change control process.

# The Database Wizard or Link Data?

Some differences exist between the Database Wizard and Link Data that can be exploited. *Link Data* only lets you create or refresh shape data, but the Database Wizard enables you to additionally link to any other cell in the ShapeSheet. The Database Wizard provides the fill patterns and colors, but it could also be used for the PinX/PinY coordinates, Width and Height, or any User-defined cells.

The new Data Graphics provides the capability to color-code shapes according to any value (including any ShapeSheet cell by use of the Custom Formula feature), but it does not provide repeatability. For example, if particular colors are associated with particular values, then you have to either manually edit the Data Graphics or provide some custom code. The Database Wizard can be used straight out of the box.

Additionally, if you are printing in black-and-white, then you may also want to use the fill patterns. Unless you take the trouble to create custom fill patterns, you have a limited set to choose from if you use Data Graphics.

The Database Wizard, however, uses the older Open Database Connectivity (ODBC) methodology for creating connections to data sources, which may be more difficult to deploy and cannot be linked to XML files or database-stored procedures.

The Database Wizard is an add-on and, as such, you do not have the same programmatic control as the newer Link Data to Shapes feature.

# Linking to a Database Table

The DBSample.mdb file contains a table called Office—Employee Details, which holds personnel data, including a Department column. You can create a new table, called Department, from the unique values in the personnel table with the following Make Table query:

```
SELECT DISTINCT [Office - Employee Details].Department
, "" AS FillForegnd
, "" AS FillBkgnd
, "" AS FillPattern
INTO Department
FROM [Office - Employee Details];
```

You should then make the Department column the primary key:

You then have a table that has all the Departments, but no Fill values.

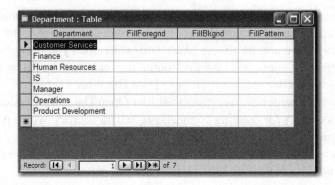

Start a new blank drawing, and add a rectangle. Use Format | Fill to change the Color, Pattern, and Pattern Color, as shown.

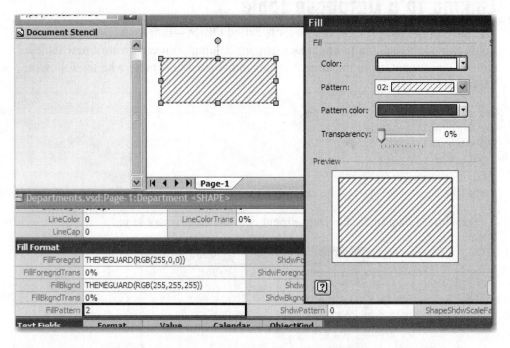

Be aware of a slight anomaly in the FillForegnd and FillBkgnd cells in the ShapeSheet when you change the Fill Pattern from 0 or 1 to any other number (and reverse). What happens is the values in the FillForegnd and FillBkgnd are reversed when you use the Fill dialog. However, the Color and Pattern Color values in the Fill dialog stay as they are. This is so that the normal user does not see the changes necessary to keep the predominant color visible when the pattern is introduced. This is important for programmers and users who intend to link the fill cells to a data source.

Then, with the rectangle still selected, select Tools | Add-Ons | Visio Extras | Database Wizard. Next, select Link Shapes to Database Records, followed by Shape(s) in a Drawing. Select the Department table in the DBSample.mdb database (via the Visio Database Samples ODBC data source), and link the Department column as the primary key.

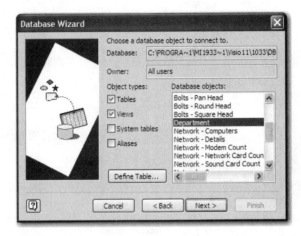

Select Customers Services as the default key value, and uncheck the Delete shape and database record right mouse option. You can let Department create the Prop, Department Shape Data item, but you then need to ensure the FillForegnd, FillBkgnd, and FillPattern database fields are mapped to the relevant cells in the ShapeSheet.

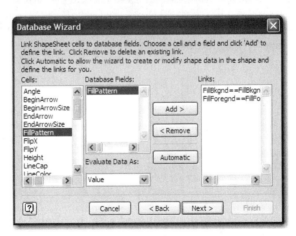

When you finish the wizard, the rectangle looks unchanged, apart from the addition of the Department Shape Data. You can use Data Graphics to display the value of the Department field as a Text item.

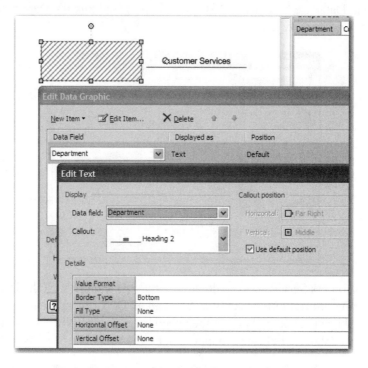

The shape now has right mouse-menu actions that can be used to Select Database Record, Refresh Shape Properties, or Update Database Record.

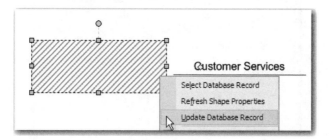

The same actions could have been performed with the Tools | Add-Ons | Visio Extras | Link to the ODBC Database option. The resultant changes to the shapes are just the same, but they provide you with a different, nonwizard interface.

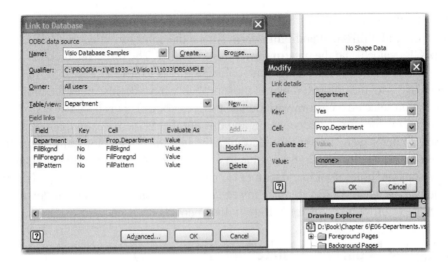

The Database Wizard has many more capabilities, as you will see, but it does not matter if you use one dialog or the other to create the link, as long as you pay attention to the settings.

## Updating a Database Table

At this point, you can choose to Update Database Record, and then view the contents of the Department table.

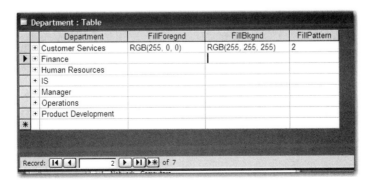

You should see that the Customer Services row has been updated with the values for the FillForegnd, FillBkgnd and FillPattern. Notice the color formulae are Red, Green, Blue (RGB) values, and the pattern formula is a number. The foreground color, Red, is thus RGB(255,0,0), and the background color, White, is RGB(255,255,255). In older versions of Visio, the color Red would most probably have been seen as the number 2, unless you selected a custom variation of the Red color. This is because Visio has a collection of colors for each document, and this number is the index in that collection. The first 24 items were always provided initially with the same color settings and the rest were custom colors, but it is possible to change the colors in the collection, and any nonstandard color used in a document is added sequentially. Therefore, it is always safer to use the actual RGB reference instead of the index number, as the index number could retrieve different colors on different documents.

## Making the Department Linked Master

Now, open the Document Stencil from the File | Shapes menu, drag the rectangle on to it, and then rename the new Master as Department. Finally, open the Master Properties dialog to check the Match Master by Name on Drop setting.

You now have a Master shape that can not only be used to select the fill colors and pattern for each Department, but also as a legend shape on any other diagram.

You may want to set the ODBC data source as read-only for normal users, so they do not inadvertently update the Department table in the database. Of course, you can copy the Master to a stencil that you issue to other users.

If you are going to deploy the Master to other users, you may need to provide them with an ODBC data source, and to edit the ShapeSheet of the Master shape accordingly. If you open the ShapeSheet, then you will see the relevant section is the User-defined cells.

| User-defined Cells | Value | | | | Prompt | | |
|---|---|---|---|---|---|---|---|
| User.ODBCConnection | "ODBCDataSource=Visio Database Samples\|ODBCQualifier=C | | | | "This cell contains the link information for the Database Wizard." | | |
| User.ODBCChecksum | "2aeb7e3" | | | | "This cell contains a checksum of the database record." | | |
| User.visDGDefaultPos | PNT(6,3) | | | | No Formula | | |
| User.visDGDisplayFormat | USE({024FE4A3-0000-0000-8E40-00608CF305B2}) | | | | No Formula | | |
| **Shape Data** | Label | Prompt | | Type | Format | Value | |
| Prop.Department | "Department" | "Shape Data Item generated from database field De | | 0 | "" | "Human Resources" | "" |
| **Actions** | Action | Menu | TagName | ButtonFace | SortKey | Checked | |
| Actions.Row_1 | RUNADDON("DBS") | "Se&lect Database Record" | "" | "" | "" | 0 | |
| Actions.Row_2 | RUNADDON("DBR") | "Re&fresh Shape Properties" | "" | "" | "" | 0 | |
| Actions.Row_3 | RUNADDON("DBU") | "&Update Database Record" | "" | "" | "" | 0 | |
| **Controls** | X | Y | X Dynamics | Y Dynamics | X Behavior | Y Behavior | Can Glue | Tip |

A closer examination of the User.ODBCConnection cell value shows it contains all the information about the database link created with the Database Wizard.

The value is one long line of text, but I have replaced the | (pipe) with a new line character, so you can see the parts of it more clearly:

```
ODBCDataSource=Visio Database Samples
ODBCQualifier=C:\PROGRA~1\MI1933~1\Visio12\1033\DBSAMPLE
ODBCTable=Department
1
Department=Prop.Department
3
FillBkgnd=FillBkgnd=0
FillForegnd=FillForegnd=0
FillPattern=FillPattern=0
```

After the ODBC DataSource, Qualifier, and Table are defined, the number 1 indicates the number of fields in the primary key, and the number 2 indicates the number of other fields that are mapped. Each of these numbers must be followed by the correct number of fields in the right format.

The mapped fields are in the format:

*database field = shape cell = evaluation type*

The common evaluation type number is usually as follows in Table 6-1.

| Evaluation Type | Description |
| --- | --- |
| 0 | Text evaluated as value |
| 1 | Text evaluated as a formula |
| 32 | Numeric |
| 111 | Currency |
| xxx | If numeric, then a list of units can be used |

**Table 6-1**   *Evaluation Types*

Indeed, having a class in code to parse the User.ODBCConnection formula has been useful in the past, so any shape can be read. You simply pass a shape, with the User.ODBCConnection cell, into an instance of the class, and you can then read the following string properties of the class:

► DataSource

► Qualifier

► Table

- ▶ NumberOfKeys
- ▶ KeyField(1-based index)
- ▶ KeyCell(1-based index)
- ▶ KeyValue(1-based index)
- ▶ NumberOfColumns
- ▶ ColumnField(1-based index)
- ▶ ColumnCell(1-based index)
- ▶ ColumnType(1-based index)
- ▶ ColumnValue(1-based index)

This class is used to rename the Department shapes in the section "Code Listing for UpdateShapeNameToDepartment".

## Code Listing for ODBCConnection Class

```
Private mShape As Visio.Shape
Private mFormula As String
Private mDataSource As String
Private mQualifier As String
Private mTable As String
Private mNumberOfKeys As Integer
Private mKeyFields() As String
Private mKeyCells() As String
Private mKeyValues() As String
Private mNumberOfColumns As Integer
Private mColumnFields() As String
Private mColumnCells() As String
Private mColumnTypes() As String
Private mColumnValues() As String

Public Property Set Shape(ByVal value As Visio.Shape)
    Set mShape = value
    mFormula = mShape.Cells("User.ODBCConnection").ResultStr("")
    Call parseFormula
End Property

Public Property Get Formula() As String
    Formula = mFormula
End Property

Private Sub parseFormula()
Dim aryFormula() As String
Dim aryElement() As String
Dim element As String
```

```
Dim i As Integer
Dim keySection As Boolean
Dim columnSection As Boolean
Dim iKey As Integer
Dim iColumn As Integer

    aryFormula = Split(mFormula, "|")
    For i = 0 To UBound(aryFormula)
        element = aryFormula(i)
        If keySection = False And columnSection = False Then
            'Must be the header section
            If IsNumeric(element) = True Then
                mNumberOfKeys = CInt(element)
                ReDim mKeyFields(mNumberOfKeys - 1)
                ReDim mKeyCells(mNumberOfKeys - 1)
                ReDim mKeyValues(mNumberOfKeys - 1)
                keySection = True
            Else
                aryElement = Split(element, "=")
                Select Case aryElement(0)
                    Case "ODBCDataSource"
                        mDataSource = aryElement(1)
                    Case "ODBCQualifier"
                        mQualifier = aryElement(1)
                    Case "ODBCTable"
                        mTable = aryElement(1)
                End Select
            End If
        ElseIf keySection = True Then
            If IsNumeric(element) = True Then
                mNumberOfColumns = CInt(element)
                ReDim mColumnFields(mNumberOfColumns - 1)
                ReDim mColumnCells(mNumberOfColumns - 1)
                ReDim mColumnTypes(mNumberOfColumns - 1)
                ReDim mColumnValues(mNumberOfColumns - 1)
                keySection = False
                columnSection = True
            Else
                aryElement = Split(element, "=")
                'Read the key field and cell
                mKeyFields(iKey) = aryElement(0)
                mKeyCells(iKey) = aryElement(1)
                mKeyValues(iKey) = mShape.Cells(aryElement(1)).ResultStr("")
                'Increment the iKey counter
                iKey = iKey + 1
            End If
        Else    'Must be the field section
            If Len(element) > 0 Then
                aryElement = Split(element, "=")
                'Read the column field and cell
                mColumnFields(iColumn) = aryElement(0)
                mColumnCells(iColumn) = aryElement(1)
```

```
                mColumnTypes(iColumn) = aryElement(2)
                mColumnValues(iColumn) = mShape.Cells(aryElement(1)).ResultStr("")
                'Increment the iColumn counter
                iColumn = iColumn + 1
            End If
        End If
    Next i

End Sub

Public Property Get DataSource() As String
    DataSource = mDataSource
End Property

Public Property Get Qualifier() As String
    Qualifier = mQualifier
End Property

Public Property Get Table() As String
    Table = mTable
End Property

Public Property Get KeyField(ByVal value As Integer) As String
    KeyField = mKeyFields(value - 1)
End Property

Public Property Get KeyCell(ByVal value As Integer) As String
    KeyCell = mKeyCells(value - 1)
End Property

Public Property Get KeyValue(ByVal value As Integer) As String
    KeyValue = mKeyValues(value - 1)
End Property

Public Property Get ColumnField(ByVal value As Integer) As String
    ColumnField = mColumnFields(value - 1)
End Property

Public Property Get ColumnCell(ByVal value As Integer) As String
    ColumnCell = mColumnCells(value - 1)
End Property

Public Property Get ColumnType(ByVal value As Integer) As Integer
    ColumnType = CInt(mColumnTypes(value - 1))
End Property

Public Property Get ColumnValue(ByVal value As Integer) As String
    ColumnValue = mColumnValues(value - 1)
End Property

Public Property Get NumberOfKeys() As Integer
    NumberOfKeys = mNumberOfKeys
End Property
```

```
Public Property Get NumberOfColumns() As Integer
    NumberOfColumns = mNumberOfColumns
End Property
```

# Creating a Linked Drawing to Update the Database

You are now ready to use the Database Wizard again to create a linked drawing that represents all the values in a database table, in this case, the Department table. Select Modify Existing Drawing and Modify Existing Page, and then check the options are as follows:

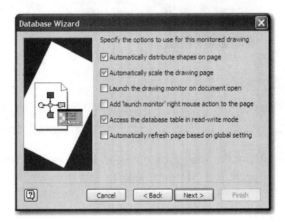

The important setting is Access the Database Table in Read-Write Mode, as you need to be able to have two-way communication.

You can then add actions to the page right-mouse menu that enables you to Refresh the shapes from the database or Update the database from the shapes.

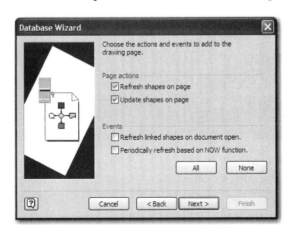

Once you complete the wizard, you will find a linked shape for each row in the Department table. Most of them appear black because they have no entries for their colors or patterns.

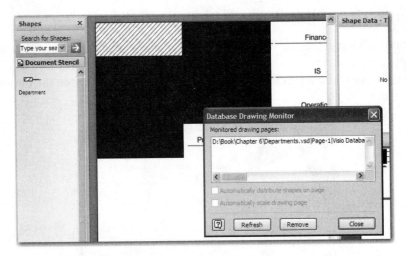

You now need to lay out the shapes on the page, and to select your desired fill colors and patterns for each of the Departments.

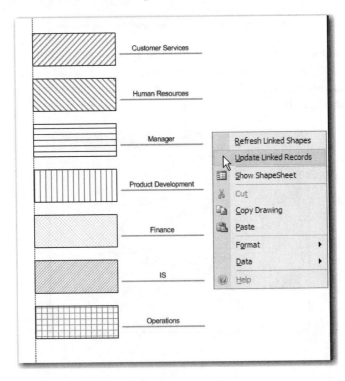

Having done this, you can select the right mouse menu of the page to update the database from the shapes. If you then examine the contents of the Department table, you will find each row has now been updated.

| | Department | FillForegnd | FillBkgnd | FillPattern |
|---|---|---|---|---|
| | Customer Services | RGB(255, 0, 0) | RGB(255, 255, 255) | 2 |
| + | Finance | RGB(102, 255, 255) | RGB(255, 255, 255) | 21 |
| + | Human Resources | RGB(0, 112, 192) | RGB(255, 255, 255) | 5 |
| + | IS | RGB(255, 192, 0) | RGB(255, 255, 255) | 16 |
| + | Manager | RGB(0, 32, 96) | RGB(255, 255, 255) | 6 |
| + | Operations | RGB(0, 176, 80) | RGB(255, 255, 255) | 3 |
| + | Product Development | RGB(204, 0, 255) | RGB(255, 255, 255) | 7 |

If you were to examine the ShapeSheet of the page, then you will find the Actions section contains two rows that call the add-ons DBRS and DBUS to refresh from the database and to update the database, respectively.

| User-defined Cells | Value | Prompt |
|---|---|---|
| User.ODBCDatabase | "Visio Database Samples" | "The database from which the drawing was created." |
| User.ODBCQualifier | "C:\PROGRA~1\MI1933~1\Visio12\1033\DBSAMPLE" | "Qualifier cell. This cell contains the name of the selected database or directory in the data source." |
| User.ODBCTable | "Department" | "The table from which the drawing was created." |
| User.ODBCStencil | "D:\Book\Chapter 6\E06-Departments.vsd" | "The stencil that contains the master used to create the drawing." |
| User.ODBCMaster | "Department" | "The master used to create the drawing." |
| User.ODBCAutoFormat | 1 | "A flag. If not 0 then the shapes will be automatically redistributed on the page when refresh is selected in the Database Dra |
| User.ODBCAutoScale | 1 | "A flag. If not 0 then the drawing page will be automatically scaled when refresh is selected in the Database Drawing Monitor. |
| User.ODBCRWAccess | 1 | "A flag. If not 0 then the database table will be accessed in Read-Write mode. Otherwise the table will be accessed in Read-( |
| User.ODBCAutoRefresh | 0 | "A flag. If not 0 then the linked shapes will be refreshed from the database periodically based on the global setting in the ODE |
| User.msvDGCalloutGap | DrawingScale/PageScale*0.0625 | No Formula |

| Actions | Action | Menu | TagName | ButtonFace | SortKey | Checked | Di |
|---|---|---|---|---|---|---|---|
| Actions.Row_1 | RUNADDON("DBRS") | "&Refresh Linked Shapes" | ... | ... | ... | 0 | 0 |
| Actions.Row_2 | RUNADDON("DBUS") | "&Update Linked Records" | ... | ... | ... | 0 | 0 |

**NOTE**

*The User-defined cells contain all the information about the ODBC links.*

This clearly indicates this methodology is only intended for a single data source, unlike the newer Link Data feature, which can have multiple data sources. However, the Database Wizard add-ons allow for the update of the data source.

Of course, you could have created a view or query definition to filter a table if you did not want to display the contents of the whole table.

## Inserting Records into a Database

You can use the Department-linked drawing to add records into the Department table. Simply add another Department shape, and enter the desired Department name, for example, Marketing, into the Shape Data. Then, select Update Database Record from the right mouse menu.

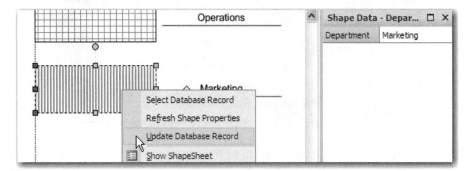

If the record does not exist, you are prompted to confirm the insertion.

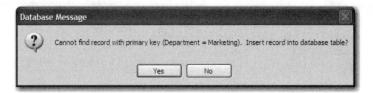

## Reviewing Records Deleted from a Database Table

If a record has been deleted from the Department table, and the shape is still shown on the drawing, then the Refresh Linked Shapes page right-mouse action informs you of any records that cannot be found in the database. It opens a dialog that identifies the shape(s) by name.

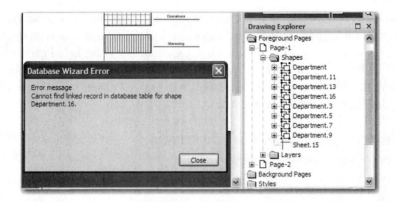

Although you can use Drawing Explorer to locate a shape by name, it would prove more useful if the shapes were named after the Department they represent. This can be done with a little bit of code, for example:

```
Public Sub UpdateShapeNameToDepartment()
Dim shp As Visio.Shape
    'Loop thru' each shape on the active page
    For Each shp In Visio.ActivePage.Shapes
        'Check that Department cells exist
        If shp.CellExistsU("Prop.Department", Visio.visExistsAnywhere) = True Then
            'Rename the shapes name
            shp.NameU = shp.Cells("Prop.Department").ResultStr("")
        End If
    Next
End Sub
```

This code simply checks each shape on the page to see if it has the Department Shape Data item, and then names the shape with its value.

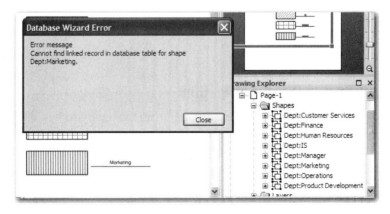

Although this code works, it is unsuitable for use on pages where other types of shapes contain the Department Shape Data item. I prefer an alternative code, which checks the shape properly by using the ODBCConnection class listed earlier in this chapter. In addition to naming the shape after the department, I added the prefix Dept: before the department value because it will make it easier to navigate the shapes in the Drawing Explorer window.

### Code Listing for UpdateShapeNameToDepartment

```
Public Sub UpdateShapeNameToDepartment()
Dim shp As Visio.Shape
Dim oDBCnx As ODBCConnection
    'Loop thru' each shape on the active page
    For Each shp In Visio.ActivePage.Shapes
        'Check that ODBC cells exist
        If shp.CellExistsU("User.ODBCConnection", _
                Visio.visExistsAnywhere) = True Then
            'Create a new ODBCConnection object
            Set oDBCnx = New ODBCConnection
            'Pass the current shape in
            Set oDBCnx.Shape = shp
            'Check if the correct ODBC linked shape
            If oDBCnx.NumberOfKeys = 1 Then
                If oDBCnx.KeyField(1) = "Department" Then
                    'Rename the shapes name
                    shp.NameU = "Dept:" & oDBCnx.KeyValue(1)
                    'Ensure Drawing Explorer also displays the NameU
                    shp.Name = shp.NameU
                End If
            End If
        End If
    Next
End Sub
```

# Deleting Records in a Database Table

You can use the Visio diagram to delete records from the database but, unless the database is your own and no one else uses it, I would not allow this option. Too much is at risk in allowing shapes to delete records because the record could also delete related records.

# Refreshing from a View

You saw how to use the Database Wizard to update the database, now you use the fill colors and patterns for each department to help you identify which department each employee belongs to.

## Create the Query Definition/View to Read

First, you should create a relationship between Department columns in the Department and Office—Employee Details tables as follows:

Finally, create a new query definition, vEmployees, with the following SQL:

```
SELECT [Office - Employee Details].Name
, [Office - Employee Details].Title
, [Office - Employee Details].Extension
, Department.FillForegnd
, Department.FillBkgnd
, Department.FillPattern
FROM Department
INNER JOIN [Office - Employee Details]
ON Department.Department = [Office - Employee Details].Department;
```

This lets you retrieve each employee record with the fill settings for their department.

## Create the Workspace Shape

Back in Visio, you should create a new drawing, with a landscape-orientation page twice the size of your normal paper. This will be an example floor plan, with workspaces for each employee on it. As before, draw a rectangle and run the Database Wizard again. Proceed in the same way, by linking the shape to a database record but, this time, select the vEmployees query definition. On the next screen, the wizard suggests you have one field in the primary key, the Name field. This is true, but you could select two (or more) fields, and then select Department as Field 1 and Name as Field 2. This enables the wizard to filter by Department before you select an employee's Name, which can make the user's task easier.

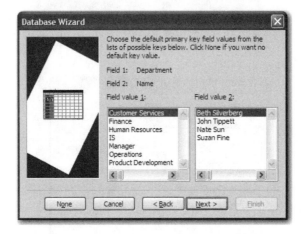

The add-on reads the table definition, if possible, to determine the primary keys, and it allows for a maximum of five fields in a combined primary key. So, use your key fields to create a cascading filter as required, just so long as the key field values determine a database record uniquely. The add-on also tries to detect the data type and suggests the appropriate evaluation type.

On the next screen, you do want to Include an On Drop event with the shape, which is to Select Record on Drop. You do not want to include the Update Database Record or the Delete Shape and Database Record right-mouse menu actions.

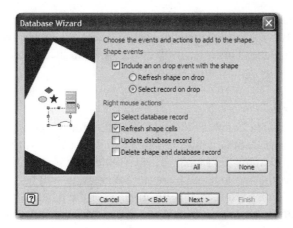

Ensure Prop.Department is the Cell for Field 1, Prop.Name is the Cell for Field 2, and then add Title and Extension as Shape Data items, and map the FillForegnd, FillBkgnd, and FillPattern fields and cells together.

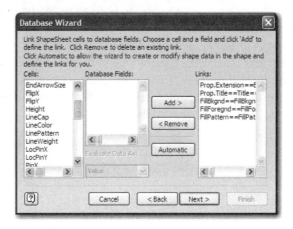

If you examine the ShapeSheet of the rectangle, you again find the User-defined cells shape data, and the Action sections were modified.

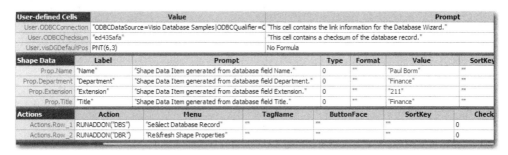

| User-defined Cells | Value | | | | | Prompt | |
|---|---|---|---|---|---|---|---|
| User.ODBCConnection | "ODBCDataSource=Visio Database Samples\|ODBCQualifier=C | | | "This cell contains the link information for the Database Wizard." | | | |
| User.ODBCChecksum | "ed435afa" | | | "This cell contains a checksum of the database record." | | | |
| User.visDGDefaultPos | PNT(6,3) | | | No Formula | | | |

| Shape Data | Label | Prompt | Type | Format | Value | SortKey |
|---|---|---|---|---|---|---|
| Prop.Name | "Name" | "Shape Data Item generated from database field Name." | 0 | "" | "Paul Borm" | "" |
| Prop.Department | "Department" | "Shape Data Item generated from database field Department." | 0 | "" | "Finance" | "" |
| Prop.Extension | "Extension" | "Shape Data Item generated from database field Extension." | 0 | "" | "211" | "" |
| Prop.Title | "Title" | "Shape Data Item generated from database field Title." | 0 | "" | "Finance" | "" |

| Actions | Action | Menu | TagName | ButtonFace | SortKey | Check |
|---|---|---|---|---|---|---|
| Actions.Row_1 | RUNADDON("DBS") | "Se&lect Database Record" | "" | "" | "" | 0 |
| Actions.Row_2 | RUNADDON("DBR") | "Re&fresh Shape Properties" | "" | "" | "" | 0 |

Actually, the Events.EventDrop cell is also modified to have the formula RUNADDON("DBS"). This prompts the user to select a database record whenever it is dropped on to the page. This is done by dragging from the stencil, duplicating, or by copying-and-pasting the existing shape.

## Adding a Data Label

Previously, we used Data Graphics to create the label for the Department shape, but I do not think any of the Data Graphics are appropriate for this Workspace shape. This is because the Data Graphic Text labels always match the width of the shape they belong to. In this case, the Workspace shape we are creating will be resized to represent the space occupied by a person, so it is unsuitable for the label to keep resizing.

If you have Visio Professional, then you can use the Tools | Add-Ons | Maps and Floor Plans | Label Shapes to create the text block containing the Name, Title, Department, and Extension Shape Data. If you have only Visio Standard, then you can use Insert | Field | Shape Data four times to achieve the same effect.

You should then use Format | Text | Text Block to change the Text Background to White Solid Color. This is because the text may need to be read when it is over the top of the colored, patterned shape.

The last thing to do is to add a control handle to the shape that you can move around to position the text label. This has to done in the ShapeSheet by adding a Control section using Insert | Section. This will include a Controls.Row_1 row, which you can rename to Controls.Text. Once done, use Insert | Section to add the Text Transform section, which you should then edit as follows:

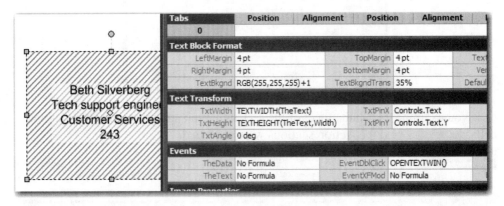

The TEXTWIDTH(TheText) formula—in the TxtWidth cell—ensures the text block is as wide as the text, and the TEXTHEIGHT(TheText,WIDTH) formula—in the TxtHeight cell—ensures the text block is as high as the text.

## Create the Workspace Master

Now you are ready to move the shape on to the document stencil to make a Master, and then rename this as a Workspace. You should check that the Match Master Name on Drop property is ticked.

Now you can simply drag-and-drop the Workspace on to the page and you are prompted for the Department, which then filters the list of employees to select.

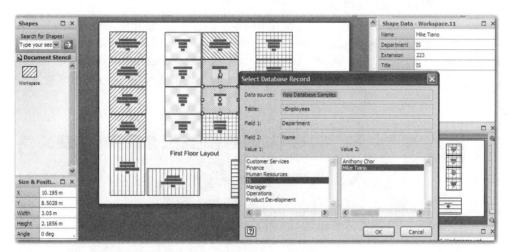

You can then easily layout, for example, a pseudo office layout displaying where everyone sits relative to each other. You can also drag the Department Master from the other drawing on to this drawing to create a legend.

You can use the Database Wizard to create right mouse actions for the page that enable you to refresh the shapes from the database.

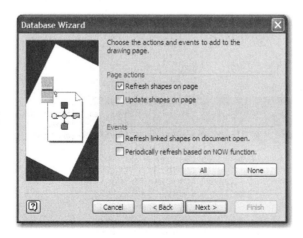

Mixing drawings used for updating the database with those used for reading from the database is not a good idea. With this in mind, it is probably worth amending the Department Master for general deployment, so it dos not include the right mouse action for updating the database, and so that it does includes the Select Database Record on Drop event.

## Renaming Workspace Shapes

In our example floor layout, there is only one workspace per employee per page, so we can automatically rename the workspace shapes according to the employee's name (see Figure 6-1). As with the Department shapes, I added a prefix, in this case "Emp:", before the employee's Name value, so the Drawing Explorer window is easier to navigate.

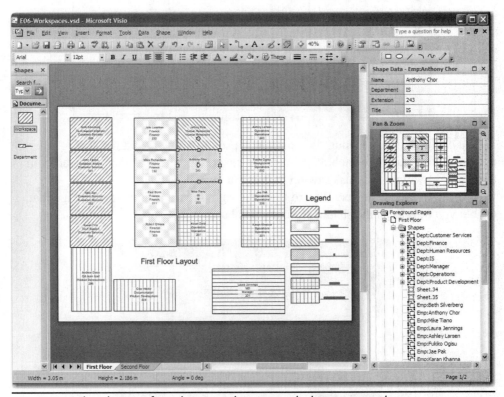

**Figure 6-1**   *Floor layout of employee workspaces with department colors*

### Code Listing for UpdateShapeNameToEmployee

```
Public Sub UpdateShapeNameToEmployee()
Dim shp As Visio.Shape
Dim oDBCnx As ODBCConnection
Dim iKey As Integer
    'Loop thru' each shape on the active page
    For Each shp In Visio.ActivePage.Shapes
        'Check that ODBC cells exist
        If shp.CellExistsU("User.ODBCConnection", _
            Visio.visExistsAnywhere) = True Then
          'Create a new ODBCConnection object
          Set oDBCnx = New ODBCConnection
          'Pass the current shape in
          Set oDBCnx.Shape = shp
          'Check if the correct ODBC linked shape
          If oDBCnx.Table = "vEmployees" Then
              For iKey = 1 To oDBCnx.NumberOfKeys
                  If oDBCnx.KeyField(iKey) = "Name" Then
                      'Rename the shapes name
                      shp.NameU = "Emp:" & oDBCnx.KeyValue(iKey)
                      'Ensure Drawing Explorer also displays the
NameU
                      shp.Name = shp.NameU
                  End If
              Next iKey
          End If
        End If
    Next
End Sub
```

## Refreshing the Whole Document

Although the Database Wizard lets you set right mouse actions to refresh the page
from the database, this action does not refresh the whole document. If you have
multiple pages, you need to have a little code to perform this. The following VBA
demonstrates one method of doing this. It can be inserted into the Visio document or
it could be in a stencil that you issue.

### Code Listing for RefreshPagesFromDatabase

```
Public Sub RefreshPagesFromDatabase ()
Dim pag As Visio.Page
Dim adn As Visio.Addon
Dim pagCurrent As Visio.Page
```

```
'Get the current page
Set pagCurrent = Visio.ActivePage
'Get the Database Refresh Addon
Set adn = Visio.Addons("DBRS")
'Loop thru each page in the active document
For Each pag In Visio.ActiveDocument.Pages
    'If the page is a foreground page
    If pag.Type = visTypeForeground Then
        'Set it as the active page
        Visio.ActiveWindow.Page = pag
        adn.Run ""
    End If
Next pag

'Return to the current page
Visio.ActiveWindow.Page = pagCurrent

End Sub
```

## Customizing the Database Refresh

When I created the large floor plans (over 500 workspaces per page) with the Sybase database using an earlier version of the Database Wizard, we found that the refresh from the database could take an extraordinarily long time (one hour to be exact), so I had to come up with a solution. I created some code to interrogate the User.ODBCConnection formula, as I did in the ODBCConnection class shown earlier, and then created an alternative Refresh from Database function that used these settings to create an ADO connection, via a login, and then to update each shape in the page that was an instance of the Master. This reduced the time taken to refresh the page to 60 seconds—a vast improvement on 60 minutes! I do believe the speed is not such a great issue now, but it is worth considering this approach if it is.

The other advantage of the custom refresh was the capability to switch from using a view to using a stored procedure with parameters. This reduced the size of the recordset being dragged across the network.

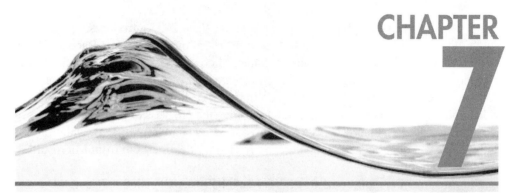

# Using Data Graphics to Reinforce Information

The new Data Graphics feature in Microsoft Visio 2007 introduces new ways to visualize information with three types of callouts: Text, Data Bars, and Icon Sets, in addition to the Color By Value. Microsoft Visio 2007 is installed with a variety of each type of callout, and you can create your own to suit your purposes. For example, you can make icons to represent the criticality of software or hardware vulnerabilities, or you can have data bars to display the progress of process steps.

In this chapter, you learn ways to create your own Data Graphic Text, Data Bars, and Icon Sets. For further reading, you can read an in-depth article from Microsoft about Data Graphics at:

http://msdn2.microsoft.com/enus/library/aa468596.aspx#Visio2007CustomData-Graphics_IntroductiontoDataGraphics.

# The Default Data Graphic Callouts

The technique for creating custom callouts is basically straight forward: choose an existing one that is the closest to what you want, duplicate it, rename it, and then amend it. Sounds easy but, first, you need to be able to see what is already there.

If you start a new drawing, then no shapes are there (usually), so Visio has nothing to apply Data Graphics to. Therefore, you need to have at least one shape in the document that contains a Shape Data item. It does not matter if this is a shape dragged from an existing stencil or you just draw a new shape and add a single Shape Data item (see Figure 7-1). This is because when you open the Data Graphic panel, using Data | Display Data on Shapes, Microsoft Visio 2007 automatically adds the default set of Data Graphic items to the document.

As you can see in Figure 7-1, no Masters are showing in the Document Stencil, but a number are in the Drawing Explorer window. This is because the Data Graphic Masters have their Hidden property set to 1. If you delete the single shape that contains the Shape Data item, then the Data Graphic Masters are not deleted from the document. These can be removed, however, by selecting File | Remove Hidden Information, and then by checking Remove Unused Master Shapes and Remove Unused Themes, Data Graphics, and Styles, before clicking OK.

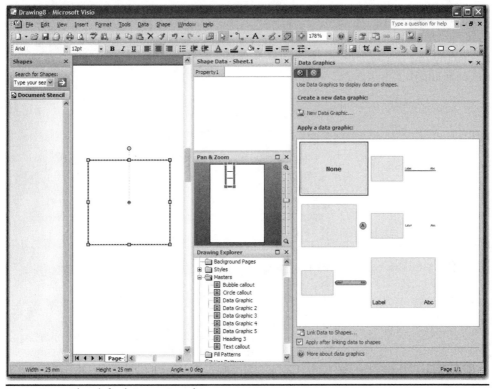

**Figure 7-1**    *The default Data Graphics*

If you examine the list of Masters in the Drawing Explorer, you will not find all the built-in Data Graphic callouts, as Visio only imports each Data Graphic callout on demand. Each time you select a different one from the Edit Data Graphic dialog, it is added to the list of Masters in the Drawing Explorer.

The Visio developers had to be clever here because, until the 2007 version, a single shape can only have one Master. But, for the Data Graphics to work, Visio developers had to find a way for each shape also to contain subshapes that are instances of different Masters. This was quite a challenge, but some caveats still exist. For example, the inclusion of Data Graphics in your drawing increases its file size, sometimes considerably, and takes longer to process any changes you make to them.

## Text Callouts

Eight Text callouts are delivered with the product, two of which are only suitable for displaying one or two characters, and three headings which only show the data value (no data label).

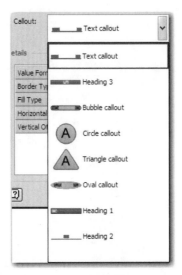

The names of the Text callouts are useful when you want to copy an existing one.

For the Text callouts that can only display one or two characters, there is the Value Length in the Details of the Edit Text dialog, where you set the maximum length of text to be returned.

If you want to do something clever, such as return the first and last character of the text, then you need to enter a formula similar to the following in the Data Field by selecting More Fields.

```
=LEFT({Status},1)+ RIGHT({Status},1)
```

## Data Bars

Eleven Data Bar callouts are out-of-the-box, most of which require a single value to change the position of the percentage indicator, but the last three (Multi-bar graph, and Stacked bar 1 and 2) can have up to five different fields to compare values.

The names of the Data Bars are useful when you want to copy an existing one.

## Icon Sets

Twelve Icon Sets are available out-of-the-box. Each set has a maximum of five icons available, and most of them are variations of red, amber, green, and blue status indicators.

The following list has the Master names for the Icon Sets, in the order in which they appear in the drop-down list on the Edit Icon Set dialog.

- ▶ Trend arrows 1
- ▶ Trend arrows 2
- ▶ Flags
- ▶ Status icons
- ▶ Colored shapes
- ▶ Lights
- ▶ Traffic signal 1
- ▶ Directions
- ▶ Ratings
- ▶ Faces
- ▶ Traffic signal 2
- ▶ Traffic signal 3

Again, the names are important when you are looking for a Master name to copy. They are listed because their names are not shown in the pull-down list.

# Creating Custom Callouts

*Custom Data Graphic callouts* are a great opportunity to express a corporate style or a product specific appearance. In addition, they can be better matched to the type of data being visualized and can, therefore, aid understanding and provide clarity. See Figure 7-2.

In this example, a custom Icon Set is in the top left of each shape, as well as a custom header Text callout—this can have different colors and corner rounding—and a custom Data Bar comprising of spheres (I resisted the temptation to make them multicolored pool balls). I show you how each are constructed in the subsequent sections.

The simplest method to create a custom Data Graphic callout is to locate a similar one in the Drawing Explorer window, and then use the right-mouse menu option Duplicate.

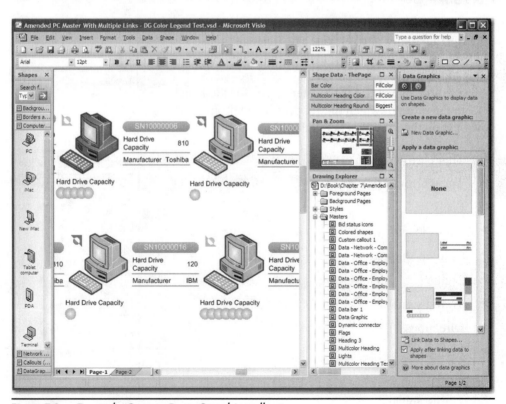

**Figure 7-2**   *Example Custom Data Graphic callouts*

This creates a new entry in the Drawing Explorer window, which you now need to rename to suit your needs.

It is quite easy for someone with ShapeSheet experience to create new Data Graphics callouts, but a few rules should be observed. Data Graphic callouts increases the file size of your drawing, and you should design any new ones with care to be efficient.

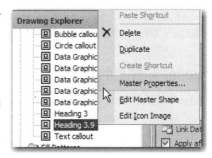

## Minimize Use of Group Shapes

If possible, always try not to create grouped shapes because Visio needs to recalculate subshapes in groups. This also means you should keep your nesting of group shapes to an absolute minimum. Do not group groups if you can possibly avoid it.

At times, you cannot avoid using subshapes in a group, for example, use of different colors or multiple text blocks requires subshapes, but a single shape can have many geometry sections (up to 255), each of which can have its visibility toggled.

I often need to create grouped shapes if an element needs to be repeated many times, for example, a port in a patch panel. In this case, I construct the first subshape with a Position Shape Data item, and then I can easily duplicate this and simply change the Position value. I demonstrate an example of this in the following Spheres bar Data Bar callout.

## Precreate Data Graphic User-Defined Cells

If you know that certain types of shapes are invariably going to have Data Graphics applied to them, then it makes sense to preload these Masters with the following list of User-defined cells. This removes the need for Visio to add these to each instance of the Master and, thus, speeds processing and may reduce the file size.

► visDGDisplayFormat

► visDGDefaultPos

► visDGCBVFill

► visDGOldColors

► msvThemeColors

► msvThemeEffects

The previous list is for Master shapes that may use Data Graphics (the target shape). This list is *not* for the Data Graphic callout Master shapes.

## General Editing Techniques

After you rename the Data Graphic Master in the Drawing Explorer window, then you should ensure Match Master by Name on Drop is checked. Choose a name that expresses the content, as you will want to be able to recognize the Master later.

Once the Master is duplicated, you can edit the shape by selecting Edit Master Shape from the right mouse menu of a Master in the Drawing Explorer window.

You likely will need to change the LockGroup cell of the Master shape to 0 while you are editing the contents of the group, but then return it to 1 when you finish. This prevents normal users from accidentally editing any of the shapes within the main group shape. The LockGroup cell is in the Protection section of the ShapeSheet.

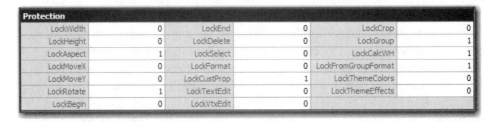

| Protection | | | | | |
|---|---|---|---|---|---|
| LockWidth | 0 | LockEnd | 0 | LockCrop | 0 |
| LockHeight | 0 | LockDelete | 0 | LockGroup | 1 |
| LockAspect | 1 | LockSelect | 0 | LockCalcWH | 1 |
| LockMoveX | 0 | LockFormat | 0 | LockFromGroupFormat | 1 |
| LockMoveY | 0 | LockCustProp | 1 | LockThemeColors | 0 |
| LockRotate | 1 | LockTextEdit | 0 | LockThemeEffects | 0 |
| LockBegin | 0 | LockVtxEdit | 0 | | |

Other cells in this section are also useful for Data Graphic callouts. In particular, the *LockAspect* and *LockRotate* ensure the aspect ratio and angle relative to the target shape are not changed; the *LockCustProp* prevents essential ShapeData from being modified; and *LockFormat, LockGroupFormat, LockThemeColors,* and *LockThemeEffects* prevent various formatting and theme effects from changing the callout.

# Text Callouts

The standard Heading callouts are fine, but I wanted to have more color choices. I also thought it would be nice to change the size of the rounding on the corners, so I decided to create the Multicolor Heading Text callout.

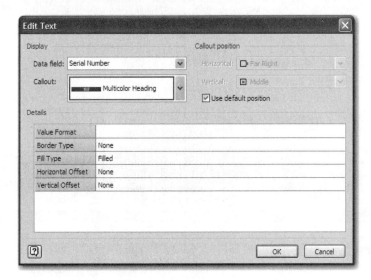

## Multicolor Heading Text Callout

First, duplicate the Heading 3 Master and rename it as Multicolor Heading, before opening the Master shape for edit. Then, open the PageSheet (the ShapeSheet of the Master Page) and insert the User-defined and Shape Data sections.

Rename Row_1 of the User-defined section as msvRHIPreventRemoval and set its value to 1. This prevents the Remove Hidden Information tool from deleting your new Master.

Rename the first Shape Data item as HeadingColor, with Type=1 and the Format

```
="FillColor;FillColor2;AccentColor;AccentColor2;AccentColor3;AccentColo
r4;AccentColor5;BackgroundColor"
```

Insert a new Shape Data row, named HeadingRounding, again Type = 1 and the Format as follows:

```
="(none);Smallest;Small;Normal;Big;Biggest"
```

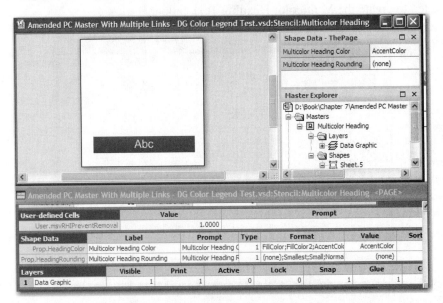

These Page Shape Data items are used to change the color and rounding of the Multicolor Heading shape itself. Master page Shape Data items are copied to the document page if they are referenced by the Master shape when it is first dropped on to a document page.

Next, you need to edit the ShapeSheet of the Multicolor Heading itself.

Setting the rounding to change is easy. Simply edit the value of the Rounding cell in the Line Format section to the following:

```
=LOOKUP(ThePage!Prop.HeadingRounding,ThePage!Prop.HeadingRounding.
Format)*0.5 mm*DropOnPageScale
```

This formula simply gets the index position of your current selection in the pull-down list, and then multiplies it by 0.5 mm (or scaled by whatever the scale of the page was at the time the shape was dropped on the page).

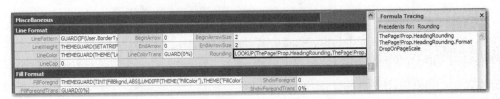

The result of the calculation means the value of rounding varies from 0 mm to 2.5 mm and, consequently, the corners of the shape change from square to completely round.

The second feature, changing the color, is more involved. The Heading shape's fill color needs to be changed whenever the user changes the value in the page Shape Data item.

The current formula in the FillBkgnd cell is:

```
=SETATREF(User.ThemeColor)
```

This means the real formula is in the User.ThemeColor cell, which is:

```
=THEMEGUARD(TINT(TONE(THEME("AccentColor2"),IF(SAT(THEME("AccentColor2"))<50,0,-
50)),-48))
```

You may think you could simply replace AccentColor2 with references to Page!Prop.HeadingColor, but this does not work (I know. I tried it.), so it is necessary to be a bit more cunning. A solution is to create a formula triggered by the change in value of ThePage!Prop.HeadingColor, which then recreates the formula in the User.ThemeColor cell with the new values. Create a new User-defined cell, named ColorTrigger, in the ShapeSheet and enter the following formula:

```
=DEPENDSON(ThePage!Prop.HeadingColor)+SETF(GetRef(User.ThemeColor),"=THEMEGUARD(
TINT(TONE(THEME("""&ThePage!Prop.HeadingColor&"""),IF(SAT(THEME("""&ThePage!Pr
op.HeadingColor&"""))<50,0,-50)),-48))")
```

You can see the cells that are affected by this formula in the Formula Tracing window. The result is that the color is changed whenever you change the value in the page's HeadingColor Shape Data.

## Data Bar Callouts

Data Bars can be split into two types—Continuous and Repeating Shape(s)—so we will create one of each.

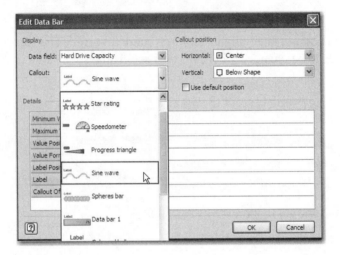

In this example, the CPU size is represented by a Progress Triangle bar, which is a continuous Data Bar, and the Hard Drive Capacity is represented by a Spheres bar, which is a repeating shape Data Bar callout.

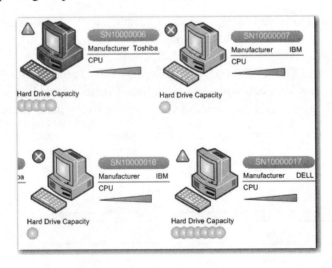

## Progress Triangle Data Bars

The *Progress Triangle data bar* is a duplicate of the Progress bar Data Bar callout, it was amended as follows.

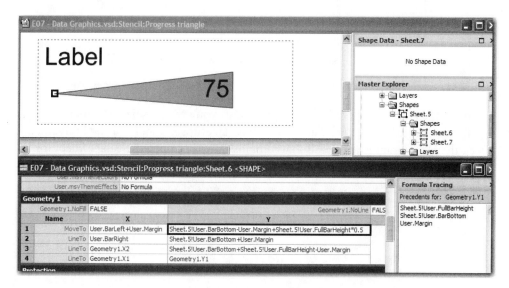

The geometry section was simply edited directly in the ShapeSheet of the previous rectangular bar. This meant deleting the last row in the Geometry1 section, and then editing the formulae of the other rows to make the closed triangle. A good practice is for closed shapes to have *X* and *Y* cells in the last row to reference to the first row. This ensures the shape will, indeed, be closed.

## Spheres Bar Data Bars

The *Spheres bar* is a bit more complicated because it is a repeating shape. It also has the capability to change color, such as the previous Multicolor Heading Text callout.

This time, you can duplicate the Star rating Master and rename it Sphere bar. You can then select Edit master shape from the right mouse menu. First, you should add a Shape Data item to the page of the Master, called MulticolorBarColor, with Type=1 and the Format

```
="FillColor;FillColor2;AccentColor;AccentColor2;AccentColor3;AccentColo
r4;AccentColor5;BackgroundColor"
```

Next, you need to open the ShapeSheet of the main shape, and delete the six Geometry sections because they contain the stars we no longer require. Instead, you need to add subshapes because this is the only way to get the spherical shading.

The shape is now prepared for the spheres, so you need to select the main shape, and then select Edit | Open Group. Then, draw an ellipse, select Format | Layer, and check the Data Graphic layer. All that remains now is to open the ShapeSheet for this ellipse, and then enter the formulae to match the following illustration:

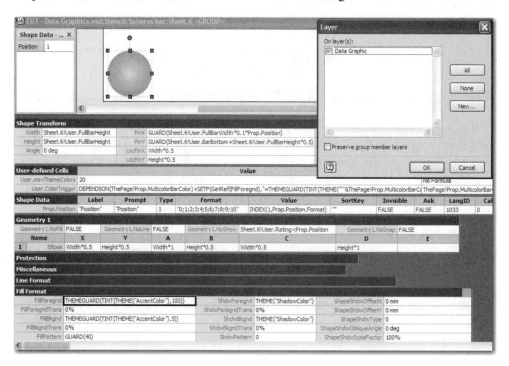

You notice there is a new User-defined cell, named ColorTrigger, with the following formula. This has a similar purpose to the ColorTrigger in the Multicolor Heading shape:

```
=DEPENDSON(ThePage!Prop.MulticolorBarColor)+SETF(GetRef(FillForegnd),"=THEMEGUAR
D(TINT(THEME("""&ThePage!Prop.MulticolorBarColor&"""),100))")+SETF(GetRef(FillBk
gnd),"=THEMEGUARD(TINT(THEME("""&ThePage!Prop.MulticolorBarColor&"""),5))")
```

In short, you have created the leftmost sphere in the row, at Position = 1. You can close the ShapeSheet, and you should have your spherical ball.

Ensure you have the Shape Data window open, then, with the sphere selected, press CTRL+D. This duplicates the shape, but the only thing you notice is the caption on the Shape Data window has changed to a new name. However, if you now select the next number from the Position pull-down list in the Shape Data window, you should see the sphere move to the second position. Thus, you just need to repeat CTRL+D and set the next position number another eight times. When you do this for positions nine and ten, you will probably not see the sphere at all because it is being automatically hidden, thanks to the formula in the Geometry1.NoShow cell:

```
=Sheet.6!User.Rating<Prop.Position
```

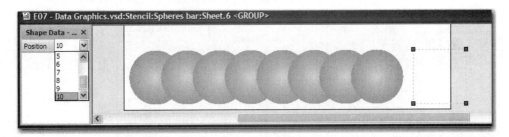

A tip for developers: copy the formula in the main group shape's User.Rating cell to User.Rating.Prompt while you manually change the values in User.Rating from 0 to 10. This enables you to check that your spheres are responding to their Position value. When you are happy that they are reacting correctly, just copy the formula from User.Rating.Prompt back to User.Rating.

You can now close the Group Edit window, and you are left with your completed Spheres bar Master.

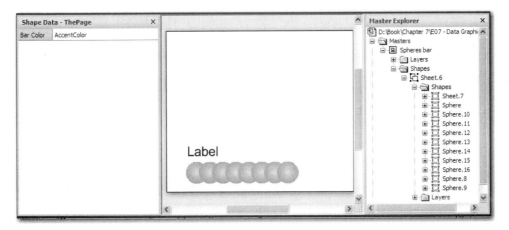

Just a reminder: Data Graphics that include many sub-shapes take more time to process and make for larger file sizes, so use them sparingly.

## Icon Sets Callouts

Two types of Icons Sets exist: the first is based on geometric changes, and the second contains images. In each case, there are a maximum of five icons.

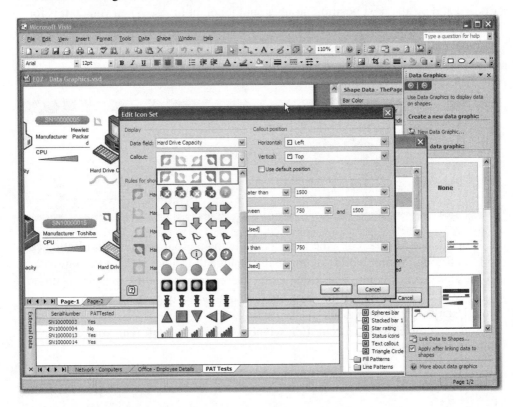

In the example on the next page, PATTested is shown with the Circle Triangle icons, which are geometry sections, and the Vulnerabilities are shown with the Bug status icons, which are images.

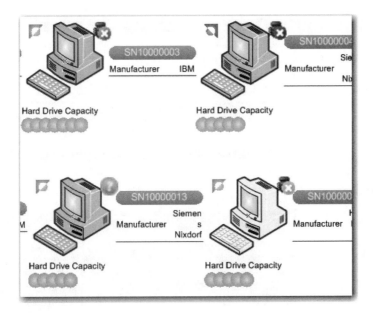

## Circle Triangle Icons

This Master is a duplicate of the Colored Shapes Master, but two extra Geometry sections were added, to make six in all. If you know you are going to print in black-and-white, then it makes sense to have icons that are geometrically different, rather than just relying on color alone. Therefore, this Icon Set has a triangle pointing to a different corner, as well as having a color change. The last one is just a neutral square for the unknown cases.

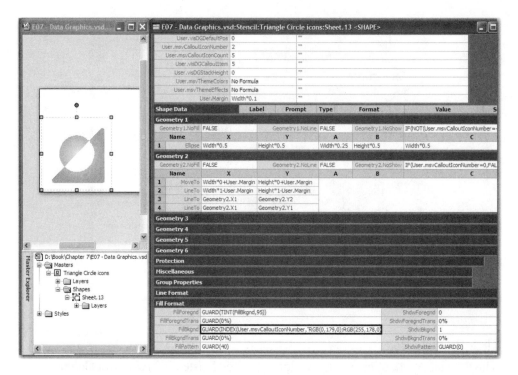

The first Geometry section is an Ellipse for the central circle, the next four are triangles pointing to each corner, and the last section is a rectangle outside the circle. The visibility of each of the last five Geometry sections is controlled by the following formula in the NoShow cell of each section (where $x$ is a number from 0 to 4):

```
=IF(User.msvCalloutIconNumber=x,FALSE,TRUE)
```

The other change is the color, so the following formula is in the FillBkgnd cell:

```
=GUARD(INDEX(User.msvCalloutIconNumber,"RGB(0,179,0);RGB(255,178,0);RGB
(105,195,255);RGB(255,0,0);RGB(185,185,185)"))
```

The FillForegnd is set to a percentage tint of the background color with the formula:

```
=GUARD(TINT(FillBkgnd,95))
```

The FillPattern is set to GUARD(40), which provides the central shading.

A tip for developers: change the value of User.msvCalloutIconNumber to between 0 and 4 to test your shape. Also, leave the number you want to have used to create the image for the Data Graphics panel display. Experienced ShapeSheet developers probably have realized that the last four geometry sections could have been condensed into just one, with the angle of rotation being varied by the value of the User.msvCalloutIconNumber.

## Bug Status Icons

This Master is also a duplicate of the Colored Shapes Master, but all the Geometry sections have been removed. Instead, images were added as subshapes within the group.

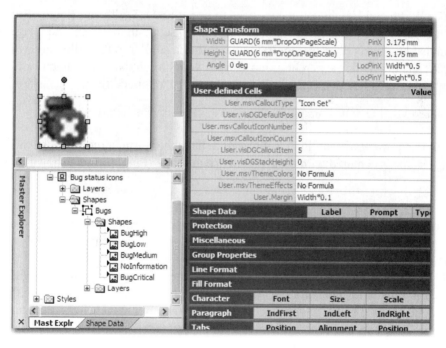

When using images as part of an Icon Set, remember these icons are going to be relatively small, so they should not be large files. Also, they should all be the same size. They can easily be added by selecting the group shape, and then selecting Edit | Open Group before selecting Insert | Picture | From File.

Then, open the ShapeSheet of the imported image because you need to edit four cells in the Shape Transform section:

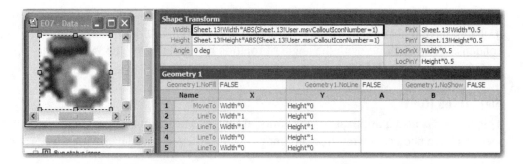

The Width and Height cell values need to be set to the Width and Height of the main group shape if this image is to be shown. Or, set them to zero, if the image is to be invisible. This is done by modifying the formula similar to the following, where Sheet.13 is the ID of the parent group shape – yours might be different, and *x* is a number between 0 and 4, (this is the formula for the Width cell):

```
=Sheet.13!Width*ABS(Sheet.13!User.msvCalloutIconNumber=x)
```

Similarly, the PinX and PinY cells need to have the formula modified, so the image shape is centered within the parent group shape (PinX formula shown):

```
=Sheet.13!Width*0.5
```

For clarity, you can rename the image shapes using Format | Special so you can recognize them more easily. Also, you should add the image shape to the Data Graphic layer using Format | Layer.

Repeat this process for the remaining four images. Do not forget to use a different value for *x* in the formulae for the Width and Height cells for each one. Close the Group Edit window, test your shape by changing the User.msvCalloutIconNumber value in the group shape, and, when you are happy with the shapes you have created, close the Master Edit window.

# Distributing Custom Data Graphic Callouts

The Microsoft Visio 2007 built-in Data Graphics are stored in a noneditable hidden stencil, and there is no way for you to add your own customizations to this stencil. You can, instead, create your own stencil that contains Masters made from shapes that contain the custom Data Graphic items. Unfortunately, your custom Data Graphic callouts will not automatically appear for your users when they select Data | Display Data on Shapes because they are not in your current document.

You could include the custom Data Graphics items and callouts in a template, so they are immediately available, which means you need to know how to copy Data Graphics from one document to another.

You can copy individual Data Graphic callouts by selecting them in the Masters branch of the Drawing Explorer window. However, it is probable that you want to copy several Data Graphic callouts at once, so you can create a Data Graphic that uses these callouts in the source document. Then, rename this Data Graphic, so it is identifiable.

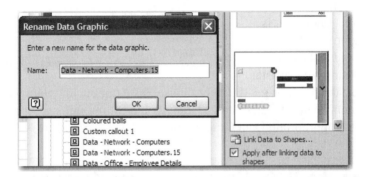

You must use the right-mouse menu item, Copy, or Edit | Copy because CTRL+C attempts to copy the current selection in the active page.

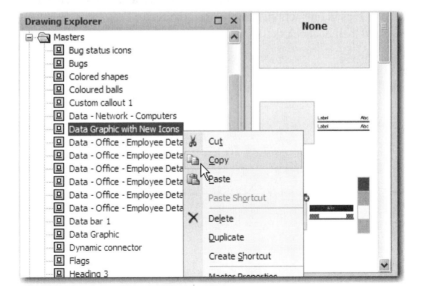

You can then open the Masters branch in the Drawing Explorer window of your target document, select a current Master, and, again, use the right mouse menu to select Paste. Otherwise, Visio will paste into the active page, rather than into the document Master.

If your target document is completely empty of Masters, then you should add a dummy Master first using New Master.

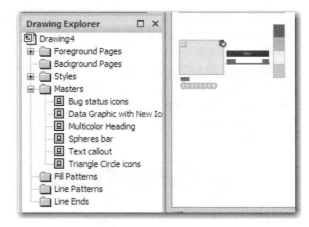

You can select this node to get the right mouse Paste option, and then you can delete the dummy Master. These new Data Graphic callout items now become available in the appropriate Data Graphic dialog.

# Changing the Data Graphics Layer Properties

You may recall that we always ensure the Data Graphic shapes and subshapes are assigned to the Data Graphic layer. This enables the user to quickly switch the visibility of all Data Graphics in one action. Simply open the Layer Properties dialog from the View menu, and then uncheck the Data Graphics Visible setting.

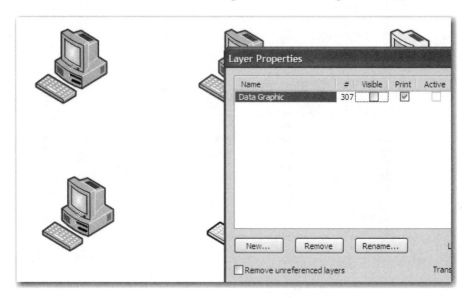

Similarly, you can change the color assigned to the Data Graphic layer, and this recolors all the Data Graphics, except for the images.

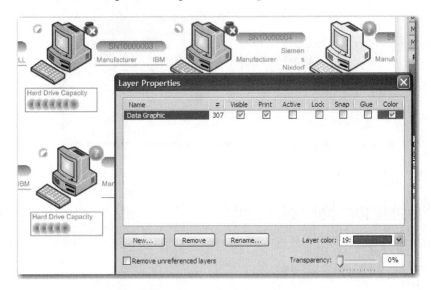

This is not a permanent change, so unchecking the color for the layer returns the Data Graphics back to their full glory.

# Recognizing Which Data Graphic

If you have the Data Graphics panel open, and then you select a shape in the drawing that has a Data Graphic applied, Visio will automatically highlight the Data Graphic which was applied to the shape in the panel. You can read the name of the Data Graphic if you hover your mouse over it in the panel, or you can rename it with the pull-down menu option.

However, you cannot easily see what Data Graphic is applied if you do not have the Data Graphics panel open. You want to see the name of the Data Graphic, along with its constituent Graphic Items, so you can recognize them in the Masters branch of the Drawing Explorer window. Therefore, I have included a short subfunction, ShowDataGraphic, which does this for you.

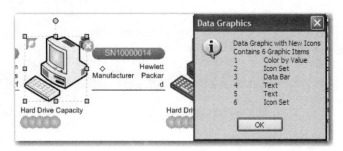

Simply select a shape and run the macro (once you add it to your document).

# Code Listing for ShowDataGraphic

```
Public Sub ShowDataGraphic()
Dim shp As Visio.Shape
Dim gitm As Visio.GraphicItem
Dim msg As String

    If Visio.ActiveWindow.Selection.Count = 0 Then
        MsgBox "Please select a shape to interrogate", vbExclamation
        Exit Sub
    Else
        Set shp = Visio.ActiveWindow.Selection.PrimaryItem
        If shp.DataGraphic Is Nothing Then
            MsgBox "This shape does not have any Data Graphics", vbExclamation
            Exit Sub
        Else
            msg = shp.DataGraphic.Name
            msg = msg & vbCrLf & "Contains " & _
                CStr(shp.DataGraphic.GraphicItems.Count) & _
                " Graphic Items"
            For Each gitm In shp.DataGraphic.GraphicItems
                msg = msg & vbCrLf & gitm.Index & vbTab & gitm.Description
            Next

        End If
    End If

    MsgBox msg, vbInformation, "Data Graphics"

End Sub
```

# Assigning Data Graphics Automatically

At times, you may need to apply Data Graphics in code, so I have included the following example of how this might be done in AddDataGraphic. The key elements are that you can apply a Data Graphic Master to either a selection or a shape, so I have shown how you can get hold of the Data Graphic Master and how you can create a selection of all the shape instances of a particular Master, in this case, PC. You may want to change the code to suit your needs by parameterizing the functions to accept different Data Graphic and Master names. Also, RemoveDataGraphic simply sets the DataGraphic property to Nothing.

## Code Listing for AddDataGraphic

```
Public Sub AddDataGraphic()
Dim shp As Visio.Shape
Dim mst As Visio.Master
Dim dg As Visio.Master
Dim mtgt As Visio.Master
Dim dgName As String
Dim sel As Visio.Selection
Dim mstName As String

    dgName = "Data Graphic with New Icons"
    'Check that the requested Data Graphic Master exits
    For Each mst In Visio.ActiveDocument.Masters
        If mst.Type = visTypeDataGraphic Then
            If mst.Name = dgName Then
                Set dg = mst
                Exit For
            End If
        End If
    Next

    If dg Is Nothing Then
        MsgBox "Unable to find the Data Graphic Master : " & dgName
        Exit Sub
    End If

    mstName = "PC"
    'Check that the requested Data Graphic Master exists
    For Each mst In Visio.ActiveDocument.Masters
        If mst.Type = visTypeMaster Then
            If mst.Name = mstName Then
                Set mtgt = mst
```

```
                    Exit For
            End If
        End If
    Next

    If mtgt Is Nothing Then
        MsgBox "Unable to find the target Master : " & mstName
        Exit Sub
    End If
    'Get a selection of the target shapes
    Set sel = Visio.ActivePage.CreateSelection(visSelTypeByMaster, _
        visSelModeSkipSub, mtgt)

    If sel.Count = 0 Then
        MsgBox "Unable to find the target shapes"
        Exit Sub
    Else
        'Apply the Data Graphic to the Shape
        sel.DataGraphic = dg
    End If

End Sub
```

# Code Listing for RemoveDataGraphic

```
Public Sub RemoveDataGraphic()
Dim shp As Visio.Shape
Dim mst As Visio.Master
Dim mtgt As Visio.Master
Dim mstName As String
Dim sel As Visio.Selection

    mstName = "PC"
    'Check that the requested Data Graphic Master exists
    For Each mst In Visio.ActiveDocument.Masters
        If mst.Type = visTypeMaster Then
            If mst.Name = mstName Then
                Set mtgt = mst
                Exit For
            End If
        End If
    Next

    If mtgt Is Nothing Then
        MsgBox "Unable to find the target Master : " & mstName
        Exit Sub
```

```
    End If
    'Get a selection of the target shapes
    Set sel = Visio.ActivePage.CreateSelection(visSelTypeByMaster, _
        visSelModeSkipSub, mtgt)

    If sel.Count = 0 Then
        MsgBox "Unable to find the target shapes"
        Exit Sub
    Else
        'Remove the Data Graphic to the Shape
        sel.DataGraphic = Nothing
    End If

End Sub
```

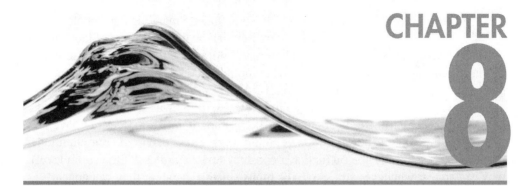

# Using Smart Tags and Actions

Y ou are probably asking yourself why I included Smart Tags in a book on visualizing information. Well, Smart Tags can be live indicators of the value of
Shape Data because they can highlight information that needs your scrutiny.
Many years ago, I used to use a UNIX computer-aided design (CAD) system
that could be linked to a database. Whenever I demonstrated color number 255, the
clients always looked on with renewed interest. Color 255 was simply flashing red,
and always successfully drew attention to the flashing item. Visio does not have any
built-in flashing colors, but it does have Smart Tags. These can grab your attention
because they can always be on (and at a constant size, regardless of the zoom level),
they can appear whenever you move the mouse over a shape, or they can appear
whenever a shape is selected. In fact, they are better than flashing red because they
can also have rollover text and a pull-down menu, and *that* is the link with Actions
on the right mouse menu!

In fact, Smart Tags provide a visible anchor for Actions that are revealed as menu
items by the down arrow on the right of the Smart Tag. These *Actions* can indirectly
run code in Visual Basic for Applications (VBA), in an Add-In or an Add-on, or they
can change the values in other ShapeSheet cells.

Just one thing, though, Smart Tags do not print and they do not show in any interface
(including the Visio Viewer control) except for Visio and the Visio Drawing control!
Therefore, they are only useful for capturing the Visio user's attention. In fact, a user
can switch off their display altogether using the View tab on the Tools | Options dialog.

# Smart Tags and Actions

Smart Tag and Action sections are not present in a shape's ShapeSheet by default,
although many Masters are delivered with Microsoft Visio that already have Action
items. I cannot think of any delivered Masters delivered with Microsoft Visio that
have Smart Tag items already present, so you need to insert at least the Smart Tag section in the ShapeSheet. This can be done by selecting
Insert | Section with the shape's ShapeSheet active.

This inserts the requested sections, so you need to
understand what each of the cells does.

## Anatomy of a Smart Tag

Smart Tag section rows can be named, or just left as
Row_*x,* where *x* is an incremental number. See
Table 8-1.

| Actions | Action | Menu | TagName | ButtonFace | SortKey | Checked | Disabled | ReadOnly | Invisible | BeginGroup |
|---|---|---|---|---|---|---|---|---|---|---|
| Actions.Row_1 | "" | "" | "" | "" | "" | 0 | 0 | FALSE | FALSE | FALSE |

| Smart Tags | X | Y | TagName | X Justify | Y Justify | DisplayMode | ButtonFace | Description | Disabled |
|---|---|---|---|---|---|---|---|---|---|
| SmartTags.Row_1 | 0 mm | 0 mm | "" | 0 | 0 | 0 | "" | "" | FALSE |

# Anatomy of an Action

Action section rows can also be named, or just left as Row_$x$, where $x$ is an incremental number. See Table 8-2.

**NOTE**

*The TagName cells in the Smart Tag and Action sections link the two sections together when a common value is used in both.*

# Button Faces

Both the Smart Tags and Actions have a cell called *ButtonFace,* in which you can put a valid value between 0 and, well, the highest value I have found is 16,178. These numbers refer to an icon within the Microsoft Office core dll, so I guess all the Office ones are in there somewhere (check out number 6,501 and onwards for some Visio button face icons). A slight bug is in Microsoft Visio 2007, though: some of the icons display as a black rectangle until you move the mouse over them (and Microsoft will not fix that problem yet). This only affects Smart Tags that are set to always display, so it is essential that you test them first.

| Cell | Description |
|---|---|
| X | The horizontal position of the Smart Tag within the shape. Usually Width*0, Width*0.5 or Width*1. |
| Y | The vertical position of the Smart Tag within the shape. Usually Height*0, Height*0.5 or Height*1. |
| TagName | Any text you want, but you must use the same text in the TagName of the Actions that will be in the pull-down menu. |
| XJustify | 0,1 or 2 means Left, Center, or Right-justified. |
| YJustify | 0,1 or 2 means Top, Middle, or Bottom-justified. |
| DisplayMode | 0,1 or 2 means display when mouse over, shape selected, or always. |
| ButtonFace | The number, from the Office dll, of the icon to display. |
| Description | The text that appears when you move the mouse over the Smart Tag. |
| Disabled | True or False. |

**Table 8-1**  *Smart Tags Section Cells*

| Cell | Description |
|------|-------------|
| Action | The action to perform when the item is selected. |
| Menu | The text that appears on the menu. Use the % character to move the text below the built-in right mouse items (it just sends the item to the bottom for Smart Tags). You can use the "_" character to include a separator line, but the BeginGroup also does this. |
| TagName | If used, then the item appears in the pull-down list with the same TagName. |
| ButtonFace | The number, from the Office dll, of the icon to display. |
| SortKey | The alphabetically sorted key. |
| Checked | If no button-face ID is defined, then this adds a check in front of the menu text if set to True. If there is a button-face ID, then the row is shown as selected. |
| Disabled | True or False. |
| ReadOnly | If True, then the menu text appears (the icon does not), but is not selectable. |
| BeginGroup | Adds a separator line before the menu text. |

**Table 8-2**    *Actions Section Cells*

The previous illustration shows the Smart Tag without a mouse over it, and this one shows the Smart Tag with the mouse over it.

But do not worry too much, because you can choose from literally thousands of icons. I was once given an Excel spreadsheet by Microsoft, which contained a macro to change the icons on a custom toolbar, 512 icons at a time. This was extremely useful for choosing a suitable icon to use in Smart Tags and Actions in the Visio ShapeSheet, but that was before Microsoft Excel 2007 and its new replacement for toolbars, called Ribbons, so I came up with a Visio only method to perform the same task.

# A Smart Tags SmartShape

To demonstrate the range of ButtonFace IDs for use in SmartTags and Right Mouse Actions, I created a Visio SmartShape that can display 25 at a time, starting from a given Shape Number value. The button-face IDs range from 0 to 16,178, although there appear to be many gaps in the range.

The SmartTags Master demonstrates some important principles. It contains a SmartTag with a pull-down menu of 25 button-face IDs. You can select one of these to change the icon displayed on the Smart Tag itself, along with the description. The currently selected button face is shown checked on the pull-down menu.

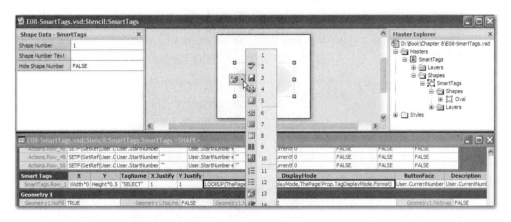

The Smart Tag is positioned to the left of the shape and is identified by the Tag-Name of "SELECT".

The current selected button face is stored in the User.CurrentNumber cell, and is put in there by the formula (where *n* is a number between 0 and 24):

```
=SETF(GetRef(User.CurrentNumber),User.StartNumber+n)
```

This formula is in each of the 25 Action rows (with *n* incremented from 0 to 24) that appear on the right mouse menu, and is repeated for each of the 25 Action rows that appear under the Smart Tag with the TagName "SELECT".

| User-defined Cells | | Value | | | Prompt | | | |
|---|---|---|---|---|---|---|---|---|
| User.StartNumber | Prop.ShapeNumber | | | | "" | | | |
| User.CurrentNumber | 13 | | | | "" | | | |
| User.Text | User.CurrentNumber | | | | "" | | | |
| User.NumberTrigger | DEPENDSON(User.StartNumber)+SETF(GetRef(User.CurrentNumber),User.StartNumber) | | | | "" | | | |

| Shape Data | Label | Prompt | Type | Format | Value | SortKey | Invisible | Ask | La |
|---|---|---|---|---|---|---|---|---|---|
| Prop.ShapeNumber | "Shape Number" | "Enter the number for the shape" | 2 | "#.####" | 1 | "" | FALSE | FALSE | 205 |
| Prop.ShapeNumberText | "Shape Number Text" | "Enter preceding text for the shape number" | 0 | "@" | "" | "" | FALSE | FALSE | 205 |
| Prop.HideShapeNumber | "Hide Shape Number" | "Enter TRUE to hide the shape number for the shape" | 3 | "#.####" | 0 | "" | FALSE | FALSE | 205 |

| Actions | Action | Menu | TagName | ButtonFace | SortKey | Checked |
|---|---|---|---|---|---|---|
| Actions.Row_1 | SETF(GetRef(User.CurrentNumber),User.StartNumber+0) | User.StartNumber+0 | "SELECT" | User.StartNumber+0 | "" | User.CurrentNumber=User.StartNumber+0 |
| Actions.Row_2 | SETF(GetRef(User.CurrentNumber),User.StartNumber+1) | User.StartNumber+1 | "SELECT" | User.StartNumber+1 | "" | User.CurrentNumber=User.StartNumber+1 |
| Actions.Row_3 | SETF(GetRef(User.CurrentNumber),User.StartNumber+2) | User.StartNumber+2 | "SELECT" | User.StartNumber+2 | "" | User.CurrentNumber=User.StartNumber+2 |
| Actions.Row_4 | SETF(GetRef(User.CurrentNumber),User.StartNumber+3) | User.StartNumber+3 | "SELECT" | User.StartNumber+3 | "" | User.CurrentNumber=User.StartNumber+3 |
| Actions.Row_5 | SETF(GetRef(User.CurrentNumber),User.StartNumber+4) | User.StartNumber+4 | "SELECT" | User.StartNumber+4 | "" | User.CurrentNumber=User.StartNumber+4 |

The ButtonFace and Description cells are, therefore, set to the value in the User .CurrentNumber cell.

The DisplayMode of the Smart Tag is set to the value in a new Shape Data item in the page, which has a type of 1 and the Format Value of "Mouse Over;Shape Selected;Always".

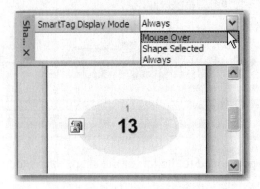

This formula for the DisplayMode is:

```
=LOOKUP(ThePage!Prop.TagDisplayMode,ThePage!Prop.TagDisplayMode.Format)
```

This enables you to test the Smart Tags in each of the three DisplayModes, just by changing the value of the page Shape Data item.

The shape has three Shape Data items, although only the first one, Shape Number, is required for our purposes. The others only exist because I wanted the shape to be compatible with the Tools | Add-Ons | Visio Extras | Number Shapes utility. It always tries to add these Shape Data items and to edit the shape text, so the Master shape also contains a subshape to display the shaded oval with currently selected button-face ID.

The Shape Number value is used as the start of the series of 25 button-face IDs to be displayed in both the Smart Tag and right mouse Action items.

When the Shape Number value is changed, the value of User.StartNumber is changed and all the relevant Action rows are automatically updated. In addition, the value of User.CurrentNumber is set to the value of User.StartNumber.

```
=DEPENDSON(User.StartNumber)+SETF(GetRef(User.CurrentNumber),User.StartNumber)
```

The top level group of the shape displays the Prop.ShapeNumber as smaller text at the top of the shape, and the subshape displays the User.CurrentNumber as larger text in the center of the shape. The text is arranged like this because the Number Shapes add-on updates the top-level text itself.

If you have not yet made a Master out of the shape, simply open the document stencil, drag the shape on to it, and rename it as SmartTags.

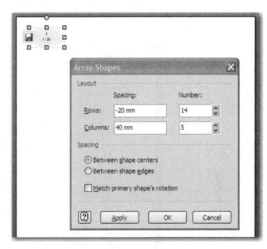

## The Array Shapes Add-On

Now that you have created the Smart Tags Master shape, you can use it in a page to help see all the button-face IDs. So, drag the SmartTags Master shape on to the top left of an empty page, and then select Tools | Add-Ons | Visio Extras | Array Shapes. This opens the Array Shapes dialog, where you can enter the number of rows and columns you want.

You should also increase the spacing between the shapes, for both rows and columns, so that they are spread out a little. The number of rows needs to be a negative number so that the shapes are arranged below the source shape. In the displayed case, there is space for 14 rows and 5 columns, with the spacing size of −20 mm and 40 mm on an A4 page.

You now have 14 × 5 = 70 identical shapes, each with a right mouse menu and Smart Tag list displaying the button faces 1 to 25.

## The Number Shapes Add-On

To quickly change the Shape Number Shape Data value for each of the shapes, you can use Tools | Add-Ons | Visio Extras | Number Shapes tool.

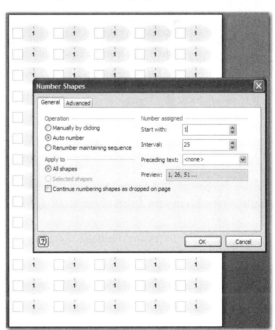

If you set Operation to Auto number, and the Number Assigned Interval to 25, then, with Apply to All shapes, press OK.

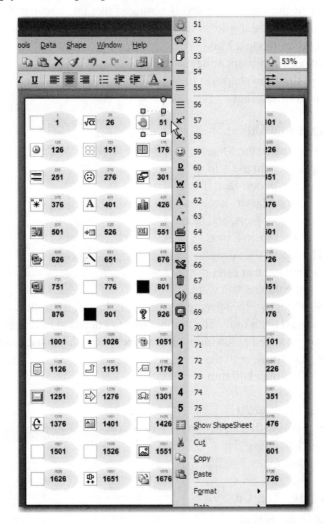

All the Smart Tag shapes are renumbered, and you can see there are 25 different button-face IDs to try from either the right mouse menu or from the Smart Tag pull-down list. So, with 70 shapes, each with 25 button-face IDs, you have 1750 possible button-face IDs to try on the page. You need to create ten such pages to review all the possible button-face IDs!

You now have a way of reviewing and testing any valid button-face ID.

# Using Actions to Change Shape Data

If you have Master shapes that have Fixed List Shape Data, then you can easily modify the Actions on the Master shape to provide a convenient method to change the values. You can also take the opportunity to add icons for each of the different choices.

For example, the Flowchart Shapes Master in the Basic Flowchart Shapes stencil has right mouse actions to change the appearance to represent Process, Decision, Document, and Data. Just drag-and-drop the shape on to a blank page, delete the shape, and open the Master for editing from either the Document Stencil or the Drawing Explorer, as usual.

This is an old shape that could use some revamping. You can first edit the shape, so it displays the same type of shape as a Shape Data Type item.

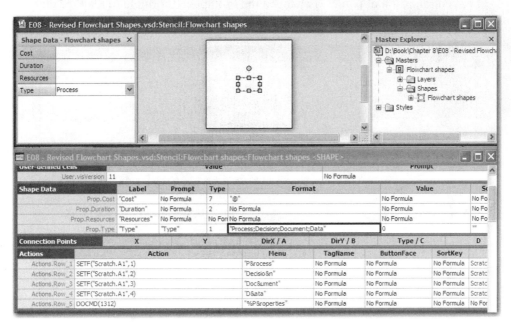

You can review the possible button faces to find icons that can represent the four different types of shape and, sure enough, these can be found as numbers 1190, 1192, 1196, and 1193 (in order, they represent Process, Decision, Document and Data).

I added a User-defined cell, called TypeIndex, with the fomula:

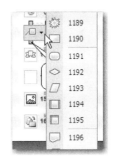

```
=LOOKUP(Prop.Type,Prop.Type.Format)
```

This just returns 0, 1, 2, or 3, depending on the selected value of Prop.Type. As I said, this is an old shape, so it has the Geometry sections Visible cells set to the Scratch.A1 cell because it was first constructed before User-defined cells were introduced into the Visio ShapeSheet. Therefore, I set a User-defined cell, TypeTrigger, to update the value in Scratch.A1 whenever the value of User.TypeIndex changes.

```
=DEPENDSON(User.TypeIndex)+SETF(GetRef(Scratch.A1),User.TypeIndex+1)
```

I changed the formula in the Action rows to use the new Prop.Type cell, so the value is changed when the Action is selected (where *n* is a number between 0 and 3).

```
=SETF(GetRef(Prop.Type),"INDEX(n,Prop.Type.Format)")
```

For centralization of names, I changed the Prompt cell formula to read the text values from the Prop.Type.Format.

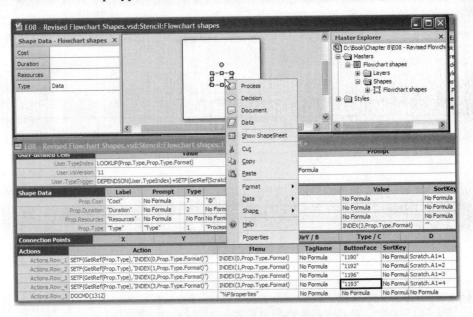

The ButtonFace is set to the numbers we discovered by using the SmartTags shape. Next, I want to have a Smart Tag with the same list of choices, so I inserted the Smart Tag section and duplicated each of the Action rows, but with the "TYPE" TagName to match the TagName of the Smart Tag.

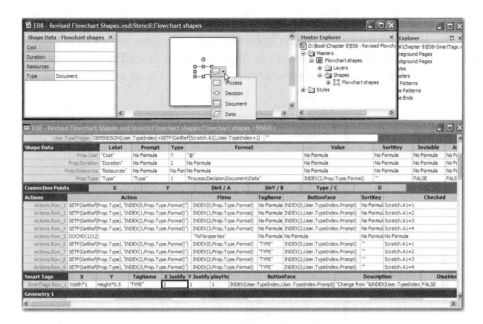

I set the Type Smart Tag to the right of the shape, and because now more than one cell needs the same button-face ID, I then put the values as a list in the User.TypeIndex.Prompt cell (I could have created a new row). Thus, the formulae in the Button-Face cells can refer to an index position within this list.

The user can now change the type of shape from a list that displays the shape appearance, but you can do even more. You could add a Shape Data Priority item, which is also selectable from a similar list to the Type Shape Data.

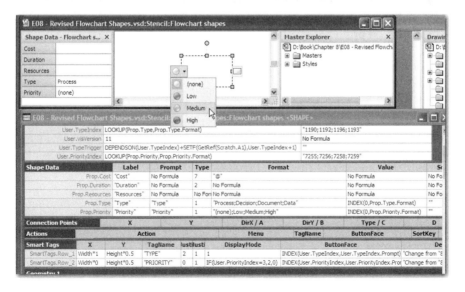

In this case, I selected items similar to those in the Colored Shapes Data Graphic Icon Set, and I set the DisplayMode to be MouseOver, unless the value is High, in which case, the DisplayMode is Always. This means the High Priority shapes will have the additional reinforcement of a Smart Tag that stays on all the time, at the same size, regardless of zoom level.

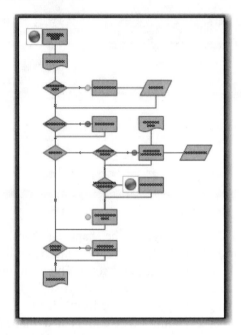

The combination of Data Graphics and Smart Tags enhances the Visio document that is visualizing information to provide an enhanced interactive environment, which can also be printed.

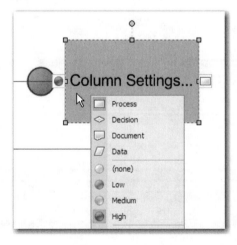

# Matching Button Faces and Icon Sets

A useful stencil Visio Extras I Icon Sets has Masters for all the built-in Data Icon Sets. You can drag-and-drop these Masters, and change the Display Icon Shape Data to show the individual icons displayed for each value. A trawl through the available button faces and the Data Graphic Icon Sets reveals that some icons look similar.

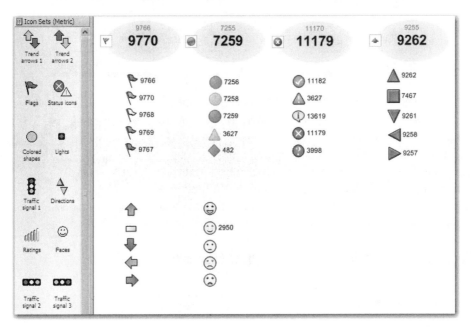

If you want to combine Icon Sets and button faces, then creating custom Icon Sets already represented in the available button faces would be useful.

# Automating Smart Tags for Icon Sets

Once you select button faces for icon sets, you could use them to highlight particular conditions. Using Smart Tags to highlight icon sets should be used sparingly, otherwise, the effect will be lost.

In the following code, the subfunction *addSmartTagRow* is an enhanced version of the one found in the Microsoft Visio 2007 SDK Code Library. The main subfunction, *addIconSet,* reads the shapes in the active page to check if the requested Icon Set is present as a subshape, and then checks to see if the requested icon number is displayed. If these conditions are met, then the $X$ and $Y$ position of the icon graphic is read and a corresponding Smart Tag is created over the top of it with the specified button face and description.

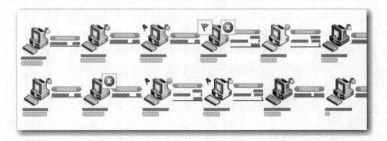

If you were to zoom in close to the relevant shapes, you would clearly see the Smart Tag over the top of the Data Graphic icon.

The second code listing enables the requested Icon Set Smart Tags to be removed from the shapes in the active page. In a production application, these functions should be called before the addIconSet is called to clear any redundant ones.

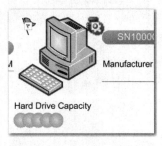

## Code Listing for addIconSet and Wrapper Functions

```
Public Sub AddNotPATTested()
    addIconSet "Flags", 0, 9766, "NOT PAT Tested"
End Sub

Public Sub AddCriticalVulnerabilities()
        addIconSet "Bug status icons", 3, 11179, "Critical Vulnerability"
End Sub

Private Sub addIconSet(ByVal iconSet As String, _
    ByVal iconNumber As Integer, _
    ByVal faceID As Integer, _
    ByVal description As String)

Dim shp As Visio.Shape
Dim subShp As Visio.Shape
Dim pinXFormula As String
Dim pinYFormula As String

    For Each shp In Visio.ActivePage.Shapes
        For Each subShp In shp.Shapes
            If subShp.Name = iconSet Then
```

```
                    If subShp.CellExists("User.msvCalloutType", Visio.
visExistsAnywhere) = True Then
                        If subShp.Cells("User.msvCalloutType").ResultStr("") = "Icon
Set" Then
                            If subShp.Cells("User.msvCalloutIconNumber").ResultIU =
iconNumber Then
                                'Add Icon
                                pinXFormula = "Width*" & _
                                    CStr(subShp.Cells("PinX").ResultIU / shp.
Cells("Width"))

                                pinYFormula = "Height*" & _
                                    CStr(subShp.Cells("PinY").ResultIU / shp.
Cells("Height"))

                                addSmartTagRow shp, Replace(iconSet, " ", ""), _
                                    iconSet, description, _
                                    pinXFormula, pinYFormula, CStr(faceID), _
                                    "1", "1", "2"
                            End If
                            Exit For
                        End If
                    End If
                End If
            Next subShp

    Next shp

End Sub

Private Sub addSmartTagRow(ByRef vsoTargetShape As Visio.Shape, _
    ByVal strRowName As String, _
    ByVal strTagName As String, _
    ByVal strDescription As String, _
    ByVal strLocationX As String, _
    ByVal strLocationY As String, _
    Optional ByVal iconNumber As String, _
    Optional ByVal xJustify As String, _
    Optional ByVal yJustify As String, _
    Optional ByVal dispMode As String)
'  Modified version of code from Visio SDK Code Library
' addSmartTagRow
'
' Abstract - This procedure adds a smart tag row and
' sets the cells to the values in the parameters.
'
' Parameters
```

```
' vsoTargetShape     Shape to add the smart tag row to
' strRowName         Name to use for the new smart tag row
' strTagName         Tag name to use for the new smart tag row
' Description        Description to use for the new smart tag
'                    row (This appears as a tool tip when the
'                    cursor hovers over the smart tag.)
' strLocationX       X location of the smart tag icon, relative to
'                    the target shape
' strLocationY       Y location of the smart tag icon, relative to
'                    the target shape
'

    Dim intNewRowNumber As Integer
    Dim vsoCell As Visio.Cell

    On Error GoTo AddSmartTagRow_Err

    ' Create the new smart tag row.
    intNewRowNumber = vsoTargetShape.AddNamedRow( _
        CInt(VisSectionIndices.visSectionSmartTag), strRowName, _
        CInt(VisRowTags.visTagDefault))

    ' Name cell
    Set vsoCell = vsoTargetShape.CellsSRC( _
        CInt(VisSectionIndices.visSectionSmartTag), _
        intNewRowNumber, CInt(VisCellIndices.visSmartTagName))
    vsoCell.FormulaU = StringToFormulaForString(strTagName)

    ' Description cell
    Set vsoCell = vsoTargetShape.CellsSRC( _
        CInt(VisSectionIndices.visSectionSmartTag), _
        intNewRowNumber, CInt(VisCellIndices.visSmartTagDescription))
    vsoCell.FormulaU = StringToFormulaForString(strDescription)

    ' X location cell
    Set vsoCell = vsoTargetShape.CellsSRC( _
        CInt(VisSectionIndices.visSectionSmartTag), _
        intNewRowNumber, CInt(VisCellIndices.visSmartTagX))
    vsoCell.FormulaU = StringToFormulaForString(strLocationX)

    ' Y location cell
    Set vsoCell = vsoTargetShape.CellsSRC( _
        CInt(VisSectionIndices.visSectionSmartTag), _
        intNewRowNumber, CInt(VisCellIndices.visSmartTagY))
    vsoCell.FormulaU = StringToFormulaForString(strLocationY)

    'DJP : Optionally add the button faces, etc
    If iconNumber > -1 Then
```

```
        Set vsoCell = vsoTargetShape.CellsSRC( _
            CInt(VisSectionIndices.visSectionSmartTag), _
            intNewRowNumber, CInt(VisCellIndices.visSmartTagButtonFace))
        vsoCell.FormulaU = StringToFormulaForString(iconNumber)
    End If

    If Len(xJustify) > 0 Then
        Set vsoCell = vsoTargetShape.CellsSRC( _
            CInt(VisSectionIndices.visSectionSmartTag), _
            intNewRowNumber, CInt(VisCellIndices.visSmartTagXJustify))
        vsoCell.FormulaU = StringToFormulaForString(xJustify)
    End If

    If Len(yJustify) > 0 Then
        Set vsoCell = vsoTargetShape.CellsSRC( _
            CInt(VisSectionIndices.visSectionSmartTag), _
            intNewRowNumber, CInt(VisCellIndices.visSmartTagYJustify))
        vsoCell.FormulaU = StringToFormulaForString(yJustify)
    End If

    If Len(dispMode) > 0 Then
        Set vsoCell = vsoTargetShape.CellsSRC( _
            CInt(VisSectionIndices.visSectionSmartTag), _
            intNewRowNumber, CInt(VisCellIndices.visSmartTagDisplayMode))
        vsoCell.FormulaU = dispMode
    End If

    Exit Sub

AddSmartTagRow_Err:
    ' Display the error
    Debug.Print Err.description

End Sub
```

## Code Listing for removeIconSet and Wrapper Functions

```
Public Sub RemovePATTest()
    removeIconSet "Flags"
End Sub

Public Sub RemoveCriticalVulnerability()
    removeIconSet "Bug status icons"
End Sub
```

```
Private Sub removeIconSet(ByVal iconSet As String)

Dim shp As Visio.Shape
Dim subShp As Visio.Shape
Dim iRow As Integer

    For Each shp In Visio.ActivePage.Shapes
        For Each subShp In shp.Shapes
            If shp.SectionExists(Visio.visSectionSmartTag, Visio.
visExistsAnywhere) = True Then
                For iRow = 0 To shp.RowCount(Visio.visSectionSmartTag)
- 1
                    If shp.CellsSRC(Visio.visSectionSmartTag, _
                        iRow, Visio.visSmartTagName).ResultStr("") =
iconSet Then
                        shp.DeleteRow Visio.visSectionSmartTag, iRow
                    End If
                Next iRow
            End If
        Next subShp

    Next shp

End Sub
```

# Creating Reports

**M**icrosoft Visio includes a basic report-writing tool, the *Report Definition Wizard,* which is a useful add-on for viewing the values in Shape Data and User-defined cells. It has limited formatting capabilities and an even more-limited programming interface, but it comes with the product and provides suitable output for numerous scenarios.

The wizard saves report definitions in eXtensible Markup Language (XML) format, which can be opened with external XML editing tools to create advanced filters. The reports can be displayed in several file types or in a Visio shape. This report shape itself can be enhanced to become a filter for selecting shapes. Thus, you can see a filtered list of shapes in the drawing, and you can use this list to select, format, move, or identify them.

# Report Definition Wizard

The Report Definition Wizard, started by Data | Reports, is the standard way to run or modify the Visio report definitions.

If you check the Show Only Drawing-specific Reports, then the available reports are limited to those that depend on Shape Data that exist in the active page. Or, you can browse for a custom-report definition file.

If you select the Run button, then you must choose among four different report outputs: Excel, HTML, Visio shape, and XML.

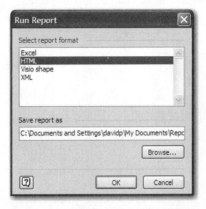

The Visio shape is, in fact, an embedded Microsoft Excel worksheet object, which you can subsequently refresh. You need to specify an output file path for the HTML and XML options. Later, in Chapter 13, you see that the HTML output can be included in the Save As Web option.

# Excel Report

The output to Microsoft Excel always creates a new workbook, which you can decide to save as a file or just discard it. The example shows the built-in PC Report with some PC shapes that are linked to data (from the previous chapter).

| | A | B | C | D | E | F | G |
|---|---|---|---|---|---|---|---|
| 1 | | | | PC Report | | | |
| 2 | *Displayed Text* | *Network Name* | *Network Description* | *Operating System* | *Memory* | *CPU* | *Hard Drive Capacity* |
| 3 | | | | | 32 | Pentium 90 | 1300 |
| 4 | | | | | 24 | Pentium 75 | 1600 |
| 5 | | | | | 16 | Pentium 75 | 1300 |
| 6 | | | | | 32 | Pentium 90 | 850 |
| 7 | | | | | 32 | Pentium 90 | 1000 |
| 8 | | | | | 32 | Pentium 90 | 810 |
| 9 | | | | | 12 | i386/25 | 120 |
| 10 | | | | | 24 | Pentium 75 | 1600 |
| 11 | | | | | 16 | Pentium 75 | 1300 |
| 12 | | | | | 32 | Pentium 90 | 850 |
| 13 | | | | | 32 | Pentium 90 | 1000 |
| 14 | | | | | 32 | Pentium 90 | 810 |
| 15 | | | | | 12 | i386/25 | 120 |
| 16 | | | | | 32 | Pentium 90 | 1300 |

All the reports appear with a similar appearance and, as you can see in the example, the built-in report probably needs to be modified to be useful.

## HTML Report

The HTML output presents the same data in a web page.

| Displayed Text | Network Name | Network Description | Operating System | Memory | CPU | Hard Drive Capacity |
|---|---|---|---|---|---|---|
| - | - | - | - | 32.000000000000000 | Pentium 90 | 1300.000000000000000 |
| - | - | - | - | 24.000000000000000 | Pentium 75 | 1600.000000000000000 |
| - | - | - | - | 16.000000000000000 | Pentium 75 | 1300.000000000000000 |
| - | - | - | - | 32.000000000000000 | Pentium 90 | 850.000000000000000 |
| - | - | - | - | 32.000000000000000 | Pentium 90 | 1000.000000000000000 |
| - | - | - | - | 32.000000000000000 | Pentium 90 | 810.000000000000000 |
| - | - | - | - | 12.000000000000000 | i386/25 | 120.000000000000000 |
| - | - | - | - | 24.000000000000000 | Pentium 75 | 1600.000000000000000 |
| - | - | - | - | 16.000000000000000 | Pentium 75 | 1300.000000000000000 |

This output demonstrates why you need to modify the format of numbers, as the default displays far too many zeros!

We look at these options shortly.

| | Memory | CPU | Hard Drive Capacity |
|---|---|---|---|
| - | 32 | Pentium 90 | 1300 |
| - | 24 | Pentium 75 | 1600 |
| - | 16 | Pentium 75 | 1300 |

## Visio Shape Report

When you run a report as a Visio shape, you need to select whether to save it with a Copy of the report definition or Link to report definition. If you decide to link to a report definition stored in the same drawing, then you need to reselect the report definition file, if it is not built-in or in a known location, whenever you select Run Report from the right mouse menu of the report shape.

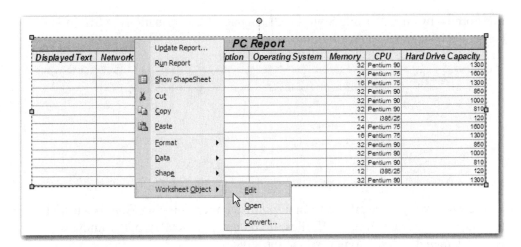

You can also select to Edit the Worksheet Object, where you can do a limited amount of formatting, which will be preserved when the report is rerun.

You cannot add anything major, such as formulae to sum column values, because they will be removed when the report is rerun.

# XML Report

The output to XML is not ready for public consumption because it presents the data, along with schema definition, in an unformatted fashion that is ready to be transformed by an Extensible Stylesheet Language Transformations (XSLT) file or consumed by another application.

```
- <xsd:schema xmlns:xsd="http://www.w3.org/2001/XMLSchema" xmlns="xsdVisioReport" targetNamespace="xsdVisioReport">
  - <xsd:annotation>
      <xsd:documentation>Visio Report Schema. Copyright 2002. All Rights reserved.</xsd:documentation>
    </xsd:annotation>
  - <xsd:complexType name="ReportProperties">
    - <xsd:sequence>
      - <xsd:element name="Title" type="xsd:string">
        - <xsd:complexType name="Font">
            <xsd:attribute name="Name" type="xsd:string" />
          - <xsd:attribute name="Size">
            - <xsd:simpleType>
                <xsd:restriction base="xsd:positiveInteger" />
              </xsd:simpleType>
```

The *XML Notepad*, available from http://msdn.microsoft.com/xml/, is a useful tool for viewing and editing XML files. If you open the XML report with XML Notepad, then it is easier to understand the structure.

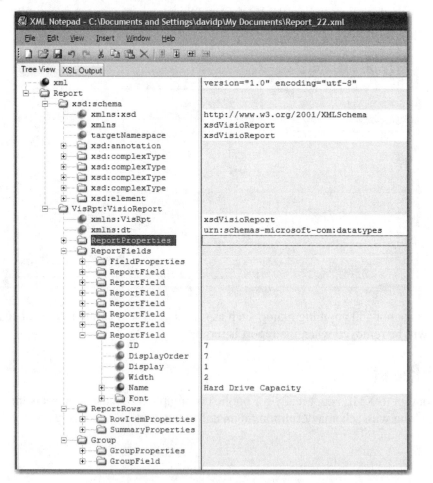

The report schema is included at the start of the file, followed by the report details.

# Creating Report Definitions with the Wizard

It is highly likely that none of the built-in report definitions will be suitable for the example where new Shape Data have been created, so, usually, you must create your own.

Start the Report Definition Wizard from a page in the Visio document that contains at least one shape with the Shape Data you need to report on, and then select New.

You need to do this, even if you choose the Shapes on All Pages option.

### Filtering the Shapes

Now, select the Advanced button to create the filter for the report.

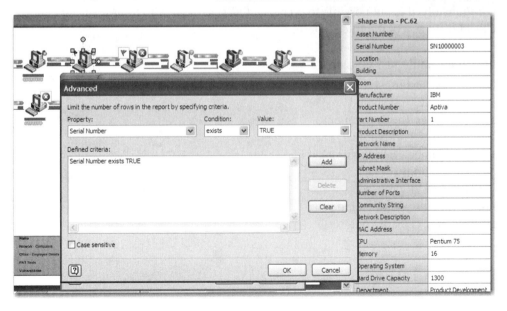

Usually best is to limit the selection to a User-defined cell or Shape Data items that exist in the shapes you are interested in. The Property pull-down list includes the following special values, in addition to the User-defined or Shape Data items.

- ▶ <Autodiscovery Shape>
- ▶ <Displayed Text>
- ▶ <Height>
- ▶ <Layer Name>
- ▶ <Master Name>
- ▶ <Shape ID>
- ▶ <Shape Name>
- ▶ <Width>
- ▶ <X Location>
- ▶ <Y Location>

The <Autodiscovery Shape> value is a relic from the past, as Microsoft retired the add-on that uses it a few years ago. Also, do not expect to find the Text callouts created by the new Data Graphics to be found in the <Displayed Text> option. And, unfortunately, it is not possible to create an OR statement with the Advanced dialog. Click OK to accept the filter criteria.

## Selecting the Report Columns

On the next screen, you need to select the columns for display.

In this case, you should select Belongs To, Department, Manufacturer, Part Number, Product Number, Serial Number, and Vulnerability.

The Show all properties option enables you to include User-defined cells in your selection.

## Setting the Report Name, Grouping, and Sorts

The next screen lets you specify the title of your report, for example, as Critical Vulnerabilities.

You can also set a value to group by, in this case, Vulnerability, and via the Options button, set the Display Options for identical rows, subtotals, and grand totals. You can also use Exclude Duplicate Rows in Group to limit the report to unique rows or totally eliminate the detail rows by setting Show Subtotals Only.

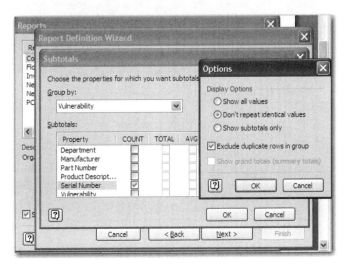

For text values, the subtotals can only be a count, but numeric or currency values can show totals, averages, maximums, minimums, and medians. Dates and times can have their minimum and maximum selected.

The Sort dialog enables you to set the sort order for columns and rows.

## Saving the Report Definition

The next screen enables you to name your report, and to add a description to help you recognize it in the future.

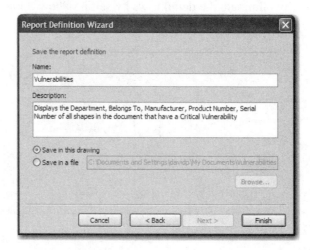

You must also decide where to save the report definition. You can save the report definition to a separate network file, in which case it will be available for use in other drawings, or by other users. If you save it to the drawing, then wherever the drawing is, it will be available.

The report definition is saved in the drawing as a value in a User-defined cell in the DocumentSheet. The DocumentSheet can be opened from the right mouse menu from drawing node (the one at the top) in the Drawing Explorer window.

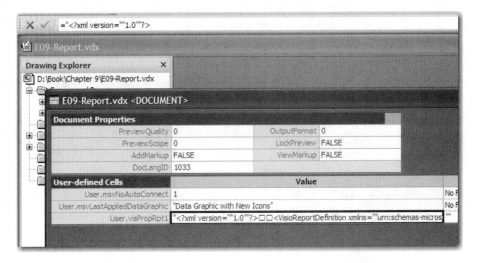

The XML definition is too large to display in the single-line display of the ShapeSheet cell editor, but you can copy the text and paste it into, say, Notepad.

Or, you could save the report definition to a file, and examine it with XML Notepad, or a similar application.

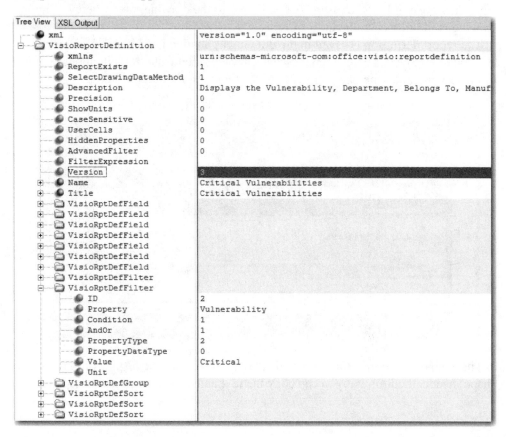

# Enhancing the Reports

The Report Definition Wizard is the standard way of creating and editing report definitions, but it is not the only way. You can use an XML editor to modify the report definition outside of Visio, so long as you keep the integrity of the file structure.

With some XML editors, you may need to change the file extension from vrd to xml to open the file. Again, I have found Microsoft's XML Notepad to be a suitable editor that does not need the file extension changed.

One note of caution: Do not change the file extension of a report definition file to XML, and then try to open it with Microsoft Internet Explorer 6. It goes into a loop that only logging off seems to close!

## Changing Displayed Column Headers

One simple thing you can do within the XML file is to change the displayed text. All you must do is locate the Display Name element and change it to whatever you want.

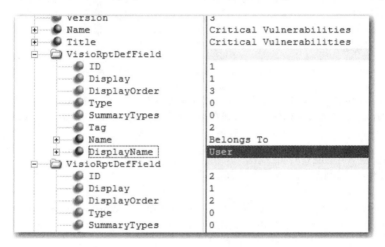

Then, on subsequent runs of the report, the column name will be different.

| Critical Vulnerabili | | | |
|---|---|---|---|
| **Department** | **User** | **Manufacturer** | **N** |
| - | Fukiko Ogisu | DELL | |
| - | Linda Leste | IBM | |
| IS | Anthony Chor | Siemens Nixdorf | |

# Creating a Variable Embedded Report

Now that you have created a report definition, you can run the report as an embedded Microsoft Excel worksheet in the drawing.

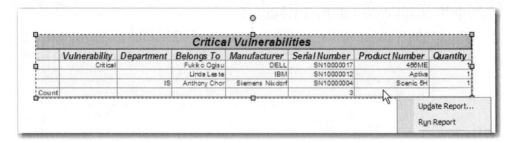

The report shape contains right mouse actions to update or run the report.

The formula in the Run Report action is the only report method that can be called from code:

```
RUNADDONWARGS("VisRpt","/rptDefName=Critical Vulnerabilities /
rptOutput=EXCEL_SHAPE /rptActionRun=")
```

If you insert a Shape Data item, called Vulnerability, which is a fixed list of the four possible values for the Vulnerability values, then you can trigger the report to run, via the new User.RptTrigger formula.

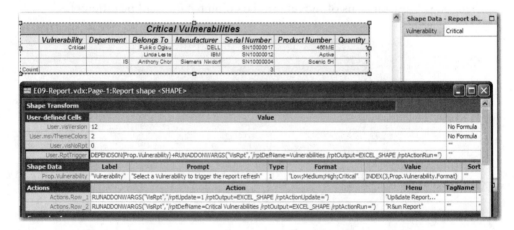

Just changing the Vulnerability value does not cause the report definition to be changed, so you need to make some adjustments in the DocumentSheet.

First, copy the contents of User.visPropRpt1 to Notepad, replace the word Critical with $NAME$, and then paste this modified formula back into User.visPropRpt1 .Prompt.

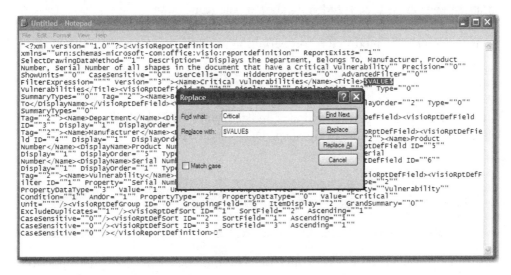

In this example, two new User-defined cells were created in the DocumentSheet. First, User.Rpt1Parameter holds the value of the selected Vulnerability from the Report shape on Page-1. Note, the formula was entered as:

```
=Pages[Page-1]!Sheet.770!Prop.Vulnerability
```

But, Visio automatically translated it to:

```
=Pages[Page-1]!Report shape.770!Prop.Vulnerability
```

This is because the shape name ID can be entered manually into formulae, but shape names cannot.

The cell User.Rpt1Parameter.Prompt holds the modified report definition with the $VALUE$ text substituted with the value of the Prop.Vulnerability on the Report shape. Note, this substitution is done on the Title and Filter, not on the Name, because the Name is used for identification by the Run action.

Finally, the User.Rpt1Trigger formula is fired whenever the Vulnerability value is changed and puts the modified report definition back into the User.visPropRpt1.

```
=DEPENDSON(Pages[Page-1]!Report shape.770!Prop.Vulnerability)+SETF(GetRef(User
.visPropRpt1),User.Rpt1Parameter.Prompt)
```

Consequently, the report definition is updated, and the report shape is refreshed whenever you select a value in the Shape Data window of the Report shape.

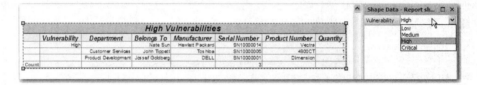

So, now you can choose which value to report on. You cannot copy this report to other pages without creating some extra formulae, as the report definition is linked to this particular shape.

To overcome this limitation, you can create the original shape with a copy of the report definition. Therefore, you can make all the ShapeSheet edits within the report shape itself and, thus, you can make a Master from the shape, so it can be reused, not only in this drawing file, but also in others! Indeed, you could take the trouble to edit the embedded worksheet a little, to highlight the different filters.

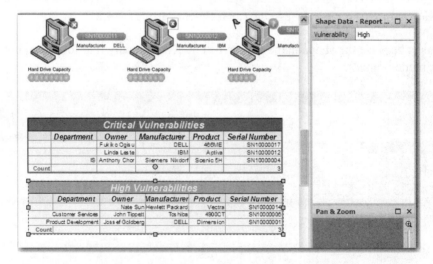

When a report definition is copied into the shape, it is stored in the User
.visPropRpt cell. So, the other cells need to refer to this cell value, and the User
.visPropRpt.Prompt contains the XML report definition with the $VALUE$ text
awaiting substitution by the value in Prop.Vulnerability.

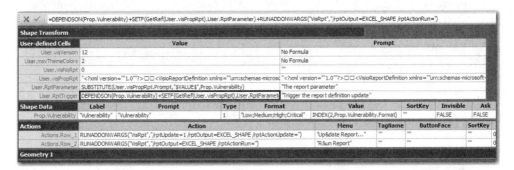

This time, there is no need to get the Prop.Vulnerability across pages, as it is
in the same shape, and the trigger can be run directly in the User.RptTrigger cell
formula:

```
=DEPENDSON(Prop.Vulnerability)+SETF(GetRef(User.visPropRpt),User.RptParameter)+R
UNADDONWARGS("VisRpt","/rptOutput=EXCEL_SHAPE /rptActionRun=")
```

### NOTE

*The name of the definition does not have to be passed to the visRpt add-on as it is within the shape.*

One caveat: in both these examples, you need to edit the report definition files if
you decide to use the Update Report action.

## Using the Advanced Filters

Strangely, Microsoft removed a button from the Report Definition Wizard in
Microsoft Visio 2003, and has not bothered replacing it. This button enabled you to
create advanced filters in XML, instead of the rather limited filters that are currently
available. Take, for example, the Shape Data values for Vulnerability in the sample
you were using earlier. There are just four values for this, Low, Medium, High, and
Critical. Earlier, you saw how you can create reports for one of these values, and how
you can create a variable-embedded report where you can choose one of these values.

However, you may want to create a report that includes both Critical and High Vulnerabilities only.

Unfortunately, the wizard will not let you do this because you can only enter AND statements—there are no OR statements.

Fortunately, you can edit the Visio report definition directly, either with Notepad or an XML editor, such as XML Notepad.

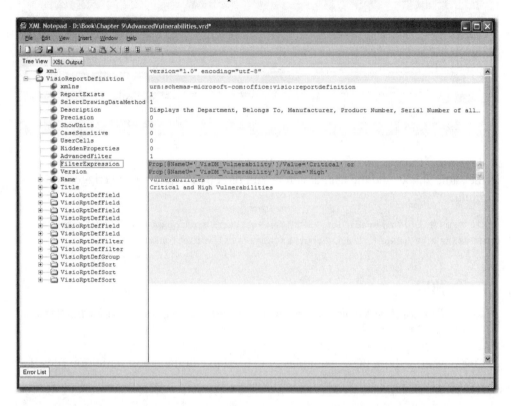

In this example, the AdvancedFilter attribute value has been changed from 0 to 1. This has the effect of telling the report-rendering engine to ignore the normal filters described in the VisioRptDefFilter elements.

Instead, you can enter an XPath expression into the FilterExpression attribute. In this case, if you enter the following, then you only display shapes that have the Prop._VisDM_Vulnerability cell with the value of Critical or High.

```
Prop[@NameU='_VisDM_Vulnerability']/Value='Critical' or Prop[@NameU='_VisDM_
Vulnerability']/Value='High'
```

The important thing to remember is that you are already at the following element before you start your XPath expression.

```
VisioDocument/Pages/Page/Shapes/Shape/
```

This opens you up to the world of XML, XSL, and XPath, which is a language for addressing parts of an XML document. Theoretically, you could use the same expression to extract shapes from the XML format of the Visio document (vdx extension). Practically, the vdx files are seven to ten times larger than the binary version, and XSL transformations of the whole document are slow, if they complete at all.

When you run the report, you will be able to see both the Critical and High Vulnerabilites.

| - | Vulnerability | Department | User | Manufacturer | Part Number | Product Description | Serial Number |
|---|---|---|---|---|---|---|---|
| - | Critical | - | Fukiko Ogisu | DELL | 1 | - | SN10000017 |
| - | - | - | Linda Leste | IBM | 1 | - | SN10000012 |
| - | - | IS | Anthony Chor | Siemens Nixdorf | 1 | - | SN10000004 |
| Count | - | - | - | - | - | - | 3 |
| - | High | - | Nate Sun | Hewlett Packard | 1 | - | SN10000014 |
| - | - | Customer Services | John Tippett | Toshiba | 2 | - | SN10000006 |
| - | - | Product Development | Jossef Goldberg | DELL | 1 | - | SN10000001 |
| Count | - | - | - | - | - | - | 3 |

This statement works because it was based on the NameU of the Shape Data item, but it could also have worked with:

```
Prop[Label='Vulnerability' and Value='Critical'] or Prop[Label='Vulnera
bility' and Value='High']
```

This filter would also select the new embedded report shape with the variable filter, because it also has a Shape Data item labeled Vulnerability. Therefore, it is better to extend the filter to include some other Shape Data item, too, one that does not exist in the report shape. The Shape Data item Serial Number is suitable for that purpose:

```
Prop[Label='Serial Number'] and (Prop[Label='Vulnerability' and
Value='Critical'] or Prop[Label='Vulnerability' and Value='High'])
```

This is perhaps easier to understand, as it is closer to the standard (nonadvanced) definition held in the report definition.

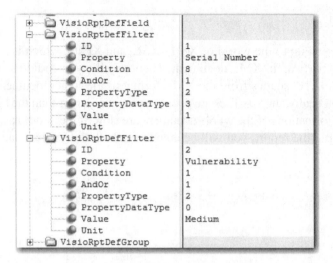

```
⊞ ⬚ VisioRptDefField
⊟ ⬚ VisioRptDefFilter
        ⦿ ID                    1
        ⦿ Property              Serial Number
        ⦿ Condition             8
        ⦿ AndOr                 1
        ⦿ PropertyType          2
        ⦿ PropertyDataType      3
        ⦿ Value                 1
        ⦿ Unit
⊟ ⬚ VisioRptDefFilter
        ⦿ ID                    2
        ⦿ Property              Vulnerability
        ⦿ Condition             1
        ⦿ AndOr                 1
        ⦿ PropertyType          2
        ⦿ PropertyDataType      0
        ⦿ Value                 Medium
        ⦿ Unit
⊞ ⬚ VisioRptDefGroup
```

The other interesting feature of using the advanced filter is that you are not restricted to the User-defined cells, Shape Data items, and the few special conditions mentioned earlier, such as layer and location. You could filter by any of the ShapeSheet cells—in fact, you are only limited by your knowledge of XPath.

Table 9-1 lists the XPath operands for text and numeric property data types (which have a value of 0 and 2 in the report definition).

| Standard Filter Value | Advanced Filter XPath operand | Valid for PropertyDataType | Description |
|---|---|---|---|
| 1 | = | 0,2 | Equals |
| 2 | != | 0,2 | Does not equal |
| 4 | < | 2 | Is less than |
| 6 | <= | 2 | Is less than or equal to |
| 3 | > | 2 | Is greater than |
| 5 | >= | 2 | Is greater than or equal to |
| 8 | (just reference it) | | Exists (Value = 1 or 0 for True or False) |

**Table 9-1** *Standard and Advanced Report Filters Operands*

Pattern matching on strings is a bit limited in XPath, but the following syntax lists all shapes where the Serial Number begins with "S".

```
Prop[Label='Serial Number' and Value > 'S' and Value < 'T']
```

# Adding SelectReportShapes to Embedded Reports

For analysis purposes, it could be useful to be able to select a report shape, and then be able to select the shapes listed in it.

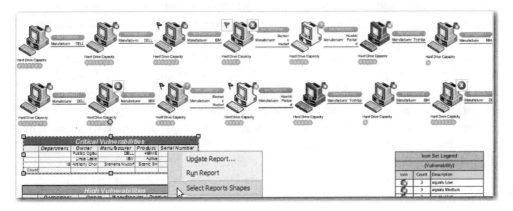

Once you select the items, you could perform a variety of actions, such as move them, format them, reapply Data Graphics, or simply see where they are.

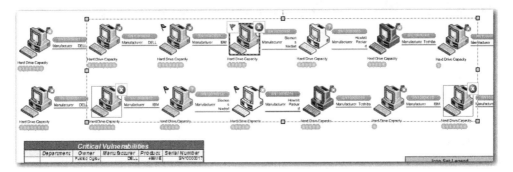

Therefore, I included the following subfunction SelectReportShapes. In this function, I handled nothing but text and numeric property data types, and I have not handled anything but Shape Data in the filter expressions. You could expand the functions to include these for production purposes, if your users require more than that.

The function can be called from a right mouse action in the report shape, with the addition of a new row.

| Actions | Action | Menu | TagName | | Button |
|---|---|---|---|---|---|
| Actions.Row_1 | RUNADDONWARGS("VisRpt","/rptUpdate=1 /rp | "Up&date Report..." | "" | "" | |
| Actions.Row_2 | RUNADDONWARGS("VisRpt","/rptOutput=EXCE | "R&un Report" | "" | "" | |
| Actions.Row_3 | RUNADDON("SelectReportShapes") | "_Select Reports Shapes" | "" | "" | |
| **Geometry 1** | | | | | |

The approach I took in the following code is to recognize that a report definition could be found in either the report shape's ShapeSheet itself, or in the document's DocumentSheet (I am not handling report definitions outside the Visio document, but you could). Then, this report definition is loaded as an XML document (therefore, the code requires a reference to Microsoft XML, v6.0, or similar). The report filters are extracted and, as they could be in either standard or advanced format, the standard ones are converted into a valid XPath statement, just like the advanced ones, and an XSL document is created in memory.

The shapes in the current page (with Shape Data) are put into an XML document in memory. Then, these are transformed with the XSL document to create an XML file in memory that contains the NameUs of all the matching shapes.

Finally, this list of shape NameUs is looped through to create a selection in the current page.

The result is you have an extremely flexible method for creating selection filters, which can be used in any Visio drawing that uses Shape Data.

## Code Listing for SelectReportShapes and Support Functions

```
Public Sub SelectReportShapes()
Dim shp As Visio.Shape
Dim rptDef As String
Dim dom As MSXML2.DOMDocument
Dim useAdvancedFilter As Boolean
Dim rptFilter As String

    If Visio.ActiveWindow.Selection.Count = 0 Then
        MsgBox "Please select a report shape first", vbInformation
        Exit Sub
    Else
        Set shp = Visio.ActiveWindow.Selection.PrimaryItem
    End If

    If shp.CellExists("User.visPropRpt", Visio.visExistsAnywhere) <> 0
Then
```

```
        'The report is stored in the shape
        rptDef = shp.Cells("User.visPropRpt").ResultStr("")
        Set dom = New MSXML2.DOMDocument
        If dom.LoadXML(rptDef) = False Then
            MsgBox "Unable to read the XML report definition",
vbExclamation
            Exit Sub
        End If
    ElseIf shp.CellExists("User.visNoRpt", Visio.visExistsAnywhere) <>
0 Then
        'The report is stored in the document
        Set dom = getRptDOM(shp)
        If dom Is Nothing Then
            MsgBox "Unable to find the report definition",
vbInformation
            Exit Sub
        End If
    Else
        MsgBox "Please select a report shape first", vbInformation
        Exit Sub
    End If

    useAdvancedFilter = CBool(dom.SelectSingleNode( _
        "/VisioReportDefinition/@AdvancedFilter").Text)
    If useAdvancedFilter = True Then
        rptFilter = dom.SelectSingleNode( _
            "/VisioReportDefinition/FilterExpression").Text
    Else
        rptFilter = getRptFilterFromNode( _
            dom.SelectNodes("/VisioReportDefinition/
VisioRptDefFilter"))
    End If

Dim xmlDOM As New MSXML2.DOMDocument
    'Load the shapes with properties into the Data DOM object
    If xmlDOM.LoadXML(getXMLText(shp.ContainingPage)) = False Then
        MsgBox "Invalid XML data file created", vbCritical
        Exit Sub
    End If

Dim xslDOM As New MSXML2.DOMDocument
    'Load the XML into the StyleSheet DOM Object
    If xslDOM.LoadXML(getXSLText(rptFilter)) = False Then
```

```
        MsgBox "Invalid Stylesheet created", vbCritical
        Exit Sub
    End If


    'Finally, transform and select the filtered shapes
    transformSelect xmlDOM, xslDOM, shp.ContainingPage

End Sub

Private Function getRptDOM(ByVal shp As Visio.Shape) As MSXML2
.DOMDocument
Dim iRow As Integer
Dim rptAction As String
Dim rptName As String
Dim iPos As Integer
Dim rptDef As String
Dim dom As MSXML2.DOMDocument

    For iRow = 0 To shp.RowCount(Visio.visSectionAction) - 1
        rptAction = shp.CellsSRC(Visio.visSectionAction, iRow, Visio
.visActionAction).Formula
        iPos = InStr(rptAction, "/rptDefName")
        If iPos > 0 Then
            rptName = Split(Mid(rptAction, iPos + 12), " ")(0)
            Exit For
        End If
    Next iRow


    If Len(rptName) > 0 Then
        For iRow = 0 To shp.Document.DocumentSheet.RowCount(Visio
.visSectionUser) - 1
            If Left(shp.Document.DocumentSheet.CellsSRC( _
                    Visio.visSectionUser, iRow, 0).RowName, 10) =
"visPropRpt" Then
                    rptDef = shp.Document.DocumentSheet.CellsSRC( _
                        Visio.visSectionUser, iRow, Visio.
visUserValue).ResultStr("")
                    Set dom = New MSXML2.DOMDocument
                    If dom.LoadXML(rptDef) = True Then
                        If dom.SelectSingleNode( _
                            "/VisioReportDefinition/Name").Text =
rptName Then
```

```
                                    'Found it
                                    Exit For
                          Else
                                    Set dom = Nothing
                          End If
                    End If
              End If
        Next iRow
    End If

    Set getRptDOM = dom

End Function

Private Function getRptFilterFromNode(ByVal fNodes As MSXML2
.IXMLDOMNodeList) As String
Dim rptFilter As String
Dim iRow As Integer
Dim fID As Integer
Dim fProperty As String
Dim fCondition As Integer
Dim fAndOr As Integer
Dim fPropertyType As Integer
Dim fPropertyDataType As Integer
Dim fValue As String
Dim fUnit As String
Dim fFilter As String

    'Create an XPath expression
    For iRow = 0 To fNodes.Length - 1
        fFilter = ""
        fID = CInt(fNodes.Item(iRow).Attributes(0).Text)
        fProperty = fNodes.Item(iRow).Attributes(1).Text
        fCondition = CInt(fNodes.Item(iRow).Attributes(2).Text)
        fAndOr = CInt(fNodes.Item(iRow).Attributes(3).Text)
        fPropertyType = CInt(fNodes.Item(iRow).Attributes(4).Text)
        fPropertyDataType = CInt(fNodes.Item(iRow).Attributes(5).Text)
        fValue = fNodes.Item(iRow).Attributes(6).Text
        fUnit = fNodes.Item(iRow).Attributes(7).Text

        fFilter = "Prop[Label='" & fProperty & "'"
```

```
        Select Case fCondition

            Case 1
                fFilter = fFilter & " and Value = "
            Case 2
                fFilter = fFilter & " and Value != "
            Case 3
                fFilter = fFilter & " and Value > "
            Case 4
                fFilter = fFilter & " and Value < "
            Case 5
                fFilter = fFilter & " and Value >= "
            Case 6
                fFilter = fFilter & " and Value <= "

            Case 8
                fFilter = fFilter & ""

        End Select

        If Not fCondition = 8 Then
            Select Case fPropertyDataType
                Case 0, 1, 4
                    fFilter = fFilter & "'" & fValue & "'"
                Case 2, 7
                    fFilter = fFilter & fValue
                Case Else

            End Select
        End If
        'Close this statement
        fFilter = fFilter & "]"

        If Len(rptFilter) = 0 Then
            rptFilter = fFilter
        Else
            rptFilter = rptFilter & " and " & fFilter
        End If
    Next iRow

    getRptFilterFromNode = rptFilter
End Function
```

```vb
Private Function getXMLText(ByVal pag As Visio.Page) As String
Dim s As String
Dim shpSel As Visio.Shape
Dim iRow As Integer

    s = "<?xml version=""1.0"" encoding=""utf-8""?>" & vbCrLf
    s = s & "<Shapes>" & vbCrLf
    'Loop thru all the shapes in the page
    For Each shpSel In pag.Shapes
        'Check that there is Shape Data
        If shpSel.RowCount(Visio.visSectionProp) > 0 Then
            s = s & "<Shape ID=""" & shpSel.ID & _
                """ Name=""" & shpSel.Name & _
                """ NameU=""" & shpSel.NameU & """>" & vbCrLf
                'Loop thru the SHape Dat rows
                For iRow = 0 To shpSel.RowCount(Visio.visSectionProp) - 1
                    s = s & _
                        "<Prop ID=""" & iRow & """ Name=""" & _
                        shpSel.CellsSRC(Visio.visSectionProp, iRow, _
                            Visio.visCustPropsValue).RowName & _
                        """ NameU=""" & _
                        shpSel.CellsSRC(Visio.visSectionProp, iRow, _
                            Visio.visCustPropsValue).RowNameU & _
                        """>" & vbCrLf
                    s = s & _
                        "<Value>" & _
                        shpSel.CellsSRC(Visio.visSectionProp, iRow, _
                            Visio.visCustPropsValue).ResultStr("") & _
                        "</Value>" & vbCrLf
                    s = s & "<Label>" & _
                        shpSel.CellsSRC(Visio.visSectionProp, iRow, _
                            Visio.visCustPropsLabel).ResultStr("") & _
                        "</Label>" & vbCrLf
                    s = s & _
                        "</Prop>" & vbCrLf
                Next iRow
            s = s & "</Shape>" & vbCrLf
        End If
    Next shpSel

    s = s & "</Shapes>"
```

```vb
    getXMLText = s

End Function

Private Function getXSLText(ByVal rptFilter As String) As String
Dim s As String

    s = "<?xml version=""1.0"" encoding=""utf-8""?>"
    s = s & "<xsl:stylesheet"
    s = s & " xmlns:xsl=""http://www.w3.org/1999/XSL/Transform"""
    s = s & „ version = ""1.0"">"
    s = s & "<xsl:template match=""/"">"
    s = s & "<Shapes>"
    'Filter the shapes
    s = s & "<xsl:for-each select=""Shapes/Shape[" & rptFilter & "]"">"
    s = s & "<Shape>"
    'Return the NameU of each matching shape
    s = s & "<xsl:value-of select=""@NameU""/>"
    s = s & "</Shape>"
    s = s & "</xsl:for-each>"
    s = s & "</Shapes>"
    s = s & "</xsl:template>"
    s = s & "</xsl:stylesheet>"

    getXSLText = s
End Function

Private Sub transformSelect(ByVal xmlDOM As MSXML2.DOMDocument, _
    ByVal xslDOM As MSXML2.DOMDocument, _
    ByVal pag As Visio.Page)
Dim outDom As New MSXML2.DOMDocument

    outDom.validateOnParse = True
    outDom.async = False
    'Transform the data to create the output DOM
    xmlDOM.transformNodeToObject xslDOM, outDom

    Dim nodList As MSXML2.IXMLDOMNodeList
    Dim iShape As Integer
    'Select all of the shape nodes
    Set nodList = outDom.SelectNodes("/Shapes/Shape")

    On Error Resume Next    'Just incase the shape is not on this page
```

```
Visio.ActiveWindow.DeselectAll
For iShape = 0 To nodList.Length
    Visio.ActiveWindow.Select _
        pag.Shapes(nodList.Item(iShape).Text), _
            Visio.visSelect
Next iShape


End Sub
```

# The Built-In Reports

There are 23 built-in reports, which can be found (usually) in C:\Program Files\ Microsoft Office\OFFICE12\1033 or similar, depending on the installation language. These reports are XML documents, but they have the file extension vrd for Visio Report Definition. Their appearance in the Report Definition Wizard depends on the filter in the definition. They are listed in Table 9-2, so you can decide if any one of them is suitable for copying and customizing, rather than starting fresh.

| File Name | Name | Description | Filter |
|---|---|---|---|
| ASSET.VRD | Asset Report | Space Plan: Belongs to, Asset Type, Name, Manufacturer | SolSH ={5D50005D-537C-4738-9C46-130C74335A6D} AND ShapeClass Exists |
| CALEVENT.VRD | Calendar Event | Calendar Event report: Start date, Start time, End date, End time, Subject, Location, Label | Solsh={FB4EACD-BEFB-4ECD-A226-1282E88A7BE7} AND Subject=1 |
| DOORSCHD.VRD | Door Schedule | Building Plan: Door Number, Size, Type, Thickness | SolSH={5D50005D-537C-4738-9C46-130C74335A6D} AND ShapeType=10 |
| EQPLIST.VRD | Equipment List | Process Engineering equipment components: Tag, Description, Material, Manufacturer, Model | SOLSH=D7D7DB7E-3668-43e5-AF97-97F58AB229A5} AND ShapeClass=Equipment |
| FLOCH.VRD | Flowchart | Flowchart report: Displayed Text, Resources, Cost, Duration -grouped by Master Name | Cost Exists |

**Table 9-2** *The Built-In Report Definitions*

| File Name | Name | Description | Filter |
|-----------|------|-------------|--------|
| GANTT.VRD | Gantt Chart | Gantt Chart report: Name, Start Date, End Date, Duration, User-defined Number, Percent Complete — grouped by Resource | End Date Exists AND Solsh Exists |
| HVACDIFF.VRD | HVAC Diffuser | HVAC: Diffuser shape, Diffuser width, Diffuser depth, Flow rate, Neck diameter, Air flow type | SolSH={5D50005D-537C-4738-9C46-130C74335A6D} AND SubShapeType=3 |
| HVACDUCT.VRD | HVAC Duct | HVAC: Master name, Duct length, Duct width | SolSH={5D50005D-537C-4738-9C46-130C74335A6D} AND ShapeType=19 |
| INSTLIST.VRD | Instrument List | Process Engineering instrumentation components: Tag, Description, Connection Size, Service, Manufacturer, Model | SOLSH={D7D7DB7E-3668-43e5-AF97-97F58AB229A5} AND ShapeClass=Instrument |
| INVENTRY.VRD | Inventory | Number of shapes on page, grouped by shape name. | MASTERINFO Exists |
| MOVE.VRD | Move | Space Plan: List where people are located | SolSh={5D50005D-537C-4738-9C46-130C74335A6D} AND ShapeClass=6 |
| NETWORK1.VRD | Network Device | Networked device list: Shape text, Net Name, IP Address, Sub Net Mask, Mac address, Net description | SolSH={BF0433D9-CD73-4EB5-8390-8653BE590246} |
| NETWORK2.VRD | PC Report | Network PC Report: Shape text, Network name, Network description, Operating system, Memory, CPU, Hard drive capacity | SolSH={BF0433D9-CD73-4EB5-8390-8653BE590246} AND ShapeType=6 |
| NETWORK3.VRD | Network Equipment | Network Equipment report: Building, Room, Shape text, Network name, Network description, IP address, Manufacturer, Product description, Product number, Part number, Serial number, Asset Number | SolSH={BF0433D9-CD73-4EB5-8390-8653BE590246} AND ShapeClass=5 |
| ORGCH.VRD | Organization Chart Report | Name, Title, Number of direct reports, Telephone — grouped by Department | Number of direct reports Exists |

**Table 9-2**  *The Built-In Report Definitions* (continued)

| File Name | Name | Description | Filter |
|-----------|------|-------------|--------|
| ORGPOS.VRD | Count Positions | Organization Chart: Count similar Titles | Title Exists<br>AND<br>SolSH Exists |
| PIPELINE.VRD | Pipeline List | Process Engineering pipeline components: Tag, Description, Line Size, Schedule, Design Pressure, Design Temperature | SOLSH={D7D7DB7E-3668-43e5-AF97-97F58AB229A5}<br>AND<br>ShapeClass=Pipelines |
| SPACE.VRD | Space Report | Space Plan: Department, Room Number, Use, Area | SolSH={5D50005D-537C-4738-9C46-130C74335A6D}<br>AND<br>ShapeType=38 |
| VALVE.VRD | Valve List | Process Engineering valve components: Tag, Description, Line Size, Valve Class, Manufacturer, Model | SOLSH={D7D7DB7E-3668-43e5-AF97-97F58AB229A5}<br>AND<br>ShapeClass=Valve |
| WDALLLNK.VRD | Web Site Map All Links | Web Diagram Report: List all links discovered | Links Exists |
| WDERRLNK.VRD | Web Site Map Links with Errors | Web Diagram Report: List all discovered links that contain errors | Error <> none |
| WINSCHD.VRD | Window Schedule | Building Plan: Window Number, Size, Type | SolSH={5D50005D-537C-4738-9C46-130C74335A6D}<br>AND<br>ShapeType=45 |

**Table 9-2**   *The Built-In Report Definitions* (continued)

# Themes, Backgrounds, Borders, and Titles

I feel these elements go together naturally because you often want to create a corporate standard for your diagrams, and the background, borders, title blocks, and themes go a long way toward establishing this.

Microsoft Visio 2007 introduced Themes to replace Color Schemes, which meant a whole lot of work for the development team because they had to go through all the Masters in the standard stencils to make them work with the new method.

In addition, Themes do some of the same stuff as Styles, but without some of the refinement. For example, *Styles* can be applied to individual shapes, but Themes are for a page or document.

# Themes

*Themes* provide you with the capability to change not only colors, but also some effects. such as line roundings and line patterns. The normal user's interface has a Theme button to open or close the Themes panel, or select Format | Theme.

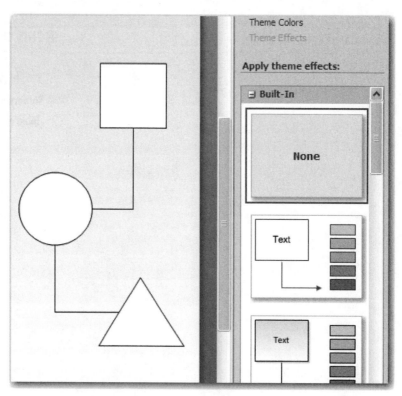

The Themes panel provides you with the capability to apply a theme, change a theme, or remove a theme. You can even create a new theme, but you should start with an existing theme that is close to what you want before duplicating and editing (see the section "Custom Color Themes").

The Microsoft article at http://msdn2.microsoft.com/en-us/library/aa445858.aspx, entitled "Designing Shapes for Use with Themes in Visio 2007," gives you more information about the intricacies of designing shapes for themes, but here is some essential information.

## Built-In Color Themes

There are 35 built-in color themes, with names like Solstice, Technic, and Paper, which are more at home in paint color-matching swatches. These themes are the same as those used in other Microsoft Office 2007 applications (Word, Excel, PowerPoint, and Outlook).

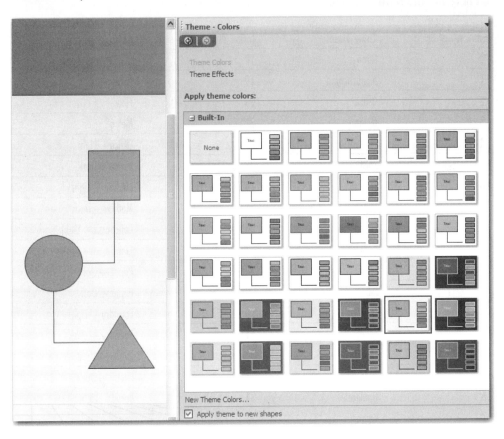

The following code lists all color themes in the active document.

```
Public Sub DisplayColorThemes()
Dim aryNames() As String
Dim i As Integer
    Visio.ActiveDocument.GetThemeNames visThemeTypeColor, aryNames
    For i = 0 To UBound(aryNames)
        Debug.Print i & "," & aryNames(i)
    Next i
End Sub
```

There is a GetThemeNamesU method, too, but no difference exists in the English interface names unless you create a custom theme. This method uses the Universal names, which remains constant across language versions, but the non-Universal name can be different.

In Table 10-1, anything listed above index number 35 is a custom colors theme, but here are the built-in ones:

| Index Number | Color Theme | Index Number | Color Theme |
|---|---|---|---|
| 0 | None | 18 | Origin |
| 1 | Monochrome | 19 | Urban |
| 2 | Office | 20 | Flow |
| 3 | Median | 21 | Metro |
| 4 | Concourse | 22 | Office — Light |
| 5 | Solstice | 23 | Office — Dark |
| 6 | Technic | 24 | Median — Light |
| 7 | Paper | 25 | Median — Dark |
| 8 | Foundry | 26 | Concourse — Light |
| 9 | Apex | 27 | Concourse — Dark |
| 10 | Trek | 28 | Paper — Light |
| 11 | Module | 29 | Paper — Dark |
| 12 | Oriel | 30 | Foundry — Light |
| 13 | Aspect | 31 | Foundry — Dark |
| 14 | Equity | 32 | Equity — Light |
| 15 | Civic | 33 | Equity — Dark |
| 16 | Opulent | 34 | Verve — Light |
| 17 | Verve | 35 | Verve — Dark |

**Table 10-1** *Built-In Colors Themes*

# Built-In Effect Themes

There are fifteen built-in effect themes that can be applied to shapes on one page or all pages in a document. You should understand what each of the built-in themes do to a shape's appearance before embarking on a custom theme.

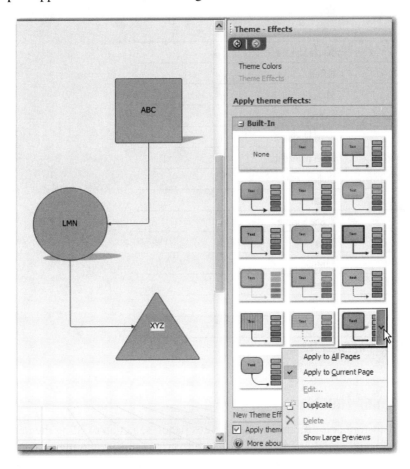

The following code lists all the effect themes in the active document.

```
Public Sub DisplayEffectThemes()
Dim aryNames() As String
Dim i As Integer
    Visio.ActiveDocument.GetThemeNames visThemeTypeEffect, aryNames
    For i = 0 To UBound(aryNames)
        Debug.Print i & "," & aryNames(i)
    Next i
End Sub
```

Anything listed above index number 15 is a custom effect theme, but Table 10-2 lists the built-in effect themes.

| Index Number | Effect Theme |
|---|---|
| 0 | None |
| 1 | Subdued |
| 2 | Simple Shadow |
| 3 | Button |
| 4 | Square |
| 5 | Pillow |
| 6 | Bevel Illusion |
| 7 | Bevel Highlight |
| 8 | Outline |
| 9 | Decal |
| 10 | Raised Surface |
| 11 | Mesh |
| 12 | Pinstripe |
| 13 | Stripes |
| 14 | Oblique |
| 15 | Toy |

**Table 10-2**  *Built-In Effect Themes*

## Custom Color Themes

To create a custom color theme, in the Themes panel, select an existing theme closest to what you want, and then choose Duplicate from the pull-down menu. Or, you can choose New Theme Colors from the bottom of the Themes panel, which creates a new theme based on the one applied to the current page.

You can rename your Color Theme, but the NameU will have been created from the theme name on which the custom theme is based, unless you change it in code.

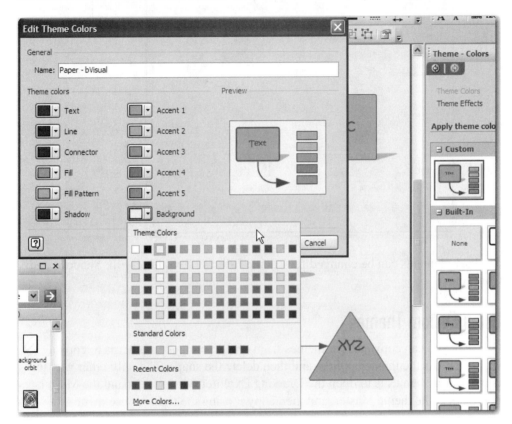

The colors presented as Theme Colors are those Microsoft suggests go together well. However, if you are confident of your graphical design skills, you can choose any color you like.

## Custom Effect Themes

Similarly, you can create custom Effect Themes.

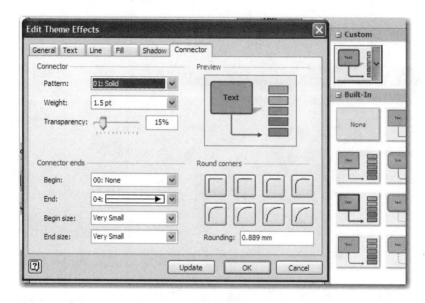

Many elements can be changed for Theme Effects (Text, Line, Fill, Shadow, and Connector).

## Using Custom Themes

One way you can copy custom themes from one drawing to another is to copy a shape that has the theme applied, and then delete the shape. The only other way to copy custom themes is to open the Drawing Explorer window, expand the Masters node, select the theme Master, and then copy it using the right mouse menu.

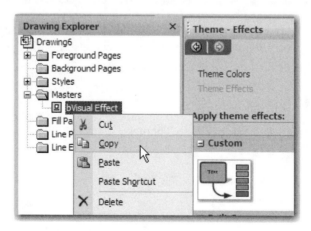

You can then go to the drawing that requires the theme, and paste it into the Masters collection in the Drawing Explorer.

# Displaying the Current Themes

The Themes panel will automatically highlight the theme currently applied to the active page, but it can be useful to extract this in code. The subfunction DisplayPageThemes uses the two new page properties—ThemeColors and ThemeEffects—which return the NameU for each theme type. So, the support subfunction getThemeIDName gets the ID number and the displayed Name of the supplied NameU.

The function displays the themes in a modal dialog, but you can adjust the code for your own purposes.

## Code Listing for DisplayPageThemes and Support Function

```
Public Sub DisplayPageThemes()
Dim txt As String
Dim nameUColor As String
Dim nameColor As String
Dim IDColor As Integer
Dim nameUEffect As String
Dim nameEffect As String
Dim idEffect As Integer

    nameUColor = Visio.ActivePage.ThemeColors
    getThemeIDName visThemeTypeColor, nameUColor, IDColor, nameColor

    nameUEffect = Visio.ActivePage.ThemeEffects
    getThemeIDName visThemeTypeEffect, nameUEffect, IDEffect, nameEffect

    txt = "Colors : " & vbTab & IDColor & vbTab & _
            nameColor & vbTab & "(" & nameUColor & ")" & vbCrLf & _
        "Effects : " & vbTab & IDEffect & vbTab & _
            nameEffect & vbTab & "(" & nameUEffect & ")"

    MsgBox txt, vbInformation, Visio.ActivePage.name & " Themes"
End Sub
```

```
Private Sub getThemeIDName(ByVal themeType As Visio.VisThemeTypes, _
    ByVal nameU As String, _
    ByRef ID As Integer, _
    ByRef name As String)

Dim aryNames() As String
Dim aryNamesU() As String
Dim i As Integer

    Visio.ActiveDocument.GetThemeNames themeType, aryNames
    Visio.ActiveDocument.GetThemeNamesU themeType, aryNamesU

    For i = 0 To UBound(aryNamesU)
        If UCase(aryNamesU(i)) = UCase(nameU) Then
            name = aryNames(i)
            ID = i
            Exit For
        End If
    Next i

End Sub
```

## Applying Themes in Code

Applying a theme in code is quite simple, as the page properties, ThemeColors and ThemeEffects, take a number or text as a value. You can set the value to the ID number or the Visio constant for built-in themes, but you cannot do this for custom themes. Instead, you can use the Name or NameU, thus, all the following lines are valid.

```
Visio.ActivePage.ThemeColors = 13
Visio.ActivePage.ThemeColors = Visio.VisThemeColors
.visThemeColorsAspect
Visio.ActivePage.ThemeColors = "Aspect"
Visio.ActivePage.ThemeEffects = "bVisual Effect"
Visio.ActivePage.ThemeEffects = "Oblique.1"
```

The last two refer to the same custom theme, in my case, because one is the Name and the other is the NameU.

The following line, however, is not valid, because 36 is beyond the range of the built-in numbers.

```
Visio.ActivePage.ThemeColors = 36
```

# Backgrounds

Backgrounds are shapes that fill the whole page, and are normally on a background page, which is the same size as the foreground page. As backgrounds are behind all the other shapes in your drawing, they should be recessive, so they do not compete too much for attention.

One criticism I have about the built-in background Masters is they are opaque. This means you cannot see the grid at all, so you may want to create a custom background master or amend one of the built-in ones.

Another issue with background pages is this: if you have pages with different sizes, scales, and orientations you may need more than one in a Visio document.

## Built-In Backgrounds

Eighteen background shapes (and one that removes the background shapes) are in the Backgrounds stencil, available from the Visio Extras category.

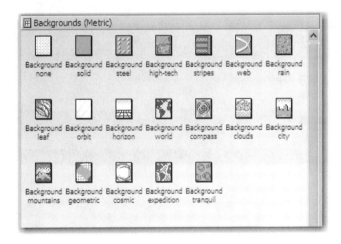

When you drag-and-drop a background Master from a stencil on to a page, it fires an add-on that does one of two actions:

If no background page exists, then it creates one, with the name VBackground-n (where *n* is a sequential number). This background page will be the same size and scale as the foreground page. Then the background shape is moved from the foreground page to the background page.

If there already a background page, any existing background shape on it will be deleted. Then, the background shape is moved from the foreground page to the background page.

This action is triggered by the following formula of the EventDrop cell of the background Master:

```
=RUNADDON("Make Background")+SETF("EventDrop",0)
```

This formula runs the add-on Make Background, and then removes the formula from the EventDrop cell, so it does not accidentally fire a second time.

An examination of a background Master reveals they are not images (as some people thought), but are instead grouped shapes.

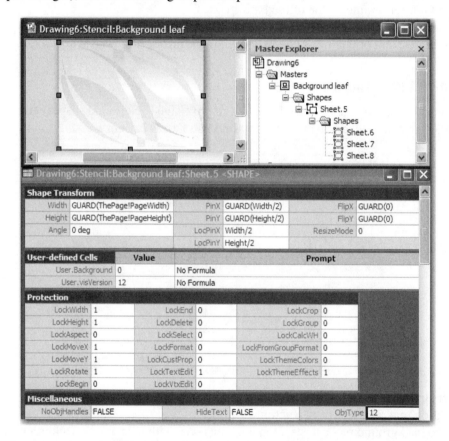

The group shape itself has formulae in the Shape Transform section cells that ensure the shape is the same size as the page and centered on it. The User-defined section contains a cell named Background, so the Make Background add-on can recognize it.

An inspection of the Line Format and Fill Format sections of the subshapes shows the colors are set with respect to the BackgroundColor theme or, if themes are not being used, to a specific shade of grey.

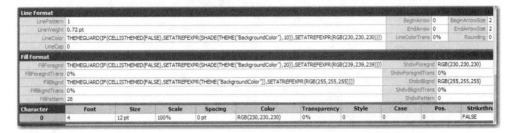

In this particular background Master, there are three subshapes, whose FillPattern cell formulae are 28, 29, and 30, but the FillForegnd cell formulae vary as follows:

Shape 1:

```
THEMEGUARD(IF(CELLISTHEMED(FALSE),SETATREFEXPR(THEME("BackgroundColor")),SETATRE
FEXPR(RGB(255,255,255))))
```

Shape 2:

```
THEMEGUARD(IF(CELLISTHEMED(FALSE),SETATREFEXPR(SHADE(THEME("BackgroundColor"),
20)),SETATREFEXPR(RGB(230,230,230))))
```

Shape 3:

```
THEMEGUARD(IF(CELLISTHEMED(FALSE),SETATREFEXPR(SHADE(THEME("BackgroundColor"),
30)),SETATREFEXPR(RGB(250,250,250))))
```

The SHADE function is used to subtly vary the shading from one shape to the next.

# Custom Backgrounds

You can use the techniques employed by the Microsoft shape developers to create your own custom backgrounds and, perhaps, improve them?

In my case, I created a grouped shape, with three subshapes, whose line and color fills are similar to those in the built-in Master described earlier. However, I set the transparency of lines and fills between 50 and 80 percent, so the user can see the page grid, if required.

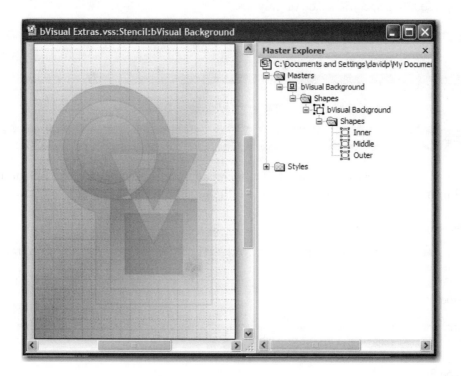

In addition, I set the whole background fill to fade away to nothing toward the top-right corner. This is because Visio pages are usually set to the bottom-left corner, so any page size changes will be to the right and to the top. This means any discrepancy between the sizes of the foreground and background pages is less noticeable.

The group shape contains the important formulae for it to behave like a background shape.

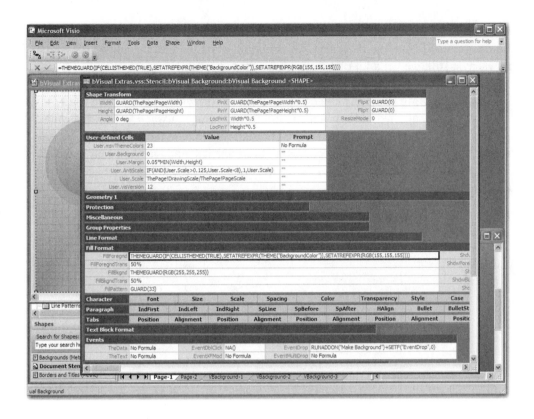

# Borders and Titles

*Borders* and *titles* are added to pages to provide a visual edge to pages or anchored positions for information about the document or page.

Border shapes do not normally go right to the edge of the page, and they may not even totally enclose the page, by providing just header and footers or edge definition.

Title blocks are traditionally in the bottom right-hand corner of a page because they should remain visible when the paper is folded (as a trainee architect, I had to fold many sheets of large paper in the print room) but, perhaps, the top of the page is more suitable for web presentation as the browser fills from the top. My career spanned the change (just) from what we called Imperial size paper and scales to the European A sizes and metric scales. The Imperial units seem to be called U.S. units nowadays, still, we get a lot of American sitcoms in return!

Both borders and titles normally contain text that can be automatically completed, such as the drawing title and subject, along with the drawing name. I have used most of the different supplied backgrounds in my time. I almost always follow the same procedure, which is to choose the desired border or title, and then to edit the Master in the local stencil to display the document title, subject, and page name automatically.

The document properties dialog holds information that can easily be accessed by a ShapeSheet function:

The Insert | Field dialog enables you to insert any of the document or page fields easily into any of the text blocks with a border or title shape.

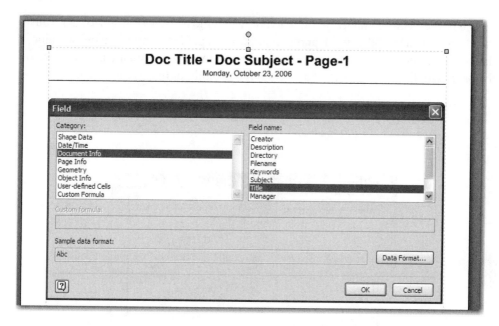

This demonstrates one reason why multiple shapes may need to be within a border Master.

The page name or number will work whether the border or title shape is on the foreground or background page. Thus, you can use the same background page, with a border and/or title that contains page information.

# Built-In Borders and Titles

The Borders and Titles stencil in the Visio Extras category provides collections of similarly styled elements.

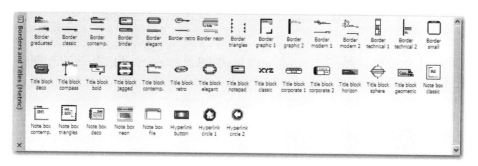

The border Masters have the same event, when the Master is dropped, that causes the shape to resize to the width and height of the page, less a multiple of the value in the User-defined cell, PageMargin. Similarly, the shape is automatically centered on the page with the setting of its PinX and PinY formula in the EventDrop cell.

```
=SETF(GetRef(Width),ThePage!PageWidth-4*User.PageMargin)+SETF(GetRef(Height),
ThePage!PageHeight-4*User.PageMargin)+SETF(GetRef(PinX),ThePage!PageWidth*0.5)+
SETF(GetRef(PinY),ThePage!PageHeight*0.5)+SETF("EventDrop",0)
```

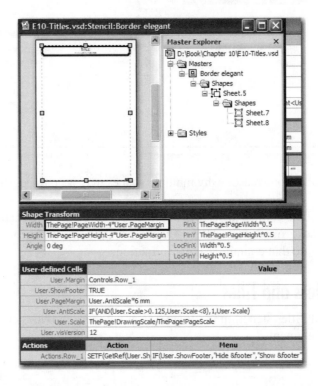

Some of the border Masters even have header and footer elements, which can be switched on or off.

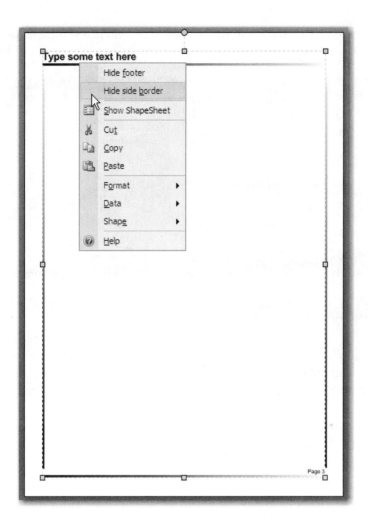

Most of the built-in title Masters have a right mouse menu to resize the shape to fit the text entered into it. The ShapeSheet for this behavior is quite sophisticated, because the top-level group shape formulae refer to cells in a subshape. Usually, this is the other way around.

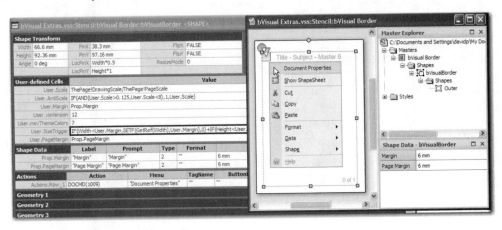

## Custom Borders and Titles

Some modifications to the ShapeSheet code can make custom borders easier to work with. For example, the formulae that set the border shape size and margin size could easily be set with relative references to the User.Margin and User.PageMargin via new Shape Data items. This lets the user enter different values than the default value.

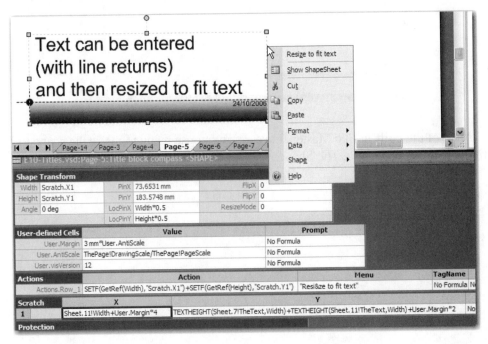

In this example, I added the Action DOCMD(1009) to provide the capability to open the Document Properties dialog directly from the right mouse menu of the border shape.

Only one subshape is in this border group shape. Thus, there are two text blocks: one at the top, which is predefined with the document title—document subject—page name, and one at the bottom, which is predefined with the page number and number of pages. The bottom text is editable as a subselection of the main shape.

In this next example, the custom border Master is designed to be dropped on the foreground page, rather than on the background, because each page in the document could be a different scale, size, and orientation. The border shape contains the company's logo at the top, but the bottom of the shape contains multiple text blocks to display information about the document and page. Earlier versions of Visio had restrictions on the length of the name of a page, so the border shape itself contains Shape Data items for the page description and revision. The right-mouse action menu was enhanced to change the page size, scale, and orientation to some recommended settings, rather than just expecting the user to play with the Page Setup dialog.

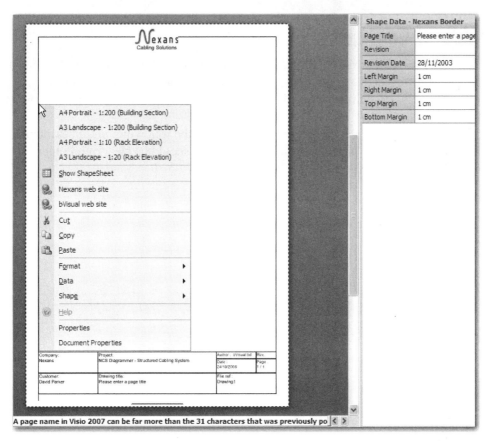

The ShapeSheet formulae behind the first four menu actions is quite long, so I listed one of them in the following code, with line breaks, although it can only be entered on a single line in the ShapeSheet itself.

```
=SETF(GetRef(ThePage!DrawingSizeType),5)
+SETF(GetRef(ThePage!DrawingScaleType),4)
+SETF(GetRef(ThePage!PageScale),0.5 cm)
+SETF(GetRef(ThePage!DrawingScale),1 m)
+SETF(GetRef(ThePage!PageWidth),42 m)
+SETF(GetRef(ThePage!PageHeight),59.4 m)
```

This formula is for Metric scale because of the scale type, 1:200 because the drawing scale divided by the page scale is 200, *A* because of the size type, 4 because the width and height are scaled values equivalent to A4, and Portrait because the width is greater than the height.

# Table of Contents

The Visio MVP (Most Valued Professional) web site (http://visio.mvps.org/vba.htm) contains code for a table of contents, which does not work for scaled or non-U.S. unit documents. In addition, it may be desirable to ignore the first page for page numbering.

The replacement TableOfContents code, listed in the following, produces a table of contents on the first page of the document, which should be clear of all other shapes before the code is run.

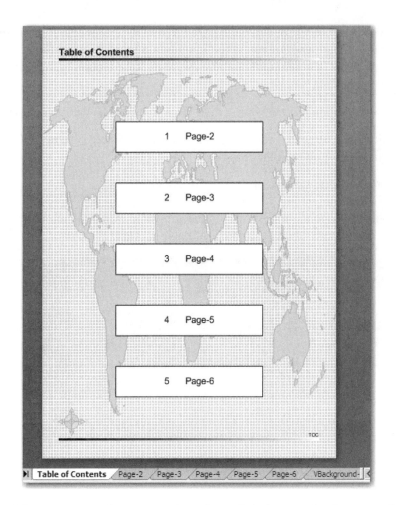

Each of the page entry shapes contains a hyperlink, in case the document is saved as a web page, and the double-click event uses the OPC (Off-Page Connector) add-on to go to the specified page. The OPC add-on is used by the Off Page Reference Master in the Flowchart | Basic Flowchart Shapes stencil. The formula uses the values in three particular User-defined cells, which are also added by the code.

```
=RUNADDONWARGS("OPC","/CMD=2")
```

The border shape on the background page has had its header-text formula modified to only show the page number part if the foreground page is not the first page, as this is used for the table of contents. The PAGENUMBER() function ignores anything but foreground pages.

```
=IF(PAGENUMBER()=1,"",PAGENUMBER()-1&" of "&PAGECOUNT()-1&" : ")&PAGENAME()
```

In addition, the footer-text formula has also been modified to show TOC on the first page and Page *x* on the other pages.

```
=IF(PAGENUMBER()=1,"TOC","Page " & PAGENUMBER()-1)
```

Thus, only the page name is shown on the first page, while all subsequent pages display the page number and the number of pages as well.

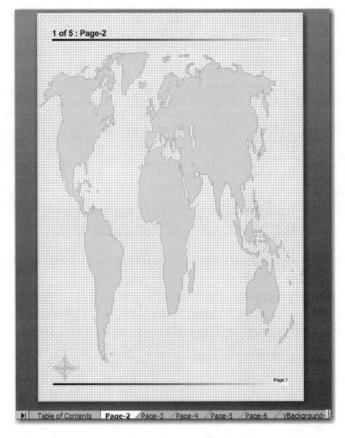

Of course, the pages would normally not be named Page-2, Page-3, and so forth.

# Code Listing for TableOfContents

```
Public Sub TableOfContents()
' creates a shape for each page in the drawing on the first page of the drawing
' then add a dbl-clk GoTo to each shape so you can double click and go to that Page

Dim PageObj As Visio.Page
Dim PageTOC As Visio.Page
Dim TOCEntry As Visio.Shape
Dim CellOjb As Visio.Cell
Dim LinkObj As Visio.Hyperlink
Dim PosX As Double
Dim PosY As Double
Dim Width As Double
Dim Height As Double
Dim PageCnt As Integer
Dim RowCnt As Integer
Dim PageCounter As Integer

' ActiveDocument.Pages.Count will give the number of pages, but we are interested
' the number of foreground pages only
    PageCnt = 0
    For Each PageObj In ActiveDocument.Pages
        If PageObj.Type = visTypeForeground Then
            PageCnt = PageCnt + 1
            If PageCnt = 1 Then
                Set PageTOC = PageObj
            End If
        End If
    Next

    PosX = PageTOC.PageSheet.Cells("PageWidth").ResultIU * 0.25
    Width = PageTOC.PageSheet.Cells("PageWidth").ResultIU * 0.5
    Height = PageTOC.PageSheet.Cells("PageHeight").ResultIU * (1 / (2 * (PageCnt + 1)))

    ' loop through all the pages
    For Each PageObj In ActiveDocument.Pages
        ' Only foreground pages and not the TOC page
        If PageObj.Type = visTypeForeground _
                And Not PageObj.Index = PageTOC.Index Then
            PageCounter = PageCounter + 1
            ' where to put the entry on the page?
            PosY = PageTOC.PageSheet.Cells("PageHeight").ResultIU - (PageCounter + 1) * 2
* Height
            ' draw a rectangle for each page to hold the text
            Set TOCEntry = PageTOC.DrawRectangle(PosX, PosY, PosX + Width, PosY + Height)
```

```
' write the page name in the rectangle
TOCEntry.Text = CStr(PageCounter) & vbTab & PageObj.Name
TOCEntry.Cells("Char.Size").Formula = "=""18 pt"""

'Add the OPC User cells
RowCnt = TOCEntry.AddNamedRow(Visio.visSectionUser, "OPCShapeID", 0)
Set CellObj = TOCEntry.CellsSRC(Visio.visSectionUser, RowCnt, Visio
                            .visUserValue)
CellObj.Formula = "=""" & TOCEntry.UniqueID(Visio.visGetOrMakeGUID) & """"

RowCnt = TOCEntry.AddNamedRow(Visio.visSectionUser, "OPCDPageID", 0)
Set CellObj = TOCEntry.CellsSRC(Visio.visSectionUser, RowCnt, Visio
                            .visUserValue)
CellObj.Formula = "=""" & PageObj.PageSheet.UniqueID(Visio.visGetOrMakeGUID)
& """"

RowCnt = TOCEntry.AddNamedRow(Visio.visSectionUser, "OPCDShapeID", 0)
Set CellObj = TOCEntry.CellsSRC(Visio.visSectionUser, RowCnt, Visio
                            .visUserValue)
CellObj.Formula = "="""""

' add a hyperlink to point to the page
Set LinkObj = TOCEntry.AddHyperlink
LinkObj.NameU = "OffPageConnector"
LinkObj.Description = "Go to " & PageObj.Name
LinkObj.SubAddress = PageObj.Name

' add a link to point to the page so you can just go there with a double-click
Set CellObj = TOCEntry.CellsSRC(visSectionObject, visRowEvent,
                            visEvtCellDblClick) 'Start
CellObj.Formula = "=RUNADDONWARGS(""OPC"","""/CMD=2"")"

        End If
    Next

End Sub
```

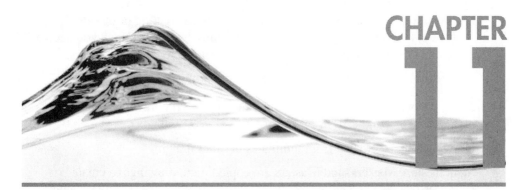

# Creating Custom Templates, Stencils, and Masters

**IN THIS CHAPTER**

Stencils and Masters

Templates

Publishing Templates and Stencils

Throughout the previous chapters, you have been creating or modifying Masters with little regard to their accessibility by others. Now, you need to understand how to make all these customizations available to others. Just to remind you:

▶ Three types of Visio document—stencil, template, and drawing—can be in binary (vss, vst, and vsd) or XML format (vsx, vtx, and vdx).

▶ Drawings can be created from templates or other drawings.

▶ Stencils store Masters, and Masters are copied on to drawings to create instances (shapes) and a copy of the Master is stored in the drawing document stencil. There is no automatic change to the copy of a Master in a document stencil, *if* you change it in the original (global) stencil.

▶ Drawings contain pages, and pages can be no scale or any particular scale.

▶ A Workspace is a drawing with optional docked (usually) stencils.

The opening screen in Visio shows templates that can be selected from a category, as you can see in Figure 11-1.

The verbose names you see are not the filenames you see in the Visio installation folder.

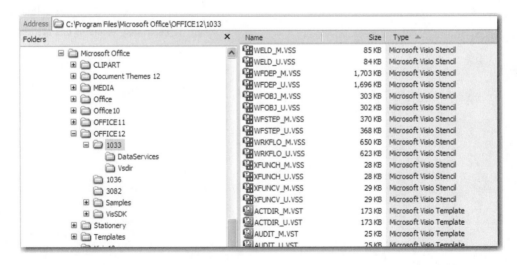

Notice vss and vst files are shown, and the filenames are in the old fashioned 8.3 format, with _U and _M alternatives for the same file. The Windows Installer holds

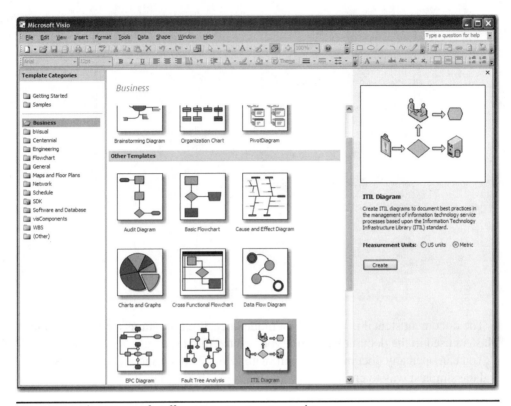

**Figure 11-1**  *The Microsoft Office Visio Getting Started Screen*

a database of the mappings from the short filenames into the verbose names you see. You need to use the Visio Publishing tool to do this, as you will see.

The alternative method of making templates and stencils available to users is to add the folders for Visio to search in, but this can cause unnecessary work for Visio, and on slow networks, it can be slow.

# Stencils and Masters

Every drawing has a document stencil. The *document stencil* is usually hidden, but it contains every Master used in the drawing. Instead, docked, read-only stencils are normally used for dragging-and-dropping Masters on to a drawing page.

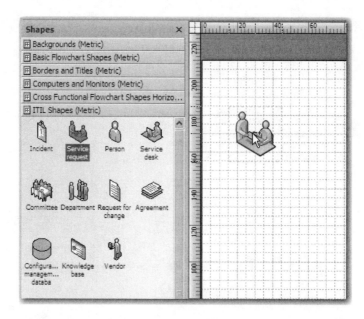

The document stencil is usually best hidden because it contains a copy of all the Masters used in the document, even if you deleted the instance!

You can open any document's stencil, with File | Shapes | Show Document Stencil, and the simplest way to create a Master is to drag a shape on to it.

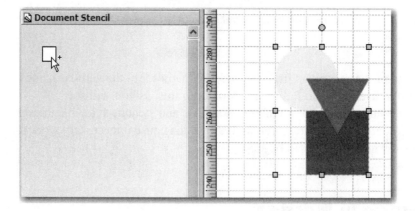

That is not the best way to distribute a Master to others, though. Instead, you can create a stencil, which you can then redistribute. This is done with File | Shapes | New Stencil.

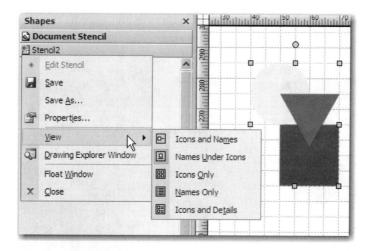

You can change the display of Master icons and names in a stencil from the right mouse menu on the stencil caption.

## Master Icons

When you create a Master, the image is created from the shape, by default. You can switch off this behavior in the Master Properties dialog.

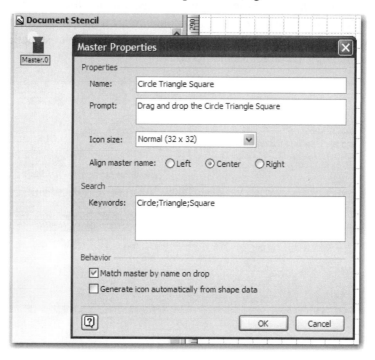

You can use the full-featured (not!) icon editor to enhance the displayed Master image.

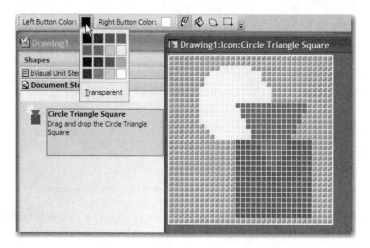

If you use the icon editor, then you must have Generate Icon Automatically From Shape Data unchecked. Otherwise, you will lose your enhanced icon.

There is a method to export the icon to a file (ExportIcon) and a method to import the icon from a file (ImportIcon), but the file must have been exported previously. It is just as easy to open the icon image on one Master manually, and then copy it to paste into the icon image of another. You could create a temporary Master icon image from an imported picture by dragging it on to the document stencil, and then copying this image to the target Master icon.

The icon can be any one of four different sizes, all are variations on 32 and 64 pixels but, be aware, different size icons in a stencil can make it look untidy.

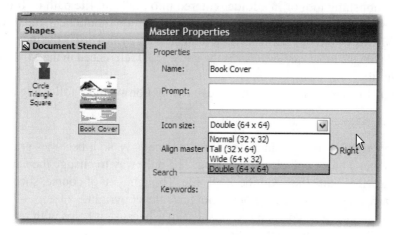

## Preparing the Master Shape

Before you publish a Master, you should open it for editing (using Edit Master), and then, with the Master shape selected, choose Format | Special. This enables you to rename the Master shape and change other properties, such as the Help file and Copyright.

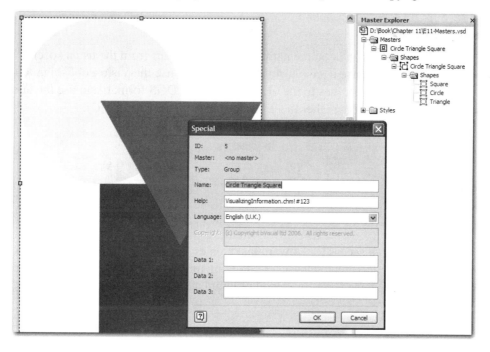

The Help file should be a Windows help file (either .hlp or .chm), and the file needs to be recognizable by Visio. This means the file must published with the Visio Publishing tool or in a folder entered into the Help file path in Tools | Options | Advanced | File Paths dialog. The Help file value should be in the format FILENAME!Keyword or FILENAME!#Number, where *Keyword* is the index term associated with the topic, and *Number* is the numeric ID referenced in the MAP section of the help file.

You can also start a Help file with an event or action with the following formula:

```
=HELP("VisualizingInformation.chm!#123")
```

The Copyright property is intended to write once only, so it becomes grayed out once you enter a value and close the dialog. The only way to change the Copyright is to save it as XML, and then edit the XML file. Though, you of course, should *not* do this with any Masters for which you do not have the copyright.

In addition, I suggest you name your subshapes because it helps with recognition, both manually and through automation.

If you have a group shape, then check the Format | Behavior settings. Usually, it is best to set the Selection to Group Only, unless you require your users to subselect shapes, for example, to edit multiple text blocks. Don't forget, it is bad practice to have too many grouped levels within a shape because it causes the Visio engine to recalculate the geometry each time.

## Stencil Names

Although little restriction is on the names for stencils, apart from the usual special characters, you should use a terse form if you intend to use the Visio Publishing tool. In this case, restrict the names to the old fashioned 8.3 DOS format, and use the last two characters to denote whether the units are Metric (_M) or US (_U).

If you do not have access to software that creates Windows installation packages and you do not need to create alternative drawing unit versions, then you have little incentive to use the terse form for stencil or template names.

# Stencil File Paths

Every user has a special folder called My Shapes, which is located, by default, in each user's My Documents folder (or just Documents on Vista). Any stencil in the My Shapes folder becomes available from the File I Shapes I My Shapes menu item inside Visio (note, the My Shapes folder is deletable, so it may not always exist). You can create Categories and Sub-categories by having folders and subfolders.

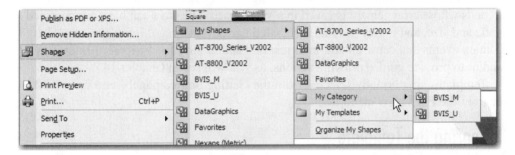

This would be similar to altering the Stencil File Paths under Tools I Options I Advanced.

Creating an installation and using the Visio Publishing Tool, however, can create categories and alternative verbose names.

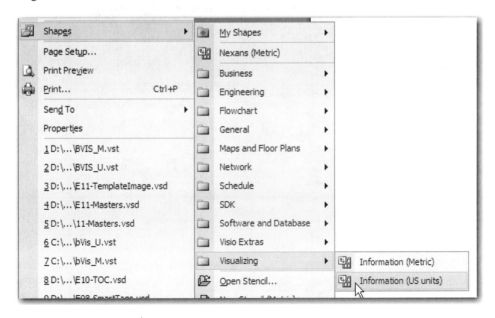

The same stencil files, with the names unchanged, are shown in the two previous illustrations. Visio has automatically appended the (Metric) and (US units) to the chosen name "Information" because the two files had the _M and _U suffix.

# Templates

A *template* is a drawing with at least one page and, usually, with a selection of docked stencils whose arrangement is saved in a Workspace. The page can have a predefined scale and size, and it may have an associated background page. Templates may also contain events that cause an add-in to respond and modify the Visio User Interface and/or to provide guided drawing actions, as you will see in Chapter 14.

Templates are normally selected from the Getting Started panel (see Figure 11-1) or from the File | New menu item.

## Preparing the Template

The text shown below the template image (as shown in Figure 11-1) is from the Description in the Document Properties dialog.

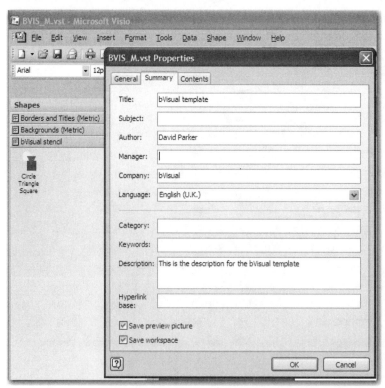

Always check that your document stencil does not contain any Masters that are not required. If you are providing Masters on a stencil, ensure you do not have copies of these in your template's document stencil, as this makes issuing updates more difficult. You should check the File Size Reduction tab of the Remove Hidden Information dialog that can be opened from the File menu.

## Template Names

If you are going to publish the templates with the Visio Publishing tool, like stencil names, you should use the terse 8.3 format with the optional measurement unit _U or _M suffix.

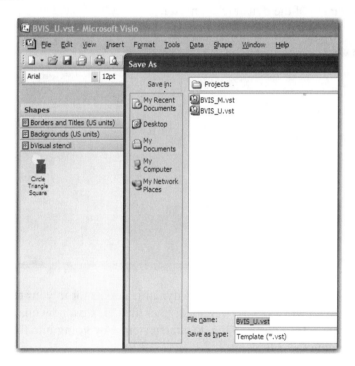

If you are not using the Visio Publishing tool, then you can use long descriptive names.

## Template File Paths

Again like stencil file paths, you can display templates in Categories or Sub-categories by altering the Template File Paths in Tools | Options | Advanced.

However, it is better to use the Visio Publishing tool if possible, because Visio has to examine all the folders and subfolders entered in the File Paths. This can be slow if there are many folders or if the folders are on a network drive, which may or may not be available.

## Custom Dynamic Connector

The *dynamic connector* is a special Master because it can be created by Visio automatically when you use certain menu items (for example, Connector tool, AutoConnect, or Connect Shapes) or use certain methods (for example, AutoConnect or ConnectShapes) in code. However, you might want your types of drawings to use an enhanced version of the dynamic connector.

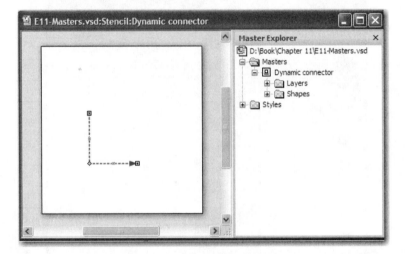

So, you can include your version of the dynamic connector in your template document, because Visio will use your version, rather than create a new one. You can hide the Dynamic connector Master in the document stencil by going into the Immediate Window and typing the following

```
Visio.ActiveDocument.Masters("Dynamic connector").Hidden=1
```

The Master will still be in the Drawing Explorer, though.

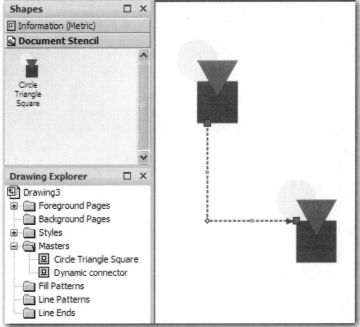

# Creating a Preview Image

The *preview image* for a document or template is generated automatically from the content on the first page. However, nothing is usually on the first page of a template, so you need to use a bit of code to copy the preview image from another document, and then lock the preview in the template, so it does not get removed accidentally.

Fortunately, Visio has a method—CopyPreviewPicture—to do just this, and the following macro CopyThisPreviewPicture should be added to the VBA project of a document that contains the desired preview, and then run while the template is active.

In this case, I inserted an image into a blank portrait-orientation page and protected the aspect ratio of the picture using Format | Protection.

This enables me to resize the image, without distorting the image, to fit centralized on the page because the preview image is square.

Any Visio document can have a preview image, and this can be locked with a check in the bottom left of the Document Properties dialog. Or, the value of the Lock-Preview cell in the DocumentSheet can be changed between 0 (False) and 1 (True).

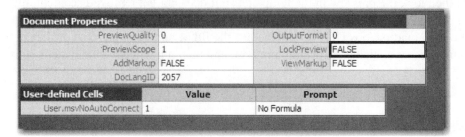

So, the code needs to change the value in this cell to 0 to allow the preview image to be updated, and then, afterward, change it to 1 to lock it.

The end result is you can update the preview picture of your template documents from any other document with its own preview picture.

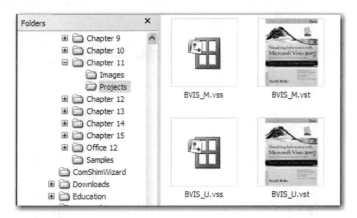

### Code Listing for CopyThisPreviewPicture

```
Public Sub CopyThisPreviewPicture()
Dim targetDoc As Visio.Document

    Set targetDoc = Visio.ActiveDocument
    If targetDoc.ID = ThisDocument.ID Then
        MsgBox "You should start this macro with the target document selected",
vbInformation
        Exit Sub
    End If

    targetDoc.DocumentSheet.Cells("LockPreview").Formula = "0"
    targetDoc.CopyPreviewPicture ThisDocument
    targetDoc.DocumentSheet.Cells("LockPreview").Formula = "1"

End Sub
```

# Publishing Templates and Stencils

Before Visio 2002, there was only one way to add categories of templates and stencils. This was to add the file paths that Visio looked in for relevant files. This capability is still present but, now, the superior method is by using the Visio Publishing tool.

## Using File Paths

The Tools | Options menu item opens the Options dialog, and the Advanced tab has a button to open the File Paths dialog.

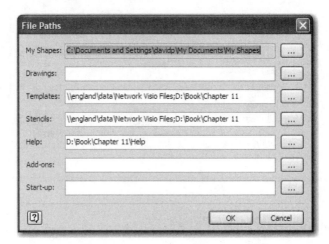

Normally, the only entry present is the one for My Shapes, which, by default, points to the My Shapes folder in My Documents (or Documents on Vista).

You can change any of the file paths with the builder button to its right, and you can have multiple folder paths, separated by a semicolon, for any of the entries except My Shapes, which can only have one path.

To create a Category within the File | Shapes menu (for Stencils) or File | New (for Templates), simply create a subfolder. The name of the subfolder appears as a Category.

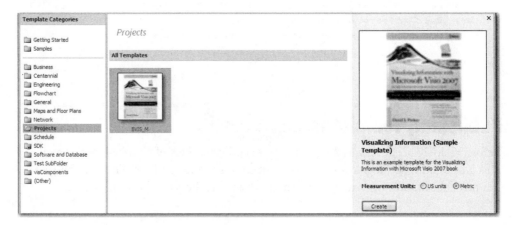

The template filename is shown within the Category, and the preview picture is displayed with the template title (and the Subject within brackets), and the Description below it, in the Getting Started panel. The preview picture will not be displayed if the file is not on a local drive because it would slow performance.

You only get the Measurement Units options if you have similarly named files, except for the _U and _M suffixes.

# Creating an Installation

The Microsoft Visio 2007 Solution Publishing tool is part of the Microsoft Office Visio 2007 SDK. The *Solution Publishing tool* works by modifying the Publish-Component table in a Windows installation file (msi file), so Visio can understand the Visio-specific elements within it. Therefore, you must have a tool, such as Visual Studio (2003 or 2005), to create it in the first place. A tool called *Orca,* which is part of the freely downloadable Windows Installer SDK could also be used.

In the following example, I used Microsoft Visual Studio 2005 to create a Windows application Setup Project. I included two stencils, two templates, and a help file.

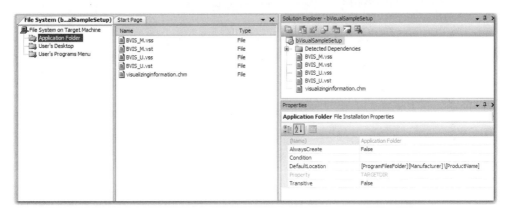

The drawing measurement units are denoted by the _U (US Units) and _M (Metric) suffix. The Visio interface does not do anything sensible like check the drawing file.

You should change the Manufacturer and ProductName values for the project because that dictates where the files should be installed within the ProgramFilesFolder.

I always set *both* RemovePreviousVersions and InstallAllUsers to True, which makes the templates available to other users than the installer by default.

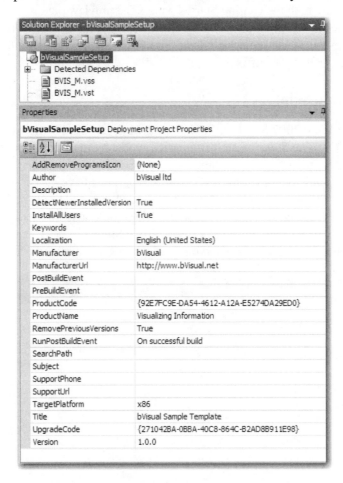

Then, check that the Active solution configuration is set to Release on the Build | Configuration Manager dialog, before you build the solution. This creates a Windows installer package, with an msi extension, in the Release subfolder.

If you were to install this package, then the files will be copied to the specified folder, but you will not see anything in Visio. To get Visio to recognize the installation, you need to modify the msi file with the Microsoft Visio 2007 Solution Publishing tool. This tool is part of the free Microsoft Visio 2007 SDK, and can be added as an external tool in Visual Studio.

## Templates and Stencils

Open the msi file with the Visio Publishing tool by starting a new project, and you should find the two stencils and two templates are listed in the Templates and Stencils tab.

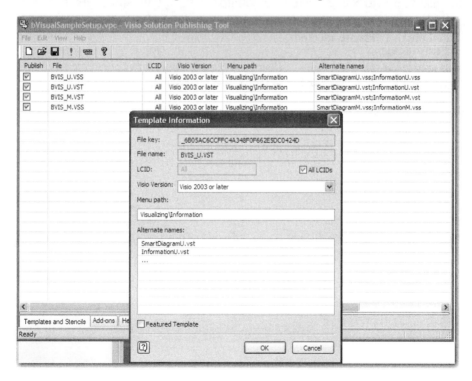

I entered the Menu Path as Visualizing\Information, so the installation creates a Category called Visualizing and the displayed name of the template is Information. This has been repeated on all the files in this tab because alternative versions exist of the same template and stencil. If you had multiple templates and stencils, you could provide different Categories (and even Sub-categories by adding extra back-slashes \ as follows Category\Sub-Category\Name) and filenames.

The Alternate Names are set in the APPData column of the PublishComponent table, which means you can use the specified alternate names in Visio automation. For example, the following code is the normal way to open a Metric copy of the example template:

```
Visio.Documents.OpenEx "C:\Program Files\bvisual\Visualizing\
Information\bvis_m.vst",visio.visOpenCopy
```

The following will not work, even though the template appears to be called Information.vst in the Visio user interface:

```
Visio.Documents.OpenEx "C:\Program Files\bvisual\Visualizing\
Information\information.vst",visio.visOpenCopy
```

Because Alternate Names were entered into the Visio Publishing tool, however, either of the next two lines of code would work because the PublishComponent table knows where the files are located.

```
Visio.Documents.OpenEx "SmartDiagramM.vst",visio.visOpenCopy
Visio.Documents.OpenEx "InformationM.vst",visio.visOpenCopy
```

Thus, the Alternate Names provide a convenient way to reference stencils and templates in automation code.

I chose to check All LCIDs, so the installed documents will work for all Locale ID language codes, rather than a specific one, such as 1033 for US, or 2057 for UK. See http://support.microsoft.com/default.aspx/kb/221435 for a list of all LCID codes.

## Help Files

Similarly, the help file is listed in the Help Files tab, where you should ensure it is set for All LCIDs. Note, the older hlp files are not supported in this tool, only chm and aw files.

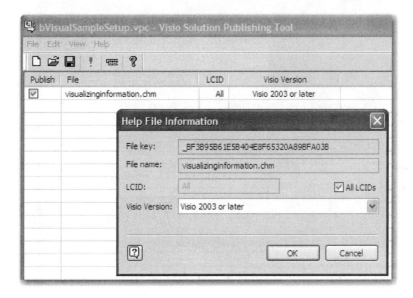

## Add-Ons

The *Add-ons tab* lists any VSL (C++ Visio Solution Library files) or Exes found in the installation package. We look at including code with Visio solutions in Chapter 14, but the important consideration is that code add-ons published with this tool automatically become a trusted source.

## Running the Installation

Once you apply the changes to the msi file, you can run the installation. During the install, you are asked to confirm the folders to copy the files into.

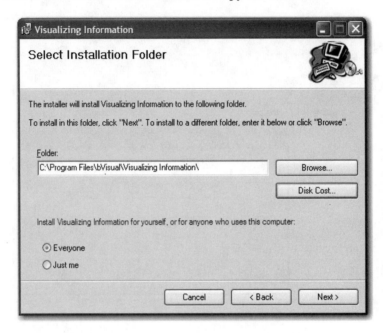

The files will be copied to the specified folder.

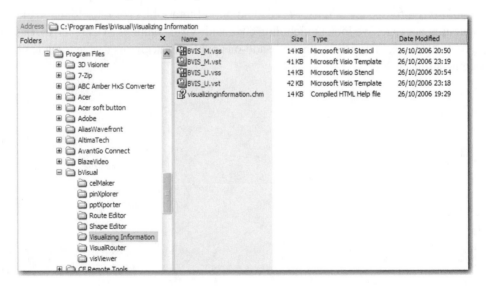

When the installation is completed, you should find a new Category— Visualizing—in Visio, with a single template, called Information. The Title, Subject, and Description are displayed on the right, under the preview picture.

Notice, although we installed two templates, we only see one, with the option to create with US or Metric measurement units.

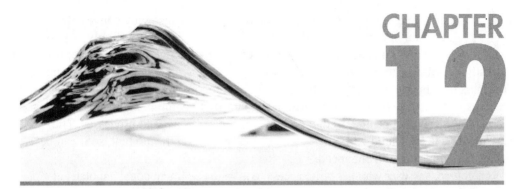

# Reviewers' Comments

**E**nterprise diagrams often need to be reviewed because they convey shared information that is required to be checked. Any document is only as good as the diagram and data it contains. Once the document is published, it is already out-of-date, unless it continues to be reviewed and kept current. Too much business information is stale, which is often only recognized when the need is greatest. Microsoft Visio provides the user with the capability to combine data and diagrams in a unique way that can be used to convey concepts, reality, and processes. The document can be shared with others who can comment on the content, so it can be refreshed, updated, and enhanced.

Of course, any user who has write access to a Visio document could annotate, at will, just by adding text, or drawing or dropping shapes. But, Visio does not know who dropped any particular shape, added a piece of text, or even when this was done.

The exception to this is the use of Insert | Comment, which does record who and when, and Visio provides Track Markup, so reviewer's comments can be displayed on their own overlay, with an assigned color. In fact, multiple reviewers can leave their own comments on distinct Markup Overlays for each page.

Although you can add, edit, delete, and view these comments easily in Visio, there is no provided solution for printing them. This chapter contains such a method.

## Annotation Without Comments

A stencil normally associated with the Brainstorming template contains symbols that can be added to diagrams to annotate such things as Priorities, Questions, and Needs Follow Up. This stencil can be opened from any drawing by selecting File | Shapes | Business | Brainstorming | Legend Shapes.

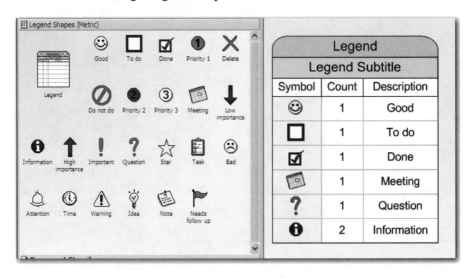

If you drop a Legend shape on to the page, then every other Master from this stencil adds itself on to the Legend shape or increments the count, if it already exists.

This is not the only stencil that contains suitable Masters for this purpose, but most of the other Masters need to be dropped on to the Legend shape first, as this registers them as a Master that should be tracked.

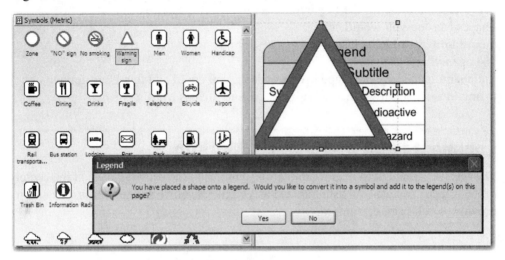

In fact, the Legend shape has more tricks up its sleeve. You can subselect the Title area to edit the displayed text, and you can open the Configure Legend dialog from the right mouse menu.

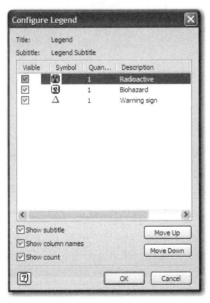

Thus, you can amend the display, change the order of icons, and even decide to omit particular shapes.

If you were to examine the ShapeSheet of a Master shape converted to work with the Legend Shapes Master, you would see the Add-on has added a User. visLegendShape cell with the value 2 (number 1 is the Legend shape itself). Indeed, you could add this User-defined cell to any Master, and it will work with the Legend Shapes Master.

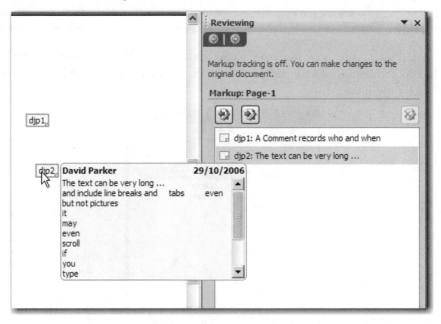

## Comments and Reviewer's Markup

The Insert | Comment tool adds annotation symbols to the drawing page at the center of the screen. You can add as much text as you like, even with line breaks, because it provides scroll bars, if required.

The Initials and the Index number are displayed on the Comment symbol, and the Name and Date, along with the annotation, are displayed when the symbol is clicked. The Reviewing pane displays the list of Markup Comments. The display of Markup

Comments can be toggled with View | Markup menu item or from the Show/Hide Markup button on the Reviewing toolbar, which also provides access to Insert Comment and the Ink tool.

A more controlled method of offering Visio documents for review is to use Track Markup. Selecting Tools | Track Markup, or the Track Markup button on the Reviewer's toolbar, performs three actions at the same time: It displays the Reviewer's toolbar, if necessary, and the Reviewing pane, plus it changes the active mode to Track Markup. See Figure 12-1.

The right mouse menu of a Markup Comment symbol enables you to edit or delete it.

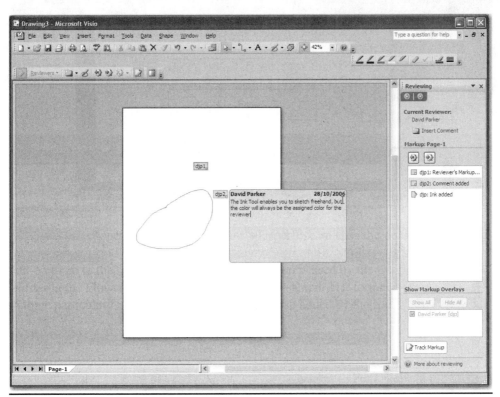

**Figure 12-1**  *The Track Markup user interface*

In fact, the Track Markup action creates a new Markup Overlay page, if it does not exist already. The Markup Overlay page, shown in Figure 12-2, is named after the Foreground page it is for, with the addition of the reviewer's initials in square brackets as a suffix.

Notice the Markup Overlay pages do not show as a page tab at the bottom of the screen, but they do appear in the Drawing Explorer, and the colored Markup tabs appear on the top-right edge of the page window, with only the reviewer's initials again. You can toggle the display of any of the Markup Overlays from the Reviewer's pull-down list on the Reviewer's Toolbar or from the Show Markup Overlays list in the Reviewing pane.

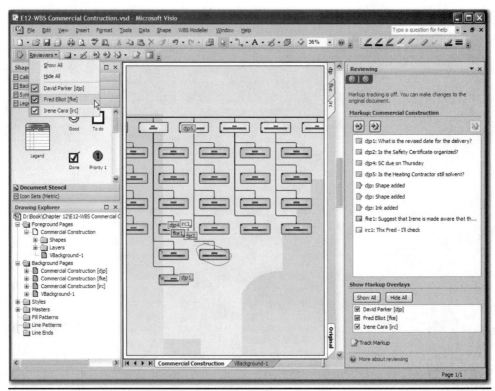

**Figure 12-2**  *Multiple Markup Overlays*

The Reviewer's Initials and Name are gleaned from a setting in the Tools | Options dialog, on the General tab.

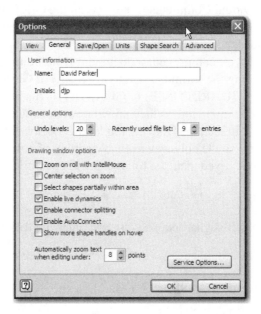

In fact, you can pretend to be another reviewer by changing these settings. Perhaps Microsoft will look into locking down the identity in future releases.

## Behind the Scenes of Markup

Each unique combination of User's Information Name and Initials causes a new Reviewer to be created in the DocumentSheet.

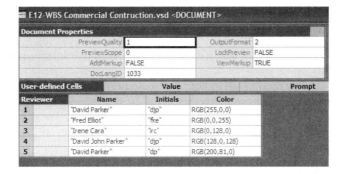

A new color formula is assigned to each reviewer and, if you do not like the colors assigned, you can change them. The color is used for the display of Markup Overlay pages, but not for individual Comments if they are on the Original page.

The Document Properties ViewMarkup cell determines whether the Markup is on show, and the AddMarkup cell tells you whether the document is currently in Markup mode. In fact, you can prevent a document from being able to switch into Markup mode by entering the formula GUARD(FALSE) or GUARD(0). You can do the reverse by entering GUARD(TRUE) or GUARD(1). This means users will only be able to review the document unless they know how to change this setting. Oops! I just told them! Or did I? In fact, the Drawing Explorer is not available for any page that is not a Foreground type, so the only way to enable editing of normal Foreground pages is to use automation code. Even then, the following will not work:

```
visio.ActiveDocument.DocumentSheet.Cells("AddMarkup").Formula = 0
```

This is because the cell is guarded, so you must enter the following:

```
visio.ActiveDocument.DocumentSheet.Cells("AddMarkup").FormulaForce = 0
```

Now, if you examine the PageSheet of a Markup page, you can see an Annotation row exists for each Markup item.

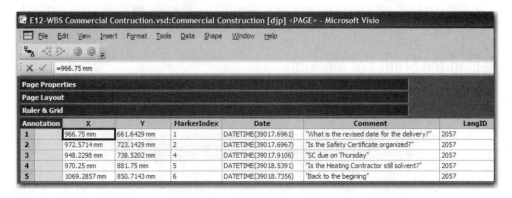

The date and time of each Markup item is stored along with the *X* and *Y* coordinate in the page, even though the user interface only displays the date. A unique Marker Index is assigned, and the Comment can be up to approximately 64k characters. Notice the illustration does not show a Marker Index 3 because this was deleted.

As a point of interest, it is possible to associate a reviewer's markup item with the location of a particular shape in the foreground page. To do this, you would need to modify the formula in the *X* and *Y* cells to refer to the PinX and PinY of the foreground shape.

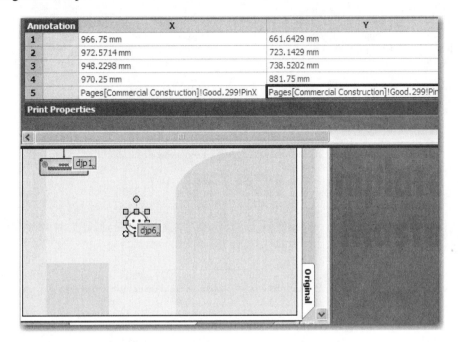

Note, the shape name was entered as Sheet.299, not Good.299, but the ShapeSheet interface changes the display.

# Listing Page Reviewers

Knowing how many Comments are there for any particular reviewer in a page could be useful, so the ListReviewer's macro lists the number of Comments made by each reviewer in the original page and in any overlay pages.

Interestingly, the ReviewerID cell in the Annotation section is hidden in the PageSheet, but it is available in code.

The macro loops through the Reviewer's section in the document, collecting the initials and names for each ID, and then it loops through the Annotation sections of the original page and the overlays pages to count the Comments for each reviewer. Finally, the results are displayed in the message box.

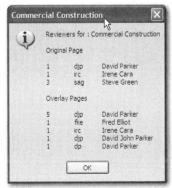

## Code Listing for ListReviewers

```
Public Sub ListReviewers()
Dim doc As Visio.Document
Dim pag As Visio.Page
Dim pagMarkup As Visio.Page
Dim row As Integer
Dim cel As Integer
Dim rvwID As Integer
Dim aryReviewers() As Variant
Dim sText As String

    Set doc = Visio.ActiveDocument
    If doc.DocumentSheet.SectionExists(Visio.visSectionReviewer, _
            Visio.visExistsAnywhere) = 0 Then
        MsgBox "There are no reviewers.", vbInformation
        Exit Sub
    End If

    Set pag = Visio.ActivePage
    sText = "Reviewers for : " & pag.Name & vbCrLf

    'Collect the potential reviewers
    ReDim aryReviewers(4, doc.DocumentSheet.RowCount(Visio.visSectionReviewer))
    For row = 0 To doc.DocumentSheet.RowCount(Visio.visSectionReviewer) - 1
        aryReviewers(0, row) = doc.DocumentSheet.CellsSRC(Visio.visSectionReviewer, _
            row, Visio.visReviewerReviewerID).ResultIU
        aryReviewers(1, row) = doc.DocumentSheet.CellsSRC(Visio.visSectionReviewer, _
            row, Visio.visReviewerInitials).ResultStr("")
        aryReviewers(2, row) = doc.DocumentSheet.CellsSRC(Visio.visSectionReviewer, _
            row, Visio.visReviewerName).ResultStr("")
        aryReviewers(3, row) = doc.DocumentSheet.CellsSRC(Visio.visSectionReviewer, _
            row, Visio.visReviewerColor).ResultStr("")
    Next row

    'Loop thru the Annotation in the current page
    If pag.PageSheet.SectionExists(Visio.visSectionAnnotation, Visio.visExistsAnywhere) Then
        For row = 0 To pag.PageSheet.RowCount(Visio.visSectionAnnotation) - 1
            rvwID = pag.PageSheet.CellsSRC(Visio.visSectionAnnotation, _
                row, Visio.visAnnotationReviewerID).ResultIU
            aryReviewers(4, rvwID - 1) = aryReviewers(4, rvwID - 1) + 1
        Next row
    End If
```

```
    sText = sText & vbCrLf & "Original Page" & vbCrLf
    'Loop thru Comments in this page
    For row = 0 To doc.DocumentSheet.RowCount(Visio.visSectionReviewer) - 1
        If aryReviewers(4, row) > 0 Then
            sText = sText & vbCrLf & aryReviewers(4, row) & _
                    vbTab & aryReviewers(1, row) & vbTab & aryReviewers(2, row)
        End If
    Next row

    sText = sText & vbCrLf & vbCrLf & "Overlay Pages" & vbCrLf
    'Loop thru Comments in any overlay pages
    For Each pagMarkup In pag.Document.Pages
        If pagMarkup.Type = visTypeMarkup Then
            If pagMarkup.OriginalPage = pag Then
                If pagMarkup.PageSheet.SectionExists(Visio.visSectionAnnotation, _
                        Visio.visExistsAnywhere) Then
                    sText = sText & vbCrLf & _
                        pagMarkup.PageSheet.RowCount(Visio.visSectionAnnotation) & _
                        vbTab & aryReviewers(1, pagMarkup.ReviewerID - 1) & _
                        vbTab & aryReviewers(2, pagMarkup.ReviewerID - 1)
                End If
            End If
        End If
    Next pagMarkup

    MsgBox sText, vbInformation, pag.Name

End Sub
```

# Printing Reviewer's Markup

Many Visio users have asked how to print reviewer's markup, and so Microsoft is-sued a method (http://support.microsoft.com/default.aspx/kb/898514/en-us), but it just creates a large rectangle with text inside it. Therefore, I suggest an alternative solution that not only enables you to print the location of the annotations, but also to use the built-in Reports system to create your own output to Excel, HTML, or XML.

## The Annotation Marker Master

This suggested method involves adding a suitable shape on the Foreground page at the exact location of each Reviewer's Comment on the Markup Overlay pages.

These shapes are instances of the Annotation Marker Master which is designed to be similar in appearance to the Reviewer's Annotation items on the Markup Overlays.

The shapes are colored the same and labeled the same, but the size cannot be exactly the same because the Reviewer's Annotation items on the Markup Overlays stay the same size, whatever the zoom level, just like SmartTags. Therefore, a Shape Data item in the page (Annotation Width) can be changed to alter the width of every Annotation Marker on the page. The value entered is the percentage of the page width that the Annotation Markers should be to make the desired print legible.

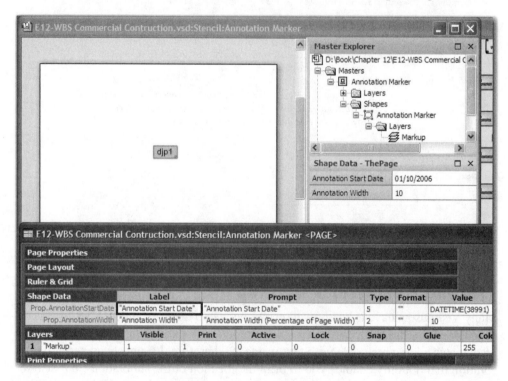

The page also has a Shape Data item—*Annotation Start Date*—so all Annotation Marker shapes that have dates before this date will automatically hide themselves. This date is also used to filter the new report: Reviewer Annotation.

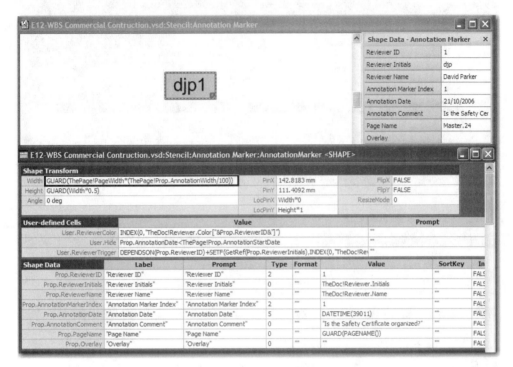

The User.ReviewerColor formula automatically evaluates the color from the document Reviewer section. A similar formula does not work for text values, though, so the User.ReviewerTrigger formula updates the ReviewerInitials and Reviewer-Name Shape Data item, whenever the ReviewerID is updated (either manually or through code).

```
=DEPENDSON(Prop.ReviewerID)+
SETF(GetRef(Prop.ReviewerInitials),
INDEX(0,"TheDoc!Reviewer.Initials["&Prop.ReviewerID&"]"))+
SETF(GetRef(Prop.ReviewerName),
INDEX(0,"TheDoc!Reviewer.Name["&Prop.ReviewerID&"]"))
```

Note, in reality, no line breaks are in ShapeSheet cells formulae. It is shown just like the previous code, so you can see the whole formula.

The *LineColor* and *FillForegnd cells* reference the User.ReviewerColor, and the *FillPattern* is guarded to ensure it does not get accidently changed.

| Protection | | | | | | | |
|---|---|---|---|---|---|---|---|
| LockWidth | 0 | LockEnd | 0 | LockCrop | 0 | | |
| LockHeight | 0 | LockDelete | 0 | LockGroup | 0 | | |
| LockAspect | 1 | LockSelect | 0 | LockCalcWH | 0 | | |
| LockMoveX | 0 | LockFormat | 1 | LockFromGroupFormat | 0 | | |
| LockMoveY | 0 | LockCustProp | 1 | LockThemeColors | 1 | | |
| LockRotate | 1 | LockTextEdit | 1 | LockThemeEffects | 1 | | |
| LockBegin | 0 | LockVtxEdit | 1 | | | | |

| Miscellaneous | | | | | | | |
|---|---|---|---|---|---|---|---|
| NoObjHandles | TRUE | HideText | User.Hide | ObjType | 4 | | |
| NoCtlHandles | FALSE | UpdateAlignBox | FALSE | IsDropSource | FALSE | | |
| NoAlignBox | FALSE | DynFeedback | 0 | Comment | Prop.ReviewerName&CHAR(9)&Prop.AnnotationDate& | | |
| NonPrinting | FALSE | NoLiveDynamics | FALSE | DropOnPageScale | 100% | | |
| LangID | 1033 | Calendar | 0 | LocalizeMerge | FALSE | | |

| Line Format | | | | | | | |
|---|---|---|---|---|---|---|---|
| LinePattern | GUARD(1) | BeginArrow | 0 | BeginArrowSize | 2 | | |
| LineWeight | GUARD(Height*0.07) | EndArrow | 0 | EndArrowSize | 2 | | |
| LineColor | GUARD(User.ReviewerColor) | LineColorTrans | 0% | Rounding | 0 mm | | |
| LineCap | 0 | | | | | | |

| Fill Format | | | | | | | |
|---|---|---|---|---|---|---|---|
| FillForegnd | GUARD(TINT(User.ReviewerColor,90)) | ShdwForegnd | THEMEGUARD("ShadowColor") | ShapeShdwOffsetX | | | |
| FillForegndTrans | GUARD(0%) | ShdwForegndTrans | 80% | ShapeShdwOffsetY | | | |
| FillBkgnd | 0 | ShdwBkgnd | 1 | ShapeShdwType | | | |
| FillBkgndTrans | 0% | ShdwBkgndTrans | 0% | ShapeShdwObliqueAngle | | | |
| FillPattern | GUARD(1) | ShdwPattern | 0 | ShapeShdwScaleFactor | | | |

| Text Fields | Format | | Value | Calendar | ObjectKind | | |
|---|---|---|---|---|---|---|---|
| 0 | FIELDPICTURE(0) | Prop.ReviewerInitials | | 0 | 0 | | |
| 0 | FIELDPICTURE(0) | Prop.AnnotationMarkerIndex | | 0 | 0 | | |

| Character | Font | Size | Scale | Spacing | Color | Transparency | Styl |
|---|---|---|---|---|---|---|---|
| 0 | 4 | GUARD(Height*0.7) | 100% | 0 pt | 0 | 0% | 0 |

The *Comment cell* is so called because this is what the user interface used to call the Screen Tip. Microsoft Visio created the current Insert | Comment method, however, and renamed the original. Therefore, the formula in the Comment cell displays the Screen Tip:

```
=Prop.ReviewerName&CHAR(9)&Prop.AnnotationDate
&CHAR(13)&CHAR(10)&Prop.AnnotationComment
```

The CHAR(9) is a tab character, and CHAR(13) & CHAR(10) are carriage return and line feed.

This Master is a good one to make invisible in the document stencil of a template because its only use is from automation.

# The AddAnnotationMarkers Code

The AddAnnotationMarkers macro should be run from the original page for which you want to have printable Comments. First, it deletes any shapes on the Markup layer before dropping an Annotation Marker at the location of every Comment for that page, including those from any overlay pages. The *AddAnnotationMarkers macro* uses the DropMany method that returns an array of all the new shape IDs created by the drop, so these arrays must be put into the array for the SetFormulas method for the Shape Data to be set on the correct shapes. See Figure 12-3.

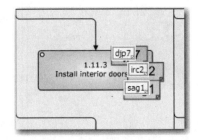

The macro adds Annotation Markers for the original page, and they are also color-coded for the different reviewers.

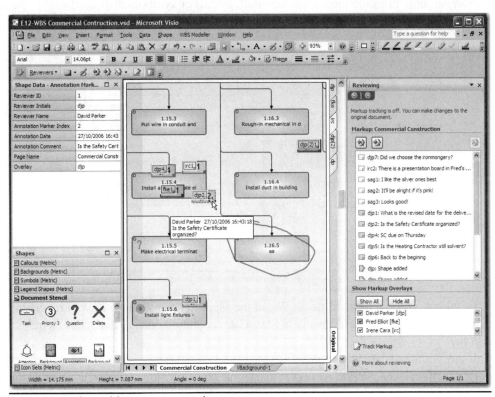

**Figure 12-3**  *The AddAnnotationMarkers macro*

You can use page Shape Data items—*Annotation Start* and *Annotation Width*—to filter the Annotation Marker shapes on display and their size.

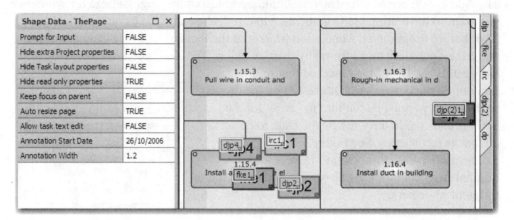

You can now print the page with Annotation Marker symbols displayed.

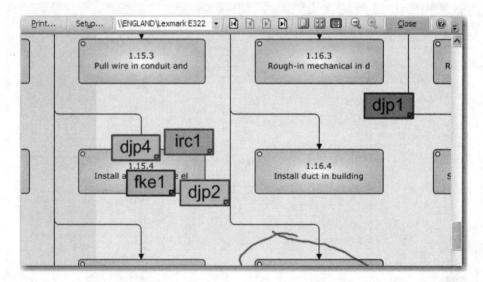

Of course, you can turn off the display of the Markup layer with the Layer Properties dialog, or you could set the Annotation Start Date to a future date, as that hides them anyway.

If any comments are edited, deleted, or added, just rerun the AddAnnotationMarkers macro, as it replaces everything on the markup layer.

# Code Listing for AddAnnotationMarkers

```
Public Sub AddAnnotationMarkers()
Dim pagMarkup As Visio.Page
Dim pag As Visio.Page
Dim shp As Visio.Shape
Dim mst As Visio.Master
Dim sel As Visio.Selection
Dim lyr As Visio.Layer
Dim iRow As Integer

Dim rvwID As Integer

Dim antX As Double
Dim antY As Double
Dim antMI As Integer
Dim antDate As String    ' Date
Dim antComment As String
Dim overlay As String

Dim countMarkers As Integer
Dim rowRvwID As Integer
Dim rowAntMI As Integer
Dim rowAntDate As Integer
Dim rowAntComment As Integer
Dim rowOverlay As String

Dim varObjectsToInstance() As Variant    'Array of Masters for DropMany
Dim adblXYArray() As Double 'Array of XY values fro DropMany
Dim aSheetSectRowCol() As Integer   'Array of SSRC for SetFormulas

Dim intCounter As Integer

Dim aintIDArray() As Integer      'Returned array of Sheet IDs from DropMany
Dim intProcessed As Integer
Dim avarFormulaArray() As Variant   'Array of Formulas for SetFormulas
Dim proceed As Boolean
Dim iCols As Integer
Dim iArgs As Integer

    Set pag = Visio.ActivePage

    If Not pag.Type = visTypeForeground Then
        MsgBox "This macro should only be run from a Foreground page", vbExclamation
        Exit Sub
    End If

    If pag.Document.Masters.Count = 0 Then
        MsgBox "This document does not have the Annotation Marker Master", vbExclamation
        Exit Sub
    End If
```

```
For Each mst In pag.Document.Masters
    If mst.Name = "Annotation Marker" Then
        'Get the required row numbers for SetFormulas
        rowRvwID = mst.Shapes(1).Cells("Prop.ReviewerID").row
        rowAntMI = mst.Shapes(1).Cells("Prop.AnnotationMarkerIndex").row
        rowAntDate = mst.Shapes(1).Cells("Prop.AnnotationDate").row

        rowAntComment = mst.Shapes(1).Cells("Prop.AnnotationComment").row
        rowOverlay = mst.Shapes(1).Cells("Prop.Overlay").row
        Exit For
    End If
Next mst

If Not mst.Name = "Annotation Marker" Then
    MsgBox "This document does not have the Annotation Marker Master", vbExclamation
    Exit Sub
End If

'Remove an previously dropped shapes
For Each lyr In pag.Layers
    If lyr.Name = "Markup" Then
        lyr.CellsC(Visio.visLayerLock) = 0
        lyr.CellsC(Visio.visLayerVisible) = 1
        lyr.CellsC(Visio.visLayerPrint) = 1
        Set sel = pag.CreateSelection(visSelTypeByLayer, visSelModeSkipSub, lyr)
        sel.Delete
        Exit For
    End If
Next lyr

iCols = 5
iArgs = 4

For Each pagMarkup In pag.Document.Pages
    proceed = False
    If pagMarkup.Type = visTypeMarkup Then
        If pagMarkup.OriginalPage = pag Then
            proceed = True
        End If
    ElseIf pagMarkup.ID = pag.ID Then
        proceed = True
    End If
    If proceed = True Then
        If pagMarkup.PageSheet.SectionExists(Visio.visSectionAnnotation, _
                                    Visio.visExistsAnywhere) Then
            If pagMarkup.Type = visTypeMarkup Then
                'Get the reviewer ID for this page
                rvwID = pag.Document.DocumentSheet.CellsSRC(Visio.visSectionReviewer, _
                    pagMarkup.ReviewerID - 1, Visio.visReviewerReviewerID).ResultIU
            End If
            'Loop thru all the annotation for this page
            For iRow = 0 To pagMarkup.PageSheet.RowCount(Visio.visSectionAnnotation) - 1
                countMarkers = countMarkers + 1
```

```
ReDim Preserve varObjectsToInstance(1 To countMarkers) As Variant
ReDim Preserve adblXYArray(1 To countMarkers * 2) As Double

antX = pagMarkup.PageSheet.CellsSRC(Visio.visSectionAnnotation, _
    iRow, Visio.visAnnotationX).ResultIU
antY = pagMarkup.PageSheet.CellsSRC(Visio.visSectionAnnotation, _
    iRow, Visio.visAnnotationY).ResultIU

varObjectsToInstance(countMarkers) = mst
'Set x,y components of where to drop
adblXYArray(countMarkers * 2 - 1) = antX
adblXYArray(countMarkers * 2) = antY

'5 Shape Data items to set, and 4 arguments
ReDim Preserve aSheetSectRowCol(1 To (countMarkers * iCols) * iArgs)
                              As Integer
ReDim Preserve avarFormulaArray(0 To (countMarkers * iCols) - 1)

antMI = pagMarkup.PageSheet.CellsSRC(Visio.visSectionAnnotation, _
    iRow, Visio.visAnnotationMarkerIndex).ResultIU
If pagMarkup.Type = visTypeForeground Then
    'Get the reviewer ID for this Annotation
    rvwID = pagMarkup.PageSheet.CellsSRC(Visio.visSectionAnnotation, _
        iRow, Visio.visAnnotationReviewerID).ResultIU
End If
antDate = pagMarkup.PageSheet.CellsSRC(Visio.visSectionAnnotation, _
    iRow, Visio.visAnnotationDate).Formula
antComment = pagMarkup.PageSheet.CellsSRC(Visio.visSectionAnnotation, _
    iRow, Visio.visAnnotationComment).ResultStr("")

If pagMarkup.ID = pag.ID Then
    overlay = ""
Else
    Dim suffixLength As Integer
    suffixLength = Len(pagMarkup.Name) - Len(pag.Name)
    overlay = Mid(pagMarkup.Name, Len(pag.Name) + 3, suffixLength - 3)
End If

aSheetSectRowCol(((countMarkers - 1) * iCols * iArgs) + 2)
                  = Visio.visSectionProp
aSheetSectRowCol(((countMarkers - 1) * iCols * iArgs) + 3) = rowRvwID
aSheetSectRowCol(((countMarkers - 1) * iCols * iArgs) + 4)
                  = Visio.visCustPropsValue
avarFormulaArray(((countMarkers - 1) * iCols) + 0)
                  = "GUARD(" & rvwID & ")"

aSheetSectRowCol(((countMarkers - 1) * iCols * iArgs) + 6)
                  = Visio.visSectionProp
aSheetSectRowCol(((countMarkers - 1) * iCols * iArgs) + 7) = rowAntMI
aSheetSectRowCol(((countMarkers - 1) * iCols * iArgs) + 8)
                  = Visio.visCustPropsValue
avarFormulaArray(((countMarkers - 1) * iCols) + 1) = "GUARD
                  (" & antMI & ")"
```

```
                    aSheetSectRowCol(((countMarkers - 1) * iCols * iArgs) + 10)
                                = Visio.visSectionProp
                    aSheetSectRowCol(((countMarkers - 1) * iCols * iArgs) + 11) = rowAntDate
                    aSheetSectRowCol(((countMarkers - 1) * iCols * iArgs) + 12)
                                = Visio.visCustPropsValue
                    avarFormulaArray(((countMarkers - 1) * iCols) + 2) = "GUARD
                            (" & antDate & ")"


                    aSheetSectRowCol(((countMarkers - 1) * iCols * iArgs) + 14)
                                = Visio.visSectionProp
                    aSheetSectRowCol(((countMarkers - 1) * 20) + 15) = rowAntComment
                    aSheetSectRowCol(((countMarkers - 1) * 20) + 16)
                                = Visio.visCustPropsValue
                    avarFormulaArray(((countMarkers - 1) * iCols) + 3) = "GUARD
                            (""" & antComment & """)"


                    aSheetSectRowCol(((countMarkers - 1) * iCols * iArgs) + 18)
                                = Visio.visSectionProp
                    aSheetSectRowCol(((countMarkers - 1) * iCols * iArgs) + 19) = rowOverlay
                    aSheetSectRowCol(((countMarkers - 1) * iCols * iArgs) + 20)
                                = Visio.visCustPropsValue
                    avarFormulaArray(((countMarkers - 1) * iCols) + 4) = "GUARD
                            (""" & overlay & """)"


            Next iRow
        End If
      End If
Next pagMarkup

'Drop the shapes on the page
intProcessed = pag.DropMany(varObjectsToInstance, adblXYArray, aintIDArray)

'Put the IDs for the dropped shapes into the array for SetFormulas
For intCounter = 0 To (intProcessed * iCols) - 1 ' LBound(aintIDArray)
                    To UBound(aintIDArray)
    aSheetSectRowCol((intCounter * iArgs) + 1) = aintIDArray
                    (Int((intCounter / iCols)))
Next intCounter
'Tell Microsoft Visio to set the formulas of the cells.
intProcessed = pag.SetFormulas(aSheetSectRowCol, avarFormulaArray,
                    Visio.visSetBlastGuards)


End Sub
```

# Reporting on Reviewer's Markup

Now that you have shapes for Comments, you can use the standard *Reports tool* to create reports or extract the information, as in the example Reviewer Annotation report, shown in Figure 12-4.

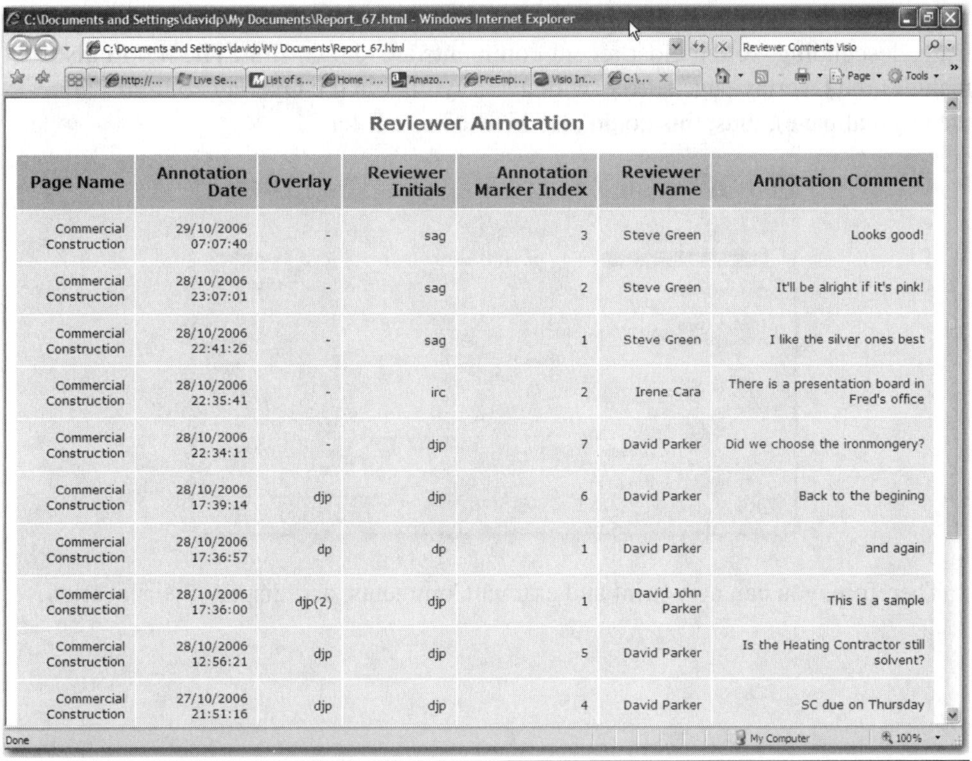

Reviewer Annotation

| Page Name | Annotation Date | Overlay | Reviewer Initials | Annotation Marker Index | Reviewer Name | Annotation Comment |
|---|---|---|---|---|---|---|
| Commercial Construction | 29/10/2006 07:07:40 | - | sag | 3 | Steve Green | Looks good! |
| Commercial Construction | 28/10/2006 23:07:01 | - | sag | 2 | Steve Green | It'll be alright if it's pink! |
| Commercial Construction | 28/10/2006 22:41:26 | - | sag | 1 | Steve Green | I like the silver ones best |
| Commercial Construction | 28/10/2006 22:35:41 | - | irc | 2 | Irene Cara | There is a presentation board in Fred's office |
| Commercial Construction | 28/10/2006 22:34:11 | - | djp | 7 | David Parker | Did we choose the ironmongery? |
| Commercial Construction | 28/10/2006 17:39:14 | djp | djp | 6 | David Parker | Back to the begining |
| Commercial Construction | 28/10/2006 17:36:57 | dp | dp | 1 | David Parker | and again |
| Commercial Construction | 28/10/2006 17:36:00 | djp(2) | djp | 1 | David John Parker | This is a sample |
| Commercial Construction | 28/10/2006 12:56:21 | djp | djp | 5 | David Parker | Is the Heating Contractor still solvent? |
| Commercial Construction | 27/10/2006 21:51:16 | djp | djp | 4 | David Parker | SC due on Thursday |

**Figure 12-4** *The Reviewer Annotation report*

Moreover, the Annotation Start Date will be respected in the filtering of the items because you can use the User.Hide value to test whether the shape is visible (Hide = 0).

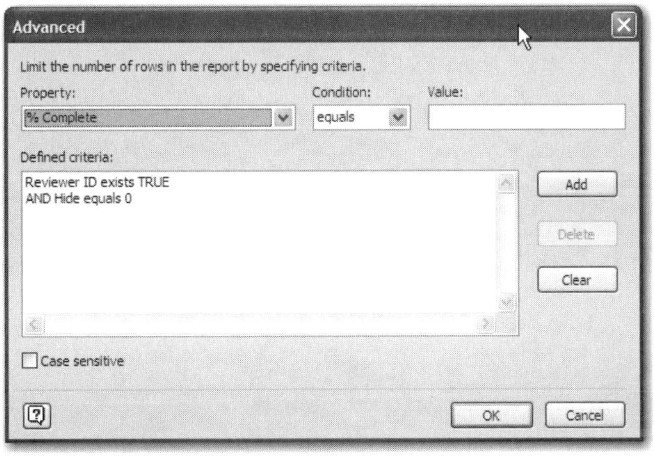

The report definition is grouped by the Page Name, sorted by the Annotation Date, descending, so the most recent comments are shown first. The report also includes the Overlay page suffix (with a "–" symbol in the Overlay column if it is the original page), thus, this could also be used as a filter.

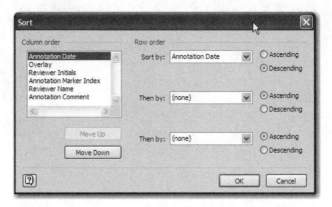

Therefore, you can now print and extract Comments, and display their location.

# Preparing for Publication

This is sad, but true: not everybody has Microsoft Visio installed on their PC. Therefore, you need a way to print your Visio document, distribute the file electronically, or place it a location where it can be viewed, such as a web site. The method of publication can affect the way you prepare your document for consumption by others.

Some electronic formats are *raster images*, which means they are built up from a number of pixels or dots, while others are *vector images*, which means they are built up from lines. A raster image does not look good if you zoom in to it. This is because the size of the pixels gets larger, giving a blocky appearance. On the other hand, vector images do not get any worse when you zoom in on them because the lines are defined between points.

A photograph is suited to raster formats, because the images are created from a number of pixels anyway: the more pixels you have, the clearer the image and the larger the file size. Visio drawings, though, like CAD files, are mainly vectors in the first place so, obviously, using a vector format for distribution is best, if possible.

The other consideration is data and hyperlinks. Visio drawings often contain data for specific shapes, and these may each contain from no data to many hyperlinks. So, if the end user for the Visio document needs to view both data and hyperlinks, then consider a format that enables access to both of these.

Other areas for considerations are the capability to see a reviewer's markup, the use of layer control, and the capability to print well locally by the end user.

# Printing

Some users get confused about printing when the printer paper size is different than the Visio page size, and they get even more confused if the Visio page is scaled. In this example, the Visio page is A3 size, and the printer has A4 paper (which is exactly half the size of A3). So, I set the Print Zoom to be 1 sheet across and 2 sheets down. The printed page has been set to Landscape because the Visio page is Portrait.

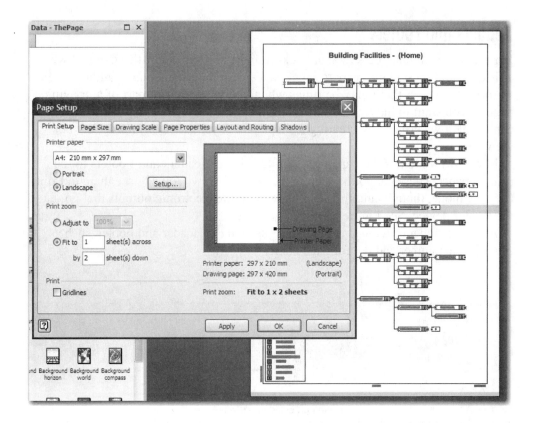

Notice you can see the Page Break as a horizontal grey band dissecting the page. This shows the overlap zone between the two pages that will be printed on both pages. View | Page Breaks toggles the visibility of this, but you will not see them displayed if you have a solid background, as are all the Microsoft-supplied Masters. Also, note, setting the Print Zoom Adjust to 100 percent would have had the same effect in this case.

Having the Visio page zoom to print on the printer paper without splitting over many pages is more normal, though, so usually the Print Zoom is set to 1 sheet across by 1 sheet down.

## Headers and Footers

In previous chapters, you saw that backgrounds, borders, and titles can provide a flexible and presentable way to label pages with their name, date, author, and so forth. However, there may be times when you need to print part of a drawing page or you want to have some information appear only when it's printed (you can create a watermark by creating a shape on a layer that is printable, but not viewable.

Microsoft Visio has the capability to add limited Headers and Footers to the printed paper. These cannot be seen in the Normal view. You can see them in Print Preview mode, though, and they can be seen on the electronic outputs that go via the Printer device. See Figure 13-1.

A small number of built-in codes can be used in the Header and Footer, such as *&p* for page number and *&n* for page name.

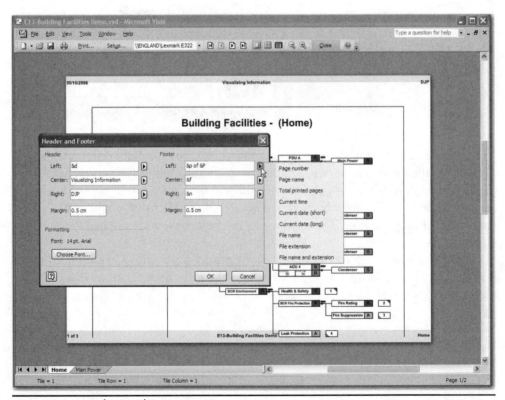

**Figure 13-1**  *Headers and Footers*

Notice the Header and Footer are at the top and bottom of the printed page, which is not necessarily the Visio page.

Although there is a CurrentDate setting, that may not be when the file was last edited and saved. Therefore, I have written a macro—UpdateHeader—to update the Document.HeaderLeft with the last modified date.

If you accept the update, then the Header is updated.

Of course, this could have updated any of the six Header and Footer positions.

The following code requires a reference to Microsoft Scripting Runtime using Tools | References.

## Code Listing for UpdateHeader

```
Public Sub UpdateHeader()
Dim fil As Scripting.File
Dim oFS As New Scripting.FileSystemObject
Dim txt As String

    If oFS.FileExists(Visio.ActiveDocument.FullName) = True Then
        Set fil = oFS.GetFile(Visio.ActiveDocument.FullName)
        txt = fil.Name
        txt = txt & vbCrLf & "DateCreated: " & vbTab & fil.DateCreated
        txt = txt & vbCrLf & "DateLastAccessed:" & vbTab & fil.DateLastAccessed
```

```
        txt = txt & vbCrLf & "DateLastModified:" & vbTab & fil.DateLastModified
        If MsgBox(txt, vbQuestion + vbYesNo, "Confirm update of Header Left") =
vbYes Then
            Visio.ActiveDocument.HeaderLeft = "Last Edit: " &
Format(fil.DateLastModified, "ddddd")
        End If
    Else
        MsgBox "This file has never been saved!", vbExclamation
    End If

End Sub
```

## XML Paper Specification (XPS)

Microsoft has launched a new portable file format—*XML Paper Specification*—which is an open specification, multiplatform, XML-based electronic paper that can be read by hardware, software, and humans. You need to download the free Microsoft Office 2007 Add-in: Microsoft Save as PDF or XPS, if you do not have it already. I hope, it is already deployed in your organization. Then, you can select File | Publish as PDF or XPS.

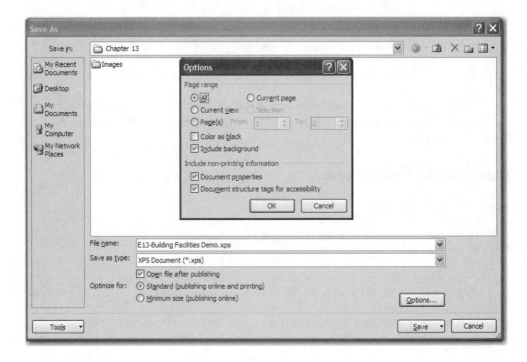

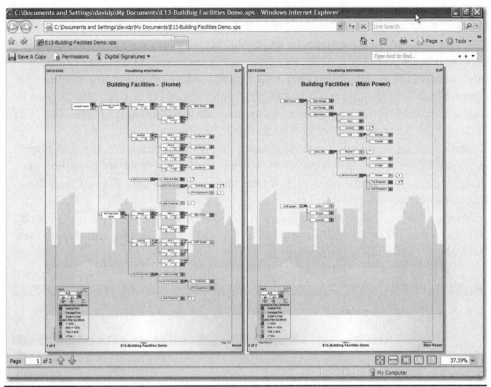

**Figure 13-2**  *The XPS File Viewer*

The file is opened in the browser, as you see in Figure 13-2.

The files are created with an xps extension, but if you change this to a ZIP file, then you can open the file to see the contents, which are comprised of folders, sub-folders and files. These xps files are only intended for viewing, not editing, and the xps files cannot be opened in Visio again.

Support is built into Microsoft Vista and Microsoft Office 2007, and can be added to Windows XP along with .Net Framework 3.

There is an API for this file format, along with the file definition, which can be extended, so developers can use these files within their own applications. In theory, the Shape Data could also be encapsulated within the XPS file, but, as yet, this is not done. See http://www.microsoft.com/whdc/xps/default.mspx for more information.

## Portable Document Format (PDF)

PDF was invented and popularized by Adobe, which provides the Adobe Reader used by a large proportion of business users. PDF is based on the Tagged Image File Format (TIFF), which is raster-based, but can do a good rendition if the dpi dots per inch (dpi) setting is high enough. Adobe also produces Acrobat, which is used to create PDF files, but now you can also use the Microsoft Office 2007 Add-in: Microsoft Save as PDF or XPS to do this. See Figure 13-3.

This creates a pretty good graphics output, but it neither includes any data nor the capability to switch layers on or off. It does preserve the primary hyperlink per shape, though. In fact, the open PDF format has fewer bells and whistles than the Adobe proprietary one.

Microsoft Visio 2007 includes a new method—*ExportToFixedFormat*—which enables you to create these Microsoft PDF files and XPS files by automation (see the section "Automating the Export").

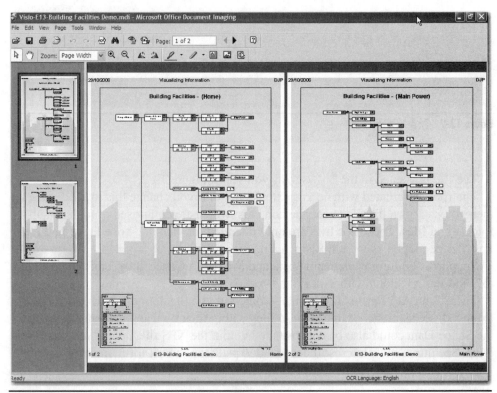

**Figure 13-3**   *PDF from Microsoft Save as PDF*

Adobe Acrobat can output both graphics and data, however, and you can maintain the layer structure.

In fact, the Adobe Acrobat conversion can create Adobe Comments from the Visio Screen Tips. Strangely, it does not convert the Visio Comments into Adobe Comments, so I can only assume the Adobe development team has not quite caught up with the change that happened inside Visio. Also, it does not appear to preserve hyperlinks. See Figure 13-4.

At press time, Adobe Acrobat 8 is being released, so I do not know if this has improved. In any case, for an extra cost, by purchasing Acrobat you can get even better PDF documents than the Microsoft tool, if it is important to display data, too. My own experience has been that Adobe PDF toolbars and menus have historically created problems in Microsoft applications, such as Visio and Excel, as well as in Microsoft Visio 2007, the menus and toolbars seem to appear at the Getting Started interface, only to disappear as soon as a drawing is opened.

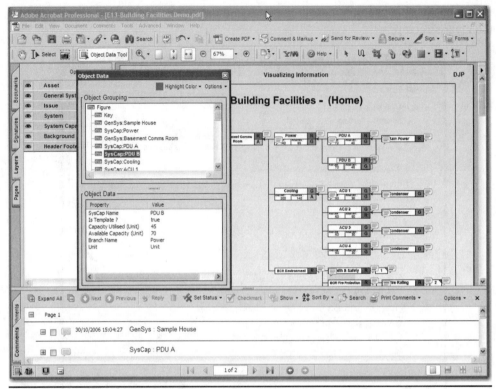

**Figure 13-4**  *PDF from Adobe Acrobat*

## Microsoft Document Imaging Format (MDI)

Microsoft Office Document Imaging uses Microsoft Document Imaging Format (MDI) format, which is also based on TIFF. This tool is part of the Microsoft Office installation and provides an electronic file that can be e-mailed and viewed, if the end user has Microsoft Office. See Figure 13-5.

MDI even has an application programming interface (API) that can be referenced for developers to control.

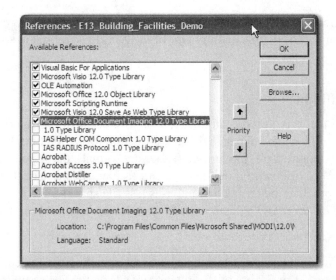

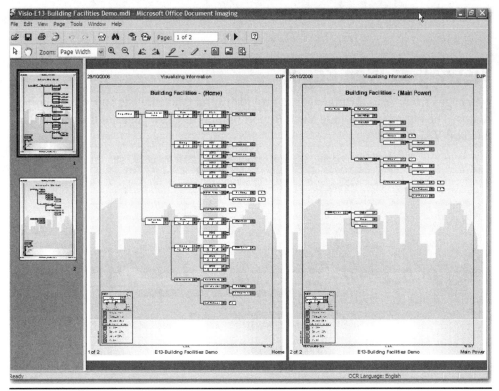

**Figure 13-5** *The MDI Viewer*

However, the quality of the image is not as good as the PDF or XPS options, and the MDI format will be deprecated in favor of the XPS/PDF format at some point in the future.

## Just as an Image

Sometimes, all that is required is an image, and Visio has many image file formats to choose from. The choice depends on the destination for the picture. For example, web pages may require a gif, jpg, or png file (raster format), but if you intend to use the picture in Word or PowerPoint, then a vector format, such as Enhanced Metafile Format (emf), produces better quality and uses less file space.

Indeed, you can even use code to export the selected shapes only to an image file.

```
Visio.ActiveWindow.Selection.Export "an image file.jpg"
```

The Export method uses the file extension of the specified file to decide on how to create the image. The quality of the image depends on the last settings used in the user interface.

# Viewing as Web Pages

Web pages from Visio documents can provide useful data analysis and visual dashboards. The output can include Visio Report outputs as extra pages at the end of the standard Visio pages.

You can choose the main output format, such as Vector Markup Language (VML) which has been supported natively in Internet Explorer (IE) since version 5 (although not in any other browser), but then you need an alternative for non-IE users, such as GIF.

You can select the destination resolution for the raster images, the style sheet to apply, and even a web page to host within, as you can see in Figure 13-6.

The VML interface provides a handy Pan and Zoom window, along with the Shape Data Details of each shape, and the capability to search them with a flashing arrow to point at the selected result. All-in-all, not bad. The Scalable Vector Graphics (SVG) alternative is almost as good, but requires the installation of an SVG Viewer control in IE, as it is not natively supported (but it is in Firefox). It does not have the Pan and Zoom window, though.

The three disappointments with the Save As Web output are the difficulty in printing (because it only uses the Internet browser print method), the lack of layer control, and the absence of reviewer's comments.

The lack of good printing can be overcome with the inclusion of an alternative printable copy, such as PDF or XPS, which you learned about in the previous sections.

The absence of reviewer's comments can be overcome with Annotation Marker shapes, as described in the previous chapter, although these comments will not be required most of the time.

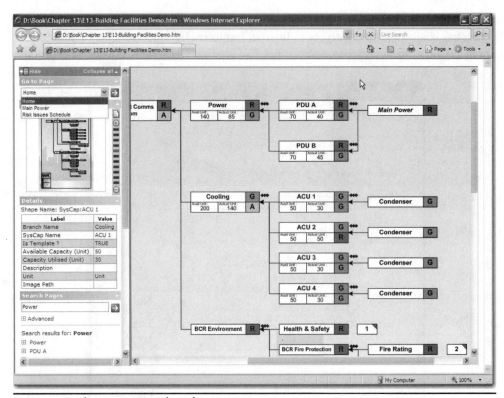

**Figure 13-6**  *The Save As Web with VML*

Layer control is missing, which is a pity, because VML and SVG both support it to an extent. However, Visio layering is more complex than anything else I know because a single element can belong to none, one, or many layers. You could save multiple PDF or XPS files with different layer settings for printing, though.

The Save As Web page creates multiple files, preferably stored in a subfolder. One of these files, called *data.xml,* contains all the visible Shape Data for the document (see Figure 13-7).

This file could be used for interrogation or reporting by your own custom web pages.

**Figure 13-7**  *The data.xml file*

# Enhancing Hyperlinks

The Save As Web with the VML format supports multiple hyperlinks per shape, but the Hyperlinks dialog (select the shape, then CTRL+K) in Visio is incomplete.

This Hyperlinks dialog does not let you set the other cells in the Hyperlinks section of the ShapeSheet, so you will need to use the ShapeSheet window to access them.

These extra cells, as shown in Table 13-1, clearly require a little explanation.

| Cell | Comment |
| --- | --- |
| Description | The Description displayed on the right mouse menu. If empty, then the Address or SubAddress is used. |
| Address | Use predefined protocols, see http://msdn.microsoft.com/library/default.asp?url=/workshop/networking/predefined/mailto.asp for more information.<br>Leave blank if SubAddress is specifying a page and/or shape within the Visio document. |
| SubAddress | If no Address, then the Name of Page in this Visio document, with option !ShapeName.<br>If Address is an Excel file, then SubAddress can be Worksheet or Range in that document.<br>If Address is a Word document, then the SubAddress can be a Bookmark in that document. |
| ExtraInfo | If used, defines the query string after the ? character, for, say, asp requests. |
| Frame | Name of target frame, if required. |
| SortKey | Alpha order, for example, 01,02, and so forth. |
| NewWindow | Default is False, but set to True if you want a new browser to open, instead of the current window being refreshed (which can be annoying if you are zoomed into a small area of a large drawing). |
| Default | Default is False, but set to True for the link you want considered as the primary hyperlink in output formats that do not support multiple hyperlinks (such as the SVG or PDF). |
| Invisible | Default is False, but set to True if you want to make a link invisible (perhaps prior to publishing to an extranet site, and the link refers to an intranet site). |

**Table 13-1**  *Hyperlinks Section Cells*

# Automating the Export

Microsoft Visio provides an API for SaveAsWeb and, now, there is a method to Export to XPS or PDF. This provides the possibility to automate the export of HTML, XPS, and PDF files in one click. This means you can get the browsability and searchability of the VML web pages, combined with the preformatted XPS or PDF files for those users who want printable output.

First, the ExportAsFixedFormat method provides the capability, using the Microsoft Office 2007 Add-in: Microsoft Save as PDF or XPS, to create XPS or PDF files for all pages, the current page, current view, or for a specified number of pages. In this example, though, I specified the whole document.

Second, I used the HyperlinkBase property of the document to define where the web page and supporting files should be published to.

Third, I specified VML as the primary web format and GIF as the secondary format.

Fourth, I modified the border shape to provide hyperlinks to the XPS and PDF files, and to a separately saved report.

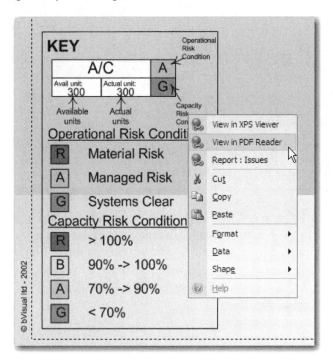

The hyperlinks have been created in the ShapeSheet, and should not be amended with the Hyperlinks dialog because it attempts to evaluate the Address formulae.

The formulae assume the XPS and PDF files are the same name as the current document, apart from the file extension, and that all the files will be stored in the subfolder created by the SaveAsWeb method.

Unfortunately, there seems to be no automation method to include specified Reports automatically, so these must be saved separately.

The CreateDocWebPages reads the active document Name and HyperlinkBase property to pass these values through to the ExportDocAsWeb function first, so it will create the subfolder, and then the ExportDocAsFixedFormat is called twice, with different parameters, so the XPS and PDF files are created.

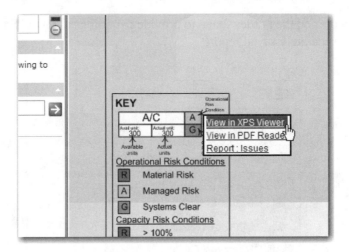

The resultant web page contains hyperlinks to printable copies of the drawing and can open reports in a separate browser. This makes it easier to have report tables and searchable graphics side-by-side for analysis, as you can see in Figure 13-8.

Moreover, the files are all contained within a subfolder for the main access web page, which means that compressing together into a zip file for e-mail, or just copying around, is straightforward.

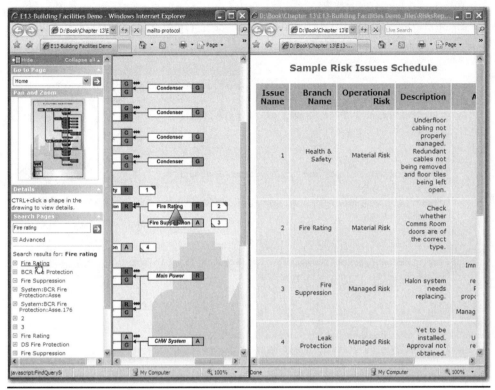

**Figure 13-8** *Searchable web page and report table*

# Code Listing for CreateDocWebPages

```
Public Sub CreateDocWebPages()
Dim doc As Visio.Document
Dim fldr As String
Dim fil As String

    Set doc = Visio.ActiveDocument
    fil = Replace(Replace(doc.Name, ".vsd", ""), ".vdx", "")
    If doc.HyperlinkBase = "" Then
        fldr = doc.Path
    Else
        fldr = doc.HyperlinkBase
    End If

    'Save As Web creates a subfolder
    ExportDocAsWeb doc, fldr, fil
    'Output XPS & PDF to subfolder
```

```
        ExportDocAsFixedFormat visFixedFormatXPS, doc, fldr & fil & "_files\", fil
        ExportDocAsFixedFormat visFixedFormatPDF, doc, fldr & fil & "_files\", fil

End Sub

Private Sub ExportDocAsFixedFormat(ByVal formatOut As Visio.VisFixedFormatTypes, _
    ByVal doc As Visio.Document, _
    ByVal folderOut As String, ByVal fileOut As String)
Dim ext As String

    Select Case formatOut
        Case Visio.VisFixedFormatTypes.visFixedFormatXPS
            ext = ".xps"
        Case Visio.VisFixedFormatTypes.visFixedFormatPDF
            ext = ".pdf"
    End Select

    doc.ExportAsFixedFormat formatOut, folderOut & fileOut & ext, _
        visDocExIntentPrint, visPrintAll

End Sub

Private Sub ExportDocAsWeb(ByVal doc As Visio.Document, _
    ByVal folderOut As String, ByVal fileOut As String)

    Dim vsoSaveAsWeb As VisSaveAsWeb
    Dim vsoWebSettings As VisWebPageSettings

    ' Get a VisSaveAsWeb object that
    ' represents a new Web page project.
    Set vsoSaveAsWeb = Visio.Application.SaveAsWebObject
    'Ensure that the passed doc object is used
    vsoSaveAsWeb.AttachToVisioDoc doc

    ' Get a VisWebPageSettings object.
    Set vsoWebSettings = vsoSaveAsWeb.WebPageSettings

    ' Configure preferences.
    With vsoWebSettings
        .AltFormat = True
        .PriFormat = "VML"
        .SecFormat = "GIF"
        .PanAndZoom = True
        .PropControl = True
        .Search = True
        .StoreInFolder = True
        .DispScreenRes = VISWEB_DISP_RES.res1024x768
        .OpenBrowser = True
        .QuietMode = True
```

```
        .TargetPath = folderOut & fileOut & ".htm"
    End With


    ' Create the pages
    vsoSaveAsWeb.CreatePages


End Sub
```

# Using the Visio Viewer

Microsoft Outlook 2007 includes the Microsoft Visio Viewer by default, and non-Outlook users can download it free from Microsoft. The *Visio Viewer control* from Microsoft lets a non-Visio user view native Visio drawings (vsd or vdx). Not only can the Visio Viewer toggle the visibility of layers, it can also switch reviewers markup on or off selectively. See Figure 13-9.

The user can pan and zoom at will, and can investigate the Shape Data on any shape. The Viewer can be used in other applications, too, which can use some of its hidden qualities. For example, the labels and values of all the Shape Data can be

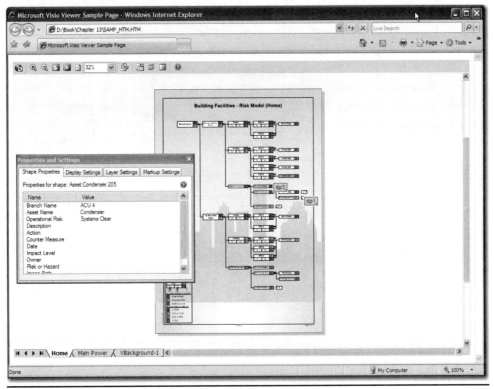

**Figure 13-9**  *The Visio Viewer in a web page*

extracted via the API, and all of the hyperlinks as well—not just the primary one, which is the case of the viewer control itself. Thus, it is possible to extract data from a Visio drawing without having Visio, even if the drawing is in binary format (vsd).

What the Viewer does not do well is print! However, now that you can easily produce printable copy in XPS or PDF, this is not too bad.

The Visio Viewer control cannot be used to edit the Visio drawing so, in that way, the document is secure, but the user does need access to the Visio file itself (or a copy of it). As security is not Visio's forte, other Visio users could copy the content and, even worse, if you have not made the file read only, modify it.

The Visio Viewer installation includes a sample web page that can be modified to include your own Visio document, and you can use the Visio Viewer at the same time you are using Visio itself.

## Sample Windows Forms Wrapper for the Visio Viewer

In this sample application, written in vb.net using Visual Studio 2005, I simply created a Windows Forms Application, and included the Microsoft Visio Viewer component, as you can see in Figure 13-10.

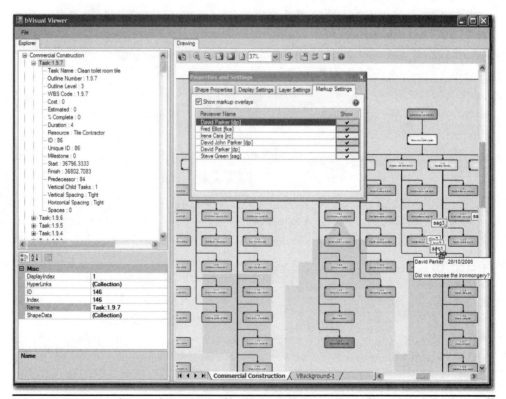

**Figure 13-10** *A simple Windows Forms for the Visio Viewer*

A straightforward Windows Forms application lets you select a Visio document from a dialog, and then loads the document into the Visio Viewer control. This loading event triggers the pages in the document to be added to the TreeView on the left, the significant shapes (those that have Shape Data) are added as elements under the page branch, and the Shape Data is listed below each shape.

If a new page is selected, either in the TreeView or in the Visio Viewer, then the shape's elements will be added to the TreeView.

The selection of a page, shape, or data item in the TreeView will fill the PropertyGrid below it, and the selection of a shape in the Visio Viewer will highlight the same shape in the TreeView (if it is a shape that contains data). Simple but effective, and, of course, something similar could be done in a web application.

The exiting user interface looks like this in Design mode:

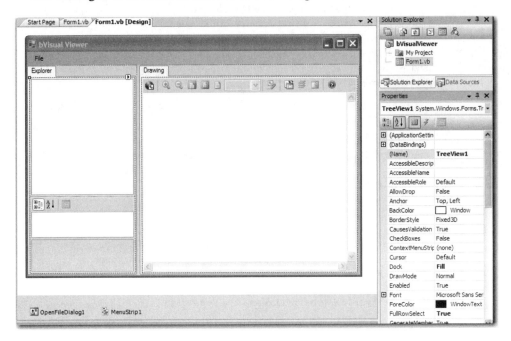

Form1 has MenuStrip1, which contains just two items: OpenToolStripMenuItem and ExitToolStripMenuItem. Form1 also has SplitContainer1 to separate the TabControl2 on the left from TabControl1 on the right. *TabControl1* contains the Microsoft Visio Viewer Control, and *TabControl2* contains SplitContainer2 that separates TreeView1 at the top from PropertyGrid1 at the bottom. All controls are set to Dock Fill.

OpenFileDialog1 has been added to enable the file open function to work. TreeView1 has HideSelection set to False, and AxViewer1 (the automatic name for the Visio Viewer control), has ScrollbarsVisible and ToolbarVisible set to True.

## Code Listing for Form1

```
Public Class Form1

    Private _pages As Hashtable

    Private Sub OpenToolStripMenuItem_Click(ByVal sender As System.Object,
                                       ByVal e As System.EventArgs)
Handles OpenToolStripMenuItem.Click
        Try
            With Me.OpenFileDialog1
                .FileName = Me.AxViewer1.SRC
                .ReadOnlyChecked = True
                .Filter = "Visio drawing (vsd)|*.vsd|Visio drawing (vdx)|*.vdx"
                .Title = "Select a Visio file to open"
                If .ShowDialog = Windows.Forms.DialogResult.OK Then
                    Me.AxViewer1.SRC = .FileName
                End If
            End With
        Catch ex As Exception

        End Try
    End Sub

    Private Sub ExitToolStripMenuItem_Click(ByVal sender As System.Object,
                                       ByVal e As System.EventArgs)
Handles ExitToolStripMenuItem.Click
        Me.Close()
    End Sub

    Private Sub TreeView1_AfterSelect(ByVal sender As System.Object,
                                 ByVal e As System.Windows.Forms
.TreeViewEventArgs) Handles TreeView1.AfterSelect
        Try
            Me.PropertyGrid1.SelectedObject = e.Node.Tag

            Dim pag As vPage = Nothing
            Dim shp As vShape = Nothing

            If TypeOf e.Node.Tag Is vPage Then
                pag = CType(e.Node.Tag, vPage)

            ElseIf TypeOf e.Node.Tag Is vShape Then
                pag = CType(e.Node.Parent.Tag, vPage)
                shp = CType(e.Node.Tag, vShape)
            ElseIf TypeOf e.Node.Tag Is vShapeData Then
```

```
            pag = CType(e.Node.Parent.Parent.Tag, vPage)
            shp = CType(e.Node.Parent.Tag, vShape)

        End If

        If Not pag.Index = Me.AxViewer1.CurrentPageIndex Then
            Me.AxViewer1.CurrentPageIndex = pag.Index
        End If

        If Not shp Is Nothing Then
            If Not shp.Index = Me.AxViewer1.SelectedShapeIndex Then
                'Would be nice to select
            End If
        End If

    Catch ex As Exception

    End Try
End Sub

Private Sub AxViewer1_OnDocumentLoaded(ByVal sender As Object,
                                  ByVal e As System.EventArgs)
Handles AxViewer1.OnDocumentLoaded
    Try
        _pages = New Hashtable

        With Me.TreeView1
            .Nodes.Clear()
            For pagCounter As Integer = 1 To Me.AxViewer1.PageCount
                Dim ap As New vPage
                ap.ID = Me.AxViewer1.get_PageIndexToID(pagCounter)
                ap.Index = pagCounter
                ap.Name = Me.AxViewer1.get_PageName(pagCounter)

                Dim nod As TreeNode = .Nodes.Add(ap.Name)
                nod.Tag = ap
                _pages.Add(ap.Index, ap)
                If pagCounter = Me.AxViewer1.CurrentPageIndex Then
                    nod.TreeView.SelectedNode = nod
                    loadPageShapes()
                End If
            Next
        End With
    Catch ex As Exception

    End Try
End Sub
```

```vb
    Private Sub AxViewer1_OnPageChanged(ByVal sender As Object,
                             ByVal e As AxVisioViewer._IViewerEvents_
OnPageChangedEvent) Handles AxViewer1.OnPageChanged
        loadPageShapes()
    End Sub

    Private Sub loadPageShapes()
        Try
            Dim nod As TreeNode = Me.TreeView1.SelectedNode
            Dim displayCounter As Integer = 0

            If TypeOf nod.Tag Is vPage Then
                Dim pag As vPage = CType(nod.Tag, vPage)
                If nod.GetNodeCount(False) = 0 Then
                    'Can only iterate shapes when page is visible
                    For shpCounter As Integer = 1 To Me.AxViewer1.ShapeCount
                        Dim shp As New vShape
                        shp.Index = shpCounter
                        shp.Name = Me.AxViewer1.get_ShapeName(shpCounter)
                        shp.ID = Me.AxViewer1.get_ShapeIndexToID(shpCounter)

                        'Collect the Shape Data
                        For datCounter As Integer = 1 To
Me.AxViewer1.get_CustomPropertyCount(shpCounter)
                            Dim dat As New vShapeData
                            dat.Index = datCounter
                            dat.Name =
Me.AxViewer1.get_CustomPropertyName(shpCounter, datCounter)
                            dat.Value =
Me.AxViewer1.get_CustomPropertyValue(shpCounter, datCounter)
                            If shp.DisplayIndex = 0 Then
                                displayCounter = displayCounter + 1
                                shp.DisplayIndex = displayCounter
                            End If
                            shp.ShapeData.Add(datCounter, dat)
                        Next
                        'Collect the hyperlinks
                        For lnkCounter As Integer = 1 To
Me.AxViewer1.get_HyperlinkCount(shpCounter)
                            Dim lnk As New vHyperlink
                            lnk.Index = lnkCounter
                            lnk.Address =
Me.AxViewer1.get_CustomPropertyName(shpCounter, lnkCounter)
                            shp.HyperLinks.Add(lnkCounter, lnk)
                        Next

                        pag.Shapes.Add(shp.Index, shp)
```

```vb
                            'Only interested in those with data
                            If shp.DisplayIndex > 0 Then
                                Dim shpNod As TreeNode = nod.Nodes.Add(shp.Name)
                                shpNod.Tag = shp
                                Dim enm As IEnumerator
                                enm = shp.ShapeData.GetEnumerator
                                While enm.MoveNext
                                    Dim de As DictionaryEntry = CType(enm.Current, _
                                                                      DictionaryEntry)
                                    Dim dat As vShapeData = CType(de.Value, vShapeData)
                                    Dim datNod As TreeNode = shpNod.Nodes.Add _
(dat.Name & " : " & dat.Value)
                                    datNod.Tag = dat
                                End While
                            End If
                        Next
                    End If
                End If
            Catch ex As Exception

            End Try
        End Sub


        Private Sub AxViewer1_OnSelectionChanged(ByVal sender As Object, _
                                        ByVal e As AxVisioViewer._
IViewerEvents_OnSelectionChangedEvent) Handles AxViewer1.OnSelectionChanged
            Dim nod As TreeNode = Me.TreeView1.SelectedNode
            Dim pagNod As TreeNode = Me.TreeView1.Nodes(Me.AxViewer1 _
                                                .CurrentPageIndex - 1)
            Dim pag As vPage = CType(pagNod.Tag, vPage)
            If pag.Shapes.ContainsKey(Me.AxViewer1.SelectedShapeIndex) Then
                Dim shp As vShape = pag.Shapes.Item(Me.AxViewer1.SelectedShapeIndex)
                Dim shpNod As TreeNode = pagNod.Nodes.Item(shp.DisplayIndex - 1)
                pagNod.TreeView.SelectedNode = shpNod
                shpNod.EnsureVisible()
                shpNod.Expand()
            End If
        End Sub
End Class


Public Class vPage
    Private _ID As Integer
    Private _index As Integer
    Private _name As String
    Private _shapes As New Hashtable


    Public Property Shapes() As Hashtable
```

```
        Get
            Return _shapes
        End Get
        Set(ByVal value As Hashtable)
            _shapes = value
        End Set
    End Property

    Public Property ID() As Integer
        Get
            Return _ID
        End Get
        Set(ByVal value As Integer)
            _ID = value
        End Set
    End Property

    Public Property Index() As Integer
        Get
            Return _index
        End Get
        Set(ByVal value As Integer)
            _index = value
        End Set
    End Property

    Public Property Name() As String
        Get
            Return _name
        End Get
        Set(ByVal value As String)
            _name = value
        End Set
    End Property
End Class

Public Class vShape
    Private _ID As Integer
    Private _index As Integer
    Private _name As String
    Private _shapeData As New SortedList
    Private _hyperLinks As New SortedList
    Private _displayIndex As Integer

    Public Property HyperLinks() As SortedList
        Get
            Return _hyperLinks
```

```vbnet
        End Get
        Set(ByVal value As SortedList)
            _hyperLinks = value
        End Set
    End Property


    Public Property ShapeData() As SortedList
        Get
            Return _shapeData
        End Get
        Set(ByVal value As SortedList)
            _shapeData = value
        End Set
    End Property


    Public Property ID() As Integer
        Get
            Return _ID
        End Get
        Set(ByVal value As Integer)
            _ID = value
        End Set
    End Property


    Public Property Index() As Integer
        Get
            Return _index
        End Get
        Set(ByVal value As Integer)
            _index = value
        End Set
    End Property


    Public Property Name() As String
        Get
            Return _name
        End Get
        Set(ByVal value As String)
            _name = value
        End Set
    End Property
    Public Property DisplayIndex() As Integer
        Get
            Return _displayIndex
        End Get
        Set(ByVal value As Integer)
            _displayIndex = value
```

```
            End Set
        End Property
End Class


Public Class vShapeData
    Private _index As Integer
    Private _name As String
    Private _value As String

    Public Property Index() As Integer
        Get
            Return _index
        End Get
        Set(ByVal value As Integer)
            _index = value
        End Set
    End Property


    Public Property Name() As String
        Get
            Return _name
        End Get
        Set(ByVal value As String)
            _name = value
        End Set
    End Property


    Public Property Value() As String
        Get
            Return _value
        End Get
        Set(ByVal value As String)
            _value = value
        End Set
    End Property
End Class


Public Class vHyperlink
    Private _index As Integer
    Private _address As String

    Public Property Index() As Integer
        Get
            Return _index
        End Get
        Set(ByVal value As Integer)
            _index = value
```

```
        End Set
    End Property

    Public Property Address() As String
        Get
            Return _address
        End Get
        Set(ByVal value As String)
            _address = value
        End Set
    End Property

End Class
```

# CHAPTER
# 14

# Using Code to Enhance Functionality

Microsoft Visio is extensible. Everything in a Visio drawing is a SmartShape, whether it is just a single line or one character of text. A ShapeSheet is behind every Shape, and a ShapeSheet contains cells with formulae. So, my first rule is:

Only resort to any coding if you cannot achieve what you want in the ShapeSheet.

My second rule is:

Encapsulate as much as possible in the ShapeSheet, and send as little chatter as you can between Shapes and Code to make it work.

I say this upfront because experience has shown me that too many good programmers ignore the power of the ShapeSheet and try to control everything in code. Then, they wonder why it starts to get complicated . . . and slow.

If you need code, then Microsoft Visio is delivered with Visual Basic for Applications (VBA) built-in. And, you can create add-ons, Component Object Model (COM) Add-ins, Visual Studio Tools for Office (VSTO) Add-ins, Add-ons, and wrapper applications. So, how do you make your choice?

# Visual Basic for Applications (VBA)

This is a great boost for productivity. Many nondevelopers in organizations can write a little bit of VBA in, say, Excel or Word. Microsoft Visio even has a macro recorder, just like the other Microsoft Office Applications, which you can use to record some actions, edit the code to make it reusable, and then run the macro when you need it. This recorder starts with Tools | Macros | Record New Macro.

Be aware that the macro recorder cannot record everything you want, especially when you are using an add-on or an add-in (although some Microsoft add-ons do write to the macro recorder). The following macro—*ToggleLayer*—recorded the switching on of the Markup layer. This is a good task for a macro because it is usual to switch both the Visible and Print columns on or off together.

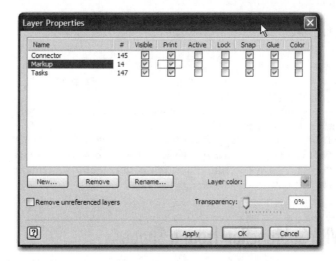

## Code Listing for ToggleLayer Recorded Macro

```
Sub ToggleLayer()
'
' Toggle Layer on/off
'

    Dim UndoScopeID1 As Long
    UndoScopeID1 = Application.BeginUndoScope("Layer Properties")
    Dim vsoLayer1 As Visio.Layer
    Set vsoLayer1 = Application.ActiveWindow.Page.Layers.Item(4)
    vsoLayer1.CellsC(visLayerVisible).FormulaU = "1"
    vsoLayer1.CellsC(visLayerPrint).FormulaU = "1"
    Application.EndUndoScope UndoScopeID1, True

End Sub
```

## Editing a Recorded Macro

What you want the recorded macro to do is turn the Markup layer on if it is turned off, and turn it off if it is turned on. The macro only detected that I chose layer number 4, but I only know it by the name Markup and the assigned number can be different on each page. So, we need to edit the macro accordingly.

### Code Listing for ToggleLayer VBA Subfunction

```
Sub ToggleLayer()
'
' Toggle Layer on/off
'
    Dim UndoScopeID1 As Long
    UndoScopeID1 = Application.BeginUndoScope("Layer Properties")
    Dim vsoLayer1 As Visio.Layer
    Set vsoLayer1 = Application.ActiveWindow.Page.Layers.Item("Markup")
    Dim currentVisible As Boolean
    currentVisible = CBool(vsoLayer1.CellsC(visLayerVisible).ResultIU)
    vsoLayer1.CellsC(visLayerVisible).FormulaU = CStr(Abs(Not (currentVisible)))
    vsoLayer1.CellsC(visLayerPrint).FormulaU = CStr(Abs(Not (currentVisible)))
    Application.EndUndoScope UndoScopeID1, True
End Sub
```

# Running a VBA Subfunction from a Shape

This could be run from the double-click event of a shape, say, a rectangle, by using the RUNADDON function.

So, double-clicking the rectangle toggles the Markup layer on/off. Even better would be if the code could read the text of the shape and use that as the layer name to toggle on/off. In this way, the rectangle, or a copy of it, can be used to toggle any layer visibility. The CALLTHIS function expects the macro it calls to have the first parameter to be a shape because it passes a reference to the shape that uses it through to the macro.

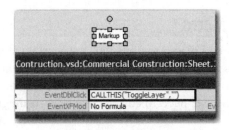

To give a visual indication of the layer status, the rectangle is colored Red if the layer is switched off, Green if the layer is switched On, and Yellow if the layer is not found.

## Code Listing for ToggleLayer Subfunction with Shape Parameter

```
Sub ToggleLayer(ByVal shp As Visio.Shape)
'
' Toggle Layer on/off - read text of shape
'
    Dim layerName As String
    'Use Characters.Text in case there are field codes
    layerName = shp.Characters.Text
    If Len(layerName) = 0 Or Application.ActivePage.Layers.Count = 0 Then
        Exit Sub
    End If
    Dim UndoScopeID1 As Long
    UndoScopeID1 = Application.BeginUndoScope("Layer Properties")
    Dim vsoLayer1 As Visio.Layer
    'To avoid an error, loop through the layers until the name is found
    For Each vsoLayer1 In Application.ActivePage.Layers
        If UCase(vsoLayer1.NameU) = UCase(layerName) Then
            Exit For
        End If
    Next vsoLayer1
    'Abort if the layer name was not found
    If vsoLayer1 Is Nothing Then
        shp.CellsSRC(Visio.visSectionObject, visRowFill, visFillForegnd).FormulaU = _
            "THEMEGUARD(RGB(255,255,0))" 'Yellow
        Exit Sub
    End If
    Dim currentVisible As Boolean
    currentVisible = CBool(vsoLayer1.CellsC(visLayerVisible).ResultIU)
    vsoLayer1.CellsC(visLayerVisible).FormulaU = CStr(Abs(Not (currentVisible)))
    vsoLayer1.CellsC(visLayerPrint).FormulaU = CStr(Abs(Not (currentVisible)))
    If currentVisible = True Then
        shp.CellsSRC(Visio.visSectionObject, visRowFill, visFillForegnd).FormulaU = _
            "THEMEGUARD(RGB(255,0,0))" 'Red
    Else
        shp.CellsSRC(Visio.visSectionObject, visRowFill, visFillForegnd).FormulaU = _
            "THEMEGUARD(RGB(0,255,0))" 'Green
    End If
    Application.EndUndoScope UndoScopeID1, True

End Sub
```

The most obvious place to store macros is in the VBA Project on the drawing, but just like Masters in the Document Stencil, this is usually wrong. If you do want to distribute macros, then put them in the VBA Project of a stencil, because the stencil can be docked in many drawings and can be included in workspaces.

Now, the rectangle shape can be made into a Master in a Stencil, and the VBA code can be put into the VBA Project. In this example, the code is put into a module called modFunctions in the Stencil Macros.

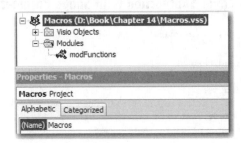

The double-click event needs to be modified to refer to the code now in the stencil.

Thus, the macro can be run from an instance of the Master, regardless of which drawing it is on, so long as the stencil is open.

VBA code runs quickly because it is running within the Visio process, and VBA is also great for prototyping code because you can test it immediately. VBA is also educational because you can try an action out to see what the recorder does. You can then decide if you could write it better yourself.

You can secure VBA code by password-protecting it, and you can distribute it with a Visio document (in fact, you can only distribute it with a Visio document). This means the code cannot run if the document is not open and it also will not work if macros are not allowed to run.

If you open Tools | Trust Center, then you can change the settings for running macros.

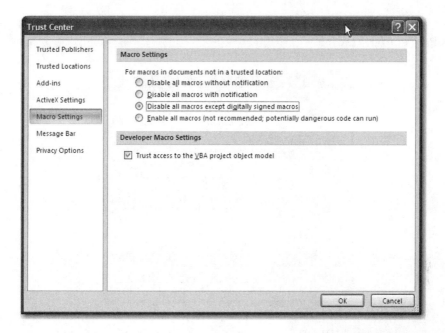

Your organization probably will not allow macros unless they are digitally signed. If so, then the macro you just created for distribution will not work, even for you, unless you add a digital signature using Tools | Digital Signature.

A SelfCert tool can create a digital signature for your own use, but you need an approved digital-signature certificate if you are going to distribute around your organization.

You should secure your code using Tools | <Project Name> Properties to lock the VBA Project from viewing.

If a digitally signed VBA Project is modified, then it must be resigned.

# VSTO Add-Ins

The Microsoft recommended method for distributing code around an organization is to use Visual Studio 2005 Tools for Office, Second Edition (VSTO 2005 SE), Visit http://msdn2.microsoft.com/en-us/office/aa905543.aspx for more information.

Visual Studio Tools for the Microsoft Office System (VSTO) is a free add-on for Visual Studio 2005 that enables developers to build applications targeted at Microsoft Office System applications. VSTO provides project templates for both Microsoft Visio 2007 and Microsoft Visio 2003 Add-ins, plus the other Microsoft Office applications. You need a license for at least Visual Studio 2005 Professional Edition to be eligible for the free download. It enables you to create managed code application-level add-ins that run in the same process space as the host application. In this example, you should name the solution ToggleLayer.

This creates a Visual Studio project with a ThisAddin class only, as Figure 14-1 shows.

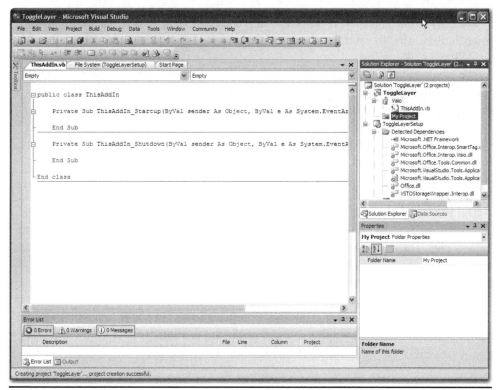

**Figure 14-1** *A VSTO blank solution*

The ThisAddin class is ready for you to enter code into the Startup and Shutdown events. These only fire when Visio starts up, and then shuts down, but all you need your add-in to do is respond to a call from the double-click event in a shape (we add a right mouse Action for good measure). The ThisAddin class includes a reference to the Application object, which can be accessed from the left-hand pull-down menu.

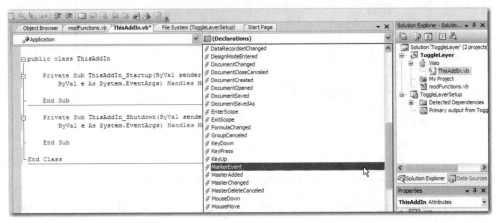

The only event you need for this add-in is *MarkerEvent*, which is a special event you can use to fire an event from a Visio document (as a persistent event) or from a ShapeSheet cell.

The MarkerEvent receives a message from Visio that is, by convention, split into multiple parameters. For example, the text is in the form /solution=ToggleLayer /cmd=1, so you need a function that can split this text into its parameters, and then decide if the message received is the correct one to run the ToggleLayer code. Thus, the parseMarkerEventContext function reads the text and returns a *Hashtable* (a list of keys and values) that can be understood. Then, the MarkerEvent subfunction can decide if the message is the correct one to pass the shape object through to the ToggleLayer subfunction.

The VBA macro code can be inserted into a new module called, say, modFunctions, but then it needs to be edited to clear all errors and warnings. The vb.net environment expects you to be more specific about any constants than the VBA Editor, so the section, row, and cell constants should now be prefixed to indicate their full, explicit name. In addition, the Abs function needs to be prefixed with its namespace.

You can develop Microsoft Visio in code in many other ways (see the examples in the Microsoft Visio 2007 SDK), but this example shows how easy it can be to move from a recorded macro through to a managed code solution.

# Code Listing for ThisAddin.vb

```
Public Class ThisAddIn

    Private Sub ThisAddIn_Startup(ByVal sender As Object, _
        ByVal e As System.EventArgs) Handles Me.Startup

    End Sub

    Private Sub ThisAddIn_Shutdown(ByVal sender As Object, _
        ByVal e As System.EventArgs) Handles Me.Shutdown

    End Sub

    Private Sub Application_MarkerEvent( _
        ByVal app As Microsoft.Office.Interop.Visio.Application, _
        ByVal SequenceNum As Integer, _
        ByVal ContextString As String) Handles Application.MarkerEvent

        Dim markerEventParameters As Hashtable = Nothing
        Dim commandCode As Short = 0
        Dim documentSource As Visio.Document = Nothing
        Dim pageSource As Visio.Page = Nothing
        Dim shapeSource As Visio.Shape = Nothing
        Dim documentID As Integer = -1
        Dim shapeID As String = ""
        Dim pageID As Integer = -1

        markerEventParameters = parseMarkerEventContext(ContextString)

        ' Check if this MarkerEvent event was fired by a document created
        ' with the template.
        If (CStr(markerEventParameters.Item( _
            ParameterSolution)) = ParameterValueSolution) Then

            ' Dispatch the event to the correct event handler.
            commandCode = CShort(markerEventParameters.Item(ParameterCommand))

            Select Case commandCode
                Case 1
                    documentID = CInt(markerEventParameters.Item(ParameterDocument))
                    pageID = CInt(markerEventParameters.Item(ParameterPage))
                    shapeID = CStr(markerEventParameters.Item(ParameterShape))
                    documentSource = Application.Documents.Item(documentID)
                    pageSource = documentSource.Pages.ItemU(pageID)
                    If shapeId.Length > 0 Then
                        shapeSource = pageSource.Shapes.ItemU(shapeID)
                        ToggleLayer(shapeSource)
                    End If
```

```vbnet
                Case Else
                    'You could add other functions

            End Select

        End If
    End Sub



    '// <summary>This function splits the components of a marker event
    '// context string into parameters and values.</summary>
    '// <param name="context">Context string from a marker event</param>
    '// <returns>Hashtable containing the parameters and values</returns>
    Private Function parseMarkerEventContext(ByVal context As String) _
        As Hashtable

        Dim returnValue As Hashtable = New Hashtable
        Dim contextParts() As String
        Dim contextPartIndex As Integer
        Dim contextPart As String
        Dim argumentParts As String()

        If (context Is Nothing) Then
            context = ""
        End If

        ' The expected format for the persistent document event string looks like
        ' "/doc=1 /event=1 /eventID=1 /solution=WBSTreeView /cmd=1"
        '
        ' The expected format for the marker context string looks like
        ' "/doc=1 /solution=ToggleLayer /cmd=1"

        '. Separate the context parts and put them into an array.
        contextParts = context.Trim().Split("/".ToCharArray())

        For contextPartIndex = 0 To contextParts.Length - 1
            contextPart = contextParts(contextPartIndex).Trim()

            If (contextPart.Length > 0) Then
                ' Separate the parameter from the parameter value.
                argumentParts = contextPart.Split("=".ToCharArray())
                If (argumentParts.Length = 2) Then
                    returnValue.Add(argumentParts(0), _
                        argumentParts(1))
                End If
            End If
        Next

        Return returnValue
    End Function

End Class
```

# Code Listing for ToggleLayer.vb

```
Module modFunctions
    '// <summary>Solution parameter used in marker event context strings
    '// </summary>
    Public Const ParameterSolution As String = "solution"

    '// <summary>Solution parameter value for the sample application used
    '// in marker event context strings</summary>
    Public Const ParameterValueSolution As String = "ToggleLayer"

    '// <summary>Document parameter used in marker event context strings
    '// </summary>
    Public Const ParameterDocument As String = "doc"

    '// <summary>Page parameter used in marker event context strings
    '// </summary>
    Public Const ParameterPage As String = "page"

    '// <summary>Shape parameter used in marker event context strings
    '// </summary>
    Public Const ParameterShape As String = "shape"

    '// <summary>Command ID parameter used in marker event context strings
    '// </summary>
    Public Const ParameterCommand As String = "cmd"

    Public Sub ToggleLayer(ByVal shp As Visio.Shape)
        '
        ' Toggle Layer on/off - read text of shape
        '
        Dim layerName As String
        'Use Characters.Text in case there are field codes
        layerName = shp.Characters.Text
        If Len(layerName) = 0 Or shp.Application.ActivePage.Layers.Count = 0 Then
            Exit Sub
        End If
        Dim UndoScopeID1 As Long
        UndoScopeID1 = shp.Application.BeginUndoScope("Layer Properties")
        Dim vsoLayer1 As Visio.Layer = Nothing
        'To avoid an error, loop through the layers until the name is found
        For Each vsoLayer1 In shp.Application.ActivePage.Layers
            If UCase(vsoLayer1.NameU) = UCase(layerName) Then
                Exit For
            End If
        Next vsoLayer1
        'Abort if the layer name was not found
        If vsoLayer1 Is Nothing Then
            shp.CellsSRC(Visio.VisSectionIndices.visSectionObject, _
                Visio.VisRowIndices.visRowFill, _
```

```
                        Visio.VisCellIndices.visFillForegnd).FormulaU = _
                        "THEMEGUARD(RGB(255,255,0))"  'Yellow
                Exit Sub
            End If
            Dim currentVisible As Boolean
            currentVisible = CBool(vsoLayer1.CellsC( _
                Visio.VisCellIndices.visLayerVisible).ResultIU)
            vsoLayer1.CellsC(Visio.VisCellIndices.visLayerVisible).FormulaU = _
                CStr(System.Math.Abs(CInt(Not (currentVisible))))
            vsoLayer1.CellsC(Visio.VisCellIndices.visLayerPrint).FormulaU = _
                CStr(System.Math.Abs(CInt(Not (currentVisible))))
            If currentVisible = True Then
                shp.CellsSRC(Visio.VisSectionIndices.visSectionObject, _
                    Visio.VisRowIndices.visRowFill, _
                    Visio.VisCellIndices.visFillForegnd).FormulaU = _
                    "THEMEGUARD(RGB(255,0,0))"  'Red
            Else
                shp.CellsSRC(Visio.VisSectionIndices.visSectionObject, _
                    Visio.VisRowIndices.visRowFill, _
                    Visio.VisCellIndices.visFillForegnd).FormulaU = _
                    "THEMEGUARD(RGB(0,255,0))"  'Green
            End If
            shp.Application.EndUndoScope(UndoScopeID1, True)

        End Sub
End Module
```

## Enabling the Shape to Call the Add-In

The only bit left to do is to create a Master shape with the following formula in the EventDblClick cell and in an Action cell.

```
=RUNADDONWARGS("QueueMarkerEvent","/solution=ToggleLayer /cmd=1")
```

Because the double-click event now performs a custom action, you could add an extra Action cell to provide quick access to the text edit window via the OPENTEXTWIN() function.

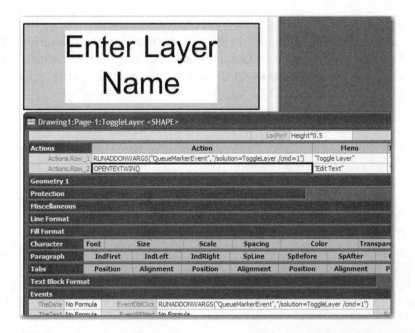

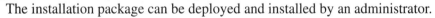

The Stencil with the new Toggle Layer Master on it can now be added to the setup project before compiling, modifying the installation file with the Visio Publisher, and installing.

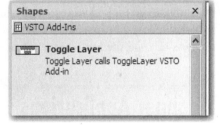

After the package is installed, the Toggle Layer Master can be added to any drawing and, after the text is edited with the name of a layer on the page, then a simple double-click toggles the named layer visible and print on and off.

The installation package can be deployed and installed by an administrator.

# COM Add-Ins

A *COM Add-in* runs in the same process space as Visio and cannot be called from the ShapeSheet RUNNADON function, but it can be called with the RUNADDONWARGS function, just like the VSTO Add-in, with the QUEUEMARKEREVENT. Visual Studio templates are in the Visio SDK to create Visio COM Add-ins with vb.net or c#, but the resultant application will be running in the same memory space as all other COM Add-ins, unless you wrap it with a COM Shim. A *COM Shim* is a C++ wrapper project that creates a separate memory space for the add-in. This primarily means, if it falls over, it will not bring down all other COM Add-ins.

As the newer VSTO is more secure, provides isolation and an immediate reference to the host application, Visio, I can see little reason for using the COM Add-in instead of the VSTO Add-in, unless you are creating an add-in that needs to be shared between multiple Microsoft Office applications.

# Add-Ons

The Visual Studio templates from the Visio SDK also enable you to create either a C++ VSL Add-on or a vb.net/c# EXE Add-on.

A VSL runs in the same process space as Visio, but an EXE runs in a different process space. Both, however, can be called from the ShapeSheet RUNNADON function.

All the supplied Microsoft Visio Add-ons are Visio Solution Library (VSLs) files. One advantage they have over either the VSTO or COM Add-ins is they do not need to be loaded at startup as they can be started on demand. However, C++ programming remains beyond the knowledge of most corporate development teams.

# Wrapper Applications

You should not forget the Microsoft Visio is delivered with the *Visio Drawing control*, which is similar to the Visio Viewer control, except you can use it to create or edit drawings. However, the client PC that uses it must have Visio installed already.

You can embed the Visio Drawing control in another application, which could be a Windows forms or web-based application, such as a web-part fronting a SharePoint service, which can have some advantages. For example, the application does not need to look like Visio. A disadvantage, however, is that neither the VBA nor the ShapeSheet is available, and certain actions cannot be performed.

One important consideration is you are always working with a copy of a drawing in the Visio Drawing control, so you have almost complete control as a developer.

The Visio Drawing control can only have one Visio document open at a time, but you can have multiple copies of the Visio Drawing control open, and each one will use the same Visio application. Indeed, it is possible to use the Visio application associated with a Visio Drawing control to open up other Visio documents invisibly.

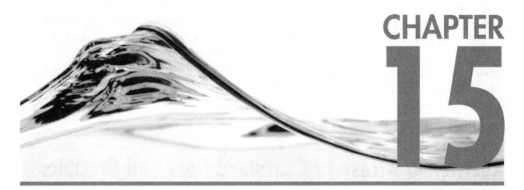

# Document Management and Security

**IN THIS CHAPTER**

Restricting Access to Contained Data and Graphics

SharePoint Integration for Document Control

Visio documents can become an important element of business processes and knowledge management, so some control needs to be exercised over authoring, editing, and reviewing them. Microsoft Visio does not have some of the more advanced management and security features that can be found in other Microsoft Office applications, although, as you learn in this chapter, you can take certain precautions.

# Restricting Access to Contained Data and Graphics

If you send a Microsoft Visio file to others, you can do little to prevent them from editing or copying the file. Visio does not have any capability (any more) to password-protect the graphics and data contained within it, but you can follow the upcoming steps to remove sensitive information and to prevent idle edits.

## Removing Sensitive Information

Microsoft Visio does include the option to remove personal information under File | Remove Hidden Information. This can include data imported using the Link Data tool.

This does not include removing Shape Data from shapes in the drawing, only the underlying data additionally stored as XML in the document. Therefore, you could accidentally leave sensitive information in the shapes unless you either remove it manually or with some code.

The subfunction CleanShapeData calls DeleteShapeData with the label of the Shape Data items that need to be cleansed. The label is used because the name of the Shape Data item could be different if you used the Link Data tool. The code loops through all the shapes on all the pages. If it finds the specified label, it forces the formula to be reset to the specified reset value.

Also, remember, you may have included embedded reports in your document, which could have included, say, Cost, before you removed the values. Either remove them or rerun them after the sensitive Shape Data is cleansed. Of course, you may want to save this cleansed file as a different name.

## Code Listing for CleanShapeData and DeleteShapeData

```
Public Sub CleanShapeData()
    DeleteShapeData "Description", """"""
End Sub


Private Sub DeleteShapeData(ByVal dataLabel As String, ByVal resetValue As String)
Dim shp As Visio.Shape
Dim pag As Visio.Page
Dim row As Integer


    For Each pag In Visio.ActiveDocument.Pages
        For Each shp In pag.Shapes
            If shp.SectionExists(Visio.visSectionProp, Visio.visExistsAnywhere) =
True Then
                For row = 0 To shp.RowCount(Visio.visSectionProp) - 1
                    If UCase(shp.CellsSRC(Visio.visSectionProp, _
                        row, Visio.visCustPropsLabel).ResultStr("")) =
UCase(dataLabel) Then
                        shp.CellsSRC(Visio.visSectionProp, _
                        row, Visio.visCustPropsValue).FormulaForce = "=" &
resetValue
                    End If
                Next row
            End If
        Next shp
    Next pag


End Sub
```

# Prevent Idle Edits

Most people who view a Visio document will not know about some of the more advanced elements, such as the ShapeSheet or automation code, so you can take some steps to make idle edits difficult.

First, the Protect Document item from the right mouse menu of the document node in the Drawing Explorer window allows some control.

You learned about the LockPreview cell in a previous chapter, but the other options in this dialog are not shown in DocumentSheet. They can, however, be set in automation as the value of the Doument.Protection property. For example, setting the value to 31 ensures the maximum protection.

However, the Shapes protection only works if the individual shape also had its Lock-Select cell set to True, and you have to save the drawing and reopen it to see the effect.

Every shape has a Protection ShapeSheet section, and almost all these cells can be accessed through the Format | Protection menu item on a shape.

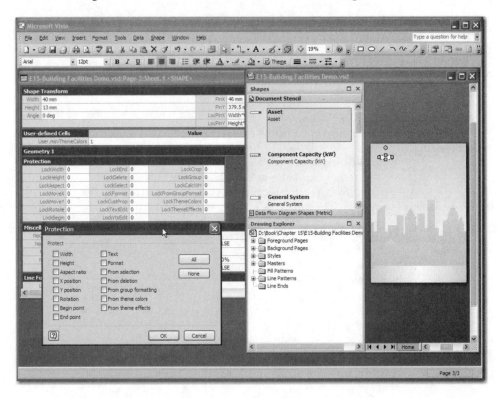

Going through each shape on each page and changing the settings is too labor-intensive, so I propose an automated solution by using the following LockDownDocument function (and UnlockDocument if you need it). This calls two subfunctions: LockDownShapes and HideMasters.

*LockDownShapes* iterates through all shapes on all pages and only changes all of their Lock cells to the passed through value (LockSelect is optional), for example, passing through "1" switches the locks on, and passing through "" (empty string) ensures the cells reinherit their values. (This is not quite the same as returning to their last value, but it does return them to their default value.)

*HideMasters* ensures all Masters (and MasterShortcuts) are either hidden or visible, depending on the passed Hide parameter value.

The effect is to have as secure a document as you can. This is a little destructive, though, so it should be done on a copy of the original. Also, a good practice is to remove all docked stencils before you save the document, preferably as read-only.

If the recipient of this cleansed file knows how to reverse some of these operations (perhaps by reading this book), nothing can stop it. At least you have made it difficult to idly edit the drawing, however.

## Code Listing for LockDownDocument, UnLockDocument, and Supporting Functions

```
Public Sub LockDownDocument()
Dim doc As Visio.Document
    Set doc = Visio.ActiveDocument

    'Remove protection temporarily
    doc.Protection = visProtectNone
    LockDownShapes doc, "1", True
    HideMasters doc, True
    'Fully protect the document
    doc.Protection = visProtectBackgrounds + visProtectMasters + _
        visProtectPreviews + visProtectShapes + visProtectStyles

End Sub

Public Sub UnLockDocument()
Dim doc As Visio.Document
    Set doc = Visio.ActiveDocument

    'Remove protection temporarily
    doc.Protection = visProtectNone
    LockDownShapes doc, "", True
    HideMasters doc, False
```

```
    'Fully protect the document
    doc.Protection = visProtectBackgrounds + visProtectMasters + _
        visProtectPreviews + visProtectShapes + visProtectStyles
End Sub

Private Sub LockDownShapes(ByVal doc As Visio.Document, _
    ByVal lockValue As String, ByVal lockSelect As Boolean)
'Pass thru lockValue= 1 to force lock down, or "" to re-inherit
'lockSelect = True means include lockSelect in changes
Dim shp As Visio.Shape
Dim pag As Visio.Page
Dim cel As Integer

    For Each pag In doc.Pages
        For Each shp In pag.Shapes
            For cel = 0 To 20
                If Not cel = Visio.VisCellIndices.visLockSelect _
                    Or (cel = Visio.VisCellIndices.visLockSelect _
                        And lockSelect = True) Then
                    shp.CellsSRC(Visio.visSectionObject, _
                    Visio.visRowLock, cel).FormulaForce = "=" & lockValue
                End If
            Next cel
        Next shp
    Next pag

End Sub

Private Sub HideMasters(ByVal doc As Visio.Document, ByVal hide As Boolean)
Dim mst As Visio.Master
Dim currentProtection As Integer
    'Store current protection value
    currentProtection = doc.Protection
    'Remove protection and hide masters and shortcus to masters
    doc.Protection = visProtectNone
    For Each mst In doc.Masters
        mst.Hidden = hide
    Next

    For Each mst In doc.MasterShortcuts
        mst.Hidden = hide
    Next

    'Restore the protection
    doc.Protection = currentProtection
End Sub
```

# SharePoint Integration for Document Control

The integration with SharePoint means you can simply impose some document management and control, as SharePoint allows an administrator to decide who can read or contribute to a project on a shared web site.

Although you can create a Document Workspace from the Document Management pane inside Microsoft Visio, I have found that uploading a Visio document, via the web browser, to a predefined Document Workspace in SharePoint is easier. See Figure 15-1.

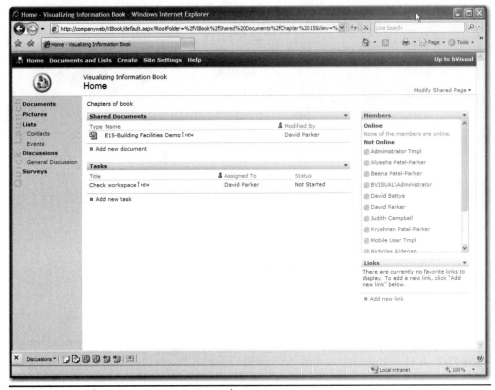

**Figure 15-1**  *A SharePoint Document Workspace*

Once you upload a Visio document to a SharePoint Workspace, it is under control. SharePoint keeps a record of who edited the document and when it was edited, and it keeps copies of previous versions, unless these settings are changed for the workspace. See Figure 15-2.

The Document Management pane also lets the user make updateable copies or alerts them when someone changes the document, for example.

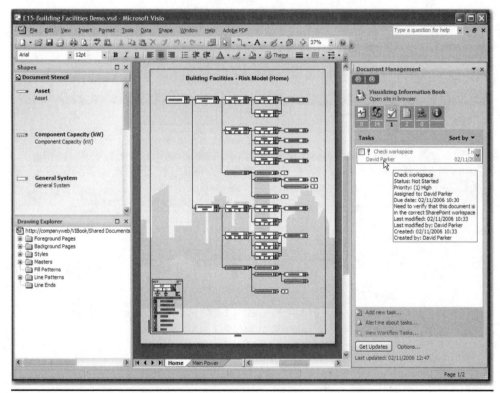

**Figure 15-2** *A Visio document under SharePoint control*

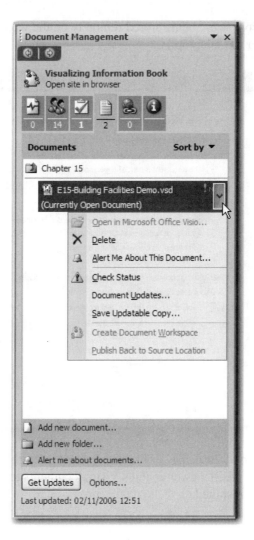

The options link at the bottom of the Document Management pane let the user customize various aspects of the SharePoint integration, including the Offline Editing Options. These options let a user take a controlled copy locally on to a computer, for example. (If the copy were being stored remotely on the web server, it may be unavailable if the user has a laptop.)

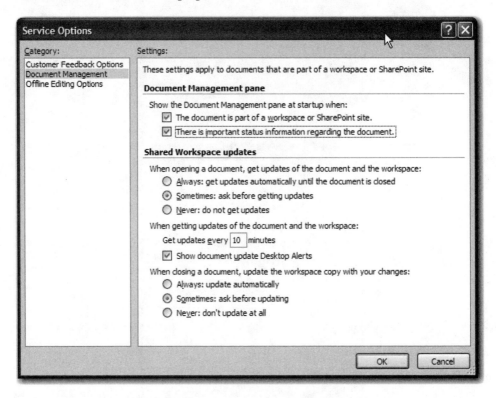

If you have SharePoint 2007 lists or libraries integrated within Microsoft Outlook 2007, then the built-in Visio viewer enables Visio documents to be previewed, without even having Visio installed.

# Scenarios

Throughout this book, you have seen ways that data can be linked to graphics using Microsoft Visio 2007 to create smarter business diagrams. This is not just for fun, but for real business benefit in a variety of scenarios, from space usage to network diagrams, and from process flows to risk analysis. In this chapter, you explore a few such scenarios where visual information can be used to real effect.

The drawing and data files used in this chapter are available from the companion web site.

# Floor Layouts

There are three ways in Visio to create floor layouts, which can be used as a backdrop to other activities, such as space usage chargeback, personnel locations, and equipment inventory. Although you could create drawings without any scale, I believe creating floor layouts to scale is preferable, so you can provide information, such as the space used by each department, the travel distance for fire escape routes, floor tiling areas, and so forth.

First, you can create floor layouts using the Master shapes in certain stencils within Visio itself, for example, with Maps and Floor Plans | Floor Plan or Maps and Floor Plans | Office Layout. If you have a large office to draw, however, then you may find the Space Plan Add-on described in the section "Space Usage" is slowed down when it recalculates the contents of each of the Boundaries and Spaces. If you find this is the case, simply save the floor layout, initially as a Visio document, and then as a suitable image file format, such as Enhanced Metafile (emf) format, subsequently using this image file as a backdrop in another Visio drawing file used for facilities management with the Space Plan Add-on. It is better to use a vector file format, such as emf or wmf, rather than a raster file format, such as bmp or jpg, so the image quality is maintained when you zoom in or out. Of course, the image file needs to be checked for scaling accuracy, as I describe in the section "Space Usage."

Second, you can embed CAD files provided by another department or company, but these CAD files must be in dwg or dxf format and they must be version 12, at the most, for Microsoft Visio 2007 to understand them. Unfortunately, the latest versions of *AutoCAD* (the most popular CAD program out there), no longer support version 12, so you may have to use an older version of AutoCAD, or another cheaper program, such as IntelliCAD, to convert to the correct version. Generally, there is no need to convert these files into Visio format as the CAD object inside Visio provides the capability to switch layers off or on within the CAD file itself, and also to change the lines' thickness and color. I have found the most successful way to embed CAD drawings to scale within a Visio page is to set the page size to what you expect it to be (you can change this later) and the page scale to the most suitable one for your purposes. For example, medium-sized office floor plans usually fit on an A1 page at 1:100 scale (if you work in Metric (ISO) units), or on a 36 in × 24 in at 1/8 in = 1 ft scale (which is 1:96 scale), if you work in ANSI Architectural units. Note, Visio does not support viewing embedded DWG files.

And, third, you could just use an image file, which could be as crude as a scanned-in paper document or as clear as a converted CAD or Visio file, but it should be scaled the same as the page. In this case, the outside measurement of the building is known (measured on the original CAD file) as 46.1994 m. The same measurement on the inserted image file is 61.62 m (as shown by the red line drawn precisely between the same two points that were measured in the CAD file). Therefore, the image must be resized to make it the correct scale.

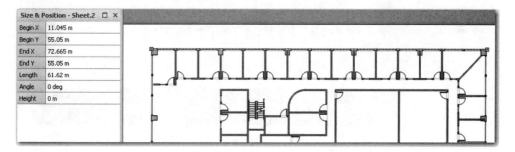

In fact, the inserted image must be multiplied by 46.1994/61.62 = 0.7497 but, first, you should protect the aspect ratio of the image file using the Format | Protection dialog. You can then enter the *0.7497 after the Width or Height values in the Size & Position window.

| Size & Position - Sheet.1 | □ × |
|---|---|
| X | 41.9375 m |
| Y | 29.75 m |
| Width | 112.409 m*0.7497 |
| Height | 79.323 m |
| Angle | 0 deg |
| Pin Pos | Center-Center |

The image file then reduces in size, but it is set to the correct scale, as you can see in Figure 16-1.

Microsoft Visio Professional 2007 includes the Space Plan template under the Maps and Floor Plans category, and this prompts for the type of file (image file, Visio drawing, or CAD drawing) to use as a floor plan. This wizard assigns an inserted image

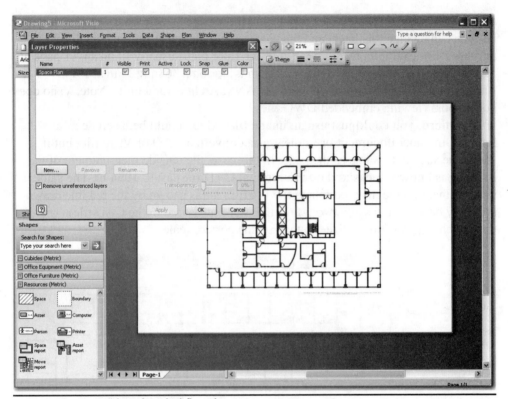

**Figure 16-1** *Inserted and scaled floor layout image*

file to a Space Plan layer, or an inserted CAD file to a CAD drawing layer. In each case, the new layer is Locked by default, so the inserted file is not accidently deleted. If you choose the Visio file option, then it is merely copied and becomes editable.

In each of these cases, the floor layout needs to be updated if there are major changes, such as walls built or removed, but the objective is to create a floor layout that does not contain personnel or equipment, as these are added later.

Note, the sample CAD file, BLDGPLAN.DWG, provided with Microsoft Visio (usually found in C:\Program Files\Microsoft Office\Office12\Samples\1033) is a poor example because it performs slowly, probably because it was created by an earlier version of Visio, and then saved as a dwg file. Most native CAD drawings do not perform this badly.

## Space Usage

The *Space Plan Startup Wizard* also offers the opportunity to import room numbers from an Excel spreadsheet as Space shapes. If you have not prepared a spreadsheet at this stage, then you can perform the same task later by using the Plan | Import Data task, but some subtle differences exist. The *Import Data task* provides you with the opportunity to specify which columns you want to import so, generally, this is the best method to choose.

In this scenario, selected database fields are exported into an Excel spreadsheet to be prepared for import into the floor plan as Spaces. The following table is an extract of this spreadsheet. It is important to use exactly the same column headings, so the Import Data Wizard does not create extra Shape Data items unnecessarily. In fact, the Floor column is not required and will be omitted during the import. Note, the Name and Space ID columns contain almost the same values, because one is used as the Unique ID and the other as the Label in the tree view of Space Explorer window initially. The Name includes the floor prefix (17/), but the Space ID omits the prefix for clarity in the display on the drawing page.

The Space Explorer can get confused over data types. More specifically, if the Name column appears to be numeric, then the Belongs To Shape Data item on shapes manually dropped on to the page from the Space Explorer will update the Belongs To Shape Data type to numeric, thus forcing enclosing quotation marks in the Shape Data values. See Table 16-1.

| Name | Space ID | Space use | Department | Occupancy | Capacity | Floor |
|------|----------|-----------|------------|-----------|----------|-------|
| 17/102 | 102 | Office | Office of the President | 1 | 1 | HQ-17 |
| 17/104 | 104 | Office | Office of the President | 1 | 1 | HQ-17 |
| 17/106 | 106 | Office | Operations | 1 | 1 | HQ-17 |
| 17/108 | 108 | Office | Operations | 1 | 1 | HQ-17 |
| 17/110 | 110 | Office | Finance | 1 | 1 | HQ-17 |
| 17/112 | 112 | Office | Finance | 1 | 1 | HQ-17 |
| 17/113 | 113 | Storage | (none) | 0 | 0 | HQ-17 |
| 17/114 | 114 | Office | Production | 1 | 1 | HQ-17 |
| 17/115 | 115 | Office | Production | 1 | 1 | HQ-17 |
| 17/116 | 116 | Office | Marketing | 1 | 1 | HQ-17 |
| 17/117 | 117 | Office | Sales | 1 | 1 | HQ-17 |
| 17/118 | 118 | Office | Operations | 1 | 1 | HQ-17 |
| 17/119 | 119 | Office | Finance | 1 | 1 | HQ-17 |
| 17/120 | 120 | Office | Finance | 1 | 1 | HQ-17 |

**Table 16-1** *The Top Few Rows of the Space Worksheet*

The Import Data Wizard asks whether you want the data to go into new shapes that are cascaded on to the page, or to store them in the Space Explorer window, ready for dragging-and-dropping on to the drawing page. The latter is usually best, as you may have quite a few Spaces to create.

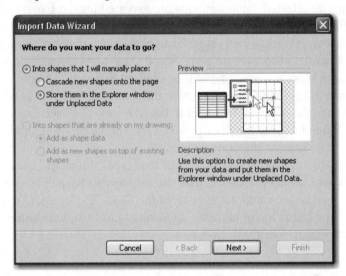

The default Space Master shape on the Maps and Floor Plans | Building Plan | Resources stencil already contains some Shape Data items and, unless you created a modified Master, restricting yourself to only these Shape Data items is best because, even though the Import Data Wizard adds more Shape Data items, the extra items are not added in the same manner as the Data | Link Data to Shapes task.

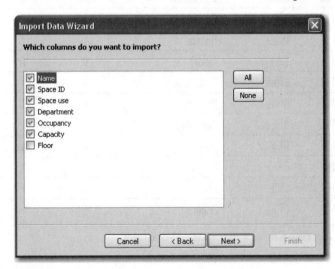

The Import Data Wizard prompts for which worksheet to use, as well as whether you want to import all columns and rows. You should only import the columns/fields previously listed, and so any others should be deselected.

You then need to select the Space shape from the Resources stencil.

You should not need to have any Label on the Space shape because it already includes a default label. But, every row appears as Unplaced in the Explorer, therefore, you need to choose the Space ID column as the Label.

You should choose the Name column as the Unique ID, as this is used as the identifier for the automatic placement of Person and Equipment shapes.

Once the first Space shape is placed, notice two call-out labels are now on it. Therefore, you can use the Plan | Set Display Options dialog to change the Spaces labels, so the Name is no longer shown (because it is already displayed on the second call-out label created by the Import Data Wizard).

The Space shapes need to be added over the top of the floor layout, in their correct location, and the vertices adjusted to suit the underlying walls and panels. Now, it is a simple matter to use Display Data on Shapes to color the Space shapes by Department, for example.

You can also now use the Link Data to Shapes task to add any further Shape Data items to each Space shape from any other data source.

In Figure 16-2, a Boundary shape is enclosing the whole of the floor plan and is labeled as the Seventeenth Floor.

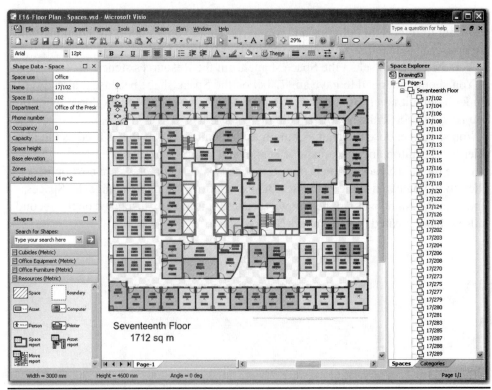

**Figure 16-2**  *Space shapes over the floor layout*

## Personnel Locations

If you have a table that has the Space ID with personnel, then you can automatically create Person shapes in the center of each corresponding Space. Table 16-2 displays the top few rows of such a spreadsheet.

Note, the column that contains the Name of the space in the drawing has been changed to Belongs To, as this ensures the Import Data Wizard matches the Person to Space correctly.

Additionally, the First Name and Last Name values are concatenated together to make a Name column, as this will be used to Label each Person shape and to appear in the Explorer window.

| ID | Name | Title | Manager | Belongs To | Phone Number | Department | E-mail Alias |
|---|---|---|---|---|---|---|---|
| AC0103 | Anthony Chor | Executive Assistant | CH0102 | 17/108 | 555-0103 | Operations | anthony@championzone.net |
| AD0114 | Andrew Dixon | A/R Manager | SW0125 | 17/124 | 555-0114 | Finance | andrew@championzone.net |
| AJ0144 | Amy Jones | Technical Manager | CW0143 | 17/311 | 555-0144 | Production | amy@championzone.net |
| AL0109 | Ashley Larsen | Senior VP Sales & Mktg | JG0100 | 17/117 | 555-0109 | Sales | ashley@championzone.net |
| BS0126 | Beth Silverberg | Controller | SW0125 | 17/280 | 555-0126 | Finance | beth@championzone.net |
| BS0161 | Brad Sutton | South America Sales | RC0159 | 17/405 | 555-0161 | Sales | brad@championzone.net |
| CH0102 | Clair Hector | COO | JG0100 | 17/106 | 555-0102 | Operations | clair@championzone.net |
| CP0168 | Carol Philips | Southern Europe Sales Manager | WV0165 | 17/461 | 555-0168 | Sales | carol@championzone.net |
| CR0150 | Cynthia Randall | Strategic Planner | SH0135 | 17/318 | 555-0150 | Marketing | cynthia@championzone.net |
| CR0160 | Claus Romanowsky | South America Sales Manager | RC0159 | 17/403 | 555-0160 | Sales | claus@championzone.net |
| CW0143 | Connie Waite | R&D Director | TM0106 | 17/310 | 555-0143 | R&D | connie@championzone.net |
| DJ0134 | David Jaffe | Marketing Director | AL0109 | 17/291 | 555-0134 | Marketing | david@championzone.net |
| DM0149 | Deanna Meyer | Game Designer | AJ0144 | 17/316 | 555-0149 | R&D | deanna@championzone.net |
| DP0167 | Daniel Penn | UK & Ireland Sales Manager | WV0165 | 17/460 | 555-0167 | Sales | daniel@championzone.net |
| DS0119 | Denise Smith | National Account Manager | HH0117 | 17/206 | 555-0119 | Sales | denise@championzone.net |

**Table 16-2**  *The Top Few Rows of the Person Data*

Use the Import Data Wizard to place the data into new shapes (Person shapes) on top of existing shapes (Space shapes). Again, you need to select the relevant worksheet and ensure only the columns that appear on the Person shape are transferred.

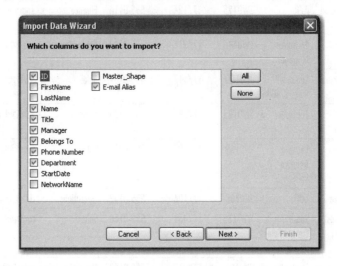

After completing the Import Data Wizard for the Person data, you should find each Space with a corresponding personnel record has a new Person shape, with the relevant Shape Data values.

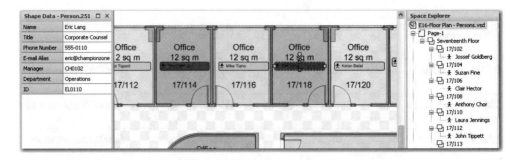

The Data Graphic used to apply the Department Color By Value to the Space shapes can now be used to apply the same colors to the Person shapes. See Figure 16-3.

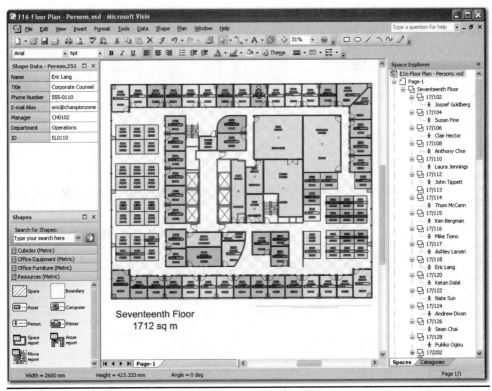

**Figure 16-3** *The Personnel automatically placed in their Spaces*

Again, you can use the Link Data to Shapes task to enhance each Person shape with information from the same or other data sources. In the following illustration, the Person table was automatically linked to the Person shapes, using the ID Shape Data value as the link. This means all other values about the person can be refreshed from the database easily, if, say, their Title or Department changes. In addition, the Space Plan Add-on can automatically move Person shapes from one Space to another if the data source used to place the Person shapes originally is changed. In this case, you select Plan | Refresh Data in Visio.

For clarity, a Smiley Face data icon was added to all Director (toothy grin) and Manager (normal grin) Person shapes.

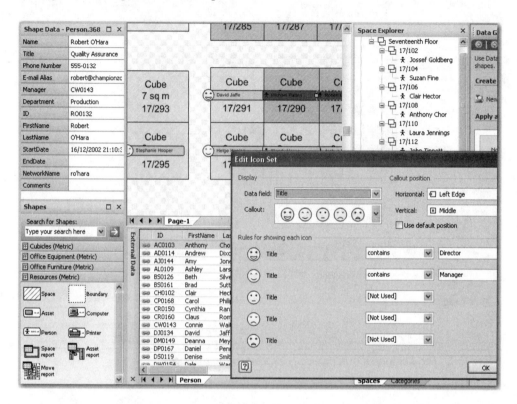

The *Pivot Diagram Add-on* can quite easily be used to create an organizational chart for the personnel within each department. In this scenario, the Person table is again used as the data source, and the PivotDiagram is broken down on Department and the ID of each Person. The Link Data to Shapes task is then used to automatically link the remaining Shape Data to each Person (using Prop.ID = Prop.Member as the match). Then, the Data Graphics are edited to Color By Value and to add the Smiley Face to each qualifying person, as on the floor layout.

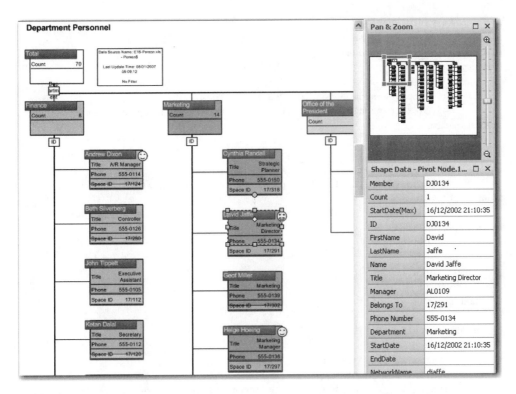

If this PivotDiagram is inserted into another page within the same Visio document as the floor layout, then it can act as a visual navigator to the Person shapes within the floor layout. The viewer can select a Person in the Organization page, then call the FindPersonSpaceFromPivot macro, and Visio then zooms to the equivalent Person shape in the Floor Layout page. This is done by modifying the FindByData code from Chapter 4 and renaming it as FindPersonSpaceFromPivot. Note, you also need the GetShapesByData subfunction, with its supporting functions, from Chapter 4.

## Code Listing for FindPersonSpaceFromPivot

```
Public Sub FindPersonSpaceFromPivot()
Dim aryCriteria() As String
'Array dimensions:
' 1 = UseName = "True", UseLabel = "False"
' 2 = Data Name or Label
' 3 = Value (as string)

Dim foundShapes() As Long
Dim pag As Visio.Page
```

```
Dim shp As Visio.Shape
Dim shpSource As Visio.Shape
Dim shapeCounter As Integer
Dim msg As String

    If Visio.ActiveWindow.Selection.Count = 0 Then
        MsgBox "You should select a Person in the Pivot Diagram first!",
vbExclamation
        Exit Sub
    Else
        Set shpSource = Visio.ActiveWindow.Selection.PrimaryItem
        If shpSource.CellExists("Prop._VisDM_ID", Visio.visExistsAnywhere) = 0
Then
            MsgBox "You should select a Person in the Pivot Diagram first!",
vbExclamation
            Exit Sub
        Else
            'Carry on
        End If
    End If

    ReDim aryCriteria(1 To 1, 1 To 3)

    aryCriteria(1, 1) = "False"
    aryCriteria(1, 2) = "ID"
    aryCriteria(1, 3) = shpSource.Cells("Prop._VisDM_ID").ResultStr("")

    If GetShapesByData(False, 2, False, aryCriteria, foundShapes) = True Then
        msg = "Found " & UBound(foundShapes, 2) & " shapes"
        For shapeCounter = 1 To UBound(foundShapes, 2)
            Set pag = Visio.ActiveDocument.Pages.ItemFromID(foundShapes(1,
                                                    shapeCounter))
            Set shp = pag.Shapes.ItemFromID(foundShapes(2, shapeCounter))
            msg = msg & vbCrLf & shp.Name & " on " & pag.Name
            If Not pag.Name = shpSource.ContainingPage.Name Then

                Visio.ActiveWindow.Page = pag
                Visio.ActiveWindow.Select shp, Visio.visSelect

                Dim dW As Double
                Dim dH As Double
                Dim dL As Double
                Dim dT As Double
                'Get the current view rectangle
                Visio.ActiveWindow.GetViewRect dL, dT, dW, dH
                'Move it to center on the Person shape
                Dim dL1 As Double
```

```
        Dim dT1 As Double
        dL1 = dL + (shp.Cells("PinX").ResultIU - (dL + (dW / 2)))
        dT1 = dT + (shp.Cells("PinY").ResultIU - (dT - (dH / 2)))
        Visio.ActiveWindow.SetViewRect dL1, dT1, dW, dH
        Exit Sub
      End If
    Next shapeCounter
  Else
    msg = "No matching shapes found"
  End If


  MsgBox msg

End Sub
```

## Equipment Inventory

You can also use the Plan | Import Data Wizard to automatically locate different types of equipment (Computer, Asset, Printer) into the Space shapes automatically.

Table 16-3 is an extract of the Computer table and the Space ID column is again renamed as Belongs To, so it is correctly understood by the wizard.

| Serial Number | Name | NetworkName | Manufacturer | Product Number | Belongs To | Department |
|---|---|---|---|---|---|---|
| SN10000001 | SN10000001 | jgoldberg | DELL | Dimension | 17/102 | Office of the President |
| SN10000002 | SN10000002 | sfine | DELL | Optiplex | 17/104 | Office of the President |
| SN10000003 | SN10000003 | chector | IBM | Aptiva | 17/106 | Operations |
| SN10000004 | SN10000004 | achor | Siemens Nixdorf | Scenic 5H | 17/108 | Operations |
| SN10000005 | SN10000005 | ljennings | Hewlett Packard | Vectra | 17/110 | Finance |
| SN10000006 | SN10000006 | jtippett | Toshiba | 4900CT | 17/112 | Finance |
| SN10000007 | SN10000007 | tmccann | IBM | PS/2 Model 70 | 17/114 | Production |
| SN10000008 | SN10000008 | kbergman | DELL | 466ME | 17/115 | Production |
| SN10000009 | SN10000009 | mtiano | Compaq | Deskpro | 17/116 | Marketing |
| SN10000010 | SN10000010 | alarsen | Compaq | Prolinea | 17/117 | Sales |
| SN10000011 | SN10000011 | elang | DELL | Optiplex | 17/118 | Operations |
| SN10000012 | SN10000012 | lleste | IBM | Aptiva | 17/119 | Finance |
| SN10000013 | SN10000013 | kdalal | Siemens Nixdorf | Scenic 5H | 17/120 | Finance |

**Table 16-3** *Extract of the Computer Data*

This particular data does not contain the computer's network name—only the last user's login name—so the Serial Number is reproduced as the Name column, to label the Computer shapes and for the display in the Explorers.

Again, you should be selective with the columns you import.

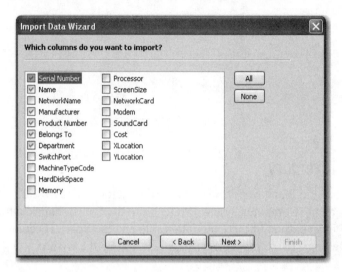

You must select the Computer shape from the Resources stencil. You will be matching the Name value of the Space shape with the Belongs To value in the Computer data.

The Computer shapes are placed into the Space shapes, adjacent to the Person shapes already there.

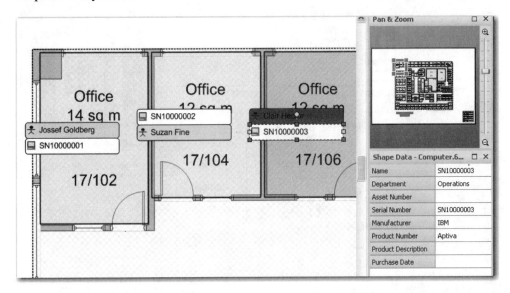

The Link Data to Shapes task can be used again to add more Shape Data items to each computer, and the PivotDiagram can be used to create a breakdown diagram by, say, Switch, Card, Port, and Connected Computers. See Figure 16-4.

# Organization Chart

Organization Charts are used for variety of purposes. An *Organization Chart* may be to display personnel relationships (optionally including photographs), department breakdowns, or team structures, for example. Microsoft Visio has traditionally used the Organizational Chart Add-on for automating the creation of charts or for providing guided diagramming. However, the new PivotDiagram provides a more flexible approach to the creation of organizational structures because, not only can you be more flexible in the way the organization is broken down, but you can also use it to roll up data, such as salaries, easily.

## Hierarchical Relationships

Microsoft Visio includes the *Organizational Chart Wizard* that can be used to display hierarchical organization charts from a variety of sources (text files, Excel files,

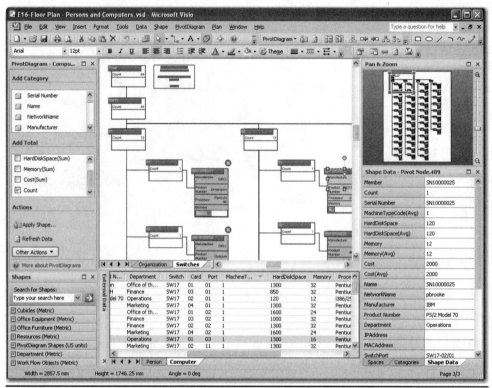

**Figure 16-4** *PivotDiagram used to breakdown Switch, Card, Port, and Computer*

Microsoft Exchange, and an Open Database Connectivity (ODBC)-compliant data source. The wizard leads you through the selection of the data source, the columns, and the breakdown across multiple pages.

I suggest you restrict the amount of fields you import with the Organization Chart Wizard, but enhance the Organization Chart shapes with the Link Data to Shapes task. This enables you to refresh the personnel data (except for hierarchical relationships) using the Data | Refresh Data task.

The Organization (Org) Chart Add-on includes the capability to include Shape Data values as text at the corners of each shape or in a central multiline block. This is distinct from the Data Graphics introduced in Microsoft Visio 2007, but there is no reason you cannot enhance the Org Chart shapes further with Color By Value, Data Icons Sets, or Data Bars. See Figure 16-5.

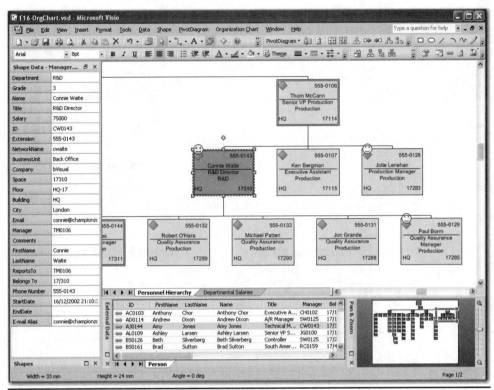

**Figure 16-5** *Personnel hierarchy with the Organization Chart Wizard*

## Automating the Organization Chart Wizard

An article titled "Create an organization chart from a data file using the command line or Run method" (http://office.microsoft.com/en-us/visio/HP010384221033.aspx) describes how you can automate the generation of organization charts from a data source. The article is for Microsoft Visio 2003, but it remains valid for Microsoft Visio 2007. If you are using HR applications, such as PeopleSoft or SAP, then you may want to automate the production of data sources that can be consumed by the Org Chart Wizard silently. For example, you can enhance PeopleSoft to output such files that can create breakdown by Department, Position, or Reports To.

# Merging Cost Data and Roll-up

As mentioned, the PivotDiagram provides the capability to provide more flexible breakdowns. The following example shows the sum of salaries for each Grade within each Department, broken down by Business Units. See Figure 16-6.

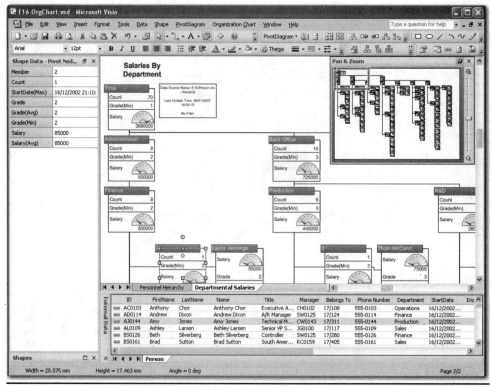

**Figure 16-6**  *Salary roll-up in an Organization Chart*

# IT System Diagrams

You have already seen how the PivotDiagram Add-on can be used to break down some network type information, but some types of network diagrams require further coding. Figure 16-7 shows an extract from a Microsoft Visio Add-in that I wrote to display the devices connected to each port of each switch within a SQL Server network discovery database.

The end devices in this database are categorized as Network PC, Laptop, Printer, and so forth, and the database collects information about the operating system (OS) and software applications, as well as what versions, patches, and licenses are present. Some custom code changes the shape outline colors according to specific data values, but the new Data Graphic Icon Sets and Color By Value are used to enhance the visual information.

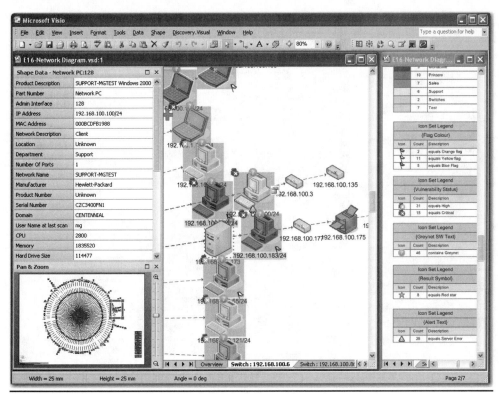

**Figure 16-7**  *Custom network diagram showing Data Graphics*

Note, you can open a second drawing window of the same page in Microsoft Visio (Window | New Window ) to enable multiple areas of a single page to be viewed simultaneously.

# Process Diagram

Microsoft Visio made much of its reputation with process flow charts, and we examined some basic flowcharts in earlier chapters. Figure 16-8 shows a custom process chart (by kind permission of Vasanthi Solaiappan at Service Net). The three main Masters (*SN Step, SN Decision,* and *SN InfoExchange*) are presented individually within the stencil, but the user can change from one to the other using the right mouse menu. The Step Severity symbol (Red, Amber, Green) is automatically updated from the weighted average of the SN Issues (Frequency and Severity) connected to it.

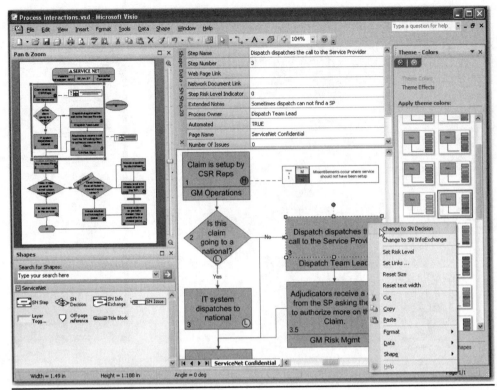

**Figure 16-8**  *A custom process diagram*

A Color By Value was applied to emphasize the different type of Master selected (using unique values of the cell User.ShapeType), and Theme colors were used, so the user can decide which theme is the most appropriate.

# Operational Risk

You saw in Chapter 7 how a Data Graphic Icon Set can be used to display the Risk value in a Shape Data item. Figure 16-9 demonstrates how Visio can be used, with custom code, to provide inherited risk levels throughout a Visio document. In this case, the ShapeSheet formulae within the Masters enable you to change the operational risk values of Issues, Assets, and Systems with the normal Shape Data window. Any parent

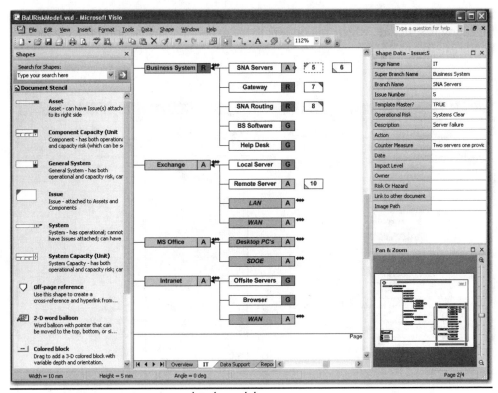

**Figure 16-9** *A custom Operational Risk model*

shapes (those connected to the left of each shape) automatically display the highest risk level of the connected child shapes (unless a Redundancy level is entered).

Moreover, Systems (which are comprised of other Systems, Assets, and Issues) can be reused throughout the model. They always show the highest criticality automatically, even if the System is described on another page in the document. Color By Value Data Graphic is used to emphasize which Systems are detailed elsewhere, as they are shown with a light blue background, rather than parchment.

# Work Breakdown Structure

WBS Modeler is a free download from www.wbsmodeler.com. This is an enhancement of the WBS TreeView, which can be found in the Microsoft Visio 2007 SDK. The WBS Modeler provides the capability either to visualize the Work Breakdown Structure from an existing Microsoft Project application, or to manually create a Work Breakdown Structure, which can optionally be exported to Microsoft Project. See Figure 16-10.

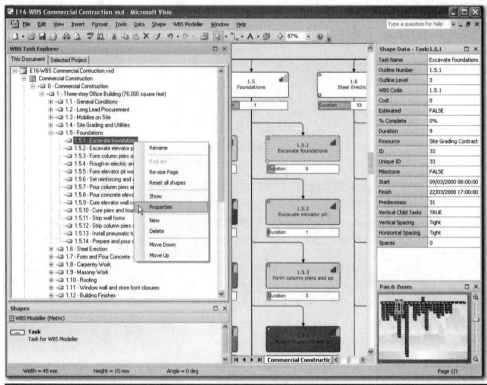

**Figure 16-10**   *A work breakdown structure*

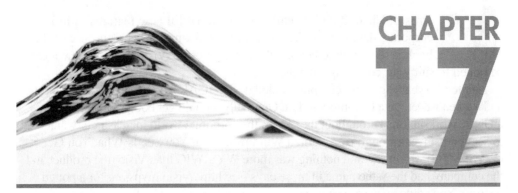

# CHAPTER 17

# Epilogue

M icrosoft Visio 2007 introduces some powerful new features to link corporate data to graphics to visualize information. The purpose of this book is to go a little beyond the out-of-the-box Visio to show how it can be honed to suit your company's needs.

I started 20 years ago with computer-aided design (CAD), on a bespoke workstation and a spreadsheet, on a Commodore Pet. Gradually, I could get both applications on a UNIX workstation. Throughout the 1990s, the corporate world increasingly wanted to see themselves through rose-tainted Windows. What You See Is What You Get (WYSIWYG) was in . . . and nothing was more WYSIWIG than Visio (the product and the company had the same name in those days (see http://visio.mvps.org for a potted history). You could even choose what the user interface should look most like among Microsoft Office, Lotus® SmartSuite®, or Novell® PerfectOffice.

I got hooked, but then a bigger fish came along and swallowed the bait (Microsoft's acquisition of Visio Corporation was its biggest at the time). Microsoft Visio emerged with a new identity, and Microsoft started the struggle to blend Visio into the rest of the Microsoft Office System. The 2007 release has continued this progression, but the Big Three of the Microsoft Office family (Word, Excel, and PowerPoint) have shiny new coats and bionic hearts, while the others look on enviously, but there are new, useful toys to play with (Link Data to Shapes and Data Graphics).

Meanwhile, PCs have become more powerful, and Microsoft has opened the vista to a landscape drawn with vectors. Web-based applications are becoming increasingly more capable, and Microsoft is planning the release of flashy operating-system(OS) independent, programmable vector components (codename WPF/E) that must challenge for some tasks currently performed by Visio today.

So, the future releases of Visio will have to raise the bar to keep its position ahead of the pack but, currently, no other application covers such a wide range of graphic types, and no other system provides such easy links to data. The intelligent use of SmartShapes makes truly smart diagrams. Visio is fully programmable and this makes it relatively simple to customize to suit most information needs. The support and familiarity of Microsoft applications is attractive to organizations that need to provide quality consistently.

It is probably easier to integrate different types of Visio data diagrams than to get the different departments within some organizations to coordinate their information. Microsoft Visio can help break down barriers by providing clarity to complex data with a myriad of relationships.

If this book inspires you to customize Visio within your own work environment, then my job is done. But this is not the only source of information for budding Visio developers looking to improve their skills in ShapeSheet or automation through code. Books and blogs by my fellow Visio MVPs (Graham Wideman, David Edson,

Chris Roth, and Senaj Lelic) that are inspirational. More details can be found on the Visio fan (oops . . . MVP) web site (http://visio.mvps.org) lovingly maintained by another MVP, John Marshall. Also, much is to be found on the Microsoft site (see http://msdn2.microsoft.com/en-us/office/aa905478.aspx) and the blogs written by the Visio Product team (http://blogs.msdn.com/visio).

The public newsgroups (news://news.microsoft.com/microsoft.public.visio and its subgroups or http://www.microsoft.com/office/community/en-us/default.mspx) are useful for asking questions and learning from the answers. Quite a few Visiophiles are out there!

Finally, please don't forget to visit the companion web site for this book (http://www.visualizinginformation.com), because you can download all the code and examples used herein.

*Be smart, be clear, be visual!*

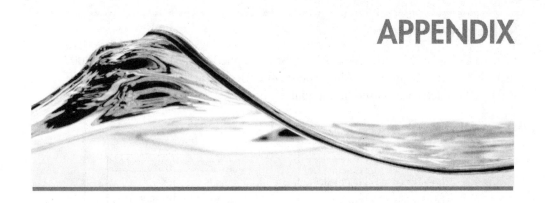

# APPENDIX

**IN THIS APPENDIX**

Schema Extract

Upsize the Visio Sample Database

## Schema Extract

Schema extract of Microsoft Access Database supplied with Microsoft Visio 2007 (usually found in C:\Program Files\Microsoft Office\Office12\1033\DBSAMPLE .MDB). This database is used throughout the book.

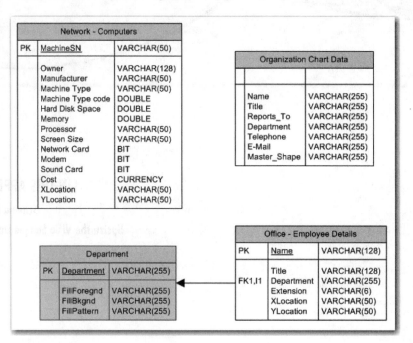

### NOTE

*The Department table has been added to demonstrate how the database can be used to store fill colors and patterns.*

## Upsize the Visio Sample Database

The Visio sample database was upsized to SQL Server, and extended to provide additional location, organizational, and network connectivity information.

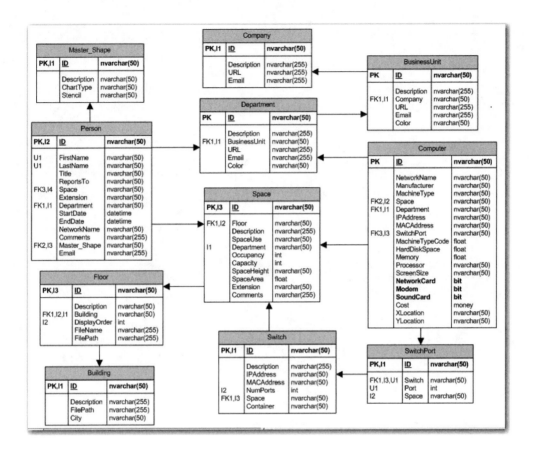

# Index

# W

# X